Contemporary Theatre Studies
A series of books edited by Franc Chamberlain, Nene College,
Northampton, UK

Please see the back of this book for other titles in the Contemporary Theatre Studies series

YURY LYUBIMOV

AT THE TAGANKA THEATRE
1964–1994

Birgit Beumers
University of Bristol, UK

Routledge
Taylor & Francis Group

LONDON AND NEW YORK

Copyright © 1997 Harwood Academic Publishers.

Reprinted 2004
By Routledge
11 New Fetter Lane, London EC4P 4EE

Transferred to Digital Printing 2004

British Library Cataloguing in Publication Data
Beumers, Birgit
   Yury Lyubimov: at the Taganka Theatre (1964–1994). –
   (Contemporary theatre studies; v. 21)
   1. Lyubimov, Yury – Criticism and interpretation   2. Taganka Theatre
   3. Theatrical producers and directors – Soviet Union
      I. Title
792′. 0233′ 092

   ISBN 3-7186-5875-5 (hardcover)
        3-7186-5885-2 (paperback)

Printed and bound by Antony Rowe Ltd, Eastbourne

Cover photograph: The Taganka Theatre by Aleksandr Sternin

CONTENTS

Appendices

INTRODUCTION TO THE SERIES

Contemporary Theatre Studies is a book series of special interest to everyone involved in theatre. It consists of monographs on influential figures, studies of movements and ideas in theatre, as well as primary material consisting of theatre-related documents, performing editions of plays in English, and English translations of plays from various vital theatre traditions worldwide.

Franc Chamberlain

LIST OF ILLUSTRATIONS

1. *The Good Person of Szechwan*, finale
2. *Ten Days that Shook the World*, Scene 26: "Shades of the Past"
3. *Ten Days that Shook the World*, Scenes 7–9: "Meeting of the US Senate Commission", "W. Wilson's Song" and "Music-hall Singers"
4. *The Fallen and the Living*
5. *The Life of Galileo*, Galileo: Vysotsky
6. *Listen!*, the five Mayakovskys: Zolotukhin, Nasonov, Khmelnitsky, Smekhov, Shapovalov
7. *Listen!*
8. *Pugachev*
9. *Pugachev*, Khlopusha: Vysotsky
10. *The Tough*, Kuzkin at court; Kuzkin: Zolotukhin, village people: Radunskaya, Politseimako, Vlasova, Grabbe, and children
11. *The Tough*, Kuzkin: Zolotukhin, Angel: Dzhabrailov
12. *The Tough*, Angel: Dzhabrailov, Dunya: Slavina, children, and Kuzkin: Zolotukhin
13. *The Suicide*
14. *Tartuffe*
15. *Tartuffe*
16. *Tartuffe*, seduction scene
17. *The Mother*
18. *What is to be Done?*
19. *Protect Your Faces!*
20. *Under the Skin of the Statue of Liberty*
21. *But the Dawns here are so Calm...*, arrival of the detachment in the truck, Vaskov: Shapovalov
22. *But the Dawns...*, sauna scene
23. *But the Dawns...*, woods
24. *But the Dawns...*, the staircase in the foyer after the performance
25. *But the Dawns...*, programme
26. *Hamlet*, close-up of curtain
27. *Hamlet*, set design
28. *Hamlet*, Hamlet: Vysotsky
29. *The Rush Hour*

PREFACE

"The most interesting thing in art is the unconscious process. Analysis starts later..."

Yury Lyubimov, 8 August 1988

The first production I saw by Yury Lyubimov was *The Possessed* in London in 1985. At that time I was an undergraduate, fascinated by theatre in general, obsessed with Dostoevsky, and about to become possessed by the idea of investigating the career of this director, who had been filling the newspapers for several years with entirely non-artistic headlines, when he was first stripped of his post, then of his Party membership, and finally of his Soviet citizenship.

When I started my research in Moscow, the name Lyubimov was taboo: his productions were shown, but there was no indication of a director in the programmes; his picture and name were removed from all new editions of theatre histories; the films in which he had acted were temporarily shelved (among them the Soviet classic *Kuban Cossacks*).

During my research, Lyubimov continued to hit the headlines: he returned to Moscow in 1988 for a visit, and was reinstated in his post and regained his Soviet citizenship in 1989. Then the Taganka theatre split and interviews with the two opponents, Gubenko and Lyubimov, filled the gossip columns of almost every newspaper in Moscow.

I have tried to characterise Yury Lyubimov through his artistic work rather than by probing the "scandals". Many people maintain that Lyubimov needed these scandals and conflicts in order to spur his creativity. I have spent a long time in archives looking at the minutes of meetings with petty bureaucrats, and have spoken to several former officials in Moscow; as a result, I dispute this view in my survey: Lyubimov's creative potential may have been strengthened at certain points by the circumstances under which he worked, but it was never enriched. His productions are tied not to the system under which they were created, but to the society he lived in and to the audience he played to. For that reason he deserves a study of this kind: his work over thirty years reflects the development of humanist and spiritual values in Soviet and post-Soviet Russia.

The Taganka theatre is a repertoire theatre. This meant that I was able to see most productions when I was conducting research in Moscow in the mid-1980s. Exceptions are: *A Hero of Our Time, Antiworlds, The Fallen and the Living, Galileo, Pugachev, What is to be Done?, The Rush Hour, Comrade, believe . . . , The Gala, Crossroads, Fasten Your Seat Belts*, and, of course, those productions which were banned or removed after interventions of the censors, such as *Protect Your Faces, Under the Skin . . .*, and *Turandot*. However, the production scripts proved a valuable source for reconstructing productions, as did conversations with actors and production assistants.

When discussing the productions, I have chosen to provide summaries of those texts which are likely to be less known, and have used the present tense for these summaries, while the discussion of the production is in the past tense to enable the reader to identify easily whether reference is made to the text or the performance.

During the writing of this book, a number of people have given me their time and assistance. Above all, I should like to express my deep gratitude to Yury Lyubimov and his family. I owe special thanks to my D. Phil. thesis supervisor, Professor Gerald Smith of Oxford University, for advice, encouragement and support during and after the writing of my thesis. While conducting research for this book, I have worked in several libraries and archives in Moscow and I should like to thank the staff of the State Theatre Library and the Moscow Party Archives for their help; the staff in the reading room of the Central State Archive of Literature and Arts of the USSR (TsGALI) and in the Theatre Workers' Union Library, especially Natalya Borisovna and Nadezhda Mikhailovna, for invaluable assistance; the actors and the staff of the Taganka theatre, especially Tatyana Vashkina, Boris Glagolin, Vladimir Guryanov, Valery Zolotukhin, Nina Shkatova, Alla Demidova, David Borovsky, Mariya Politseimako, Veniamin Smekhov, and Galina Aksenova; Svetlana Sidorina who has put material at my disposal; Rimma Krechetova, Marina Perchikhina, Mikhail Shvydkoy, Tatyana Bachelis and the late Konstantin Rudnitsky, Vladislav and Mariya Ivanov, Lena Ivanova, Yury Karyakin, Yury Kononenko, Yury Pogrebnichko, and Olga Trifonova. I am obliged to the photographers Viktor Bazhenov, Aleksandr Butkovsky, Valery Plotnikov, and especially Aleksandr Sternin for making their photographs available. I am thankful to the University of Cambridge for facilitating a trip to the première of *Zhivago* in Vienna in 1993. Finally, I should like to express my deep gratitude to Gordon McVay for reading my manuscript so thoroughly.

Without the support of my mother and my late grandfather neither my thesis nor this book could have been written.

Transliteration, abbreviations and translations

The transliteration system of *Oxford Slavonic Papers* has been used for the bibliography and footnotes; in the text, the soft and hard signs (' and ") have been omitted and Vasil'ev is given as Vasiliev. Names of foreign origin (e.g., Schnittke) have not been transliterated.

Abbreviated forms of the titles of productions have been used in the bibliography and the tables.

Lyubimov's memoirs published in France are referred to as *Feu* in the notes.

All translations are my own, unless otherwise indicated.

Sources

Informal interviews were conducted with Galina Aksenova (theatre critic and wife of the Taganka actor V. Smekhov); David Borovsky (stage designer); Alla Demidova (actress); Aleksandr Efimovich (administrative director of the Taganka Theatre from 1989 to 1990); Boris Glagolin (director, later administrative director, at the Taganka Theatre); Paul Hernon (set designer); Yury Kononenko (stage designer for *Three Sisters*); Yury Medvedev (actor); Bulat Okudzhava; Yury Orlov (Faculty of Theatre Management, State Institute of Theatre Arts [GITIS]); Igor Petrov (actor); Yury Pogrebnichko (director of *Three Sisters*); Mikhail Shvydkoy (theatre critic, editor of *Teatr*, deputy Minister of Culture); Veniamin Smekhov (actor); Olga Trifonova (widow of Yury Trifonov); Tatyana Vashkina (literary department, Taganka Theatre) and Boris Vasiliev (writer).

Archival sources are as follows:

The Central State Archive of Literature and Art of the USSR [Tsentral'nyi gosudarstvennyi arkhiv literatury i iskusstva SSSR, TsGALI, now Rossiiskii gosudarstvennyi arkhiv literatury i iskusstva, RGALI] contains documents concerning the Taganka Theatre between 1964 and the present in the second and the fourth inventory of fond 2485. Fond 2329 contains documents about the activity of the USSR Ministry of Culture.

The Archive for Contemporary Documentation [Tsentr khraneniya sovremennoi dokumentatsii, TsKhSD] contains documents concerning decisions at Central Committee level and correspondence with the Ministry and the KGB in fond 5 (cultural department).

The United City Archives [Gorodskoe ob"edinenie moskovskikh arkhivov, GOMA] contains documents pertaining to Mossovet's decisions and policy making with regard to all Moscow theatres subordinated to Mossovet in fond R429; however, according to the staff of the archive, most documents concerning the Taganka were removed to an unknown destination in about 1984.

References to all archival sources are as follows: fond/inventory/unit.

The cover photograph is by Aleksandr Sternin. All the other photographs are by Aleksandr Sternin (Taganka Theatre), except nos. 1, 3, 4, 15, 21, 24, 39–40, 43–5, 47, 50, 58, 61–3 (Viktor Bazhenov); 28 (Valery Plotnikov); 64 (Aleksandr Butkovsky); 10–12 (Yury Feklistov); 67 (Johann Klinger, courtesy of Wiener Festwochen); the photographers of 34, 35 and 39 are unknown to me.

INTRODUCTION

Yury Petrovich Lyubimov: a child of the October Revolution?

Yury Petrovich Lyubimov was born in Yaroslavl on 30 September 1917, in the very year of the October Revolution. However, Lyubimov's background was far from revolutionary: his grandfather was a *kulak* who would flee to Moscow to escape arrest during the collectivisation in the 1930s; his parents, Petr Zakharovich, a merchant, and Anna Aleksandrovna, a schoolteacher, moved to Moscow in 1922 where his father worked for a Scottish company. During the New Economic Policy (192–1928) both father and mother were arrested, and the three children, Natalya, David and Yury, were left to fend for themselves. Since he was not of proletarian origin, Yury was barred from higher (other than technical) education, and therefore trained as an electrician at the Institute for Energy near Taganka Square. In 1934 he joined the Second Moscow Arts Theatre Studio, founded by Mikhail Chekhov, reciting for his admissions interview the recalcitrant speech Yury Olesha had just delivered at the Writers' Congress, in which he had opposed the new parameters for Socialist Realist Literature. When the Second Studio was closed by Stalin's order in 1936, Lyubimov transferred to the studio of the Vakhtangov Theatre.

Having been an underprivileged member of a socialist society for the first twenty years of his life, Lyubimov suddenly found himself on the side of the Soviet system: during the war he was drafted to work for the Ensemble of Song and Dance organised by the minister for Internal Affairs, Lavrenty Beriya.[1] This ensemble produced shows for the entertainment of officers at the front; here, Lyubimov met the satirist Nikolay Erdman and the composer Dmitry Shostakovich. In 1935 Lyubimov had married the actress Nina Zorina, whom he divorced a few years later to marry the dancer Olga Kovaleva in 1940. After the war, he returned to the Vakhtangov Theatre where he became a successful actor.[2] In 1952 he won the State Prize of the USSR and by 1953 joined the Communist Party; in 1954 he was awarded the title "Merited Artist of the RSFSR". At the Vakhtangov Theatre, he met Lyudmila Tselikovskaya,[3] the Vakhtangov theatre's leading actress and wife of one of Stalin's favourite architects, Karo Alabyan. Tselikovskaya became Lyubimov's common-law wife.

In spite of his success as an actor, Lyubimov was dissatisfied. He abhorred the pompous sets and costumes demanded by the stage realism still prevailing in most Soviet theatres at the time:

> The coarsely daubed backdrops, all the stage properties such as goblets, beards, wigs; all decor which imitates real life such as bushes, clouds, hammocks, lawns, … are as irritating as the general belief in the necessity of make-up, the use of paint and powder on one's face, which is most often nonsensical, and quite repulsive on men.[4]

To Lyubimov, all this merely served to create a verisimilitude which he considered undesirable. He rejected the uniform style of Soviet theatres, which held the Moscow Arts Theatre's concepts of emotional experience (*perezhivanie*) and psychological realism as ideal:

> At that time, all theatres without exception were trimmed in the selfsame manner; that is good for an English garden, but in the theatre, it is disgusting.[5]

He therefore turned to pedagogical activity at the Vakhtangov Theatre's Shchukin School in 1958. In 1963 he staged with the course graduating in 1964 Brecht's *The Good Person of Szechwan*. This production established Lyubimov as a director, and he was subsequently appointed to the post of "artistic director" of the Theatre of Drama and Comedy, located on Taganka Square (on the fringe of central Moscow, unlike other "established" theatres). The theatre had been founded in 1945 by A. K. Plotnikov who had mainly staged mediocre plays which complied with the prevailing concept of Socialist Realism. Therefore, the repertoire was in a lamentable state and failed to attract audiences. The theatre had debts amounting to 70,000 roubles, which had to be paid off before Lyubimov could build up his own ensemble and repertoire.[6]

Lyubimov added to the name of the theatre the designation *na taganke*, derived from its location. The word *tagan* means 'trivet' and indicates that the building is in the centre of a proletarian area; a red flame in a square henceforth formed the new emblem of the theatre. The new name was not officially acknowledged (the theatre was listed as "Theatre of Drama and Comedy", omitting the words *"na taganke"*) which, of course, drove supporters to refer only to "the Taganka".[7] This change of name is indicative of Lyubimov's protest against the standardization of theatres named after great writers or directors (Pushkin Theatre, Stanislavsky Theatre) or with a reference to their repertoire (Satire Theatre), and speaks of his wish to address the (local) people. This controversy over the new name was the first, albeit small, occasion on which the Moscow City Council showed its opposition to the theatre.

Since Soviet theatres had the function of disseminating current ideology, they had to be firmly controlled: both state and Party exercised control over the theatres. The Ministry of Culture received directives both from the Council of Ministers and from the Secretary for Ideology in the Central Committee of the Communist Party.[8] The immediate responsibility for theatres was delegated to the Main Administration of Culture of the Moscow City Council Executive Committee, thus to a lower level in the state apparatus.[9] This placed power in the hands of innumerable, often low-ranking bureaucrats.[10] The Main Administration of Culture controlled the theatre repertoires, allocated budgets for the general management of the theatre and for each individual production, gave preliminary consent to each new play for its inclusion in the repertoire, and final consent to the stage production after a viewing. It was also in charge of sending unpublished texts to the literary censorship board, *Glavlit*,[11] which, strictly speaking, was authorised only to censor matters pertaining to state and military secrets, but in fact objected to anything that seemed ideologically unsound. The Main Administration could make mandatory requests for changes, omissions, and additions; these would be specified in a licence which granted permission to open the production to the public.

The state organs liaised closely with the Administrative Director of the theatre (Nikolay Dupak), who would be held responsible for any infringement of the procedures for passing a production and who was in charge of the orderly running of the theatre. In addition, the Party exercised direct control over the theatre through the Party organisation which is part of any large institution.[12] As Artistic Director, Lyubimov was thus exposed to the control of both state and Party organs. He therefore relied heavily on the Artistic Council, which functioned as an advisory board, stimulus and defence organ for the theatre. Lyubimov often "enlarged" the Artistic Council of the Taganka, calling on selected, prominent members of the (often dissident) intelligentsia. He thus rapidly assembled leading writers and critics, artists and scientists in the Artistic Council to help him oppose state and Party demands. Both Lyubimov's non-conformist, unorthodox, formalist and "avant-garde" production style and the composition of the Artistic Council made the representatives of Main Administration fear discussions at the Taganka and created for Lyubimov a reputation of an "enfant terrible".

At the Taganka theatre, Lyubimov formed a new ensemble and created his own repertoire, eventually consisting of more than thirty productions. They included not only plays, but adaptations of works in prose and poetry, ranging from classical to very contemporary writing, and including all forms of theatrical art: lighting, set design, music, choreography, mime, song, dance, and, of course, acting. Between 1964 and 1984 Lyubimov established the Taganka theatre as one of the major venues of "avant-garde" art in Moscow. In 1978 he married the Hungarian theatre critic Katalin Koncz; together with her and their son Petya he was exiled in 1984 following his outspoken criticism of the theatre censorship. A socialist at heart, Lyubimov was disappointed in the perversion of the ideals of the October Revolution by Soviet bureaucracy; he returned to Moscow in 1988, after Gorbachev's *perestroika*.

Lyubimov as a theatre theoretician

The portraits of four great directors of this century not only dominate the foyer of the Taganka theatre, but also Lyubimov's work; they are Stanislavsky, Meyerhold, Vakhtangov and Brecht. Yet to trace their influence on Lyubimov would be a rather unproductive exercise, since elements of their theory and practice can be found in the work of most Russian directors. Lyubimov's approach is not an amalgam of these four directors, but is idiosyncratic. Lyubimov proceeds from exterior to interior, from the form of a dramatic text to its content, from movement and action to the right feeling or sub-text for the actors' performance. An essential feature of all his productions is their fragmentary structure. Such a structure can, above all, be found in the plays of the "founder of epic theatre", Bertolt Brecht; but it can also be created by using prose of an episodic nature or by collating poems. Lyubimov has directed many productions which he has classified as "montage", "collage", or "spectacle", where he mixes several works by one author; or he combines the works of different authors and adapts them for the stage; or he commissions writers and collaborates with them.

Lyubimov's approach to theatre has no declared theoretical foundation. He has published his memoirs and some articles, the most important being "In Defence of the Acting Profession and Professionals", "The Algebra of Harmony", and "I am for Anti-decor".[13] Lyubimov's production concepts are subject to development and change, and depend on his choice of author: "Each author requires a particular solution for his own theatrical manner, his style".[14] However, a number of basic ideas emerge from his theoretical writings and characterise his working principles.

First, Lyubimov re-defines the function of theatre. He wishes, like Brecht with his epic theatre, to create an awareness in the spectator of being in the theatre.

> We must not forget for a minute that we are in the theatre, we must not try to act with untheatrical means, we must not imitate reality; then, the feeling of truth and of life on stage will be stronger, and the spectator will believe us ... We immediately propose [to the spectator] the rules of the game.[15]

Since the spectator is aware of being in the theatre, there is no need for the actor to pretend complete identity with his role or to evoke emotions in himself artificially. On the contrary, the actor is asked to bring his own personality into the role: he is supposed not to play-*act*, but to re-*act* with his personality both to the role and to the reaction of the audience.

> The link of the actor with everything that surrounds him on stage, plus the constant awareness of the auditorium as a living partner imposes special requirements on the range of the actor's capabilities. . . . The actor at the Taganka . . . is able to shift his stance and to define it anew at any moment in the performance; the character, the personality of the actor and their reception by the spectator meet and merge in this stance.[16]

The role of stage design deserves particular attention in such an approach. On the one hand, the set should make hypocrisy, "false" acting, and pretending by the actor impossible, and should ensure sincerity.

> [Borovsky's] method presupposes the utmost truth of immediate physical interaction of the actors and the world of the scenic object.[17]

> The natural item taken from everyday life set by the designer into interaction with the actors makes any falsehood in acting impossible.[18]

On the other hand, set design provides a central image for the concept of the production, thereby promoting the role of the designer, who assumes a vital and active part. This preoccupation with image, and consequently form, dominates Lyubimov's approach to the theatre. For the representation of a concept on stage, Lyubimov and his set designer David Borovsky use a central metaphor, which concentrates the contents of the literary material in a formal image.

> We are accustomed to start from everyday truth and verisimilitude. Yet in art not the truth of everyday life in itself is important, but the *artistic image*; the underestimation of the role of *form* in search of imagery is a strange but widespread prejudice. The psychological mood of the actor, if not expressed in a clear *scenic form*, is unconvincing and diffuse to the audience.[19]

The pace of contemporary life plays another vital role in Lyubimov's work. Historical and social developments, technical progress have changed the pace of human life; man is now able to grasp information at greater speed, and this requires a different rhythm for the events on stage.

> Along with our rhythm of life, our perception of the theatre has changed. The fragmentation, the acceleration of communicative movements have sharpened our senses and have made us insensitive to certain traditional forms in the theatre: exposition, heroic monologues, never-ending dialogues. Time on stage has to change, too.[20]

With this change of pace, not only a different rhythm of stage events is introduced, but also fragmentation and simultaneity of action. The literary material for such treatment on stage has to be episodic as in the adaptation of prose or the montage of poetry, which give "... more possibilities for the creation of a multiple-layer dramatic composition than a play".[21]

Lyubimov's theatre is therefore an *avtorskii teatr*: the director assumes the responsibilities of an author both in writing or assembling texts, poems and songs to form a play by means of collage, and in adapting material and directing the production with a right to impose a personal interpretation on the chosen material: "the director must ensure both the construction and the articulation of the production himself".[22] In such a theatre, the role of the actor also acquires another dimension: the actor becomes an executor.

> Theatre is a collective art, but it is naive to think that in the process of the creation of a production actor and director work on an equal footing. They have different jobs. The director thinks up the concept, while the profession of the actor is an executive profession.[23]

Lyubimov's ideas changed in accordance with social and cultural changes which he reflected and also generated – intentionally or not – with his productions. It is thus important to investigate the form chosen for the expression of ideas, and the relation of form and ideas to the cultural, social and political context. The role of the audience should not be neglected since the form of address depends on the ideas expressed. Finally, Lyubimov attributes different functions to theatre arts at different times: theatre is a means to appeal to society, a means for philosophical reflections and the expression of ideas, or serves purely aesthetic purposes.

Form and content

Lyubimov's work at the Taganka theatre falls thematically into three phases: the socio-political agitation of the 1960s, the tragic perception of the 1970s and the musical visions of the 1980s; the last phase had been prepared by his work in the opera, where there are, analogous to the development in the theatre, three stages: formal innovation, the theme of a tragic human existence, and religion.

Lyubimov is first and foremost an innovator of theatrical form. To him, form itself is an aesthetic principle: "art is pure creation of form. And without form, there can be no profundity in content"[24] and consequently "form is the only expression of truth in art".[25] Theatrical devices, like mime, choreography, music, light, and dance, were activated in the first productions. Formal and thematic innovation was achieved by the integration of the historical context, by the introduction of the author as a character, by fragmentation or the restoration of original versions. The device of several actors playing one complex character to enhance his multi-layered personality was discovered. The form of a production thus attains a vital importance in Lyubimov's theatre. The rhythm of movement and word, the pace and the tempi of the production help to preserve the idea expressed on stage, even if the actors are not in their best form.

In his attempt to innovate in theatrical form, Lyubimov revived some theatrical traditions of the 1920s, as developed by Meyerhold and Vakhtangov, which were repressed under Stalin and forcibly replaced by the Stanislavsky 'system' as used by the Moscow Arts Theatre (MKhAT); these policies continued in the Brezhnev era. Lyubimov's style was frequently criticised by orthodox and conservative critics for lack of psychological portrayal and for superficiality, since his theatre was not a psychological theatre, but an intellectual one: it was based on Brechtian *predstavlenie* (demonstration) rather than Stanislavskian *perezhivanie* (emotional experience).

The set concentrates on essentials only, and all properties are real. Lyubimov almost always chooses props carefully and insists that they must be real. This principle is based on the tradition of Stanislavsky and Vakhtangov, for whom in acting the reality of the object is vital to help the actor in his role. Otherwise, the stage for Lyubimov is stripped of what can only imitate reality – in opposition to Stanislavsky. Lyubimov also dwells on the reality of the existence of the character on stage, and often there would be a real physical danger. The actor thereby experiences for himself the situation of the character he plays. This closeness to reality in these two points, the actual danger and the real properties, is characteristic of "poetic theatre", as defined by the poet David Samoilov in an article in *Literaturnaya gazeta*:

> [Poetic theatre] is above all a theatre which is able to make of the poetic detail an element of the stage action, of the theatrical show. Poetic thought is metaphorical. The theatre takes from poetry the metaphor. It does not try to imitate reality by recreating on stage a reality of properties. It seeks, like poetry, the exact and bright detail in which the idea of the whole is condensed. This detail is not a property, but the original: the original material of life, habits and time.[26]

The major innovations Lyubimov has brought to theatrical history are thus the creation of a new theatrical genre, the poetic theatre, in which all evolves around one metaphor, and the creation of a new form of dramatic material, which refrains from limiting itself, but incorporates the historical and biographical context, and, if applicable, restores original versions of the chosen text.

Lyubimov never engaged in political theatre as such; he was preoccupied with ideas of the time, with the establishment of a direct link to the audience, with collective creation (ideas often emerged from meetings with the intelligentsia). However, the Taganka theatre created with and for the dissident intelligentsia and existed in conflict with officials.

Lyubimov developed concepts and ideas on the basis of a contemporary reading of texts. Texts would be adapted or reduced to these ideas: it is not the literary work that stands in the centre, but the *idea* the director developed from a contemporary reading of a text. Lyubimov's technique of adapting prose or other texts for the stage is therefore idiosyncratic. The stage versions are tailored for Lyubimov, if not written or co-written by him. It is difficult to imagine other productions on the basis of these versions or adaptations.

At the beginning of his activity as director of the Taganka theatre, Lyubimov set out to appeal for the activity and solidarity of the audience as a social group. Group solidarity would strengthen the individual and at the same time equip the social group with the power and energy to bring about changes in social and political life.

Towards the end of the 1960s, in a climate of stagnation, the hope for any effects of this appeal lessened. As the conflicts with censorship grew, society was no longer perceived as a force able to generate actions and changes, but as a group of individuals lacking mutual respect and personality, incapable of putting socialist theories into practice. The appeal now was to demonstrate at least responsibility for each other. The protagonists of this phase were negative: they were egoists and hypocrites. The individual, deprived of the support of others, failed to be socially active.

In the 1970s, as no change in cultural politics occurred, Lyubimov turned to the individual, isolated in the social mass, and appealed to his conscience, his honesty, his sense of truth. The individual was first isolated from the social mass and established as a unique human being; then, man was perceived as tragically alone in an evil society; finally, the existence of the artist in an aggressive social setting was investigated. Values such as truth, tradition and creativity were asserted.

At the end of the 1970s, at a time when stagnation had reached its climax, Lyubimov invited other directors to direct in his theatre, while he went abroad to work in opera, and at home experimented in quest of a new concept. Thematically, he was concerned with ends and means, with conscience in thrall to ideas, and with memory. The audience was challenged and attacked in this period; it was deprived of hope; its notions of reality and fantasy were challenged. The creative and imaginative world of the poet became more real, with more right to exist, than the real world.

Finally, man was seen as a being in the hands of fate; however, this does not condemn him to passivity and make him an object. At this point, a new concept for Lyubimov's theatre emerged: aesthetics. In a world which has deprived itself of all human values, of humanist tradition, in which man has, without resistance, become a marionette of corrupt systems, there is no longer any need to appeal or be appalled, to criticise or pass moral judgments. The form, visual and musical, contains everything the director has to say. Lyubimov refrained from his favourite device of addressing the audience. He demonstrated, in a perfect form, the metaphor which contained the idea he perceived as the core of the work. Ethics were replaced by aesthetics.

PART I

AGITATION IN THE 1960s: SOCIETY AS A GENERATOR OF CHANGE

1

THE DEVELOPMENT OF A POETIC THEATRE

The history of the Taganka Theatre of Drama and Comedy is intrinsically linked to the political history of the Soviet Union. Founded in 1945, it had been one of the many theatres severely affected by the absence of high-quality dramatic writing and by the levelling in the arts under Zhdanov. It was to be the last of several theatres to profit from the Khrushchev "Thaw", which affected cultural life first and foremost.

In his "secret speech" at the XX Party Congress of February 1956, Khrushchev had admitted to the falsification of history, and had rejected the cult of personality. However, Khrushchev's liberalism was met by a strong Stalinist opposition, as demonstrated by the violent crushing of the attempted revolution in Hungary in November 1956. Khrushchev's fight for his liberal programme against the old Stalinists was reflected in the USSR's cultural politics, repressive one day and liberal the next: in 1958 Boris Pasternak was forced to refuse the Nobel Prize, while Aleksandr Tvardovsky was reinstated as editor of the literary magazine *Novyi mir*.

In the theatrical season immediately following the XX Party Congress (1956/57) Mariya Knebel, a pupil of Mikhail Chekhov, was appointed Chief Artistic Director of the Central Children's Theatre in Moscow. Here she promoted the careers of Oleg Efremov (who, in the same season, organised the "Studio of Young Actors", which later became the *Sovremennik* Theatre) and Anatoly Efros, who was to emerge as a leading theatre director in the 1960s. In the same season Meyerhold's pupil Valentin Pluchek was appointed Chief Artistic Director of the Satire Theatre, Moscow; and the talented, young Georgy Tovstonogov filled the same post at the Gorky Bolshoi Drama Theatre, Leningrad. A second wave of liberalism in the arts occurred at the very end of the Khrushchev era, in the 1963/64 season, when the *Sovremennik* was established as a theatre, and Efros was given the artistic directorship of the Theatre of the Lenin Komsomol, Moscow.

The Taganka theatre is the last child of a short period of relative liberalisation in Soviet history, opening only a few months before the Thaw came to a formal end with the forced retirement of Khrushchev in October 1964 and the beginning of the conservative politics of Brezhnev.

At this point, the Taganka theatre had just premièred its first production, *The Good Person of Szechwan*, in which Lyubimov reflected the hopes raised by the Khrushchev era. He used agitational elements, inviting the audience to participate actively not only in the theatre, but also in social life, in a fight against the system.

Epic theatre: *The Good Person of Szechwan*

Brecht's *The Good Person of Szechwan* was produced in the Shchukin School of the Vakhtangov Theatre in 1963 with the third-year students of the course taught by Anna Orochko,[1] who had invited Lyubimov to stage a play as the diploma work of her course. The initially hostile attitude of the School and critics changed completely once the positive review by Konstantin Simonov had appeared in the Party organ *Pravda*.[2] Thanks to the production's success, Lyubimov was established as a director; this subsequently led to his appointment as "artistic director" of the Taganka theatre.[3] Lyubimov transferred *The Good Person of Szechwan* to the Taganka stage, where it opened on 23 April 1964, with a new cast, including several actors from the Shchukin School production.[4]

The very fact that a Brecht play was produced in that place and at that time is remarkable and deserves comment. There had been few productions of Brecht's plays in the Soviet Union, partly because of the presumed incompatibility of the Stanislavsky method prevailing in Soviet theatre with Brecht's theory of epic theatre. Brecht had, up to that point, been known in the USSR mainly for his theoretical works on theatre, and only a few plays had been staged in the Soviet Union before Lyubimov's production.[5] The only live contact for Soviet audiences with Brecht occurred during a tour of the Soviet Union by the Berliner Ensemble in 1957. Surprisingly, Lyubimov had missed those performances,[6] and hence had not seen Brecht's work prior to his own production of *The Good Person of Szechwan*, so that any influence by Brecht must be attributed to theoretical rather than practical sources.

Lyubimov was the first Soviet director to attempt to apply the theories of epic theatre to a Brecht play. Reviewing the production, many Soviet critics expressed amazement at the fact that the actors were so young; they had viewed the production as "merely" the diploma work of a class in drama school. They were then forced to recognise that these actors trained by Lyubimov had bypassed the "classic" Russian actor's training and were thus fitter to put into practice his own stage theory.

The Good Person of Szechwan is about three Gods who descend to earth and search in the region of Szechwan for a good person who will give them a justification for not changing the world. They believe they have found that person in Shen Teh, a prostitute, who has offered them shelter for the night. They pay her, since she has no money, and she buys a tobacco shop, where not only friends seek shelter, but where all the poor come to ask for alms, and where Shen Teh herself is put under constant pressure from the house-owner. Unable to be good to everybody without ruining herself, she creates a fictional stepbrother, Shui Ta, who says "no" where she would have been incapable of doing so. He rescues her shop, saves her from a marriage with Sun, who was only interested in her money, and protects her unborn baby by opening a tobacco factory which creates financial security for the child. He is then accused of having killed Shen Teh, and the Gods – who are the judges in his/her trial – finally drive Shui Ta to giving up his disguise. The Gods insist, however, that they have found a good person and take off on a cloud, leaving everything as it is – and Shen Teh in despair.

The ending is open: in the song which forms the epilogue to the play, all the actors address the audience with a plea to help create "a good ending" and thereby establish a kind of solidarity with the audience. The audience is asked to participate actively in the ideas developed during the course of the play, and to decide how goodness may be found.

Lyubimov's production took place on a virtually bare stage (Figure 1). The set was limited to an orange wall at the back, while the sides of the stage were decorated with a poster of Brecht and a placard with a tree and the words "street theatre" (both painted by the designer Boris Blank). This set embodied Brecht's idea that theatre should be drawn from everyday occurrences presented on stage by actors aware that they are only showing what has happened to somebody else. The props consisted of only chairs and tables. A critic noted that this might originally have been due to financial constraints, which forced the collective to resort to the furniture of their lecture theatres (hence the absence of shelves for the Tobacconist);[7] but this minimal use of props has subsequently been maintained on the professional Taganka stage for more than twenty years.

The audience was not only faced with the two permanent side placards, "Brecht" and "Street Theatre", but the location of the action was also indicated by means of placards ("Judge", "Cheap Restaurant", "Tobacconist", "Carpets", etc.). Special use was made of the Brecht placard at the side: it was lit by a spotlight between episodes. A placard saying "scene change" was used for episodes which involved a change of set, so that actor and audience should be aware of being in the theatre, as Brecht stipulated: "If the theatre scene follows the street scene, then the theatre no longer hides that it is theatre".[8]

At the side of the stage, a slight elevation served as a catwalk for the actors to present themselves and enhanced the demonstrative element in their performances. A key element for the actor to alienate himself from the character he represents (Brecht's *Verfremdungseffekt*, or alienation effect) is the actor's direct address to the audience, requesting analysis of his actions. This indeed happened in the production; even more frequently, the passages an actor was supposed to address to the audience were taken up by the musicians, who sang them.

The musicians played a very important role. Although Brecht intended that songs should be used, Lyubimov's use of song in this production went beyond the dramatist's original intentions. The musicians accompanied individual scenes and acts, endowing them with rhythm and thereby with a unity of form. A striking example was the scene at the tobacco factory, where the workers sat on stools, with backs to the audience, and clapped their hands rhythmically to the song, indicating the monotony of their work, and thus taking rhythm beyond its usual, purely formal function. Other examples were the rhythmical beating by the police of the boy who has stolen bread, which was performed in dance-like movements; and the movement of Sun abandoning Shen Teh while awaiting Shui Ta on the wedding day. Music invariably accompanied exits and entrances as well as changes of scene.

In addition, Lyubimov replaced many verbal passages entirely by mime. Wang's despair at not finding a night shelter for the Gods was expressed by his repeated running against the wall; Shu Fu's declaration of love to Shen Teh was presented in the form of a dance. Mime could also accompany words, for example when Shen Teh is talking to Sun; Shin's imitation of Shu Fu's restlessness; or Shen Teh's mime with her unborn baby son, where movement and gesture gave meaning to her words.

Exits and entrances were choreographed in a disciplined, military manner, often describing rectangular movements on stage, thus precluding any illusion of an accidental or naturalistic occurrence. An excellent example was in the first scene, where more and more "relatives" came to seek shelter in Shen Teh's shop, or the exit of the wedding guests.

Lyubimov developed particular techniques for ridiculing certain characters. Inna Ulyanova, who played the house-owner, employed a series of ironic gestures to define her role. She tried to use her female charms on Shui Ta by pulling up her skirt when seated on the table, and by indicating her silhouette when referring to her "business affairs" (*delovye otnosheniya*) with him. The manners of the old woman (the carpet seller's wife) were ridiculed by gesture: she was led off stage by the end of her kerchief, or would need a touch on her shoulder when she stumbled over words and kept repeating them. The family of eight was referred to as sheep when they "baa" with the pronunciation of "smile" (*uliba-a-a-isya*).

But most important was the satirical portrayal of the Gods. They appeared as bureaucrats in suits; they had milk delivered to them on a cloud lowered from above; they could not remember their prayers without the help of a printed copy; they were cowardly and submissive: they "froze" when Shen Teh told them to do so; they played cards and got black eyes when involved in arguments. The Gods are preservers of a power which refuses to perceive and accept the needs of those subject to it, which refuses to face up to the necessity of changing the existing order. Since these Gods neither see nor act, the individual must take action to bring about change; the individual not in isolation, – like Shen Teh, who failed, – but together with society as a whole. An individual like Shen Teh may be good, but she is isolated in her fight; this isolation forces her to produce an *alter ego*, Shui Ta, if she wants to survive. In order to prevent the individual from revealing and using his *alter ego*, he must be supported – not attacked – by others, and the representatives of the system must not demand of an individual that he carry the burden of society, as the Gods demand of Shen Teh.

There was a strong element of social and political agitation in the play, and Lyubimov's production underlined that aspect. The whole of society would need to fight for good if anything was to be achieved; if society does fight, then it will win. Society was seen as a force to make things happen, even if there were superior authorities who neither wished nor were able to change things. The relationship between actors and audience was one of friendly unity; the audience and the company formed one single "we".

Staged before the end of the Khrushchev Thaw, Lyubimov's production of *The Good Person of Szechwan* suggested that the individual as part of a broader social movement might generate the hope and energy required to realise reforms. The keynote of the production was optimistic; the notion of goodness as a gift from above was challenged, and it was society in the form of the audience that was asked to define and create goodness.

This production laid the foundation for much future development of theatrical theme and form at the Taganka. It outlined the interest in Brecht's theatrical theory and practice, in theatre as a form of communicating with the audience, and as a means of conveying ideas.

None the less, however significant this production might have been for the Soviet theatre of its time and for the repertoire of the Taganka, it now seems somewhat pale when measured against subsequent Lyubimov productions. This may be partly explained by the fact that a dramatic text offers less scope for interpretation than, for example, the adaptation of a prose work for the stage, which involves a high degree of condensation – and thereby interpretative selection – of the original material. But it also reflects the aptitude of the actors: the play was staged with trainee actors, not professionals, – a factor which Lyubimov bore in mind when opting for *The Good Person of Szechwan*.[9]

Prose adaptation: *A Hero of Our Time*

When Lyubimov was offered the post of "artistic director" of the Taganka Theatre, he made one condition: the right to select his own ensemble and to build a new repertoire.[10] He rapidly reduced the performances of Plotnikov's productions, often played *The Good Person*,[11] and invited other directors to work at the theatre.

The second production of the newly-founded theatre was *A Hero of Our Time*, which opened in October 1964. The première coincided with Khrushchev's fall from power. The adaptation of Lermontov's novel had been written by Nikolay Erdman and Lyubimov for the 150th anniversary of Lermontov's birth.[12] The production was not considered successful and remained in the repertoire for a relatively short period of time.[13] However, *A Hero of Our Time* was Lyubimov's first adaptation for the theatre, and basic principles for his technique of transferring prose to the stage were established here. Moreover, elements from *The Good Person of Szechwan* were developed further, and new devices were discovered.

Lermontov's *A Hero of Our Time* (1840) describes the phenomenon of the nineteenth-century superfluous man in the figure of Pechorin, and uses a highly complex narrative technique. The novel consists of five separate stories; the first two, "Bela" and "Maksim Maksimych" are told by a first-person narrator who meets Maksim Maksimych on a journey in the Caucasus. Maksim Maksimych relates the story of his friend Pechorin's adventures with the Circassian girl Bela, whom he had abducted and whose heart he won. A jealous local suitor, Kazbich, attempts to seize Bela, but fails; nevertheless, Bela dies, leaving Pechorin in distress. During a second encounter, Maksim Maksimych passes Pechorin's diary to the narrator, and the publication of the diary forms the remaining three sections of the novel: "Taman", "Princess Mary", and "The Fatalist".

In "Taman" Pechorin watches some smugglers, a young girl assisted by a man and a blind boy. Noticing that they are being observed, the girl attempts to drown Pechorin. However, Pechorin is concerned not with the serious danger to his life, but with the fact that it would have been ludicrous had he been killed by a young girl. In "Princess Mary", written in diary form, he demonstrates a similar indifference for life. Pechorin plays with the feelings of two women: Vera, his former mistress, whom he rejects, and Princess Mary, whom he is trying to attract. Yet he does not love Princess Mary, and destroys the prospects of Grushnitsky whom he challenges and kills in a duel. In "The Fatalist" Pechorin suggests a wager challenging the concept of predestination: Captain Vulich takes a revolver, but it misfires as he aims at his head, showing that he is not in control of his life (and death). Yet he is killed the same night by a robber in the street.

Pechorin is an anti-hero, yet he is symptomatic of his time. He is gifted, has considerable potential, but seems doomed to merely destructive activity.

Lyubimov's adaptation restructures the novel to a certain extent. The stage version is divided into two parts; the first comprises "Bela", "Maksim Maksimych" and "The Fatalist", the second "Princess Mary"; "Taman" has been omitted. The first part observes more or less the sequence of events in the narrative, whereas the second part omits some of Pechorin's diary entries and condenses events to enhance the dramatic tension.

Apart from these structural changes in the narrative, some additions have been made for the stage version. Lyubimov employed a theatrical device equivalent to the narrator's function in the novel: he created the figures of "the Author" (the first-person narrator) and "the Poet" (Lermontov, the real author) on stage. The Author, together with Maksim Maksimych, were omnipresent on stage, narrating events, commenting on them and providing the links between episodes. Frequently, scenes were enacted to his and/or Maksim Maksimych's narrative, so that both the Author and Maksim Maksimych function as commentators and narrators who introduce episodes. This underlines a demonstrative element in the acting. In the first part, Maksim Maksimych is doubled by a second actor for some scenes (e.g. the wedding scene), when he himself sits with the Author, and his double enacts what he is relating.

The narrative structure is thus effectively transferred onto the stage: the threefold breakdown of the distance at which the reader is introduced to Pechorin (first through Maksim Maksimych, then through the Author, and finally through Pechorin's own mind) has been maintained in the stage version: Pechorin is seen by the Author through the narrative of Maksim Maksimych; he is a marionette, first appearing only in spotlights when mentioned, then re-enacting what is told. The scenes with him can even be stopped when the light is shifted abruptly to Maksim Maksimych and the Author to provide further information on other characters: narrative and dramatic scenes thus run in parallel. The Author merely passes remarks to Maksim Maksimych in "Bela". At the end of "Bela" he steps forward to announce his second meeting with

Maksim Maksimych and produces a notebook (the diary) to read to the audience. Maksim Maksimych disappears, and the Author only comments on Pechorin, now starting to act independently in "Maksim Maksimych", but even more so in "The Fatalist". It is in the latter section that Pechorin reflects for the first time on his actions, on the notions of life and death (narratively speaking he is able to do so only now as the author of his own diary). The Author and Maksim Maksimych merely figure for a short exchange at the end of the episode. In the second part, the Author virtually disappears. Pechorin tells us what happens; he is fully in charge of and responsible for his actions; he relates his thoughts upon leaving Mary alone after she has declared her love for him. At this point, the Author also steps in and comments on the "hero of our time", drawing largely on the text of Lermontov's foreword to the second edition, in which he explains that he wishes to show the illnesses of his time without offering any cure.[14]

Whereas the distancing from the characters was created by the overlapping narrator–commentator (Author and Maksim Maksimych) in the first part, in the second part, Pechorin steps back from his role to comment by means of the alienation effect. At the end of the second part, Pechorin himself stops the action with the words "Finità la commedia". Then the two letters are read: the first by Doctor Werner, after which the parting scene with Mary is re-enacted, and the second by Vera. As Pechorin tears up Vera's letter, Vera continues to speak: a letter can be destroyed, but the impressions she made on Pechorin cannot be effaced. His desperate attempt to catch up with Vera after she has left is narrated by the Author, who reads the account from Pechorin's notebook.

Moreover, an epilogue and a prologue have been added; here, the figure of Tsar Nicholas I is introduced. In the prologue, the Tsar forces Lermontov to read his poem "The Death of the Poet" to a musical accompaniment, then enquires about the poet's behaviour in general, and finally insists on his punishment. The Author relates that Lermontov was thereupon sent to the Caucasus. At the end, again, the Tsar appears with his ministers, followed by the characters of the play, to comment on *A Hero of Our Time* with words taken from a letter the Tsar wrote to his wife.[15] This forms a frame round the adaptation, but it also dwells on the importance of the poet's life.

> The idea of the director Yury Lyubimov and the theatre he heads is very clear – to tell people today how great artists had to cringe, how they were broken, tormented and finally killed by tyrants.[16]

The theme of the poet, or author, in conflict with the ruling classes was not only extremely important for this production, but was to remain at the forefront of Lyubimov's attention for some time. Lyubimov laid the foundation here for his concept that the life of an artist is as relevant as his works.

As with *The Good Person*, this production, too, was set on a bare stage; a minimum of props and decor was used. The stage was separated from the auditorium by a "light curtain" (*svetovoi zanaves*)[17] at the beginning and end of the production, as well as for set changes; this underlined the temporal distancing of the stage events. A rectangle on the right of the stage was slightly elevated and served for the enactment of certain scenes: a small theatrical stage, it resumed a metatheatrical function. The costumes were relatively modern and neutral: the actors playing Pechorin and the Author wore black frock-coats, the military men wore a kind of *zanni* instead of uniforms.[18]

Music was used for the prologue and epilogue, the Tsar usually being accompanied by choral music. The wedding scene, set to local Caucasian music, and the shouting of the Ossetians during the journey stood therefore in sharp contrast to the pompous music for the imperial world. A special sound effect was used in "The Fatalist", where a voice from above announced the wager; it could also be heard when Pechorin attempted to arrest the murderer – that is, when he challenged his fate.[19]

Choreography was effectively employed, as in *The Good Person of Szechwan*. During the scene in which Mary and Pechorin entertain people in the park of Pyatigorsk, groups were formed around each of them. Gradually, Mary was deserted, while a large crowd gathered round Pechorin. Furthermore, Bela's death was performed in dance-like movements. Indeed, a definite rhythm underlay the whole production:

> The action seems to follow a metronome, set to the pulse of a troubled time going by, and we in the auditorium distinctly hear this metre at various points, underlined in "Bela" by the throwing of the daggers, in "The Fatalist" by the amplified sound of the heated cries of the gamblers, and in "Princess Mary" by the dissonance of the instruments of the brass trio, invalids of the Caucasian wars.[20]

Satirical elements prevailed in the portrayal of Pyatigorsk society, both at the well in the park and at the ball, which resembled a "roundabout of mime".[21] However, the acting, particularly of Pechorin, played by Nikolay Gubenko, was criticised: he was accused of acting too flatly and coldly, with excessive distance and evil; the actors were condemned for being inadequately trained.[22] Indeed, Lyubimov seems to have had doubts about the acting ability of his ensemble.[23] Yet it has to be borne in mind that Lyubimov deliberately cut out the childhood memories from the part of Pechorin, the reflections and doubts about his existence which can be found in the diary. He deliberately deprived Pechorin of any trace of romantic feeling or self-analysis. Instead, he turned Pechorin into a passive and phlegmatic superfluous man. Therefore, the insufficient training of the actors was not the reason for the failure of the production. In a Brechtian approach, the actor comments, reflects, and acts, which is essentially what Pechorin cannot do: he is predestined to continue a superfluous existence; he only longs for a termination of his suffering. Pechorin is destructive, and although the audience observes him, the spectator remains at a distance. Hence the theatre can merely show and ask the audience to view the hero objectively. Yury Aikhenvald reflected in his criticism that the production actually conveyed this interpretation: "... I was shown the process of self-knowledge, I lived through it, but at the same time I looked as if from the side".[24] It seems that it was not the lack of profound psychology in Pechorin, so much criticised in the press, but another reason that caused the failure of this production: Brecht's theories were known, but their practical application left much to be desired in the Soviet Union. Yet Pechorin in a Brechtian theatre could only be the Pechorin chosen by Lyubimov, a Pechorin who looks at his life coldly and objectively, without fervour or despair, doubt or uncertainty. Moreover, the material chosen offered itself formally and structurally for experimentation on stage because of its complex narrative structure and stance, which must have attracted Lyubimov. Yet as far as the content is concerned, the "hero" had little to say to the audience of "our" contemporary time; he was a character formed by his time, and although the philosophical question of existence is still topical, it is placed in a different philosophical context, which has already seen the emergence of existentialism at the turn of the century and the rebirth of the "superfluous man" as the sufferer of *mal du siècle* with Sartre's *Nausea*.

Finally, and most important, there was no bond with the audience apart from the actors' turning to the auditorium, since the theatre had not yet found its own audience. The critic Maryamov noted that in 1964 mainly young, local people went to the theatre, since it was close by.[25] The audience for *The Good Person of Szechwan* had been a special one: theatrical circles and critics for the performances in the Shchukin School, which actually took place in a gymnasium; later, after moving to the Taganka theatre, the production attracted mainly liberally-minded intellectuals. *A Hero of Our Time* was the first production by a new ensemble in a new theatre, which had lost its former audience in two ways: those who had frequented the traditional productions of Plotnikov stopped going to the Theatre of Drama and Comedy, and the spectators of the Shchukin School production had turned to other new school or studio productions, and were not attracted enough by *A Hero of Our Time* to make the journey to Taganka Square.

However, the technique for adapting literature revealed basic principles, such as the creation of an author or narrator figure, the introduction of historical context and the use of documentary material for the purpose of literary adaptation. The theatrical devices of the production confirmed elements already used in *The Good Person*: the bare stage with basic props only, choreographed movement, music to accompany or counterpoint. Furthermore, the light curtain was used for the first time in this production, replacing the traditional theatrical curtain.

Poetic montage: *Antiworlds*

Antiworlds was the first "poetic performance" at the Taganka theatre, premièred on 2 February 1965; it was originally presented under the title *The Poet and the Theatre*. Andrey Voznesensky read his poetry at the beginning of the performance, and then the poems were presented and enacted on stage. As time went on, Voznesensky stopped reading, and the whole performance was created by the actors, now under the title *Antiworlds*.[26]

Lyubimov had no intention of working with one particular playwright, as was the custom in many Soviet theatres, which had "house writers".[27] Instead, the intellectual élite he assembled in the Artistic Council frequently composed montages or adaptations, sometimes jointly with Lyubimov. Voznesensky happened to be a rising star at the time, with a growing national and international reputation. His poetry has a formal link with futurism; yet it is thematically innovative and original. His preoccupation is twentieth-century Man, who exists in an industrial and materialist age of progress which threatens traditional values of beauty, truth, and ideals.

Lyubimov used Voznesensky's poetry to create a bridge to the long-standing tradition in Soviet theatre of poetry readings on stage. However, Lyubimov did not content himself with having the poet merely declaim: he attempted to find a visual correspondence to illustrate and intensify the meaning of the poetry, and often poems would be enacted in the form of dialogue. Furthermore, he embedded the text into the personal experience of the actor as a method of acting.

The elaborate use of mime in *Antiworlds* coincided with extensive experiments in this genre under the guidance of circus artists for the production *Ten Days that Shook the World*, which was premièred two months later. Thus, in the search for new expressive means, poetry offered itself as a suitable textual base for experimentation with a variety of theatrical devices, for experimentation in the area of what critics started calling a "synthetic" theatre: "Plasticity, music, mime, poetry are a *synthesis*, which is created by the performance".[28] In *Antiworlds*, mime served to illustrate the poems "Rock'n'Roll" and "Striptease". The music varied: a choir emerged for "Ophelia's Song"; the "Internationale" sounded out for the poems about Lenin; carnival masks and masquerade music were used for "New Year in Rome"; march music, together with the sound of Hitler's soldiers marching, were heard for "The Masters", during which a swastika and the fences of Maidanek were projected onto the back wall. Brechtian "street theatre" proved helpful: the titles of the poems were given on a blackboard. The actors were omnipresent on stage, like "a wandering street group, which hardly ever parts; all are together – all in black circus outfits".[29]

The text was composed by Voznesensky; it draws on the cycles "Parabola", "Triangular Pear", "Antiworlds" and "I do not renounce!", and the long poems "The Masters", "Longjumeau", and "Oza". These poems were largely uncut, with the exception of the longer poems, of which only sections were selected. The poems were assembled in two sections. The first deals with examples of spiritual or physical death as a cause of the state of the civilised world: the destructive and dehumanising elements in Western culture ("Rock'n'Roll", "Striptease"), suicide ("Monologue of Marilyn Monroe"), experimentation and automatisation ("Oza"), and violence for the sake of progress ("A Woman is Being Beaten", "The Skull Ballad"). The second section discusses ways of seeing: parabolic and linear perception ("Parabolic Ballad"), the absolute rejection of the old for the new ("Paris without Rhyme", "New Year in Rome"), the multifaceted identity as perceived in existentialist philosophy ("I am Seven"). Whereas the poems of the first part are examples of the decline of the humanist tradition, the poems of the second section are warnings of further dangers for human values if progress is blindly pursued. Time therefore plays a vital role in a world dominated by the race for progress. Despite the increased speed of evolution, human life is composed only of moments of eternity, and is futile.

> The clock ticks quietly, in no hurry, but this peace is alarming, false, striving ... each of your days, each word, thought and act, each goes into eternity.[30]

The theme of "Antiworlds" was seen by certain Soviet critics as an opposition between capitalism and socialism, an interpretation to which Voznesensky's poetry indeed lends itself. This theme enabled him fairly early in his career to gain permission to travel abroad, and it almost certainly helped the production to pass without major problems:

> The sense of the production is to oppose the bourgeois world of money, conceit and lies to the world of good and humanity.[31]

The distorted gnashing, barking and convulsing of the robot civilisation...
interrupts... the human, eternal motive of the love and brotherhood of people
(whom the civilisation of the "free world" tries to convert to robots).[32]

Antiworlds, however, also investigates the conflict in Voznesensky's poems between human tradition and technical progress. Voznesensky does not merely oppose capitalist and socialist worlds in order
to classify one as bad and the other as good. There was an undertone of
challenge in the poem "Paris without Rhyme", where the reputation of
Paris as a unique capital was challenged by the actor, speaking as if this
might be Moscow or Leningrad too.[33] The contrast between old and new,
human and material values was symbolised on stage by the image of a
Rublev-style madonna on the right and the picture of a cosmonaut on the
left; these images were carried out after the prologue, when they were
split into halves, and one of each joined together to form a face.[34]
Tradition, merged with contemporary life and progress, stood as a
preamble to the production. Voznesensky's poetry is critical of all
progress which disregards human life: "All progress is reactionary, if
man is destroyed" was the final phrase of the production.

In *Antiworlds*, Lyubimov experimented with theatrical form.
Furthermore, he found in poetry a suitable material for experimentation
in the direction of a theatre combining all available devices, and which
may properly be called "synthetic". Lyubimov made no direct appeal to
the audience in this production. He used Voznesensky's poetry to
formulate in theatrical terms the threat man is subjected to by blind faith
in progress and technology; he perceived the audience not as a mass, but
as a community of individual voices, and underlined the value of the
individual personality.

Revolution as a spectacle: *Ten Days that Shook the World*

In April 1965 the theatre premièred its second highly successful and
much acclaimed production. It was a spectacle loosely based on John
Reed's *Ten Days that Shook the World*, and was subtitled "a popular
performance in two parts with mime, circus, buffoonery and shootings...
with songs based on texts by B. Brecht, A. Blok, F. Tyutchev,
D. Samoilov, N. Maltseva, V. Vysotsky". The adaptation was written by
Yu. Lyubimov, S. Kashtelyan, I. Dobrovolsky and Yu. Dobronravov.[35]

It is necessary to emphasise that the adaptation is *loosely* based on
Reed's account of the revolution and on motifs from his book. The only
incidents taken directly from Reed are the argument about the existence
of two classes between the soldier and the student Panyin at Tsarskoye

Selo railway station and the ideas of the counter-revolutionaries which render the arguments presented to Reed on his visit to the counter-revolutionaries' hideout.[36] The popular ideas, the opinions of the crowd and the revolutionaries narrated by Reed have been inserted into the adaptation without any coherence. The themes of the fall of the Romanov empire, or the suffering of the prisoners have been added to the information provided by Reed.

The role of John Reed as a character, not just an observer of the revolution, but as an American citizen and communist, has been introduced into the adaptation. Not only is the production preceded by Lenin's comment on Reed's book, but several scenes are devoted to the reactions provoked by Reed's account in the United States, including Reed's trial for spreading revolutionary ideas. Apart from that, Reed appears as an observer of the diplomatic gathering.

The information on which the adaptation is based is drawn from several additional sources. Many speeches by Lenin have been added, the Reed theme inserted, the fall of the tsarist regime taken into account. Sources used for dialogues supplementary to Reed's account are Maksim Gorky's *The Life of Klim Samgin* and Leonid Andreev's *Tale about the Seven who were Hanged*.

Despite the fact that little of Reed's text was used for the adaptation, and that there is no correspondence in coherence or chronology of events between Reed's *Ten Days* and the theatre version, the adaptation managed to catch the spirit and the atmosphere of Reed's account, in which the people are shown as active and energetic, as the driving force of the revolution. In the production "the protagonist is the revolutionary people".[37]

The text of the adaptation is thus basically new, drawing on the literature of the time, and attempting to capture on stage what stimulated Reed to write his account. Ideas and atmosphere are expressed by and large in *theatrical* rather than verbal language. It draws on devices like song, mime, projection, voice-over, shadow-play, buffoonery, images, allegories, in other words, all the theatrical and literary devices available. The production is "the free and creative arrangement of the book in theatrical language".[38] The adaptation devotes long sections to the instructions for mime or stage directions, which is not common for other playscripts of the Taganka Theatre.

The text of the adaptation is very neatly structured: it is divided into two parts, containing 26 and 16 scenes respectively, each scene bearing a title.[39] The first part provides an exposition of the revolutionary atmosphere, followed by a series of scenes devoted to the character of Reed, his attitude to the revolution, and his trial in the U.S., forming a prologue to the events in Russia. The state of affairs in Russia is first shown by quoting examples of the individual sufferings of the proletariat, and by citing individual attitudes to the politics of the nobles and bourgeoisie. Then, the political events are focussed on the fall of the tsarist empire and the emergence of the Provisional Government under Kerensky. Finally, individuals have become crowds, which are portrayed in the last section, referring both to the bourgeoisie and the proletariat. The second part provides first an insight into the "old guard": the Duma, the counter-revolutionaries and the diplomats. Then, it gives the opinion of the common people, soldiers and crowds, representing the "new guard". Finally, it looks at the political effects of these attitudes: the fall of the Provisional Government and the triumph of the Bolshevik revolution.

As far as the revolutionary theme is concerned, there is a logical principle of cause and effect on which both parts are based: in both parts, the people are the cause; the effects are the February and October revolutions respectively. The cause has, on each occasion, two sides: the worker and the bourgeois, the counter-revolutionary and the Bolshevik. It is this contrast between thesis and antithesis, in Marxist terms, that leads to the historic synthesis: revolution. The principle of two contrasted and opposing forces forms the aesthetic principle of the production: the thematic contrast between reactionary and revolutionary forces is represented in the stylistic contrast of comic and tragic, grotesque and pathetic, satirical and serious, which determines the aesthetics of the production.

Theatrical devices employed to underline this contrast were used either for one or both forces simultaneously, so that there was no stereotyping in the usage of any theatrical devices for a particular type of expression.

Mime was used both for comic and tragic, revolutionary and anti-revolutionary scenes. It was employed to portray the revolution in symbols or images, such as the rise of the red flame of the revolution, which cannot be suppressed by black – conservative – forces, or the beating of the anvil as a symbol for the power of the workers in the revolution, sparking off the revolutionary fire in the introduction and finale. Mime was also deployed for the silent expression of the heavy burden of the people in the time preceding the revolutions: the straining work of a peasant, ploughing the soil; or the queue for bread. The imprisonment of revolutionaries was symbolised by the prisoners' holding their arms in the form of a rectangle around their faces, which were lit by a spot, creating thus the impression of heads behind bars. The busy "hive of the revolution" was shown in the form of a fast moving mime.

Mime also rendered the exploitation by the bourgeoisie in allegorical form. In "The Bureaucrat and the Dignitary" both figures were reduced to puppets, moving to the tune of a musical box and talking only when a halt in the music caused their movements to stop. After the third repetition of the order by the dignitary to continue pushing the workers further to increase production, the music speeded up and lost its rhythm, as did the movements of the two men: their ideas were as much out of time and pace as their movements. The fall of the Provisional Government was also executed in the form of a mime: sailors came onto the stage one after the other, pulling the bench on which the ministers of the Provisional Government were seated, occupying one seat after the other, and at the same time pushing the ministers off the other end of the bench, where they collapsed in a heap, falling over each other.[40]

A variation of mime was the shadow-play, or theatre of silhouettes. In the scene "Shades of the Past", several representative members of society passed behind a huge white screen covering the whole of the stage. They acted through their shadows, which were original, enlarged or diminished in size. Paperboys, nuns, alcoholics, prostitutes, bourgeois passed along, elements of a society that was about to crumble (Figure 2). Three Red Guard soldiers were enlarged to a size that even extended beyond the screen, nearly wiping away all these "elements". One guard engaged in an argument with a little man, the student Panyin of Reed's account, about the theory of two classes; the soldier crushed his opponent both by his size and by his argument, which was repeated several times over an amplifier.

> It is as if the soldiers wipe out those shades of the past. Thus the theatre hyperbolically summarises the idea of the great force of the revolution.[41]

Light played another vital part in the production, creating images, such as the columns of the Petrograd exchange, or columns separating the mother from her imprisoned son. The light curtain was used to distance events, to serve, for example, as a trench, or to deprive the soldiers of the White Guards of head and body, concentrating on their step by having them march along in front of the light curtain.[42]

Buffoonery was a vital component for the portrayal of counter-revolutionary and bourgeois scenes, and it occurred largely in connection with verbal irony or satire. In the scene where the U.S. Senate interrogated Reed, the senators stood in front of Wilson's animated portrait, and behind their lecterns and robes, wearing *zanni*. Only their hands and faces emerged behind their robes, a device used in Meyerhold's production of *The Puppet Booth*.[43] They were reduced to masks, to façades, hiding behind their profession and position, and shrinking to insignificant little men when emerging from behind them. The scene also ridiculed the senators textually, while Reed remained superior to them with his wittiness. When the senators pretended to "see through" Reed, he countered "Dr. Roentgen, presenting to the world the radiology machine, would have simply envied you, Sir".[44] In their enthusiasm to fight the revolution and Reed's book, the senators were not only ready to "arrest" the book, but to ignore the revolution entirely and pretend it never happened.[45] When Reed gave an account of what he said to Lenin about future economic relations with the U.S., he was told not to repeat these words, only to point out that they stem from George Washington,[46] thus highlighting the senators' ignorance of the history of the country they represent. Their session was followed by a song sung by Wilson from behind his animated portrait, and by an ensemble of music-hall singers emerging in hats, red boots, black net tights, shorts and waist-coats, with a portrait of president Coolidge attached to their bottoms (Figure 3).

The nobles' meeting was constructed similarly: the nobles, a banker, a priest, a nobleman and an industrial manager, all wearing *zanni*, dined – fictionally – at a table consisting of a tablecloth placed over two ropes pulled across stage. They were exposed to ridicule, requiring a waiter to tell them about table manners. Similarly, the scene of the diplomats parodied their manners when they sipped their drinks audibly. They also wore masks. The Duma was represented literally as a "headless" government: the members sat at a black table, they were covered by the cloth, with only their hands emerging, gesturing in the void.

Kerensky and the Provisional Government were satirised. After the fall of the Tsar, expressed by the backdrop of his upside-down portrait on the back wall, the banner was dropped over the portrait, with the red part extending to the workers and revolutionaries on one side, the white to the White Guard and the clergy on the other, and the blue section covering the centre stage, from which masked bourgeois society emerged with Kerensky. Kerensky was symbolically carried on the shoulders of a bourgeois. Kerensky's Provisional Government ministers appeared with their cases and folders already packed, placing the cases bearing the words "provisional" (*vremennoe*) and "government" (*pravi-tel'stvo*) along the stage. As they sat in line, the military member of the government fell asleep, completely drunk, and when woken up, he passed a bottle of vodka to Kerensky, thus alluding to the problem of alcoholism at the time of the revolution, described by Reed. The cases were then piled up to construct a podium for Kerensky's speech, during which he collapsed along with the podium. The women's battalion put

at Kerensky's disposal was ridiculed by the undisciplined manner in
which it marched around, by the ambiguous comments of the women on
their reasons for joining the army, and by the execution of the command
"Lie down!" upon which they all took off their skirts. Their officer even
gave up training them, and showed indifference in his command
"Forward, backward, where you want".[47]

The last meeting of the Provisional Government showed again the
masked ministers with cases and folders, this time to be pushed off the
bench. The conversation is full of irony: the ministers are wordy, but
inactive; they play with words.

> FIRST MINISTER: "Gentlemen, our situation is not that dangerous."
> SECOND MINISTER: "We have two situations, an inner and an outer one." ...
>
> SIXTH MINISTER: "We have a peak (*pikovaya*) situation."
> SEVENTH MINISTER: "We have a delicate (*pikantnaya*) situation."
> EIGHTH MINISTER: "Thank goodness, we are still in a vertical situation."[48]

Kerensky got completely muddled towards the end, and, closing the
meeting, called it – nonsensically – a *"predsedanie zavitel'stva"* instead of a
"zasedanie pravitel'stva" (government meeting). He was left vainly asking
his headless ministers (whose heads slipped under their mantillas), to
think about new "measures", and urging that a "formula" be found.[49]
Aleksandr Fedorovich Kerensky's flight was illustrated by him changing
behind a partition screen into the nurse Aleksandra Fedorovna.

Three devices directly taken from Brecht were the use of song,
placard and projection. Songs commented on the action, summarised,
linked episodes, and created transitions. At the same time, the singers led
the audience through the production, providing a bond with the spectators. The voice of Maksim Straukh (who played Lenin in a number of
now classical films of Soviet Socialist Realism) filled the auditorium with
comments by Lenin on the Bolshevik revolution; this device connected
episodes to the historical context.

Slides of Lenin, smiling, frowning, as child or grown-up, were
frequently projected either on the back or the side wall, underlining his
role as leader of the Bolshevik revolution. Furthermore, the Reed memorial plaque on the Kremlin wall near the mausoleum, Reed's pass for the
Smolny, the Statue of Liberty, a portrait of Breshkovskaya and the icon
of the Virgin Mary were projected onto the walls either to document or
create the atmosphere of a particular scene.

Placards provided headlines: "Popular performance" (*narodnoe
predstavlenie*) was the heading for the prologue, when all the actors were
training or exercising on stage, getting ready for the production which

was about to start. It was opened by a shot from three soldiers at stage right. "Revolutionary matter" (*Delo o revolyutsii*) was the title of the senators' folders. "Provisional Government" (*Vremennoe pravitel'stvo*) was written on the cases of the ministers, cut to *"vrem[ya]"* (time) and *"prav[a]"* (rights) for the Duma-scene by the overlapping tablecloth, possibly indicating that *time* for the Duma had run out as much as the *right* to exist. "No bread" (*Khleba net*) signposted the queue for bread. "No paraffin and not known" (*Kerosina net i ne izvestno*) echoed the lack of fuel during the revolution. The soldiers in the trenches appealed to their opponents with the placard "Let's be brothers – come for friendly chats and snacks" (*Budem brat'yami – vykhodite na druzheskie razgovory i zakuski*).

The production was, however, not limited to the stage and the auditorium. It started outside the theatre, where amplifiers emitted revolutionary songs. The tickets were checked and piled on bayonets by Red Guards. Programmes were sold by ladies wearing red kerchiefs. Red bows were pinned to the spectators' jackets. Red banners with revolutionary slogans decorated the walls of the foyer, preserving in their spelling the old letter "yat": "All power to the Sovets!"; "Welcome the revolution of workers, soldiers and peasants!"; "Proletarians of all countries, unite!" and Mayakovsky's slogan "Eat pineapples and chew grouse, your last day is coming, bourgeois louse!". The musicians appeared twice in the foyer before the performance to create the revolutionary atmosphere with song and dance, before leading the audience into the auditorium. The audience was thus integrated into the festive atmosphere of the production. It was also asked, upon leaving, to vote for or against the production: "Dear citizens, we ask you, at the end of the production, to insert your ticket: if you liked the production – into the red box; if you did not like the production – into the black box. No abstaining. Bye-bye". The integration of the audience, its participation, were vital to the production, as was pointed out by several critics:

> The most interesting thing in it [the production] is the auditorium, its joyfully raised spirits . . . such a production is simply unthinkable in a politely indifferent audience.[50]

> The exceptional contact between actors and spectators performs a miracle: the spectators feel like contemporaries of those heroic days.[51]

> The theatre fulfilled one of its most important missions – it awakened all our feelings and at the same time gave relaxation.[52]

The topicality of the production lay not only in the festive atmosphere, in the enthusiasm of the young ensemble, but also in the way in which the text was performed, and in additional lines spoken to update the text. In April 1990, the following modifications had been effected: the senator commented on the entertainment of the music-hall singers that "This is what our people need"; in the conversation of the nobles, the priest remarked "again you are asking for pluralism"; Kerensky expanded his speech from "Democracy is discussion" to "Democracy is, up to now, only discussion";[53] the musicians sang about the "freedom of parliamentary elections"; in the discussion of newspapers by the diplomats, a paper was named as the "organ of Lithuanian separatists"; Kerensky was supposed to say "I am anointed by the people to raise Russia from her grave" (*Ya pomazan narodom podnyat' Rossiyu iz groba*), but garbled it to "I come from the masses of people" (*ya iz mass naroda*),[54] thus converting his speech to the argumentation of his opponents, the Bolsheviks. The production of 1990 thus mingled the revolutionary past with the present, drawing open parallels or hinting at hitherto hidden similarities between past and present.

> Everything is subordinated to a definite ideological and artistic task –... synthetically to unite the revolutionary past and the socialist present.[55]

Lyubimov challenged history in making it tangible to a contemporary audience, rather than putting it on a pedestal.

> Yu. Lyubimov deprived history of its magnificence and private life of its seclusion. He achieved this thanks to a generous use of abstraction and purely fictional elements.[56]

The production drew on elements of Brechtian theatre in the use of placard, projection, and song, as well as the mode of *predstavlenie* (demonstration) rather than that of *perezhivanie* (emotional experience) of the Moscow Arts Theatre. The carnivalesque, playful elements echoed Vakhtangov's theatre; the notion of the ensemble of actors as a means to express the director's idea was reminiscent of Meyerhold.[57] Critics commented on the influence of Petrushka theatre and the tradition of icon-painting (covering all but hands and face);[58] and on the use of cinematic techniques in the episodic treatment of the production and the use of the device of foregrounding and backgrounding.[59]

Yet a production like *Ten Days* deserves to be considered as idiosyncratic, as an entity rather than an amalgam of styles and traditions. Certainly, many devices can be traced back to theatrical history, and certainly, Lyubimov connects to the style of Meyerhold and Okhlopkov, which had been lost in the 1940s. But Lyubimov's use of different theatrical methods is not so much a statement of belonging to a certain school, but more an attempt to create a form which corresponds to the ideas he wishes to express in the production.

Ideas come in various guises in Lyubimov's productions; in *Ten Days*, the idea of an active people creating major changes was put forward in an original form. The attempt to create the festive atmosphere of those revolutionary days, to re-create the enthusiasm was an ideal mode to appeal to the audience to continue, in the present, the active and creative role it played in the past, and to take part in the revolutionary process. A production like *Ten Days* was only possible in the initial phase of the Taganka, at a time of political "Thaw", with a young collective ensemble, and in a phase when theatrical creativity was dominated by a positive attitude to the people, the audience, who are asked to bring about changes.

War poetry: *The Fallen and the Living*

The Fallen and the Living is a montage of Russian war poetry composed by David Samoilov, Boris Gribanov and Yury Lyubimov. The production was intended to mark the 20th anniversary of the victory over fascism on 9 May 1965. The montage was presented without an interval, and the programme only named the sections of the composition as "novellas", composed of poems, letters, memoirs and other authentic material.

The composition begins with a prologue (a recital of poems by Vladimir Mayakovsky, Nikolay Aseev, Mikhail Svetlov, and Aleksandr Tvardovsky) which is followed by the dedication of the performance to those fallen in the war in the form of an "eternal flame" being lit, a minute of silence, and Samoilov's poem "The Fatal Forties". The "Novella of the Three Poets" gives an account of the fate of the poets Vsevolod Bagritsky, Pavel Kogan, and Mikhail Kulchitsky, who all died in the war. Then a novella based on Viktor Nekrasov's *Zemlyanka* ("The Dug-Out") tells about the dominating role of war experiences in the memories of the participants and the danger of forgetting the past for those who were not involved in the war. The "Novella about Four Soldiers" deals with writers in the war. The scene "Dictator–conqueror", based on Charles Chaplin's autobiography, is about the bomb threats after the filming of "The Great Dictator", and Chaplin's appeal for the formation of a Second Front. Chaplin turns into Hitler to comment on culture and politics. The mime "This must not be repeated" forms the epilogue to the excursion into history. The novella about the "Prisoners of Fascism" remembers the engineer Dmitry Karbyshev, the poet Musa Dzhalil, and the Czech national hero Julius Fucík, who died in concentration camps, and includes the song "The Ten Grumblers" (a variation of the German folk song *Zehn kleine Negerlein*). The "Novella about Leningrad" is based on Olga Berggolts's memoirs of the blockade. The "Liberated City", Berlin, is remembered with poems and diary excerpts by Konstantin Simonov, Vsevolod Ivanov and Boris Pasternak. The novella "You must not pity us" deals with the poet Semen Gudzenko, who died of his wounds after the war had ended. The last section contains poets' comments on the war, and ends with poems by Boris Slutsky and Yury Levitansky.

Apart from poetry, documentary materials have been used for the composition; they were presented in the production by characters like the "documentalist", the "radio speaker", the "leader", or a figure speaking "on behalf of the author".

The Fallen and the Living was set on a bare stage; the actors wore neither make-up nor costume (Figure 4). The musical arrangement contained pieces from Schubert and Shostakovich, and there was guitar accompaniment for some Russian folk songs[60] and for Bulat Okudzhava's songs "Along the Smolensk Road" (*Po Smolenskoi doroge*) and "Song of Soldiers' Boots" (*Pesnya o soldatskikh sapogakh*). Mime operated in the interludes and in the Chaplin section. The light curtain was used for scenes of war.

Critics were unanimous in their judgement that the theme was important, especially for young people. The production sounded as if it came not from the past, but from the present: it was contemporary and topical.

> The very title of the production formulates an appeal to the present. The aspects of Soviet history which become visible in the life and experience of those poets are, for Lyubimov, not closed, but open, in process, and are tested today for their validity.[61]

> [The production] purifies and elevates us above everyday life, evoking silent and bitter tears about those who were taken by the war. It preserves and confirms the memory of the fallen in the hearts of the living.[62]

The poetry was recited in an unusual manner: poems seemed to be filtered through the individual personality of the actor, and the experiences of each actor seemed to be genuine. There was no stilted declamation, as so frequently happened in Soviet theatre. Therefore, the production was compared to a requiem in its musicality and sincerity.[63] The theme of individual loss, the loss of poetically and artistically gifted people because of the war is not entirely compatible with the contemporary official view of the war as a heroic deed by the Soviet nation as a whole; nor is the idea that soldiers fight not *for* their country, but *against* the idea of fascism compatible with the official reading of the Great Patriotic War.

> The fallen did not only fall for the sake of military victory; their fight on the battlefields was not just the fight of a soldier fulfilling his military duty. It was the opposition to a concept, the fight against the very idea of fascism.[64]

However, the production was criticised for containing "no formal innovations"; attacks were launched on the actors for their lack of psychological portrayal; and the composition was criticised for a lack of profundity.[65] This had to do with the official view of the production and the tightening up of censorship at the time. In the first years the Taganka theatre still profited from the presence of liberals in the relevant positions in the state apparatus. There were no conflicts over any of the Taganka's previous productions. But there were serious difficulties with the authorities over this production.

Two issues gave rise to controversy. First, fascism was equated with Stalinism and the personality cult. Fascism was not sufficiently barbaric and not associated closely enough with Hitler's Germany. Moreover, Hitler's caricature in the production was seen to weaken his barbarism:

> Lyubimov does not confuse anything, but quite consciously attempts in this montage to divert the anger of the audience away from the fascists, who killed the Leningrad woman mentioned above, and focus it on the gunmen of the 1937 tragedy which has no connection with the Leningrad blockade whatsoever.[66]

Furthermore, the choice of poets featured numerous Jewish writers at a time when the Jewish question was a particularly delicate issue. F. Evseev of the Main Administration accused Lyubimov of choosing only Jewish writers, naming the Russian Kulchitsky along with Pasternak, Samoilov, Kogan and Kazakevich, but forgetting the seemingly Ukrainian, but in fact Jewish, Semen Gudzenko.[67] This instance showed the incompetence of the state representatives who were in charge of the theatre.

Secondly, the material incorporated texts which were either controversial or unpublished. These included: Olga Berggolts's "Duma" of 1940 which, apart from being unpublished and censored from an edition of Berggolts's poetry prepared in 1965,[68] contained a reference to the Kolyma prison camp. Similarly, the mention of a camp caused objections to the scene between the poet Vsevolod Bagritsky and his imprisoned mother. The poems by Pasternak came mainly from *Doctor Zhivago*, which had been refused publication in the Soviet Union and had subsequently been published in Italy. In 1958 Pasternak was awarded the Nobel Prize, but forced to refuse it. Although some of the Zhivago poems had been published in 1954, the central one used for the production, "Hamlet", had not been one of them. Lyubimov was accused of sensationalism for selecting this poem.[69] Emmanuel Kazakevich's letters to his wife were also unpublished. The Main Administration requested the deletion of the appropriate passages and the inclusion of the poem "Ten Grumblers", with its description of the disappearance of people in the Third Reich, and the figures of Karbyshev, Fucík and Dzhalil, to strengthen the theme of "barbarism" under fascist régimes; the last novella with poems by Sergei Narovchatov, Aleksandr Mezhirov, Yaroslav Smelyakov and Mikhail Lukonin (all survivors of the war) was added to redress the balance between Jewish writers and Russians.

Discussions of the *The Fallen and the Living* were carried out at five different levels of the Party and state apparatus: the Main Administration of Culture, the Kirov District Committee of the CPSU, the Ministry of Culture, the Central Committee, and the Writers' Union's Committee on Matters of the War; they included personal meetings between Lyubimov and Yury Andropov of the Central Committee, and the Minister of Culture, Ekaterina Furtseva. *The Fallen and the Living* was viewed by the Main Administration of Culture in March, June and September 1965, and by the Ministry of Culture in October 1965. Nineteen changes had to be made before the production could be premièred on 4 November 1965,[70] and finally cleared by the Main Administration thanks to the support of Anastas Mikoyan.[71] However, it came under attack in the press once the hardliners had resumed power in 1968.[72] The modifications and procedures reflect the cultural climate of the time, the process of stagnation and the regression to conservative politics rather than the continuation of liberalism.

With respect to these two major issues, the theatre had gone against the Party line. However, it remains doubtful whether Lyubimov was aware that the age of liberalism had passed, whether he could anticipate the change to hard line politics which had only just begun to manifest itself openly: in the Kremlin meetings of 1962/63 when Khrushchev met the intelligentsia, and blamed it for the failure of his liberalism in the aftermath of the Cuban Missile Crisis; in the arrest in 1964 of the Leningrad poet Iosif Brodsky during Khrushchev's campaign against "parasites"; in the arrest of Andrey Sinyavsky and Yuly Daniel' for publishing abroad under pseudonyms in February 1966; in the temporary suppression of a number of controversial productions during the XXIII Party Congress in 1966 (including Tvardovsky's *Terkin in the Other World* at the Satire Theatre); in the ousting of Fedor Burlatsky and Len Karpinsky from the editorial board of *Pravda* following their article in favour of liberalism in cultural politics with regard to the theatre in June 1967;[73] and finally in the intervention of Soviet troops in Prague in August 1968.

Restoration of original versions: *The Life of Galileo*

In 1966 the ensemble returned to Bertolt Brecht. This time it was *The Life of Galileo*, based on the life of the great seventeenth-century physicist who was forced by the Inquisition to renounce his theory that the earth moved around the sun. The play demanded a more subtle psychological portrayal than *The Good Person of Szechwan*, particularly as far as the protagonist was concerned.

Brecht wrote *The Life of Galileo* in 1938/39, when it ended on the pessimistic note that Galileo, after renouncing 'iis theory of the universe, is merely interested in his bodily health, and sends his former pupil Andrea Sarti away when the latter comes to say farewell. In 1945/46, Brecht changed this ending into a more optimistic one: in a long speech, Galileo assumes responsibility for mankind as far as his discoveries are concerned, and passes his manuscripts on to Andrea. This change followed the dropping of the first atomic bomb on Hiroshima:

> The atomic bomb is both as a technical and as a social phenomenon the classic result of his [Galileo's] scientific achievements and his social failure.[74]

The standard text consists of the modified, later version, in which Galileo's long, final speech is appended to the earlier version.

The Taganka theatre preserved this double ending in its production. Galileo, played by Vladimir Vysotsky, sent Andrea away at the end of the play. Then the actors returned, the stage was dimmed in red light; Vysotsky–Galileo pulled Andrea back with his walking stick in order to give him the manuscripts. Then Vysotsky pronounced the speech, while standing in a spotlight on the bare stage: all the props that belonged to the play and its time were removed to illustrate the lapse of time in order to make allowance for this speech, written "after the bomb", and to refer the audience to the 1940s.

The theatre added yet another note to these two endings, creating a third finale, which was built up from the beginning of the production: Soviet Pioneers with red ties peered out of the "windows" of the set, introducing the audience to the play which the players of the theatre are about to show; they were chased off by some monks. The same Pioneers, only more in number, emerged at the end of the production with globes, which they turned round while encircling Galileo: even if he had been destroyed, as the first version said, he had`assumed responsibility for enlarging mankind's horizon, and his ideas have survived.

The set designed by Enar Stenberg consisted of walls made out of egg cartons (Figure 5). They could be modified by red lighting to form the sides of narrow streets, folding into two parts, or to define rooms, functioning as a wall. The structure of the egg cartons was broken up to create windows. Again, the set was simple, consisting only of what was essential for the action, and giving an indication of place and its nature: open or closed, oppressive or liberating.

Galileo emerged in the first scene performing a handstand and standing on his head as part of his morning exercises: the world was turned upside down in front of his mental eye, just as he would, symbolically speaking, turn the notion of the world upside down.[75] A further symbol was Galileo's making the sign of the cross over the body of his daughter Virginia, who fainted: he destroyed her future marriage by pursuing his studies.

Galileo was supported by two choirs: the Pioneer boys formed a choir in support of Galileo, representing hope.[76] They stood on one side of the stage, while a choir of monks was placed on the other; this one was endowed with the function of repeating the threats to Galileo. The profiles of the monks were drawn on a screen covered with black velvet, with their faces emerging through holes. Whereas the boys had angelic faces, the monks covered theirs with masks made from photographs. Yet at the same time, the two choirs represented the duality of Galileo's personality:

> Not only the words of their songs conflict, but even their voices – the heavenly voices of the children and the coarse and mundane voices of the monks. In the confrontation of the choirs, the aim and idea of the tragedy of Galileo becomes clearer... Precisely these two sides fight in Galileo's great soul.[77]

Galileo fights not only against external, but also internal forces. These external forces are, as Brecht suggests, not only the Church, but any form of authority: "In the original the Church was shown as a lay authority, with an ideology in principle exchangeable with many others".[78] Hence spy scenes occur frequently: Galileo is under constant overt or covert surveillance from the authority with which he is in dispute.

In the play, Galileo is tempted by earthly and bodily health and pleasures, which lead him to renounce his discovery in the first version. In the Taganka production, it was society that broke Galileo's character, not his flesh; he did, in fact, not age during the performance.[79]

> The Galileo of the Taganka theatre searches for a compromise not because he is driven by the commands of his flesh, but because society compels him, breaks him, violates him.[80]

The responsibility he assumes lies not just with him, but with everybody:

> If Galileo has such a responsibility for mankind, then contemporary man has as high and as great a responsibility.[81]

Society at large and the audience in particular share this responsibility:

> We experience a community between us and those who so audaciously and with such conviction give up their rights for the freedom of thought.[82]

Carnivalesque elements were used as stipulated by Brecht when people celebrate on the street after Galileo has taken up research again.[83]

> Galileo's audacity and happiness are emphasised in the production by means of folk scenes. The actors of the touring theatre pour out onto the square . . . their dance, their smart acrobatic figures, the round dance in bright colours, the ragged costumes – all is like a holiday, like a break from everyday life, an example of the people's solidarity.[84]

Brecht himself indicated that "the 'hero' of the work is not Galileo, but the people...".[85] If the people are the "hero", and have the power to destroy the freedom of others, then it lies within their capacity to change an abuse of power.

The people, rather than the individual, were the protagonist in the production, although the popular mass was composed of individuals. Again, the idea of people's power carried an optimistic overtone, and a positive appeal underlay the concept of the second Brecht production at the theatre.

Homage to a poet: *Listen! Mayakovsky!*

On 16 May 1967 the Taganka theatre premièred another poetic performance, this time about Mayakovsky. The production had first been given the provisional title *Alive with the Living*,[86] but was eventually entitled *Listen!*, after Mayakovsky's poem of 1914.

The composition was written by Yury Lyubimov and Veniamin Smekhov, and consists of two acts, with four thematic sections: Love, War, Revolution and Art. These sections are differentiated by means of light (green, red/black, red and rainbow colours respectively), by illustrative poses of the artists and by quotations, from Shakespeare, Marx, Engels and Hugo respectively. The first act contains a prologue about the exhibition of twenty years of Mayakovsky's work, the introduction of the four themes, and the sections "Love", "War" and "Revolution". The second act deals with the section "Art", covering also the conflict of the artist with bureaucrats and opponents; it also covers a recital competition of Mayakovsky's poetry as held in Soviet schools, and a conversation between Pushkin and Mayakovsky. The acts represent the convergence of personal and political in the poet, and their divergence.

The composition draws on famous poems by Mayakovsky, as well as on documents, letters and statements, which are assembled in an associative rather than chronological manner: "The lyric montage is based . . . on subjective whimsical associations".[87] The excerpts are mainly from the love poem "About That" (1923); the poems on Lenin and the revolution "Left March" (1918), "An Ode to the Revolution" (1918), "V. I. Lenin" (1924), "War and the World", "Lenin is with us!" (1927), "Very Good!" (1927); the poems on the power of words "Jubilee" (1924), "A Conversation with the Inspector of Taxes about Poetry" (1926), "Epistle to the Proletarian Poets" (1926); the early poems "Listen!" (1914), "Cloud in Trousers" (1914/15); the satirical poems "On Trash" (1920/21), "Paper Horrors" (1927), and "Veterans" (1928) and the autobiographical poem "I Myself"; the plays *Vladimir Mayakovsky*, *The Bath-House*, *Moscow Burning* and *Mystery Bouffe*.[88] The production thus combines literary materials of different style and tone to create a theatrical entity:

> The poetic show is gripping, and you begin to forget that you are watching a montage, and not a play. Document, poem, reply, words from papers, from Mayakovsky's polemical debates blend with the music of the poetic symphony, with the symbol of detail, with the drawing of the mise-en-scène. The picture of the poet's life is created with different elements – pathos, agitational placard, lyrics, anger, irony, delight.[89]

The approach was comparable to *Ten Days* in its combination of different theatrical and literary techniques to form a synthesis; the term "synthetic" once again proved more than adequate for Lyubimov's style.

Mayakovsky's poetry was treated as an industrial product, as indeed it was perceived by the poet himself: "[Words] establish Mayakovsky not as a literary legend, but as the worker of the poetic production line".[90] The set was directly derived from this interpretation: Enar Stenberg's design consisted of cubes bearing the letters of the alphabet, out of which walls, chairs, tables, tribunes, benches, a catwalk and pedestals for statues could be built (Figure 6); they were "the construction material for the performance".[91] But the letters could also be assembled to form words like *lyubof* ("love", misspelt), *Misteriya Buff* (Mystery Bouffe), *pech'* (Oven), or "Mayakovsky". Symbolically, the letters "M" and "B" of the title of Mayakovsky's play *Mystery Bouffe* could fall away when problems with the permission for rehearsal were mentioned, leaving the word "hysteria" (*isteriya*) instead of "mystery" (*misteriya*), and "phew" (*uff*) instead of "bouffe" (*buff*).

The atmosphere of work was further underlined by the use of white and red aprons worn by the poet-figures and the characters in those scenes where the work aspect was emphasised, such as the section on "Revolution" and the mention of Mayakovsky's activities at the Smolny. The metaphor in which creating poetry was likened to cooking[92] was symbolised on stage by the construction of a cube-tower of the letters P, E, Ch, ', (stove, oven) on which the poets, wearing aprons, worked.

On the back wall, a lion – an enlarged drawing by Mayakovsky – was shaped from black metal bars; it could move its tail, smile or pout, and weep by means of a light bulb functioning as a tear (in the scene "War"). It could also roar in protest at the action on stage, when Mayakovsky was under accusation or at the recital competition.

The role of Mayakovsky was distributed between five actors (Figure 6), a device to be repeated in the 1973 production *Comrade, believe...* with Pushkin. The five Mayakovskys were based on a description Mayakovsky gave of himself in 1915 in a piece entitled "About the Different Mayakovskys" in which he characterises himself as "self-advertiser", "cabby", "cheeky fellow," "cynic," and "haughty" respectively. Valery Zolotukhin played the "pupil of the painting school, young, naively delighted, in love with life"; Boris Khmelnitsky was "in a striped yellow jacket and top hat, young, mischievous, lanky, boy-like, awkward"; Vladimir Vysotsky was "in a white shirt, without jacket, with cloth cap, with billiard cue and chalk in his hands, as he looked at the billiard table, on the platform of the Polytechnic, when, taking off his jacket, he read his poems and engaged in polemics with the audience"; Veniamin Smekhov, the "representative Mayakovsky, in an elegant American suit, as he was in the last years of his life, as known in America and Europe"; V. Nasonov, was the "silent, victorious" Mayakovsky.[93] The motives for the suicide were also differentiated at the end: Nasonov left first, excluding himself from the poets; Zolotukhin went out when judged to possess an "iron" character; Vysotsky left third after – accused of being a demagogue – he recited "Listen!"; Khmelnitsky, the fourth, left because he felt misunderstood by his own country; finally, Smekhov ran away from the "trash", the Soviet bourgeois audience.[94]

This division proved helpful for revealing the multi-faceted character of the poet. However, all the actors together represented a unified character, since no differentiation was made in the texts they spoke. The lines of each Mayakovsky did not reflect the division made by the outer appearance, and therefore the approach remained on a rather superficial level. Shakh–Azizova argued that the device was not successfully realised until Pushkin in *Comrade, believe...*

Analytically splitting Mayakovsky, the theatre did not achieve a synthesis. We do not see the traits of a powerful, difficult and solid character, but a group of like-minded people, in agreement with each other. Instead of algebra, there is arithmetic; the play "by various Mayakovskys" did not take place.[95]

Mime illustrated certain themes: the killings during the war were represented by men falling off the catwalk formed by cubes to a musical accent set by a kettledrum; the mood of the poet in "Love" was underlined by a leap-frog exercise by the five poet-actors; and the theme itself was announced in the form of a mime in which women embrace the poets.

The use of satire in the production was highly effective and made it sound most topical. Characters who glorified or attacked Mayakovsky were portrayed satirically or grotesquely. The themes of religion, the education system and bureaucracy were exposed to satire, since they were perceived as "enemies of the revolution". In the scene in which angels invited the poet for coffee, the angels had haloes formed by the butterfly nets which they carried in their rucksacks (Figure 7); bureaucrats read *Sovetskaya kul'tura* and scribbled on little tables made of cubes, having paper thrown at them from above; they also performed morning exercises to a song with the words "Two steps right, one to the left, one to the front and two to the back".[96] The recital competition was ridiculed by having a boy and a girl speak seemingly meaningless words at high speed, both dressed in a rather casual manner, not at all like Soviet schoolchildren.

Further targets of satire could be found in the treatment of other "enemies of the revolution": the philistine (Rasmi Dzhabrailov) walked around with a girl (Nina Shatskaya), who was much taller than he was; a drunkard, Mayakovsky's opponent, splashed vodka across the stage. The economy was satirised: shoes and caps from Mosselprom were demonstrated on stage; they were left there after a tap dance as if to "advertise" a new economic policy, or agitate against the New Economic Policy. Even Lenin was mocked when Mayakovsky claimed to be the author of the phrase "Party allegiance is above all discipline". The poet halted when he came to the mention of Stalin in one of his poems, and instead the tune of a song about Stalin was played.[97]

The grotesque and satirical treatment of bureaucrats made the production topical even in the 1980s. Moreover, Mayakovsky's conflict with the authorities was implicitly compared to the theatre's own conflicts. In a discussion with the authorities, Lyubimov made the point that "Mayakovsky fought against bureaucracy, and we fight against those bureaucrats, too".[98] The theatre also referred to its own conflicts with rehearsals, when Mayakovsky–Vysotsky pretended that the rehearsals of *Mystery Bouffe* had taken place in the Taganka theatre,[99] or with the allusion to the editor Yury Zubkov and the Main Administration in the poem "Epistle to the Proletarian Poets".[100]

Mayakovsky frequently appeared as a statue. A pedestal was formed out of the cubes, and the actors stood on them to illustrate the "glorified" Mayakovsky in contrast to the living human being, or to copy the monument erected in Moscow on Mayakovsky Square. The statue was swept with a brush at the beginning of the production as if to point to the need to "freshen up" the image of Mayakovsky. The dialogue with Pushkin, adopted from "Jubilee", was enacted between the Pushkin monument on Pushkin Square at Tverskoy Boulevard and the Mayakovsky monument; it was broken off at the break of dawn, when the whistles of the militia put an end to the nocturnal meeting of the two poets. Mayakovsky's portraits were shown at the beginning and end; at the end of the performance, the black mourning ribbons were removed from the portraits by the five actors who played Mayakovsky. Homage was thereby paid to the poet and the man Mayakovsky. Yet the theatre was always concerned with the man rather than the political agitator, poet, and "official" Mayakovsky.

> Before us ... is not a historical biographical play, but the spiritual world of Mayakovsky ... [Lyubimov] introduced Mayakovsky's poetry ... into the poetry of theatrical art. Mayakovsky's poetry appears in the performance as something independent, live, material. Poetry is here not just verse: it is humanised, it mingles with Mayakovsky's personality.[101]

Hence the spectator already met with Mayakovsky's portraits in the foyer, as if to get acquainted with him even before the production started.

In standard Soviet literary history Mayakovsky had been turned into a static monument, a proletarian, yet heroic poet. The Taganka production showed him as alive and human, a victim of the constant opposition from the bureaucratic apparatus. The poet was taught in schools, but the man was driven into suicide last and not least by the politics he had fought for all his life. Mayakovsky was thereby lifted off the pedestal he had been placed on by Stalin's edict; the "unofficial" side of Mayakovsky, Mayakovsky the lonely man emerged.

> Who knows what Mayakovsky was like alone with himself? The theatre wants to penetrate precisely into this "loneliness", hence the tone of the poet's lyrical confession dominates the performance.[102]

Even if Soviet teaching has always considered Mayakovsky to be a revolutionary, for whom personal life came somewhere in "tenth place", the theatre doubted that this was a correct reading. No poet lives independently of people and of appreciation. The lack of support from his own country, his fellow revolutionaries and in real life from his fellow poets and the women he loved, finally destroyed him as much as disappointment with the revolutionary Russian people, who have, after fighting for the revolution, lost their feelings for each other.

> By telling us to protect our poets and appreciate them the theatre reminded us with the whole content of the play, and with the everyday simple title "Listen!", and with the lyric lines which were repeated throughout the performance as a leitmotif that [*the personal life*] *was closer, much closer than* [*in the tenth place*].[103]

This emphasis on the personal life certainly did not correspond to the prevailing official reading of Mayakovsky's life. The production was severely attacked for the omission of the theme of the future, and the portrayal of Mayakovsky as lonely and vulnerable.[104] The Main Administration and the Ministry criticised the production for its unorthodox view of Mayakovsky. Many changes were demanded, especially in the choice of revolutionary poems. The inclusion of Pasternak's poem "The Death of a Poet" (1930), recited at the end of the play, was severely criticised, as were other references to contemporary poets.[105] Furthermore, the production seemed to pose a question about the motives for the poet's suicide, which remained unanswered within it.

> The theatre did everything possible to create the impression that the persecution of Mayakovsky was deliberately organised and led not by a "gang" of poetic self-seekers and rogues, not by a claque of "intellectual" philistines, but by the organs, representatives and agents of the Soviet régime, by the officials of the state apparatus, the Party press.[106]

> Lyubimov maintained a tactful silence on the question of his interpretation though there can be no doubt in the minds of the spectators after the finale that there were political reasons for the poet's suicide and that his death could not be attributed solely to his own emotional vulnerability and deep depressions.[107]

Yet even if Lyubimov remained silent on the interpretation, and incorporated most of the comments made by the authorities in the discussions, the authorities showed much opposition to the unorthodox reading, and interfered heavily with the making of the production. The theatre, which had been under Lyubimov's control for only three years, had already encountered difficulties with poetic productions, and Lyubimov aired his anger to the representative of the Ministry of Culture on 17 May 1967:

> You, Mikhail Sergeevich [Shkodin] argue like that. Why do you not pay attention to any of the comments made by some of the greatest figures in Soviet culture? You are not an old man. You ignore the speeches of recognised authorities – Shklovsky, Chukhray, Lev Kassil'. All your comments have upset me tremendously for the three years during which I have been head of the theatre. Not a

single production passed without your RSFSR Ministry of Culture tendentiously hitting the theatre from one side all the time. We have documented facts about each production. We listen, change, have already changed a number of things; we listen to you, but you do not listen to us, you do not take us into consideration, you do not trust us... Not one production passed without thousands of debates, with the theatre improving, altering, removing, inserting... What makes you think that you are always right? You take upon yourself the unusual audacity to speak in the name of all Soviet people, of the Party and of all Soviet spectators... But why do you never have any doubts, why do you never think that you may possibly be wrong... You are the manager of all the theatres in the RSFSR, but fortunately an acting manager.[108]

This opinion, entirely justified in view of the course of the debate, was the first of a series of attacks by Lyubimov on the authorities, and the beginning of a conflict that would escalate over the next decade, culminating finally in the closure of several productions and Lyubimov's eventual public statement about the destructive role of the authorities in *The Times*[109] that is thought to have led to his expulsion.

With *Listen!*, the conflict with the authorities was begun. At the same time, the theatre found a poetic style, which placed the life of the poet or writer in focus together with his work in the form of collage or montage. The satirical or grotesque treatment of "negative" characters was developed in this production to an extent previously seen only in *Ten Days.*

Historic documentation: *Pugachev*

The staging of Sergey Esenin's *Pugachev* based on the eighteenth-century cossack rebel led to further difficulties with the authorities. This time, they concerned not the choice of play by the theatre or the actual dramatic text, never staged in the Soviet Union before, but the "intermedia" or interludes written by Nikolay Erdman and based on the works of the Empress Catherine the Second.[110] At Lyubimov's request Erdman had written two interludes to reflect the atmosphere at Catherine's court: her desire to write operas and engage in literature and the arts rather than make politics (Interlude I), and the attempt of her ministers and Prince Potemkin to pretend to her that life in her country was perfect, by constructing the so-called "Potemkin villages" (Interlude II). These interludes showed life at court in a comic and ironic manner and thereby created a contrast to the coarse reality of peasant life. At the same time, they embedded the plot in its historic context and provided a new dimension for the play, which in itself contains little scope for dramatic action.

The contemporary theatre knows how to be poetic and documentary... On the one hand, we perceive poetry from the stage as documentary testimony of the

> spiritual life of its time, its inner contradictions, conflicts and social forces. On the other hand, the document, included in the system of dramatic writing, appears for us as artistic detail, the artistic image taken from real life and carrying not only information, but also a certain artistic function in the production similar to the function of a metaphor.[111]

However, *Glavlit* and the Main Administration of Culture refused to grant permission for the interludes; the Main Administration stopped rehearsals on 20 October 1967 after the "Commission for the Immortalisation of the Memory of the Poet Sergey A. Esenin" in the Writers' Union of the RSFSR and the poet's elder sister Ekaterina had protested sharply against any tampering with Esenin's text (although *Pugachev* itself had remained unchanged) and against the insertion of material of "minor literary quality".[112] Erdman advised Lyubimov to withdraw the text of the interludes in order to gain permission for the production,[113] and only then was the production premièred on 17 November 1967. However, Lyubimov managed to preserve the contrasting court atmosphere essentially in the form of a mime with some text spoken.[115] In the production, the empress Catherine appeared with her court, who would stand below the stage, in front of the first row of the auditorium, thereby creating a bond with the present.

Apart from this addition Lyubimov had the production start by a jester who created a comic contrast to the plot. At the beginning of the performance, he rolled heads down the platform on the stage. He was a figure of the court, but at the same time he brought an element of popular *balagan* (low farce) into the court atmosphere and thereby created a link with the simple peasants. He recited lines from Esenin's "The Song of the Great Campaign".

Furthermore, Lyubimov added some choirs of a folk tradition rather than with a commenting function as in epic theatre. A choir of three men, who played the balalaika, the pipe and wooden spoons, represented the simple man; the text for their songs was written by V. Vysotsky. A choir of boys, dressed in white shirts and holding candles, sang folk songs and a psalm, which made their whole appearance reminiscent of that in an oratorio.[116] Finally, a choir of lamenting women sang old folk songs, whose texts have been preserved, but the music stylized by Yury Butsko. A most impressive sound was created by authentic church bells, ringing during the production.

The set designed by Yury Vasiliev consisted of a wooden platform, sloped at 30–40 to the audience (Figure 8 and 9). At the front there was an executioner's block, into which axes would be thrust to form a throne for Catherine during the interludes.

> [Lyubimov] invented this platform of blank wooden boards which goes down from about four metres high at the back wall to floorlevel at the frontstage. In front of the platform is a block, a real block into which axes have been thrust. Sometimes this block is covered with gold-threaded cloth and turned into a throne in front of the audience; the axes become the armrests of the throne. The empress sits down and holds a conversation with her court.[117]

At the back, darkness reigned. Red spotlights could be directed at characters on the platform to symbolise bloodshed or death. This use of artificial light contrasted with the candles held by the boys; such a juxtaposition of natural and artificial light would be developed during the 1970s (*Crime and Punishment*). The props, all belonging to the time of the action, were real: axes and heavy chains.[118] All the actors playing Pugachev and his rebels were naked to the waist, wearing only trousers made out of sacks; they were barefoot.

The combination of real objects instead of artificial props, together with the exposure of the actors' semi-naked bodies, created real danger. Vysotsky remembered:

> In this production I play Khlopusha, a fugitive convict; held in chains, I am tossed backwards and forwards on the platform. When you throw your naked body against these chains, it sometimes hurts. Once, some new actors played in a performance and almost beat me half dead. They did not know how to work with the chain, ... which has to be held tight. But they simply beat me on the chest with this real, metal chain. We also have real axes, which are thrust into the floor... In one word, there might be pain at times, but art requires sacrifices.[119]

Their dress was contrasted to that of the boys (in white) and the lamenting women (in black) and that of the pompous and vulgar style of the court. Costumes were also hung up on the sides of the stage, peasant costumes on one side, court garments on the other; they were frequently moved into the centre to reflect which group had the upper hand at any given point during the uprising: state or people.

Vysotsky was particularly praised for his interpretation of Khlopusha and the way in which he articulated Esenin's text. Vysotsky had never heard a recording of Esenin reciting the text, but had read about Gorky remembering how Esenin dug his nails into his palms, until they were almost bleeding, so closely did he identify with the character. The other actors followed Vysotsky's style.

Pugachev emerged from the people, which was at the centre, and virtually ever-present on stage. Both for Esenin and for Lyubimov, the people was the chief protagonist; interest was focussed on the uprising rather than on Pugachev as an individual:

> [Esenin] is more interested in the *Pugachevshchina* [the spirit of the Pugachev revolt] than in Pugachev, more in the psychology of the movement than in the psychology of the personality.[120]

> The inner theme of [Lyubimov's production] is the tragedy of popular movements, based on their belief in "good Tsars".[121]

Once again Lyubimov manifested his interest in social movements rather than the individual. He was attracted by the power of such social movements, and here quoted an example from the past to generate a feeling of solidarity in the present audience to form a similarly homogeneous social movement.

Lyubimov proved with this production that documentary material could usefully provide the historic context, thus continuing an experiment started in *A Hero of Our Time*. Furthermore, he used the principle of contrasting comic and tragic elements to create an aesthetic harmony. Finally, the acting principle became clear in this production: a set with the basic and natural objects provided the actor with the means to realise and experience what the character experiences; what he demonstrates on stage thereby becomes true and honest rather than pretended and hypocritical.

In these early productions Lyubimov defined a new approach to theatre: he created form with all the elements available to theatre. Experiments with form also determined the choice of material: poems and prose texts were tailored to suit these experiments. The combination of a poetic text with historic material proved ideal to create poetic metaphors on stage; but forms of popular entertainment struck the balance with this lyricism.

Optimism characterised these productions, which formulated an appeal to act, endowing the audience with the power to create society, history and politics. The performers were in a solidarity with the on-lookers, which strengthened both sides, as Rimma Krechetova explained:

> Lyubimov's theatre wanted to educate the spectator, to open in him new sources of individual energy... The spectator was, above all, a participant in complex social processes, a person on whom not only the development of such processes depended, but also the realisation and the solution of highly important contemporary problems.[122]

Lyubimov still believed at this point that the spirit of the Thaw could be revived if only society would be unanimous in supporting liberal attitudes and opposing conservative ones.

2

1968 AND AFTER:
THE CRUSHING OF A REPERTOIRE

The late 1960s were characterised by a perseverance of the reactionary politics that had begun already under Khrushchev with the campaign against "parasites", and which had led to the arrest of the Leningrad poet Iosif Brodsky in 1964. In 1965 Andrey Sinyavsky and Yuly Daniel were arrested for publishing their works abroad under the pseudonyms Abram Terts and Nikolay Arzhak. During the XXIII Congress in 1966, several critical and controversial productions were banned. Lyubimov's *The Fallen and the Living* was permitted only after numerous viewings and the support of a Politburo member. Tvardovsky's *Terkin in the Other World* was removed from the repertoire of the Satire Theatre for the duration of the Congress; Tvardovsky himself had to resign as editor of *Novyi mir* in 1970. Eduard Radzinsky's play *A Film is Being Shot* with explicit sexual references and comments on censorship in the cinema was excluded from the repertoire of the Theatre of the Lenin Komsomol. In 1967 Solzhenitsyn wrote a letter against censorship to the IV Congress of the Writers' Union and was ousted from the Union. Fedor Burlatsky and Len Karpinsky, editors of *Komsomolskaya pravda*, published an article in which they favoured a liberalisation of cultural politics with regard to the theatre;[1] they were dismissed from the editorial board of the paper. Yury Rybakov was removed from his post as editor of the magazine *Teatr* in 1969 for his liberal editorial policies; he had printed largely positive reviews of the controversial productions removed from the repertoire between 1966 and 1968. The liberally orientated writers Evgeny Evtushenko, Viktor Rozov and Vasily Aksenov were dismissed from the editorial board of the journal *Yunost*. This wave of reaction in the cultural sphere ran parallel to the crushing of any liberalisation in politics by the intervention of Soviet troops in Prague in August 1968. Pessimism and resignation pervaded the entire Soviet intelligentsia.

On the theatrical front, in 1967 Anatoly Efros was dismissed as Chief Artistic Director of the Theatre of the Lenin Komsomol for "ideological shortcomings" and given the inferior post of mere director at the Moscow Drama Theatre on Malaya Bronnaya. Efros' productions of Arbuzov's *The Promise* (*My Poor Marat*) and Chekhov's *The Three Sisters* were banned in 1968. He ran into further difficulties with *Seducer*

Kolobashkin by Radzinsky, about a modern Don Juan, which was considered an unsuitable concept for a socialist society.

Touring by theatres, even within the USSR, became impossible:
the Taganka Theatre did not leave Moscow until it was invited to Kiev
in 1971, after Shelest (First Secretary of the Ukrainian SSR) had given
a positive evaluation of a Taganka production. At the Taganka itself,
the authorities refused to pass Lyubimov's production of Boris
Mozhaev's *The Tough*: *From the Life of Fedor Kuzkin*, a text which asserts
that action and resistance are needed even if the system remains
unchanged.

Put on ice: *The Tough* (*Fedor Kuzkin*) and *The Suicide*

The short novel *The Tough*: *From the Life of Fedor Kuzkin* is set in a village
in central Russia in the early 1950s and deals with the collective farm
(kolkhoz)[2] worker Fedor Kuzkin's problems to feed his family with his
income on the farm, and the bureaucratic problems he encounters when
trying to seek employment outside the farm. Written in 1956, the novel
had been severely attacked, after its publication in *Novyi mir* in July 1966,
for its critical view of kolkhoz life and it was not published in book form
until 1973 with the title of *The Tough*.[3] The controversy about the novel
had arisen from its setting against the background of agricultural politics
in the 1950s under Stalin and Khrushchev: mismanagement, irregular
payment, and the inefficiency of work were exposed in a critical way
rather than in line with the Socialist Realist view of the kolkhoz as the
perfect form of farming.

Lyubimov's attention was drawn to the novel by the theatre's
advisor and friend, the dramatist Nikolay Erdman.[4] The first internal
discussion of the play took place as early as January 1967.[5] On 5 February
1968 the Main Administration of Culture gave permission for the author's
adaptation and *Glavlit* passed the play on 18 March 1968. On 19 April
1968 a rehearsal took place in the presence of the French director and
actor Jean Vilar, who had been invited by Lyubimov to attend. This led
to an argument between Lyubimov and the Administrative Director,
Nikolay Dupak. Lyubimov was summoned to the Kirov District Committee. Rumours were spread about a suspension of Lyubimov from his
duties, and both the theatre's Party organisation and the actors drew up
a letter of support, for which they were sharply criticized.[6] On 23 April
1968, Lyubimov read out a letter to Brezhnev at a Theatre Conference at
the Theatre of the Lenin Komsomol after having been subjected to severe
attacks from the participants. The letter had the effect of restoring to him
his permission to work, as Mozhaev summed up ironically:

> The director was expelled from the Party and relieved of his post for the "defamatory" production. He wrote to Brezhnev, who showed mercy: let him work.[7]

There are no documents which support the assertion that Lyubimov was expelled from the Party or relieved of his post at this point. However, it is likely that documents had been prepared and were destroyed once the dismissal had aroused public attention and was withdrawn. Yet both written and oral memoirs support the fact of his dismissal.[8] On 26 April 1968, a Party official from the Kirov district attributed the rumours of Lyubimov's suspension to Western propaganda and confirmed Lyubimov as Artistic Director. Boris Rodionov, the head of the Main Administration, later held Lyubimov responsible for spreading these rumours. However, on 30 April 1968 the Main Administration of Culture stopped the rehearsals and asked Mozhaev to make alterations to the text in accordance with the recommendations of the Main Administration.

A second attempt to get the production passed was launched on 6 March 1969 with the permission of the USSR Ministry of Culture. The Minister Ekaterina Furtseva watched the production in person and condemned it after the first act for its alleged apolitical, anti-Party and anti-Soviet attitude.[9] Viktor Grishin, head of the Moscow Party Committee, had strongly objected to the production, but in spite of this, Furtseva had allowed rehearsals. Grishin's anger about the production and the theatre is expressed in a letter to the Central Committee of 14 March 1969, which is characteristic of the use of Party terminology for the condemnation of a work of art:

> Dealing with the torments of this man and the people around him, the theatre shows our kolkhoz villages *tendentiously*. The characters, leading figures of Party and state, are shown in a *negative* light. The brigadier, the kolkhoz chairman, the chairman of the District Committee are *insincere, malicious* people, petty tyrants who are, in all their actions, guided only by *selfish* interests. The secretary of the District Committee is *passive* and *indifferent* to the fate of others. ... And although, in the end, there is an improvement in Fedor Kuzkin's and the kolkhoz's life, the theatre insists that these improvements have a *personal* character. The director introduces into the production the allegorical figure of the angel, who appears every time that something good comes from above. ... The Artistic Director of the theatre and director of the production, Yury Lyubimov, behaved *aggressively* in the discussion of the production and *categorically* rejected the critical remarks, announcing his intention to complain to higher organs.[10]

In subsequent years Lyubimov wrote several letters to such higher organs. In 1972 Furtseva repeated her prohibition on rehearsals of the production and Viktor Grishin suggested that Lyubimov "make a trip to America".[11]

In 1975 Petr Demichev, newly appointed Minister of Culture, allowed rehearsals again. A last attempt to stage *The Tough* was made on 24 June 1975, when the Deputy Minister of Culture, K. Voronkov, appeared in the theatre with a delegation of kolkhoz directors and agricultural workers; they decided unanimously that the performance "did not correspond to reality and truth", that "the decisive rôle of state and Party cannot be felt" in the play, that "the production does not reflect the reality we want to see"; the editor of an agricultural journal concluded that "even if it really were the way it has been presented, we would consider it not to have been like that!".[12] Voronkov instantly wrote a letter to the Central Committee, remarking that "the whole concept of the production contradicts historical truth". Vasily Shauro of the Central Committee's Department of Culture reproached Voronkov for having allowed the rehearsal at all and for having conducted the discussion in the presence of the audience.[13] Shauro asked the Ministry to keep in close contact, to consult with the Party organs and to observe the procedures of viewing and discussion in the process of authorising productions, particularly with regard to the Taganka.

At the end of the debate in 1975 Mozhaev wrote a letter to Brezhnev, complaining not so much about the ban itself, but about the way in which it was carried out:

> You have the impression that some workers in the apparatus – under the guise of defending the Party line – defend something completely different. They defend, and actively propagate, their most narrow, conservative views. They create an oppressive atmosphere of suspicion, insincerity, nervousness. They use not their authority, but their power: they shout and command. And since they act directly in the name of the Party, their activity, objectively speaking, discredits Party policy with regard to literature.[14]

When *The Tough* finally opened in 1989, its production history was added to the account of the novel's history in the prologue. Lyubimov reflected the struggle with the authorities in a provocative manner in this production – even if it was done with a delay of some twenty-odd years.

> Boris Mozhaev: From the Life of Fedor Kuzkin. The Tough. Fedor Fomich Kuzkin, called in the village "the tough", was forced to leave the kolkhoz on Frol's Day... I wrote this story in 1956. Wrote it and put it aside. Was it necessary to put it aside? In 1968, *The Tough* was adapted for the theatre. The production was closed by the Minister of Culture of the USSR. "You should not be put on trial for the *ogorod*, but for the production", she said and put the production aside for 21 years.[15]

Fedor Kuzkin, called "the tough" in the village of Prudki, has decided to leave the kolkhoz, since he gets neither sufficient goods in return for his work, nor adequate money. His attempt to earn more money by accepting supplementary work brings him punishment: the District Committee excludes Kuzkin from the kolkhoz and imposes levies. Since Kuzkin is unable to pay, the District Committee confiscates his bicycle. Kuzkin writes a complaint to the Province Committee, whose inspectors find him in extreme poverty. Thereupon, Kuzkin is called to the district, where the head of the social department unsuccessfully tries to bribe him, and where he finally gets a passport. Kuzkin finds a job guarding tree trunks, but the kolkhoz refuses to help him rescue the trunks during a storm; then, he can no longer buy bread from the kolkhoz and is threatened with being deprived of his garden (*ogorod*). Kuzkin swiftly plants potatoes in the garden, upon which he is accused of illegally seizing kolkhoz property (i.e. his own garden). A trial takes place, which establishes that Kuzkin had not been properly informed about the decision of the kolkhoz and Kuzkin is acquitted; the garden remains his. During the winter, Kuzkin is busy making wicker-baskets; while cutting osier-switches, he has an accident and contracts injuries. Once recovered, he is sacked by Motyakov, the former District Committee chairman, who now appears as his boss.

Mozhaev's novel is episodic in nature, and hence suitable for direct transformation for the stage. But it is prosaic, not dramatic, and ends on a sad note: Kuzkin is sacked by Motyakov and is unable to accept work elsewhere since he has a house and family in Prudki. And yet he concludes that "it is possible to live now", misunderstanding the phrase "it is possible to live everywhere".[16] Apart from shortening the family history narrated at the beginning of the novel, the dramatisation therefore excludes Kuzkin's accident in the snow and the loss of his job in order to create a positive ending with Kuzkin's victory over the district administration.[17] Indeed, Mozhaev intended to strengthen the optimistic tone that the production of 1968 was to have:

> Optimism above all! However difficult the situation might be, he [Kuzkin] believes that he will not fail... for the stage version, I changed the ending... So – utmost optimism, comrades![18]

This concern with optimism reflects Mozhaev's thematic preoccupation: Kuzkin is a rebel against bureaucracy, and it is his victory which is more important than the theme of peasantry and nature. This interpretation was viewed with hostility both by the literary and the theatre censorship.

The function of the omniscient, third-person narrator of the novel, who is a commentator on Kuzkin's actions and speaker of Kuzkin's thoughts, was taken up on stage by Kuzkin himself: Kuzkin spoke the passages of the "author" by stepping back from his role and presenting them in Brechtian manner. Thus, the narrator function was not only integrated with the character, but moreover theatrically transformed into the alienation effect. This alienation was enhanced by the transformation on stage of the actor Valery Zolotukhin into Fedor Kuzkin: Zolotukhin came on stage, where a scarecrow with a copy of *Novyi mir* on top was wearing his peasant costume. Zolotukhin took the magazine, read a few passages from it while dressing, then continued with the prologue. Similarly, at the end of the performance, he left his garments on the scarecrow, tore off the end of his scarf and thus gave up his role to exit as the actor Zolotukhin again.

The set was designed by David Borovsky and consisted of about 15–20 birch tree trunks which could be driven into the stage floor (Figure 10). They were decorated variously with a letter box attached to the trunk, a starling house, a cuckoo clock, miniature houses that could be lit from the inside, or an orb on their top. The trees could be carried or held still; they were shaken to mark the storm during the night before the first of May; they threatened Kuzkin when the judge retired to reach his verdict, implying that even if the verdict was in Kuzkin's favour, the threat would not be removed for good from Kuzkin's life, thereby alluding to the events in the final chapters of the novel; they all bent forth in curiosity, imitating Kuzkin's movement, during the trial, in which the accused Kuzkin stood behind a barrier formed by one of the trees.

A line of chairs could be lowered on a flying bar from the top down to the front of stage for the scenes at the District Committee, limiting the space on stage to a small corridor at the front and barring the peasant setting from the sight of the audience. The world of the bureaucrats was thereby contrasted with nature; this contrast was asserted by the costume: all the actors wore original peasant costume, except for the higher ranking bureaucrats, who appeared in suits.

Nature and civilisation, outside and inside, were juxtaposed throughout the production in terms of symmetry and asymmetry: while the commission which inspected Kuzkin's hut walked symmetrically through the woods, and the chairs were neatly lined up, as organized by the human mind, the arrangement of trees on the stage was asymmetrical, as in nature. Many devices underlined the close link of peasant life to nature, such as the imitation of the sound of the arrival of spring by the actors' clapping their fingers into their palms wetted with spittle; when Filat and Kuzkin talked about the fish at their favourite fishing place, a goldfish was carried along the light curtain in a polythene bag. A cow mooed when Kuzkin dreamt about owning a cow. The letter Kuzkin sent to the Province Committee was transmitted by Kuzkin's little boy, who ran across the stage and put the letter into a letter box hanging on a tree, where it was "transformed" into a butterfly: the boy received a paper-butterfly on a stick, which he then delivered directly to the committee members standing on the side of the stage.

The space underlay the principle of conditionality or conventionality (*uslovnost'*): locations were not specified, but indications and symbols defined the conditions of the play. Kuzkin's hut – indicated by the tree with a cuckoo clock on top – was marked by an invisible border, which was visible to the commission from the District, who waited on the threshold. Distances were shown by panels which Kuzkin's children carried across stage, running in the opposite direction to Kuzkin, as he walked to the town. The sign for the village of Prudki served simultaneously as a frame for the scarecrow in the prologue, reminding the audience permanently of Kuzkin's roots.

The use of light emphasized the contrast between the peasant community and bureaucracy. Light was essentially of natural colours: white, blue or yellow with green, as well as ultraviolet light with the effect of making white styrofoam patches (representing the frozen river) glow blueishly in the dark. The white back wall of the theatre was usually lit by green and blue spotlights to differentiate seasons in the village scenes; or to characterise the interior with yellow light for committee scenes. The legendary light curtain was used when Kuzkin and Filat were cutting the hay with their sickles: both moved along the light curtain and cut the beams of light. Also, when people helped Kuzkin to plant the potatoes in his garden, ploughing it with their horses, horses' feet and tails were moved along the light curtain.

The music, arranged by Edison Denisov, provided a leitmotif for the worlds of nature and bureaucracy. The musical leitmotif for Kuzkin consisted of a phonogram with variations on the folk tune "A Birch Tree Stood in the Fields ... ", which varied in tempo and tone to reflect the comic or tragic, optimistic or pessimistic, threatening or calm aspects of the stage events. A threatening tune played on an old, rusty horn accompanied the appearances of bureaucracy. Most important, however, for the peasant world was the use of the *chastushka*, a rhymed four-line folk refrain, which usually deals with the theme of love or social issues, and has been a popular form of peasant lyric poetry for the last century. The village community, frequently present on the stage, was no monolithic, anonymous mass; individual voices were singled out by means of the *chastushka*, sung by one or two actors without accompaniment. The villagers left the stage after both the first and the last scene singing a *chastushka*. The *chastushki* related the plot to contemporary society; they mocked and criticised the politics of the Soviet Union and commented on "taboo" aspects of Soviet life, such as alcohol, sex and emigration. At the beginning of the production, the village people sang *chastushki* about kolkhoz life and agricultural issues concerning the collectivisation of the Soviet Union, such as the slogan of the 1930s to catch up with America in agricultural produce, which were echoed by Khrushchev in the 1950s; the impossibility for kolkhoz farmers of keeping cows because of the taxes imposed and the subsequent slaughtering of livestock in the early phase of collectivisation; the model kolkhoz proposed by Stakhanov; the competition to increase the production of grain.

My Ameriku dognali *Po nadoyam moloka* *A po myasu ne dognali –* *Os' slomalas' u byka.* (Voronin, I, 1)	We have caught up with America in yields of milk; but we haven't caught up in meat: the axle on the bull's cart got broken.
Mne by Stalina uvidet' – *Ya skazhu emu v glaza –* *Ran'she bylo tri korovy,* *A teper' odna koza.* (Nastya, I, 1)	If I were to see Stalin I'd tell him straight: I used to have three cows but now I've just got one goat.
Ya gulyala s brigadirom *S predsedatelem spala* *Na rabotu ne khodila* *A Stakhanovkoi byla.* (Tsyplakova, I, 1)	I went out with the brigadier, and slept with the chairman. I didn't go to work, but I was a Stakhanovite.
Vashe pole kolosisto *Nashe kolosistee* *Vashi parni kommunisty* *Nashi kommunistee.* (Timoshkin, I, 1)	Your fields are full of corn Our fields are fuller Your lads are communists Ours are more communist.

In the finale, the *chastushki* were concerned with Soviet history and politics in general terms:

Kommunisty prosyat krupki, *My poidem na vse ustupki,* *Na ustupki vy poidete,* *A ubitykh ne vernete...* (Antipov, Finale)	The communists ask for grain, we'll make any concession. You'll make concessions too, but you can't bring back the murdered people...
Ya uchebniki zubril, *Vsyu istoriyu uchil,*	I've mugged up all on history from the schoolbooks;

A nado by istoriyu	but I should have studied our history
uchit' po krematoriyu.	from the lists in the crematorium.
(Shapovalov, Finale)	

Serdtse radostno volnuetsya	Our hearts beat with joy
Vnov' idem golosovat'.	as we go to vote again;
Samykh chestnykh,	we will elect only the most honest
samykh luchshikh	and the very best this time.
Nynche budem izbirat'.	
(Lukyanova, Finale)	

Bili nas, roga slomali	We were beaten, our horns were broken
A my vse-taki zhivem	But we are still alive.
Deputata izbirali	We have elected our deputy
A teper' ne izberem.	But this time we won't vote.
(Vlasova, Finale)	

Children were also singled out by means of a *chastushka*, theirs being concerned with school life.

S neba zvezdochka upala	A little star has fallen from the sky
I razbilas' na kuski –	and broken into pieces.
Nasha molodost' prokhodit	Our youth passes by
V srednei shkole u doski.	in front of the blackboard at school.

These *chastushki* however varied: Lyubimov often checked the list and adapted it to the contemporary situation (for example he would change a reference to the length of the period of Soviet communism to the exact number of years: 72 years in 1989).[19]

The device of demonstration (*predstavlenie*) prevailed throughout the production over the naturalistic and psychological portrayal (*perezhivanie*). The scenic translation of events was illustrative and summarised the action often at such speed that the effect was similar to fast-motion in the cinema. The story of Kuzkin's life previous to the narrative occupies a whole chapter in the novel; on stage, Zolotukhin said a few words about Kuzkin's life; when he came to the point of telling how many children he has, he kissed Dunya several times as the cuckoo clock sounded, and, upon each kiss, a child ran onto stage and joined them to illustrate the growth of the family in a speeded-up version. Similarly, the scenic translation of some descriptive passages of the novel was treated in a humorous manner: Kuzkin put on a sack as shelter against the rain when he went to the District Committee; this proved to be dripping wet by the time he arrived; on his way, he had been watered by a man with a watering can who followed him, with a silver Christmas tree in his hands (Figure 11). This figure represented the "heavenly" forces in the production. Such elements of the phantasmagorical came into play for Kuzkin's imagination: his cellar was empty, since it was ruled by spirits: the house-spirit (*domovoi*) in the form of a huge rat emerged from the ditch in Kuzkin's hut when the commission inspected his stocks. Kuzkin sent him away with the words "Go away, my dear, otherwise they will confiscate you, too".[20] When Kuzkin dreamt of "manna from heaven", it was sent in the form of sand, delivered by an "angel": an actor "flew" onto the stage, tied to a rope, with little angel's wings and the tin with the "manna" around his neck; he was dressed in shirt and boots only (Figure 12). He then crossed the stage, stopped by the orb to make the sign of the cross, and continued his flight in a frozen position, announcing the interval. The phantasmagorical was an additional element to enhance the contrast with the world of the bureaucrats by dwelling on folkloric, superstitious beliefs and the belief in goodness and justice.

The production opposed to the lyrical and folkloristic treatment of the peasant theme the satirical and grotesque depiction of bureaucracy. The contrast with nature made the bureaucrats look even more ridiculous and reduced their capacity to frighten: "Taken out of the walls of offices, Motyakov is ridiculous rather than frightening for Kuzkin".[21] In contrast to the satirised and caricatured bureaucrats, Kuzkin was presented as a witty and clever person: he was ready and able to contradict the authorities to ensure his own survival. He clearly perceived the mechanisms of corruption, immediately seeing through the ploy of Varvara Tsyplakova from the Social Department of the District who was subjected to extreme satire: her fatness described in the novel was matched by that of the actress Ekaterina Grabbe; her tremendous sneeze after taking snuff was perfectly performed and exaggerated to the extreme. Moreover, she laughed at Kuzkin's wittiness in an excessive way and pushed him off his chair, making him fall off the stage into the auditorium.

Journalists were ridiculed, too: a correspondent ran back and forth under the chairs on the slightly elevated flying bar, asking Kuzkin to say the equivalent of "cheese" (in Russian this equivalent is *izyum*, a raisin, an item which Kuzkin has certainly never even seen before) to make him look like a contented little farmer rather than a worried family father.[22] The correspondent, ironically, had a copy of *Ogonek* in his pocket and was thus a caricature of a progressive left-winger of the late 1980s.

When Timoshkin and Kuzkin met at the District, both thought they were correct. Accordingly, they sat on the slightly elevated chairs on the flying bar, and as one triumphed with a new argument, he jumped onto the seats and made the other fall down. This see-saw game continued through the entire scene and its comic effect masked the gravity of Kuzkin's situation. Kuzkin remained strong as long as he was active and his opponents were ridiculously inactive or placed out of their context, as the legal officer Fateev, who was shown polishing the floor with a brush tied to his foot and rolling up a red carpet. Fateev took a bureaucratic approach to Kuzkin's affairs: when he found Kuzkin unwilling to compromise, he asked for his name, address, etc., which he already knew very well. His meticulous behaviour was underlined by the monotonous tapping of a typewriter in the background.

The Committee meetings were caricatured: some members scribbled something down while others cleaned their suits or read, indifferent to what was going on at the meeting. When Demin was called to the phone after interviewing Kuzkin in a kind manner, he left Kuzkin to the committee with the word "Sort things out" (*Razbiraites'*), upon which all the members assailed Kuzkin with verbal and physical attacks. The satire also applied to the use of language. At the trial, there was confusion over addressing the judge as comrade (*tovarishch*) or citizen (*grazhdanin*): Kuzkin should call him "citizen", whereas the others should use the official form of address "comrade", since Kuzkin – as the accused – was deprived of his civil rights. However, the address "citizen" is a compliment, since it enhances the individuality of a character.[23] The verdict itself was mocked: as the judge pronounced the verdict, he received a phone call which obviously embarrassed him, before acquitting Kuzkin. It was implied that the judge was subject to guidance from some other bureaucrat in reaching his verdict.

The committee members were shown as uneducated or stupefied by the monotony of their work: Guzenkov had to give a report on Kuzkin; he stood at the lectern, mumbled, and drank water before he began to speak. Then he forgot his words. Similarly, Demin could not remember the word for "work". Kuzkin, on the other hand, in his accusation of Timoshkin, could not think of the word "signature" and was prompted by a voice from the audience. When a question was put to a committee member, he would pass it on to his neighbour, leaving the last one in the line with nobody to refer to. Fedor Ivanovich twice told his assistant Albert to be quiet, calling him by his name only; another committee member then used the word "Albert" to tell his neighbour to be silent. Such stereotyping caused man to lose all capacity for thought and for the thoughtful use of language.

The status quo was illustrated by the use of chairs to replace people at the committee meetings:

> The people, the people are not the point, insists Lyubimov [with this produc-
> tion]: some are sacked, others are transferred to another post, but the chairs,
> there they are – already waiting for new agents of grief.[24]

The most important agents of the bureaucratic apparatus were absent, their chairs were empty. The chairs represented the system, which was more harmful than the people who represented it and who filled the chairs. Thus the production was not merely a portrayal of kolkhoz life, but a satire on an entire system ruled by bureaucracy. In the novel, Kuzkin is a victim of this bureaucracy; in the stage version, Kuzkin defeated the corrupt administration and won the fight for justice.

The Tough, seen in the context of 1968, was an expression of profound despondency and despair together with an attempt to be optimistic at all costs. The audience which attended the performances in 1968 had been specially invited to the viewings arranged for the representatives of the Moscow City Administration and the Ministries of Culture and Agriculture; it was thus not the regular and typical Taganka audience. Lyubimov always tested his productions on a chosen intellectual-dissident audience, and his early productions all address such an audience. However, the audience of the Taganka changed over the decades: in the 1960s, mainly intellectuals and dissidents were attracted to the theatre; *blatnost'*, the jargon of prisoners, was understood among the audience. In the 1970s tickets became a matter of prestige among the party élite, and the percentage of tickets distributed to the *nomenklatura* rose steadily until the end of the 1970s, reaching a peak in 1977/78 with the ticket distribution for *The Master and Margarita* almost entirely among state and Party officials. The ensemble played more and more to an audience with little solidarity or understanding, but with a certain degree of animosity. After *perestroika* and *glasnost'*, the channels of information were opened and the theatre lost its purpose for those who considered it exclusively as a place where the otherwise unspeakable could be pronounced.

It was interesting that Lyubimov returned to his aesthetic con-
cepts of 1968 in a period of liberalisation in the political sphere. It can be seen either as a return in style to the 1960s, or as a new appeal to society to act *at present* against corruption. It may seem doubtful, however, that the theatre audience required such an agitational function of the theatre in the late 1980s. However, *The Tough* was undoubtedly the most popular and favoured production of the 1989/90 season, as is evident from

reviews in the press:

> This truly popular performance expresses with pain and joy the truth about the Russian village, giving rise to power and faith in the people and in Russia.[25]

> It was evident that the artists of the Taganka kept this unperformed production in their collective consciousness for these two decades. It was evident that today too the problems of the village stand before us as acutely as before.[26]

Lyubimov himself pointed out his amazement at the popularity of the production: "It seems, that *The Tough* today is even sharper than in the past. I cannot understand why that is so".[27] However, kolkhoz life was a topical issue around 1989, with privatisation of the land being discussed.

In agreement with his aesthetic principles of the sixties, Lyubimov addressed the audience directly in the production. Kuzkin was not only prompted from the auditorium when words escaped him. The audience was also criticised: when Kuzkin said that people need to be fed, he made a gesture at the audience of 1989; food supplies remained, after all, a problem under Gorbachev. On tour in Berlin in 1990, Kuzkin's invalidity pension of 120 roubles was quoted in dollars at the current exchange rate: 50 cents; in the same performance, the passport he asked for was an international one (allowing travel abroad). The Moscow audience was integrated into the production: when the actors talked about provincial people, they looked at the audience; talking about pensioners, Varvara Tsyplakova said that there were a lot of them while staring at the audience. The audience was even threatened: Andryusha held the artificial limb of his amputated leg like a gun pointed at the audience when advising Kuzkin to hide his gun before the inspection; one spectator was made to look up at the stage by having his or her head lifted up with the sickle held by Andryusha and Kuzkin when they discussed the size of a fish's head, thus implying that the audience was dumb like fish. These addresses to the audience emerged naturally from the chosen artistic form and harmonized with the popular style of the production.

Lyubimov employed once again the technique of "holding a mirror to the audience to show the age its real face... ".[28] He challenged the audience to recognise itself in the situation, not the character. This not only allowed the comic and satirical effects to work in a tragic situation, but also allowed the parallels between the system in the 1950s, 1960s–1970s and 1980s–1990s to emerge. The fight against bureaucracy was as important in the 1990s as it had been in the 1960s. Mozhaev attributed the universality of his protagonist to the fact that Kuzkin could be anyone other than a kolkhoz worker, as long as his sense of justice was preserved.[29]

The destructive effects of stereotyping and bureaucracy made both Kuzkin and Lyubimov victims: "And where is the difference: the serf asking the landowner [for freedom], the kolkhoz worker asking the chairman, the director asking the minister".[30] The idea of a destructive bureaucracy as encountered by Kuzkin offended the representatives of the bureaucracy in general and the USSR Minister of Culture in particular when they were asked to pass the production in 1968: "She [Furtseva] took the production as a personal insult".[31] The bureaucratic system continues to threaten: the reforms of both Gorbachev and Eltsin are crippled by the remnants of the old system.

[The production] says – look: in 1954, when this happened, and in 1956, when Mozhaev wrote it, and in 1968, when Lyubimov staged it, and today all is as usual, as before![32]

It is a paradox, however, that a production based on the theme dominant in Lyubimov's theatre in the 1960s should have achieved such popularity and topicality in the Moscow of *perestroika* and *glasnost'*, of reform and democracy, in many respects reminiscent of the Khrushchev "Thaw" which had given birth to the theatre. The question remains whether it was a longing for solidarity necessary to defend the reforms or the attraction to a myth, a legend of two decades ago, which made *The Tough* so popular with the audience and the critics.

The Tough has at first sight very little in common with *The Suicide*. However, both were rehearsed in the 1960s and then banned, opening only in 1989/90. Both protagonists, Fedor Kuzkin and Semen Podsekalnikov, are simple men from a peasant and urban environment respectively; and both are materially speaking not well off. Furthermore, both works satirise bureaucracy and aspects of life under socialism, and this appears to have been the reason for their prohibition. Satire had become an almost extinct genre in Soviet literature (except for writers who emigrated), since to make others laugh may mean to expose to criticism, which was incompatible with the dogma of Socialist Realism, stipulating that life under socialism had to be portrayed in a positive way.

Nikolay Erdman had been drawn to the Satire Theatre as co-author for its opening revue in 1924. His first play, *The Warrant* (1925) was performed at Meyerhold's Theatre. *The Suicide* was written for Meyerhold's Theatre, where it was rehearsed in 1932 and closed by the *Glavrepertkom* censor L. Kaganovich.[33] At the Moscow Arts Theatre Stanislavsky, who had been given the text by Maksim Gorky, also made an attempt to stage the play and even wrote a petition to Stalin, but Stalin considered the play harmful.[34] Erdman was arrested in 1933 and exiled to Siberia for anti-Soviet writings. Between 1940 and 1948 Erdman was drafted to the NKVD Ensemble of Song and Dance as a dramatist, in charge of writing sketches. It was here that Lyubimov had met Erdman,[35] who later lived in the same house as Lyubimov and Tselikovskaya, opposite the American Embassy in Moscow. Erdman became a consultant to Lyubimov from the early days of the Taganka onwards, although he was never officially designated as literary advisor. He worked with Lyubimov on *A Hero of Our Time*, and wrote the interludes to *Pugachev*. Lyubimov made several attempts to stage *The Suicide,* but knew perfectly well that it was pointless to start rehearsing an unpublished text.[36] The play had no licence from *Glavlit* and was only published in 1987, followed in 1990 by a book with documents, letters, sketches and other writings. Until then, little was known about Erdman, to the extent that his date of birth was given as 1902 instead of 1900, and that he was generally believed to have never returned from exile.

After Lyubimov's return to the Taganka theatre in 1989, it had become possible to rehearse *The Suicide* thanks to the abolition of theatre control in 1987. The premiere took place on 24 July 1990. There were very few reviews at the time, since critical attention had been drawn to the earlier production at the Satire Theatre (1987) which was the first theatre in the country to obtain a licence for the play when the old system of control was still operative.

The Suicide is about the unemployed Podsekalnikov, who is suspected by his wife Masha and his mother-in-law Serafima of being about to commit suicide because of his hopeless situation (he has to rely on his wife to make a living). However, Podsekalnikov had merely wanted to eat some sausage in the middle of the night, and the thought of suicide had not occurred to him at all, since for him, the solution to his dilemma was obvious – he will learn to play the horn and then earn a living as a musician. Unfortunately, the manual "Teach Yourself to Play the Horn" also requires the use of a piano to learn the scales. Meanwhile, the news about Podsekalnikov's "suicidal" tendencies has spread, and his neighbour Kalabushkin has set up a business – he takes money from those who need publicity, promising them that Podsekalnikov will leave a farewell note claiming to have killed himself for the relevant cause. Thus, Aristarkh Goloshchapov wants him to die for the Russian intelligentsia; Kleopatra Maksimovna needs Podsekalnikov to kill himself out of love for her, hoping thereby to outdo her rival Raisa Filippovna and to draw their common lover's attention to herself; Egor expects Podsekalnikov to commit suicide for the Marxist cause; Pugachev, a butcher, represents the cause of tradesmen and Elpidy, the priest, represents the interests of the church; finally, the writer Viktor Viktorovich hopes to attract attention to his profession. Flattered by all this attention, Podsekalnikov agrees to die for any of their ideas, even though he had no intention of killing himself in the first place. However, it is too late: the wreaths, coffin and mourners arrive, and Posekalnikov hastily hides in the coffin. During the funeral speeches, however, he is so moved that he rises, only to be blamed for being alive. After he has affirmed his desire to live, a message comes with the news that an unseen character, Petunin, has committed suicide and left a note saying that Podsekalnikov was right: it is indeed not worth living.

Lyubimov used the entire text of the play and followed essentially the (fuller) Meyerhold version, with very few and minor omissions.[37] Moreover, Lyubimov inserted some interludes about Erdman's life. At the beginning of the production, the members of the NKVD ensemble were called up by a guard and some circus numbers, such as those written by Erdman at that time, were performed. Then, Stalin's voice (Lyubimov) sounded, demanding that this nonsense should stop; panic broke out, in the midst of which Semen was heard calling for Masha (intending to ask her for the sausage) on the pitch dark stage. Thus, information about Erdman was integrated into the play and a bond created between Stalin and the fate of both writer and play: it had indeed been Stalin who finally barred the play from the stage in his letter to Stanislavsky, which was read by a voice over the loudspeaker system as Podsekalnikov acquired a revolver. Another circus number was performed when Podsekalnikov completed his will; again, the tragic situation was contrasted with the comic style of the writer Nikolay Erdman. The first part concluded with an episode commenting that life is more frightening than death, as our era has shown.

The second part began in the foyer, where Meyerhold's portrait (displayed alongside those of Stanislavsky, Brecht and Vakhtangov) was taken off the wall and carried onto the stage. Erdman appeared, this time in exile and remembering his work at the Meyerhold Theatre and his invitation to Gorky's dacha, where he could have met Stalin, but which he had turned down.[38] During the funeral scene, a piece from Erdman's interlude to *Hamlet* was inserted "To Dig or not to Dig ... ".[39] Bulgakov's letter to Stalin asking for permission for Erdman to be allowed back to Moscow was read over the amplifier.[40] The production ended with a reading of Meyerhold's letter to Molotov asking for permission to work,[41] and Erdman remembering how he bowed instead of Ostrovsky at the end of Meyerhold's premiere of *The Storm*. Extracts from letters Erdman wrote to his parents from exile were interspersed throughout the production. These inserts had a dual purpose. They informed the audience about the writer, his relationship with Meyerhold, and his involvement with the Meyerhold Theatre, thereby paying tribute to Meyerhold as much as to

Erdman. They placed Erdman within the context of his colleagues and friends of the 1930s and thereby within the literary and artistic establishment, from which he had subsequently been barred. Moreover, they underlined the tragic dimension in Erdman's life and brought out the tragic dimensions of *The Suicide*.

The set design by David Borovsky comprised a curtain with Karl Marx's face printed on it. This curtain had a theatrical function, separating the stage from the auditorium at the beginning and at the end, as well as for the interludes which were performed on the frontstage. A guard turret could be moved across the frontstage from one side to the other when information about Erdman in exile was provided. However, even for the scenes from *The Suicide*, the curtain was never fully raised, but only by a third, so that both the actors and Marx's eyes remained visible. Marx's eyes could be lit up at the mention of revolution, socialism, leadership, state, or government. Goloshchapov pointed to Marx, expecting his name to be Podsekalnikov's answer to his question "Who do you blame?"; Podsekalnikov blamed Theodor Hugo Schultz, the author of the wretched manual "Teach yourself to Play the Horn".

Behind the curtain was the Podsekalnikovs' flat, represented by lines full of washing (Figure 13). Characters would sometimes become entangled in sleeves, or their shadows would be visible behind the sheets.[42] For the second part, the washing was replaced by curtains and a slightly slanting table for the party and the funeral. The costumes matched the setting: in the first part, the characters wore underwear or nightshirts (the action takes place at night); later they wore suits.

The stage was pitch dark for the scenes at night, and only a candle would be lit occasionally, as stipulated in the text. Shadow play could be performed behind the sheets which also functioned as doors: Podsekalnikov's mother-in-law Serafima eavesdropped on the conversation between Podsekalnikov and Kleopatra while holding on to the end of Kleopatra's scarf and pulling her away from Podsekalnikov from behind the sheets. When Masha knocked at Kalabushkin's door for help, believing Podsekalnikov to have killed himself, the sheets formed a door. This allowed the audience to see both sides; at the same time, the transparency of the walls could also be read as a reference to the lack of privacy throughout the Soviet era.

The musical arrangement for the production was achieved by Edison Denisov. The music provided leitmotifs for the tragic and the farcical themes: circus music for the scenes performed by the NKVD ensemble, which, in a stylised form, also paces the action for the grotesque episodes. Prison songs accompanied the glimpses of Erdman in exile, and a funeral march the tragic moments. Finally, tunes on a horn parodied Podsekalnikov's failure to master that instrument. Sounds underlined the action: a toilet flush could be heard when Serafima reported that Podsekalnikov was not hiding in the bathroom, as they had thought. A shot sounded when Podsekalnikov was believed to be shooting himself.

The characters who ask Podsekalnikov to die for their cause were all caricatured: Aristarkh Goloshchapov lisped; Egor carried a folder with the title "Karl Marx. Das Kapital"; Viktor Viktorovich wore a band around his head all the time (black for the funeral), which looked as though he had a toothache. The funeral was also parodied: it was a red funeral by analogy with the red wedding in Mayakovsky's *The Bedbug* which parodied the attempt to adapt rituals to socialism. Here, the coffin was red, and the wreaths had red bands.

The topicality of the production arose from the text itself. Written at the end of the period of the New Economic Policy when market economy structures were introduced to improve living standards, the play disclosed many parallels to the situation in the Soviet Union under *perestroika*. Some phrases were slightly adapted to make them even more pointed: the "20th century" became the "eve of the 21st century"; when Podsekalnikov read the paper to have a rest when preparing to shoot himself, he always quoted a headline containing an ambiguous reference to current issues. At the premiere he quoted as a headline the meeting of Eduard Shevardnadze and George Shultz, where Schultz also was the name of the author of "Teach yourself to Play the Horn". In 1991 Podsekalnikov mentioned a meeting of Bessmertnykh (then Minister of Foreign Affairs), the word *bessmertnyi* meaning immortal. The ambiguity of words was also underlined by action: as Podsekalnikov explained that the Kremlin has "hung" up the receiver, he was pulled up by a rope from above and "hung" from the ceiling.

The production was amusing and entertaining, but mainly because of Erdman's lines rather than the interludes or the topical references. Lyubimov could certainly not be accused on this occasion of overdoing the farce and neglecting the tragic dimension, or of sacrificing the text to the interludes. The production came, however, in many ways too late to have a spectacular effect, since by 1990 the play had already been staged and published. Moreover, there was little scope in this text for any outstanding directorial intervention as is typical of Lyubimov's style.

Towards the end of the 1960s the scandal over *The Tough* and the prolonged exclusion of Erdman from the repertoire gradually led Lyubimov to change his atti- tude to the audience (which was itself changing), and therefore also his choice of material. For a while, he almost withdrew to the classics, both Soviet and foreign, beginning with *Tartuffe*.

A press campaign: *Tartuffe*

The press had always played an important role in the cultural life of the Soviet Union. Itself controlled by *Glavlit*, it was used to present the Party line on ideological or current issues and to promulgate new ideas. This was the case, for example, when the "drama without conflict" theory was declared outmoded in an editorial in *Pravda* in 1952, opening new paths for Soviet dramatists. All the Soviet papers and journals were official organs of state and Party organisations: *Pravda* was the organ of the CPSU, *Izvestiya* that of the government, etc. The same applied to specialized journals: the monthly *Teatr* was the organ of the USSR Ministry of Culture and Writers' Union, the bi-monthly *Teatralnaya zhizn* the organ of the Russian Federation Ministry of Culture, the All-Union Theatre Society (VTO) and the RSFSR Writers' Union. Certain journals had already defined their attitude to the Taganka theatre; *Teatralnaya zhizn* and its chief editor Yury Zubkov had always manifested a hostile view towards innovative productions, as opposed to the liberally orientated *Teatr* under its editor Yury Rybakov.

Tartuffe had a very difficult production history in its own time. Molière showed a first version of the play, which is believed to have consisted of the first three acts of the text as now known, to Louis XIV on 12 May 1664. The King prohibited the play, and a hostile pamphlet by the curé Pierre Roullé condemned the play in August. In the same month, Molière wrote his first petition to the King asking for permission to perform *Tartuffe*. On 5 August 1667, a modified version of the play was presented under the title *Panulfe*, with the authorisation of the King, but in his absence. Although Molière had disguised the pharisee *Tartuffe* in civilian clothes, the play was closed, and some days later the Archbishop of Paris, Hardouin de Péréfixe, threatened all readers or spectators of the play with excommunication. Molière wrote a humble second petition to the King in August 1667, again pleading for permission to perform the comedy. After consultations with theologians, the King finally gave his consent and *Tartuffe* (in five acts, as it is known today) was performed on 5 February 1669.[43]

Lyubimov integrated Molière's own dispute over *Tartuffe* into his production, which opened at the Taganka on 14 November 1968. The performance started in the foyer, where pictures of Molière and his contemporaries were exhibited to recreate the atmosphere of the time. At the beginning of the production, the actors, dressed in French costumes of the 17th century, assembled on stage. Molière (the actor who would later play Orgon, the part that Molière himself played in *Tartuffe*), stepped forth, wearing a wig (a sign that he is Molière and not

Orgon) to present his first petition to marionettes of Louis XIV and the archbishop Hardouin de Péréfixe, which were placed in pompous golden frames at either side of the stage while the actors knelt on stage in support of this plea. First, the Archbishop made a negative gesture, but finally the King gave permission with a nod of his head. Red velvet curtains closed inside the frames, the marionettes disappeared. Then followed the first three acts (i.e. the 1664 version) which constituted the first part, terminated by the intervention of the *exempt*, a Royal Police Officer, who stopped the performance: historically speaking for three years, theatrically speaking for the duration of the interval. The second part started in the same way as the first: Molière assembled the actors, read his second petition to the King who gave his consent, after which followed a speeded-up mimed "playback" of the first part: the first three acts were repeated, before acts IV and V (as in the 1669 version) were shown. In accordance with the events in Molière's time, Tartuffe was a priest in the first part; in the second, he wore lay clothes. This change was made by Molière before the presentation of *Panulfe* to avoid offending the ecclesiastical censors. At the end of the performance, as both the King and the Archbishop applauded, all the actors knelt again, asking indulgence for Tartuffe and the director of this production, from the King and the audience.[44] They appealed to the audience not to take for granted the *deus ex machina* appearance of the *exempt*: "The theatre winks at the spectator, so that he should not forget where this polished ending comes from".[45]

Apart from these structural changes in the play, Lyubimov employed a number of theatrical devices to render his interpretation viable for the stage. The production was set on a bare stage with the two golden frames at either side. The set (designed by Mikhail Anikst and Sergey Barkhin) consisted of eleven framed portraits of the characters of the play (Figure 14). Yet they were not simple portraits on canvas, but painted on elastic straps vertically stretched inside the frames. These elastic blinds could be stretched for entries and exits of characters, or characters could insert their faces, hands and feet or legs through them to replace the painted parts of their bodies (Figure 15). The frames could be moved into various formations – diagonal or in a semicircle – to indicate in an abstract manner whether the place of action was a closed room or an open space; they could also be placed in a horizontal position to form tables or screens. The frames symbolically indicated the fainting of characters by being sloped backwards, or, when Orgon talked about the future marriage of Mariane and Tartuffe, the frames in question were placed together in the centre. They were all covered in linen sacks for the interval. Thus in terms of their representation on the paintings, all the actors were omnipresent on stage, even if the actors themselves were absent.

> With his basic approach to the production, Lyubimov doubled, or, more precisely, divided into two all the characters. There is the immobile portrait-screen of each character ... and the character himself – a living individual person, an actively acting actor.[46]

The part of Cléante was considerably reduced: the "raisonneur" had little to say in Lyubimov's production, and continued his speech by blabbering "bla-bla-bla", underlining that words were an inefficient means to fight hypocrisy. Other additions to the text were made in French. At the beginning, when the actors entered via the centre aisle, they all introduced themselves in French, thus doubling the alienation effect: they commented on their parts and did so in a language foreign to the audience. During the production, they occasionally referred to the technical staff in a mixture of Russian and French ("Davai lumière"), or inserted replies in contemporary language ("Ciao, Papa", "Fantomas"). Molière commented on the rehearsal, and finished the first part with the words "Voilà, c'est tout, entracte!"[47]

Lyubimov often rendered the comic elements as implied by Molière in his stage directions in an exaggerated manner. Dorine was not just a maid, but she dominated those who live in Orgon's house: she dusted their faces at the beginning, openly overheard scenes by sticking her head through her portrait; she provoked Orgon when he attempted to make her leave. Yet she was also shown as a go-between for Mariane and Valère: she joined their hands stretched out through the portraits and made them kiss behind the pictures, so that both emerged with bright red lipstick around their mouths, looking like clowns.

When Tartuffe is tempted by the breasts in Dorine's décolleté, he covers them with a handkerchief. In Lyubimov's production, this temptation was caricatured: Tartuffe touched Dorine's breasts on her portrait as Dorine emerged through it. He then hastened to cover them with a handkerchief of towel size that he folded to a minute patch of material. The seduction scene which Elmire plotted to convince Orgon of Tartuffe's intentions took place behind two pictures placed horizontally on stage (Figure 16). Tartuffe undid the ribbon of Elmire's dress, which was endlessly long, so that he had to wind it up; then he threw the ball of ribbon to her. These elements turned the production into a farce:

> Lyubimov has evidently not hesitated to have recourse to the devices of farce, Punch and Judy show, and American comics in a perpetual chassé-croisé between the actors and their doubles. ... the shift from the dialogue to the gestural, the movement, the pantomime bring the production even closer to farce, circus, music-hall.[48]

The actors continued the double play with which they had introduced themselves: they demonstrated their roles with all aspects of the alienation effect, stepping back for comments either into their existence as actors, or, in the case of Orgon, into his second role of Molière. In this alienation from their parts, they revealed their attitudes to their roles:

> The actors have a twofold function: each of them plays the actual character of Molière as well as ... his own slightly mocking attitude to that character.[49]

> The living characters either merge with their conventional figure or swiftly break free from it.[50]

The tempo of the performance was very fast, dialogues were not intimate, but aimed at the audience, which was helped by the translation of Mikhail Donskoy. To a large extent, the production indeed resembled a speeded-up version of the play, yet it should be borne in mind that the idea of the play itself alone was not what attracted Lyubimov to it; he was drawn to it because of the dispute that surrounded the play in its time, the difficulties Molière had with its presentation, and only in that context did the actual contents of the play matter. Lyubimov was interested in the topic of the artist in conflict with the system, and for this he was criticised by Zubkov.[51]

Lyubimov's textual interpretation relied on his reading that it was not merely Orgon who was responsible for the success of Tartuffe's deception, but everyone. The audience was told not to rely on some saviour to rescue them from deception. Everybody has to look out for false friends, who may peer round every corner, like Tartuffe, or people who can easily be deceived and believe that everyone has a good core, like Orgon. Therefore, both of them were under constant supervision by the other characters of the play.

> Not just the head of the family is guilty, but also his daughter, the daughter's fiancee, his wife and so on, who reveal themselves to be incapable of a successful fight against hypocrisy. The responsibility for the anti-social phenomenon never lies with one person, but with the entire surroundings. It is not, therefore, sufficient to be merely a 'good person' – one has to be active and ready to withstand evil in all its forms.[52]

In the production, all the characters spied on one another: Dorine on Orgon and Tartuffe, Tartuffe on Orgon, Orgon on Elmire and Tartuffe etc. Yet all this supervision was in vain. It was only by the intervention of an authority (the Royal Police Officer) that the deceiving party could be uncovered and retribution made. The people on stage were incapable of bringing about a change or an improvement in the deception undermining their society. The audience was thus called upon by a "negative" appeal to act: they should *not* behave like the characters on stage. This form of appeal stood in sharp contrast to the positive appeal urging the audience to join in with the principles defended on stage (*The Good Person of Szechwan*). Therefore, all the other characters were of minor impor-tance; they were only there to be the victims of either Orgon or Tartuffe, who were – apart from Dorine – the main protagonists in Lyubimov's production.

The schematisation of the characters was thus intentional: "In the production, the personality of each character is schematised and bears only one, and for him the most noteworthy, trait".[53] Yet the production was criticised for negligence in the psychological portrayal of the characters and for lack of psychological realism. Yet Molière himself had pointed out in the "First Petition" that he had drawn a black-and-white picture without any nuances: "I have removed everything that could confound good with evil, and I have used nothing but very striking colours and vital features in this painting".[54] Such a black-and-white portrayal was exactly what Lyubimov had been looking for above all in Brechtian plays, judging that his actors were not fit for profound psychological investigation of the characters:

> I started to go into depth and chose plays which asked for psychological elaboration rather than continue the sharp contrast between light and shade, black and white, that exists in Brecht's plays.[55]

Lyubimov had integrated in a shortened and simplified, but comprehensible way the historical conflict surrounding the play. But he also implied that such quarrels with censorship still existed and were relevant to the contemporary theatre, thereby making a direct comment on the situation of the artist in Soviet society and accusing censorship of infringing artistic freedom. It was this interpretation which caused a hostile reaction, this time not from the censors, but in the press, ensuing a battle resembling that of Molière for his play.

Tartuffe was condemned by the critic Evgeny Surkov (editor of *Iskusstvo kino*) in an article in *Ogonek*[56] for lack of respect for Molière in distorting his play and misusing it for allusions to the (contemporary) fight of the artist with the régime; for formalism and lack of content; for lack of profundity in the character portrayal; for lack of philosophical content; and, subtly and indirectly, for pornography in the seduction scene between Elmire and Tartuffe. Following a favourable article by the critic S. Velikovsky in *Teatr*,[57] Surkov wrote another hostile article in which he attacked Velikovsky for unfounded enthusiasm and for failing to draw the necessary conclusions from the one critical remark he did make. Surkov also addressed the issue of the interpretation of the classics in general, approving of any contemporary reading based on profound analysis, but not for the purpose of allegory. Letters to the editor and reactions by students supplemented the attack. The student N. Lavrenyuk wrote an article for *Sovetskaya kul'tura*,[58] condemning the production for failing to fulfil her expectations of Socialist Realist art and accusing the theatre of reducing the repertoire to the theme of the eternal conflict between the artist and the régime. Galina Kuzko agreed with Lavrenyuk and Surkov, concluding a letter to the editors of *Ogonek* with the exclamation: "But if [the productions] are useless, then it means that they are *harmful!*"[59]

The campaign against *Tartuffe* had, however, a twofold purpose: to attack the contemporary interpretation of a classic, especially by Lyubimov, and to discredit the editorial policy of *Teatr* and its chief editor Yury Rybakov. He was attacked by Tolchenova in *Ogonek*[60] for having published positive reviews of those controversial productions which were banned during the XXIII Congress or removed from the repertoire by the end of the decade. At the end of 1968, Yury Rybakov was dismissed from his post. *Ogonek*'s campaign also attacked Lyubimov's aesthetic principles. Indeed, many hostile reviews of *Tartuffe* could partly be explained by the fact that critics had no recent experience of a classical dramatic text being interpreted in relation to Soviet reality and were unwilling to see on stage more than a textual representation with room for emotional experience in the style of the Moscow Arts Theatre.

> It is a proclamation of a certain approach to the classics in general, in which the main aim is the programme of "allegory" as a method for the reading of ancient plays...[61]

These reactions reflected widespread open hostility to the theatre, particularly in 1968/69, when Lyubimov was in danger of losing his post at the theatre because of *The Tough*. Reviews of *Tartuffe* became more understanding and focused as time went by, but even then they did not appear in the Moscow press.[62] The "contemporisation" of the classics in order to make a comment about the very complex situation of the late 1960s at a time of American superiority in space and the Soviet intervention in Prague was not tolerated; therefore, a theatre where the director absorbed the function of author, an *avtorskii teatr*, where "the director has the right to broaden the tale and the subject matter, to open up what is covered in them, to give his interpretation of the ideas in the production"[63] inevitably caused controversy.

"Soviet" classics in the grip of censorship: *The Mother* and *What is to be Done?*

The scandal which ensued from *Kuzkin* and *Tartuffe* had revealed the fragility of Lyubimov's position. In the following years, the theatre turned to seemingly "safe" works embodying the ideals of Socialist Realism: the novels of Gorky and Chernyshevsky. Indeed, the repertoire plans of the Taganka theatre seemed to result largely from suggestions (not in a compulsory form) of the Main Administration so as to avoid further bans and thereby waste time and energy on work that would not reach a broad audience.[64] However, Lyubimov's unorthodox treatment of the texts prolonged the conflicts with the authorities and even sharpened them.

Maksim Gorky's *The Mother* is about a young worker, Pavel, who engages in revolutionary activities. His mother, Nilovna, supports her son for purely maternal reasons at the beginning, but later, when Pavel is under arrest, she adopts his cause. Although Gorky's novel is a landmark in Soviet literature in terms of Socialist Realism – the ideal of socialism is at the centre of attention, predominating over family bonds –, Lyubimov's interpretation received three viewings and the theatre effected seventeen changes before the production could be premièred on 23 May 1969. The points criticised in the discussions largely concerned an insufficient depth in the psychological portrayal of Nilovna and Pavel; a diminution of the rôle of the revolutionaries, especially their educational goals; and the absence of the theme of international brotherhood which should, the Administration argued, be given greater prominence in the production.[65]

The Mother was adapted for the stage by Yury Lyubimov and Boris Glagolin,[66] and is, like the novel, divided into two parts. However, the first part of the dramatisation is much longer than the second. The adaptation follows the events of the novel with few and minor exceptions which all serve the purpose of ensuring a dramatic flow of the action.

A clear dramatic structure has been imposed on the first part by dividing the revolutionary activities into three stages: the formation of opinion among the soldiers, the people and Pavel; the formation of the revolutionary movement culminating in arrests; and finally, the public demonstration in the May Day parade. At this point, both the play and the novel break up. The second part of the novel has been severely pruned in order to make it suitable for the dramatic structure; it is reduced to the long-term effects on those revolutionaries who have already been introduced (Rybin, Nikolay Ivanovich, Egor, Nilovna and Pavel), leaving out the description of Nilovna's life in town. The figure of Rybin is demoted: his departure for the village to bring the new ideas to the peasants, and his request for leaflets and books for the peasants are omitted, as well as his escape from prison. The theatre thereby under-lined the neglect of the peasantry in the early stages of the formation of a revolutionary movement and pointed at the lack of involvement of the peasants in the revolution.

Human relationships between the activists are not elaborated as much in the play as they are in the novel. The discussions of political issues are pared to their core; the theme of religion, which so preoccupies the mother, is curtailed; the descriptive and impressionistic parts of the trial have also been suppressed, so that no court scene takes place on stage. Instead, only some reactions to the trial are given. Although these omissions are numerous, they help to concentrate on Pavel and Nilovna, while other characters play a minor, largely functional role. This is also highlighted by the fact that Nilovna, who gives inspiration to both the action and the production, has been played uninterruptedly by Zinaida Slavina since 1969, whereas most other parts have been taken over by younger actors or understudies. She assumes at the same time an acting and a narrating function, in line with Brecht's theory of alienation from the character played.

Several scenes have been added, mainly concerning the armed forces: four scenes, in which an officer and a general comment on their attitude to life and the revolution, have been inserted. The scenes with the officer make it clear that he assumes a role attributed to him by the ruling class and exercises power over the indifferent; he is tired of the job, as he confesses to the audience.[67] He keeps repeating the same sentence,[68] since he has nothing more to say. The scenes with the general draw an ironic portrayal of the military: the general comments on the ideas that are permissible in society; he reduces man to the function of a brick for the construction of the state; and he repeats the clichéd opinion that revolutionary ideas have been influenced by the West and take no account of the Russian mentality. The textual base for these additions lies in other works by Gorky, in which he pays more attention to the oppressors than in *The Mother*.[69] These additions help to sharpen the conflict between oppressors and oppressed. They also emphasise that the submissiveness and indifference of the people make them an easy prey to dictatorship. Even the revolutionary ideas fall on barren soil in Russia, since the population is so passive and indifferent, as the general points out. This comment is certainly not limited to Russia's popula-tion at the beginning of the 20th century; some of these remarks are ad-dressed directly to the audience and sound very topical. At the same time, the inserted scenes help to create a dramatic balance, for the novel provides a one-sided account of the life of the workers only, not juxta-posing it to the empty attitude of those who rule the people, and whom the people fear. Also, the ironic manner in which the military is portrayed makes it seem ridiculous, and thus lets the enemy appear more feeble.

As with many productions at the Taganka theatre, *The Mother* started off in the foyer, where the audience was confronted with a small exhibition of old photographs of the models for the protagonists of Gorky's novel, with commentaries on their roles in history: Gasher (Sasha), Petr Zalomov (Pavel), Garinov (Rybin), Zalomova (Nilovna), and some participants of the May Day parade in Sormovo in 1902.

The need to illustrate and balance two opposing forces influenced the production's set, designed by David Borovsky, who had recently joined the theatre from Kiev; this was his second work for Lyubimov, after *Kuzkin*. Since Lyubimov's idea of the opposition between police and people was clear from the start, Borovsky developed a set to go along with this interpretation. First, he thought of a wooden parqueted floor with inlaid patterns in the style of Russian baroque, onto which workers and revolutionaries would fall, lying in their own blood. He then designed the existing set, departing from the bare stage.[70] The back wall was covered with red bricks; the windows and doors at the sides of the proscenium were also cluttered with brickwork to underline the atmosphere of Russia as a prison. A bridge was built diagonally across the far right corner; on it, Pavel was seen when he was in prison, and another revolutionary was killed there. Metal bars could be lowered from above to assume numerous functions: they could be tables on which the mother ironed or served tea, a coffin for the funeral scene of one of the revolutionaries, covered with a red flag, or the production lines of the factory when work was stopped for Pavel's speech. Props were few: a steam whistle, which called every morning for work and sounded at critical moments; a wheel, to which Rybin was tied for the tortures he underwent after his arrest; red flags were used in the parade; a samovar, a suitcase and a gramophone playing Chaliapin's "Dubinushka", served as symbols of the time, as well as paraffin lamps mingled with the theatre lighting equipment.

However, the most important element of the set design was the soldiers. An entire detachment of soldiers (usually from the neighbouring district of the Taganka theatre) was almost continuously present on stage, and its movements were choreographed in such a way that it could assume multiple scenic functions, such as the formation of walls, corridors, and curtains, which could be either transparent or opaque, permeable or impermeable for people (Figure 17). For example, they formed a circle around Pavel and his revolutionary friends for the scene of the house-search, overwhelming them in number, before leading two of them off for their arrest.

Another important role was played by the people, the *narod*: they appeared first of all on stage for the performance of the quadrille, illustrating, between scenes, the habits, manners and ways of their everyday life, both in general and with individual examples (drinking, marriage, physical violence). The mother and Pavel emerged out of the crowd, clearly highlighting their origin.

> Lyubimov loves mass scenes, knows how to show the people, revealing their very soul. However, for the director, the masses never appear monolithic; he sharply distinguishes in the masses what is special, often dramatically conflicting.[71]

Thus the people as a cradle for revolutionary ideas and as the origin of the revolutionaries themselves was very important here; this aspect would be elaborated in later productions. However, even if people were evaluated as a positive social force, they can only act as a group. Individuals fail. Yet a group needs to be composed of many strong individuals, and Lyubimov's hope for such a force began to decline from now on.

Lyubimov changed the tone of his appeal: in *Tartuffe*, he had shown the audience a negative example in order to emphasise the responsibility of each individual in society. Here, he dwelt on the individual's need for support from the masses if new ideas were to be put into practice.

The troubles with the authorities which had led Lyubimov to stage *The Mother* also made him turn to Chernyshevsky's *What is to be Done?* two years later. The novel, written in 1863 and compulsory reading for every Soviet citizen, was one of the first revolutionary novels in Russia, written by Nikolay Chernyshevsky in prison after he had been arrested for his activity as a journalist on the *Sovremennik* and his contacts with emigrants like Herzen. With *What is to be Done?* Chernyshevsky wrote a classical 19th century novel but in a utopian, socialist setting: the heroine, Vera, is saved from an unhappy marriage by the medical student Lopukhov. She is given the opportunity to set up her own life and help other women to do the same, thereby putting socialist principles of equality for women into practice. Her marriage with Lopukhov is a model relationship in socialist terms also: she is free to have an affair with his friend Kirsanov.

Nevertheless, two viewings were necessary before the production was accepted. Objections were made to the choice of the extract on the theme of slavery from Lenin's "About the National Pride of the Great Russians". Originally, some poems by Nikolay Nekrasov were recited or sung to music composed by Yury Butsko, but the Main Administration opposed the inclusion of Nekrasov's works since such a step could be interpreted as an allusion to the low quality of Chernyshevsky's novel, necessitating the inclusion of other material.[72] Nekrasov's *Elegy* with its theme of the suffering of the people as eternally important, which was directly addressed to the audience, had to be omitted. In accordance with the taboo on matters of artistic control, both the mention of censorship and the figure of the censor – anachronistically shown *not* wearing a uniform – were removed. The scene in bed between Vera, the emancipated socialist, and her lover Kirsanov, was considered to lower the ideas represented by the characters; it also has to be borne in mind in this context that any direct allusion to sexuality was taboo and subject to state censorship. Concerning the set which consisted of the wooden benches of a lecture theatre decorated with portraits of philosophers and thinkers, the Main Administration asked for Marx and Lenin to be placed higher than other figures, such as Herzen, Einstein, Voltaire, Socrates, Newton and Chernyshevsky.[73]

What is to be Done? had a very long and difficult path to the stage. In December 1969, the Main Administration of Culture accepted its inclusion into the repertoire; in January 1970, the text was sent to *Glavlit* for approval; in April, *Glavlit* denied competence on the ground that no permission was needed for a published text. Meanwhile, the theatre modified the text in accordance with the requirements of the Main Administration and the Ministry. In June the text was again sent to *Glavlit*, which again denied competence. The Ministry then tried to gain approval from the Gorky Institute of Literature and the Institute of Marxism–Leninism.[74] These procedures reflect the uncertainty on the part of the Main Administration and the Ministry, and their wish to receive approval for their activities from higher organs.

The novel contains many subplots, and therefore requires considerable pruning to adapt it for the theatre. Moreover, it is a novel of ideas and thoughts rather than action and intrigue. Finally, the role of the author is peculiar in *What is to be Done?*, since he presents the novel and debates with the reader on style and content. The novel consists of a prologue with two crucial scenes revealing later events of the plot to incite the reader's interest; it is followed by six chapters, dealing with the themes of Vera's impending marriage to Storeshnikov, Lopukhov's arrival as Vera's saviour from that marriage, the developing relationship between Vera and Lopukhov, and the acquaintance of Vera and Kirsanov.

The dramatisation[75] consists of a prologue, an introduction, two parts and an epilogue. The prologue of the dramatisation maintains the function of the prologue to the novel in presenting the scene of

Lopukhov's bogus-suicide (he pretends to drown himself in order to allow the relationship between Vera and Kirsanov to develop). In the introduction, the main characters are portrayed with a characteristic incident. The sequence of events has basically been preserved, with the exception of some characterisations given towards the end of the novel, which have been transferred to the introduction of the theatre version; and Kirsanov's attempts to withdraw from the Lopukhovs have been drawn together. Any dramatisation would necessarily have to omit or shorten large parts of the novel in order to condense the material into the time available for a normal theatre production. The omissions mainly concern Vera's ideas on freedom, the theme of women's equality and the utopian vision of society; Lopukhov's background and the changes of his personal plans in order to help Vera; Kirsanov's visits to the Lopukhovs.

The dramatisation concentrates, in the first part, on the relationship between Vera and Lopukhov, in the second on that between Vera, Lopukhov and Kirsanov. Little insight is provided into Lopukhov's character, and his return to Russia after the bogus-suicide has been entirely omitted. Almost no attention is paid to Vera's ideas and their realisation, both as far as the workshop and as far as women's rights are concerned. The adaptation diminishes the role of Kirsanov, but expands proportionally that of the student Rakhmetov. Furthermore, the dramatisation maintains the figure of the author interfering in the reading of the novel, resuming the function of a commentator and critic of his readers. In the stage version, he not only comments and functions as "leader" of the action by prompting the enactment of scenes or rendering the thoughts of the characters, but his life becomes to some extent the subject of the production.

The prologue mingles students' comments on Chernyshevsky's work, quoting from Valentinov, Lenin, Marx and Lunacharsky, with Golytsin's notes on Chernyshevsky's literary activity and with scenes from the trial based on archival documents.[76] Chernyshevsky's life is foregrounded at the beginning of the second part, which opens with documents from the trial and scenes of the indictment of Chernyshevsky for editing the *Sovremennik* and corresponding with Herzen. The plan for Chernyshevsky's arrest is drawn up at the end of the second part. In the finale Chernyshevsky is honoured by students after his arrest, and his ideas of progress continue to be promulgated. The author is thus at the centre of attention in the dramatisation: his life and his work *What is to be Done?* are placed on the same level. The author himself introduces scenes from his work, commenting on the action. At the same time, he conducts an argument with the potential reader of the novel and with the "Philistine", a character created for the dramatisation.

The author-figure, played by Leonid Filatov, was indeed a more central figure than Vera, Lopukhov or Kirsanov, who were reduced to puppets; they all merely served to illustrate his thoughts, and to provide a basis for him to air his views on the reader in discussion with the Philistine. Yet the theme of the novel *What is to be Done?* was reduced to a minimum.

> The theatre finds the drama not in the peripeteia of the subject-matter. The true drama, for the theatre, lies in the strained inner life of the author, who is, in the production, protagonist and intermediary between stage and auditorium. The theatre moves the subject-matter to the background, showing it through the prism of the author's perception.[77]

However, the dramatisation reduced the subject-matter of the novel not always according to a logical pattern. The selection of scenes sometimes lacked any principle, some scenes only filling gaps of silence.

The role of the author was twofold. He was both commentator and critic of the reader. This double function was represented by the two voices of the author:

> One [voice] trustfully addresses those who can, and, in the belief of the author, want to understand; the other, facing the aggressive and bad manners of the philistine, plays the buffoon in order to puzzle with his "acumen". The part of the first voice is taken by Filatov, the second voice is given by the director to the ensemble of actors.[78]

The production contained a certain amount of topicality, for instance by having Storeshnikov refer to his service in the "Tagansky" regiment. The use of language also allowed a character to speak the truth unwillingly, like Pavel Konstantinovich calling Storeshnikov an "idiot" when Marya Alekseevna called him one, taking her words as a prompt and thereby revealing not only his true opinion of Storeshnikov, but also illustrating his dependence on the thought of Marya Alekseevna.

The set by David Borovsky consisted of a university lecture theatre, a construction of wooden benches, which could be moved apart. Portraits of thinkers such as Herzen, Chernyshevsky, Einstein, Newton, Voltaire, Socrates, Lenin and Marx were painted on the benches, and Latin phrases were written on them: "Memento mori", "Cogito, ergo sum", "Docendo discimus" (Figure 18). The characters sat on the benches with a copy of *What is to be Done?* The benches could represent any place of action: a room, with a samovar and trays on the benches, a street, etc. The benches could move apart for Vera's dreams and for the finale with the verdict, to let the spire of the Peter and Paul Fortress emerge in the background. This set had a twofold meaning: Chernyshevsky himself studied literature, and considered it a means to spread ideas; second, the novel was considered a "guidebook" for life, and students continued reading the novel in that way.

A side-effect of the set was that the action proved rather static, an impression that was furthered by the concentration on the author, who prompted the action. The production was reproached for being too illustrative: "The illustrativeness comes into collision with the actor's desire to act, it impoverishes his acting".[79] This effect was further facilitated by the fact that Chernyshevsky's ideas on literature were placed at the centre of attention; the plot was reduced to a means of passing ironic comments on the author's opponents. The production did not dwell on the theme of the novel as a guidebook to life and the set was therefore an ironic contradiction to such an interpretation of the novel.

The ideas of socialism, as practised in the workshop, were omitted, as well as the theme of equality: both themes were apparently considered as dreams of the past, which should have been "achieved" in the present. The same was true for the utopian vision in Vera's dream:

> The production of Chernyshevsky's novel is no song of praise about a better future, i.e. our present. Unfortunately, the theatre failed to present itself with such a task.[80]

Lyubimov's audience had experienced disappointment in the realisation of socialist ideas, and in such a context the novel as guidebook could only be a subject of irony and ridicule. Even the moral qualities praised in the novel were bound to seem false in that perspective. The attempt to make an enthusiastic work about socialism sound enthusiastic at a time when the principles of socialism had manifestly failed was inevitably doomed. The honesty of both author and characters was not elaborated. The static action did not render the author's optimism and his belief in the future. It seems that the theatre should either have concentrated on the novel, – with its theme of honesty of character – or on the author and his ideas about literature and socialism, with illustrations from several works. The combination chosen by the theatre did not satisfy either as a production about the author's life or as a version of the novel, and indeed received only a few and not very positive reviews. *What is to be Done?* had an annual run below average, and was removed temporarily for two years from the repertoire, until it was cancelled completely in 1982, after ten years in repertoire.

Both productions of standard works of Russian and Soviet literature, *The Mother* and *What is to be Done?*, proved somewhat unsuccessful, and did not serve the intended purpose of satisfying the authorities and avoiding problems with the censorship.

The theatre thus failed in its attempt to reveal the faults of the contemporary socialist system by means of "classics" of socialist literature. Its appeal to the audience was unsuccessful. There was no scope for optimism or hope to generate change by looking at the past and at the origin of a theory and a system that had now clearly failed. However, the device of introducing the author into the plot of the production, of merging work and life, that had emerged from *Listen!* was developed further with *Tartuffe* and *What is to be Done?*

The problem of improvisation: *Protect Your Faces!* and *Under the Skin of the Statue of Liberty*

Improvisation is not really controllable, since the actor has a degree of freedom that enables him to explore and expand the part. As such, improvisation was generally prohibited in the Soviet theatre, since it excluded preliminary control through the organs of censorship. Experiments with improvisation and form had, however, started at the Taganka theatre with the production *The Poet and the Theatre*, a preliminary version of *Antiworlds* (1965). This experiment with the open form of a theatrical production was then pursued in various productions. At a time of growing opposition from the state to free interpretations of the Russian classics, whether Soviet or not, the Taganka theatre again had recourse to the form of poetic montage and improvisation as a non-finalised form.

Protect Your Faces!, which received its only performances on 10 February 1970, was the second montage based on Andrei Voznesensky's poems.[81] The production was based solely on improvisation and experiment, and had the form of an open rehearsal, which could be stopped for the director, Lyubimov, to intervene at any time. Actors could try alternative versions of their parts. Since a vital and essential element of the production was improvisation, it is difficult to establish, particularly after such a lapse of time, the final text version of a production which has, moreover, never been performed officially.[82]

Protect Your Faces![83] concentrates on the theme of the face: an artist, the "master", wants to create the Face of Time. A face is represented in a mime performed by several actors at the back wall. Features of the face become alive: lips, tears, tongue, but also facial expressions like humour or temptation, are the acting characters. Negative features or expressions (tears, sorrow and grief) are rejected by the master. There is no democracy in a face: one feature always dominates and dictates. The memory of the past, of fascism is also part of the face ("Call of the Lake").

Tongues are vile since they spread rumour and lies ("Tongues"). In the West, human faces degenerate: the truth is concealed, the world is perceived from below, finally everything seems to be drawn into the void in a spiral ("New York Badges", "Sea Song", "Jerry's Dialogue"). The master concludes that the Face of Time cannot be constructed, but that it must create itself; it is composed of many individual faces, the faces of the spectators: the audience must be protected from the schematised face created by the master.

Antiface first presented the raw material of the artist: colour, musical notes and alphabet. Music and composition determined the set: the lines of the musical staff were fixed to the back wall (Figure 19). The creator-poet underwent a crisis ("I cannot write", "Lament about two Unborn Poems"), and finally the master decided to create a face. The second act dealt with themes of Western society and culture: football ("Football"), manipulation of time ("Time on Restoration"), President Kennedy, the Last Judgement ("Jerry's Dialogue"), influenza ("Hongkong Influenza '69"); references were made to the moon and the Vietnam war in this connection. The actors asked the audience to protect their faces, faces of the 20th century, and held a mirror to the auditorium.

In *Protect Your Faces!* Vladimir Vysotsky sang, for the first time to a large audience, his famous *The Wolf Hunt*, which provoked what in official language was described as "uncontrollable reactions": applause and enthusiasm in the audience.[84] Furthermore, the play contained a line from Voznesensky with the palindrome *"a luna kanula"* (the moon sank),[85] which was understood by the authorities as a reference to Soviet failures in space shortly after the first successful American mission of Apollo 9 to the moon.[86]

> Mocking remarks are made, such as "The moon was covered", "the moon sank", "mechanics – so what?" which clearly allude to the priority of the Americans in these matters and ignore the achievements of Soviet science.[87]

Apart from *The Wolf Hunt*, there was little at first sight which made the production open to attack: Voznesensky's poems had been published, and hence the text was cleared from the point of view of censorship. Yet officials put forward ridiculous objections in the discussions on 3 and 6 February 1970, as did Tarasov, Head of the Theatre Department in the USSR Ministry of Culture, in a letter where he complained that the distinction between the socialist and capitalist worlds was not sharp enough.[88] The Head of the Main Administration, Boris Rodionov, criticised the enumeration of exclusively Jewish names at the beginning and end of "Call of the Lake" (a poem dedicated to the victims of fascism), and the ghetto of the lake reminded him all too much of a labour camp.[89] Viktor Grishin of the Moscow Party Committee sharply attacked Rodionov for having let the production reach this point, and complained to the Central Committee both about the Main Administration's rash consent to a public showing of the production and about the lack of communication between his Committee and the Ministry, which had commissioned the text without prior consultation with the Party organs. Rodionov was reprimanded on 18 February 1970 for irresponsible and unprincipled conduct. He was dismissed from his post and failed to obtain his expected promotion to the position of Soviet Deputy Minister of Culture.[90] The Ministry was advised to review the reliability of the Theatre Department.

> The production is permeated with ambiguity and allusions, with the help of which alien ideas and views are propagated (about the failure of Soviet scientists to conquer the moon, the renaissance of socialism, about people not knowing what is Left and what is Right, according to which time they live – Moscow time? Beijing time? New York time?). The actors address the audience with a challenge: Don't be silent! Protest! Go to the executioner's block as Pugachev did! etc.[91]

The discussions on *Protect Your Faces!* ended with a ban on the production. On 19 February 1970, Mossovet's Main Administration of Culture charged Lyubimov with "coarse violation of the procedures for showing new productions" and with "ideological mistakes committed in the production *Protect Your Faces!* at the Theatre of Drama and Comedy".[92] Although Lyubimov had obtained permission from the Main Administration of Culture to try out the production on the audience on 7 February 1970, he had put on another matinée and an evening performance on 10 February without authorisation.

The closure of this production marked a heightening of Lyubimov's conflicts with censorship: until *Protect Your Faces!*, only *The Tough* had been banned. However, lengthy debates with the censors before the opening of productions had by 1970 become the rule for Lyubimov, as the next poetic montage should demonstrate.

Under the Skin of the Statue of Liberty opened on 18 October 1972. It was based on Evgeny Evtushenko's poem of 1968 with the same title. The poem follows a very precise structure in recounting Evtushenko's impressions of a visit to the United States. First, the theme of absence of liberty, slavery and spying is introduced in general terms. Then, victims who were striving for freedom are cited: Martin Luther King; a surrealist painter and magician; Dostoevsky's hero Raskolnikov; the Mexican revolutionary and guerilla leader Pancho Villa; Robert and John F. Kennedy;

the ex-SS officer Rauf and the Abkhazian Pilia. The conclusion is drawn that those who strove for goodness and freedom and were murdered have become martyrs or Christ-figures. The poem ends with the description of a journey into the Statue, and the assertion that freedom can only be achieved with time, by evolution.

The theatre version[93] does not adhere to this structure. It embeds the theme of freedom in the context of the 1968 student protests in the United States. In the course of the play, students take up the roles of political leaders or literary figures. The Statue is represented by a student girl, holding a cigarette in her hand. In the first section, the murders of John and Robert Kennedy are described, followed by an enumeration of all the murdered American presidents. Simultaneously, the metatheatrical layer is initiated with the theatre staff beginning the production and is continued with a consideration of the audience's expectations on the basis of "Corrida", and brought to a close later with a comment on the state of the theatrical profession in "Monologue of a Broadway Actress". The poem "About the Cemetery of Whales" forms a transition to the accounts of Bohemian life, and comments follow on fortune and the morality of American life. The first two sections are framed by the poem "Two Towns" (1964). Then victors and victims of freedom are cited: Raskolnikov, the magician, Martin Luther King, the Indian chief Hiawatha and Pancho Villa. The theme of spying provides the frame work for this section. The "Monologue of Dr. Spock" is followed by students' comments on the state of the world with lines from poems by Evtushenko of earlier years: "Monologue of an American Poet" (1967), "Come on, boys!" (1959), "Other Times have Come" (1963), "Beloved, sleep..." (1964), "White Snow is Falling" (1965), "People Laughed behind the Wall" (1963), "Curse of the Century" (1967). Christ appears in the finale for his crucifixion, accompanied by an opinion poll on belief and religion.

During the production, all the actors sat in front of a metallic wall, which limited the stage to a small path frontstage. On the wall, the ending of a slogan ("... the war") was painted. The actors wore clothes as worn by American youth at the end of the 1960s. Placards with slogans against the Vietnam war were held up, and papier-mâché skulls lay about, serving as a pedestal for the statue (Figure 20). American policemen, helmeted and with sticks, were seated in the first row of the auditorium. The limitation of the stage to the extreme front by David Borovsky's design and the immediate presence of police created an atmosphere of no escape.[94] A guitarist, a children's choir and rock music accompanied the text.

The playscript for *Under the Skin of the Statue of Liberty* seems to be completely unsuccessful in its structure. This is largely due to the changes required in the course of several viewings, followed by discussions, between March 1971 and October 1972.[95] Eventually, the production was mutilated to such an extent that it remained in repertoire for less than two years.

Apart from Evtushenko's poetry, the theatre used extracts from works by John Donne, Kurt Vonnegut, Boris Pasternak and Bulat Okudzhava, as well as Gallup opinion polls.[96] To ensure the balance of American and Soviet sources and to counterbalance the portrayal of imperialism with that of socialism, the state officials demanded the insertion of Gorky's "On Dullness" into Robert Kennedy's monologue of the same title. The addition of characters such as the political anarchists Sacco and Vanzetti and the martyr of the American labour movement Joe Hill was required to strengthen the presence of the working class. References to spies had to be omitted: the sentence "He who does not spy, does not exist" was deleted. The theme of Christ was highly controversial, as one would expect in an officially atheistic state: Christ had to be represented as a member of the student movement to underline the anti-clerical theme, and should not provide solutions for social problems. The theatre was asked to change the costumes of the students to avoid them resembling hippies; at the next discussion the new clothes were rejected in favour of the costumes used previously. Similarly, the layout of the programme was at first rejected, only to be reverted to later. The licence drawn up after the viewing on 9 June 1972 requested a change of the title from *The Arms of the Unarmed* to *Under the Skin of the Statue of Liberty*.

The production was postponed so often that not only the director and the author stressed the need to open the production, but also a Party representative:

> The theatre is being held back from further work, and that affects the fulfilment of further plans by the theatre and even, if you like, the moral condition of the entire ensemble.[97]

Few Soviet critics reacted to the production, while American reviewers were preoccupied with the so-called anti-American stance of the production. Evtushenko protested: "Neither I nor Yuri Lyubimov, the director, could ever produce an anti-American production, since genuine art, as we understand it, cannot be anti-people".[98]

In spite of the attempt to create a "requiem" for those pacifists who fell victim to violence, as Evtushenko formulated the intent of the production,[99] the production failed. The poetic structure had been subjected to so many changes that it eventually broke down, reducing the production indeed to a mere political statement with anti-American overtones. The attempt to create a requiem for individual fighters for justice and liberty, who stand out from the common mass, reflects the ideas pursued during the phase when Lyubimov was preoccupied with the theme of the tragic individual in society.

Both productions show a certain preoccupation with American themes, and this reflects the time of the Strategic Arms Limitation Talks (SALT) between 1969 and 1970, culminating in the signing of the agreement during Nixon's visit to Moscow in 1972. The authorities' handling of the two productions similarly shows the wish on the Soviet side not to read too much into the rapprochement of East and West.

By the early 1970s the authorities had managed to crush a substantial part of Lyubimov's repertoire: his attempt to move into the satirical genre had been thwarted by the categorical prohibition of *The Suicide*; his exploration of village prose was held up with the ban on *Fedor Kuzkin*, until he eventually turned to Fedor Abramov in the mid-1970s. Prose adaptations, even of accepted, socialist novels, seemed to be a slippery road for the theatre in two ways: the material did not really lend itself for the illustrative and episodic style of the Taganka, and at the same time there was no guarantee of a licence. Poetry, which had proved to be such suitable material for Lyubimov in the 1960s, now seemed too topical for the censors and inappropriate for the present times – the general climate was pessimistic in the aftermath of 1968 and with the gradual understanding that a return to more liberal politics, in the arts and elsewhere, could not be expected for the foreseeable future.

Figure 1 *The Good Person of Szechwan*, finale.

Figure 2 *Ten Days that Shook the World*, Scene 26: "Shades of the Past".

Figure 3 *Ten Days that Shook the World*, Scenes 7–9: "Meeting of the US Senate Commission", "W. Wilson's Song" and "Music-hall Singers".

Figure 4 *The Fallen and the Living.*

Figure 5 *The Life of Galileo*, Galileo: Vysotsky.

Figure 6 *Listen!*, the five Mayakovskys: Zolotukhin, Nasonov, Khmelnitsky, Smekhov, Shapovalov.

Figure 7 *Listen!*

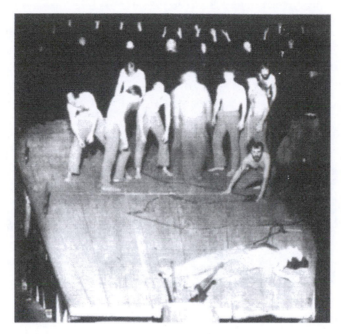

Figure 8 *Pugachev.*

Figure 9 *Pugachev*, Khlopusha: Vysotsky.

Figure 10 *The Tough*, Kuzkin at court; Kuzkin: Zolotukhin, village people: Radunskaya, Politseimako, Vlasova, Grabbe, and children.

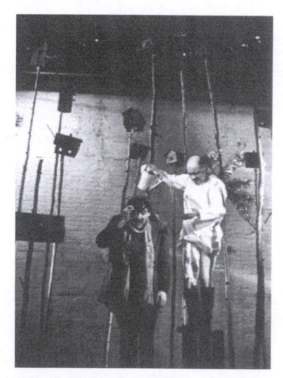

Figure 11 *The Tough*, Kuzkin: Zolotukhin, Angel: Dzhabrailov.

Figure 12 *The Tough*, Angel: Dzhabrailov, Dunya: Slavina, children and Kuzkin: Zolotukhin.

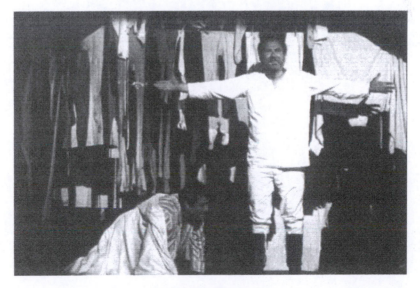

Figure 13 *The Suicide.*

Figure 14 *Tartuffe.*

Figure 15 *Tartuffe.*

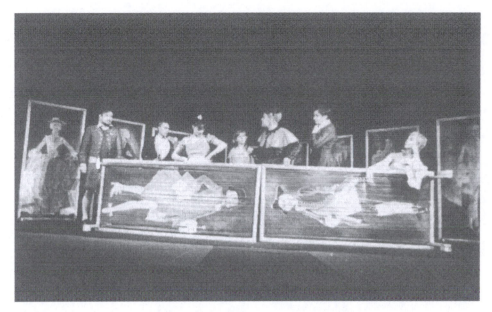

Figure 16 *Tartuffe*, seduction scene.

Figure 17 *The Mother*.

Figure 18 *What is to be Done?*

Figure 19 *Protect Your Faces!*

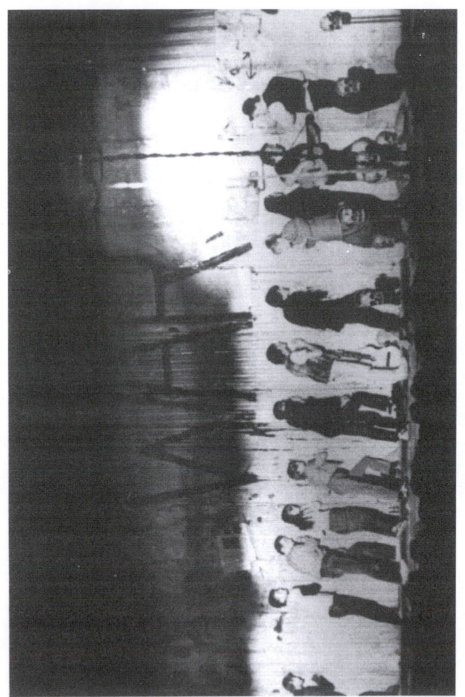

Figure 20 *Under the Skin of the Statue of Liberty.*

PART II

THE TRAGIC DIMENSION OF THE 1970s:
THE INDIVIDUAL AND SOCIETY

3

THE INDIVIDUAL IN THE PRESENT AND IN THE PAST

By the early 1970s Lyubimov's attitude had changed: whereas in the first years he had seen society as an instrument to bring about reforms and change, he now began to perceive society less as a cohesive social force than as a group of individuals who have neither respect nor responsibility for each other; the individual therefore is tragically alone in a hostile environment. At the same time Lyubimov perfected the formal innovations he had embarked upon in the 1960s: the focus on the author, the integration of the audience, and the importance of the people (*narod*) as participants in social and political movements. Both thematically and formally Lyubimov had developed a series of devices which essentially served one sole purpose: to strengthen the sincerity of the individual in society as much as that of the actor on stage.

In the 1970s, Lyubimov gave prominence to the sincerity of the individual, both in his acts and his thoughts: the individual who had failed to make "the ending", the social and political history of his own country a "good one", was more and more withdrawn from that society which had failed to support him in his actions, and concentrated on his responsibility for his actions and his conscience. The individual stood alone with the problems of his time, and this isolation turned his existence into a tragedy.

In the productions of the 1970s, the individual was set apart from social movements or groupings; it was left to him to resolve the conflict between his action and his conscience. A conscientious and honest stance was advocated even in extreme circumstances, such as war (*But the Dawns here are so Calm...* and *Crossroads*), illegal seizure of power (*Hamlet*), Stalinism and the purges, collectivisation and cosmopolitanism (*The Wooden Horses, House on the Embankment*), or banal, everyday problems of suspected illness or curtailed living space (*The Rush Hour* and *The Exchange*). The role of the people not as a social mass, but as a popular force, emerged more and more strongly. At the same time, the tradition of honouring artists, begun with *Listen!*, was continued as a means of paying homage to the courage of the artist who expressed the truth despite unfavourable circumstances.

The individual's responsibility: *But the Dawns Here are so Calm ...* and *Crossroads*

But the Dawns Here are so Calm ... (1971) deals with the Second World War, its effect on the individual, and the conflicting interests of human conscience. In this respect, *Dawns* went back to the attitude established in *The Fallen and the Living* where Lyubimov had interpreted World War II not in terms of the heroic contribution of the Soviet nation to ensure the victory of socialism over fascism, but in terms of the personal dimension, the effect of war on the lives of individuals. This interpretation, however, contradicted the official Soviet policy to the War.

The adaptation of Boris Vasiliev's story *But the Dawns Here are so Calm...* was written by Yury Lyubimov and Boris Glagolin, with the consent of, but no collaboration from, the author himself.[1] The tale deals with the fate of five women soldiers in World War II. The young widow and mother Rita Osyanina, the beautiful Zhenya Komelkova, the hunter's daughter Liza Brichkina, the orphan Galya Chetvertak and the Jewish student Sonya Gurvich, under the command of Sergeant Vaskov, cross a marsh and woods in Northern Russia to stop some German soldiers from reaching the strategically important White Sea Canal and the Kirov railway line. As they reach their point of destination, they discover the enemy's superiority and the women soldiers all die, leaving Vaskov in grief over the deaths of Russia's "future mothers", but able to defeat the remaining German soldiers.

The story, first published in *Yunost* in 1969, was dramatised in 43 scenes, separated from each other by musical and visual effects.[2] The adaptation follows the sequence of events of the subject-matter of the story, which in its turn follows chronologically the events set in May 1942. The story contains flashbacks into the past on the occasion of the deaths of Liza, Sonya and Galya. The flashbacks into the lives of Vaskov, Rita and Zhenya are set apart from those of the other women soldiers in order to illustrate the original motivation for their commitment to the war and their better qualification as fighters.[3]

The play re-structures the chronology of the story. The adaptation starts off in the present, and proceeds to the past, which emerges from the conversations of the women and from Vaskov's monologue.[4] The plot then continues in the present. The past is referred to in talks between the women and Vaskov as their worlds come closer. Finally, the worlds of Vaskov and the women, of past and present, are merged: Vaskov will live with an eternal memory of the women soldiers, and their deaths make the women part of the past. They are united with those they loved when they die on stage: Liza is united with her father and the hunter,

Sonya with her parents, Galya with the orphanage and her imaginary mother, Zhenya with her mother and Luzhin, and Rita with Osyanin.[5] The adaptation thus finds a coherent treatment of flashbacks into the past for all the characters, and imposes a new principle of temporal structure that brings past and present close together.

Thematically, the story has a circular structure, in four layers. In the central circle stand Liza's, Sonya's and Galya's deaths together with their memories (Chapters 7–11). In the second circle the Germans, who formerly seemed inferior, have gained a superior position (Chapters 6 and 11). Whereas the women marched through the marsh with the aim of fighting off the Germans, they now retreat or seem to meet death deliberately. Thirdly, Rita's and Zhenya's past has caught up with them: they are killed (Chapters 2 and 13/14). In the fourth circle, Vaskov, who used to be dissatisfied with his soldiers, has changed his attitude to the women soldiers (Chapters 1 and 14), and the son he lost in the past has been replaced: in the epilogue, he seems to have adopted Rita's son.

Whereas the story merely juxtaposes past and present, the dramatisation has a distinct structure in its thematic organisation. Scene 1 explains how Vaskov came to command a women's detachment. Scenes 2–7 consider the situation of the women soldiers and Vaskov's attitude. Attacks follow, in which the women show courage (Scenes 8–13), and continue their lives cheerfully, revealing their reasons for taking part in the war (Scenes 14–17). These scenes form the exposition. Scenes 17–21 see reactions upon the arrival of the German soldiers. In Scenes 22–27, the women go into the marsh to stop the Germans from reaching the railway line; these scenes illustrate the conflict, which reaches its climax when it becomes clear that the Germans are numerically superior (Scene 27). The reversal of their fortunes follows in Scenes 28–42: the women are killed one by one in an attempt to hold up the Germans. The effects of the conflict emerge in Scene 43 (epilogue), when Vaskov remembers the women soldiers.

The dramatisation omits parts of Vaskov's thoughts, his attitude to regulations, and his military strategy. It also cuts Galya's fantasies in the orphanage, Vaskov's persecution by the Germans, the stealing of the guns and Vaskov's arrest of the remaining German soldiers, as well as geographical descriptions. The dialogue follows by and large the text of the story. Insertions or changes have been made, though they are of minor significance and serve the purpose of replacing descriptive passages of the prose text, as for example chats by the women about their age or queries regarding rights and regulations for women soldiers. Noteworthy additions are the letter Sonya receives from her friend of university days, which serves to highlight her past; or Rita spotting the

Germans, who are not hiding in the woods but have just been dropped from a plane to make the audience instantly aware of their superiority in number. Furthermore, Sonya's parents, of Jewish nationality, are killed when Vaskov remembers Sonya's mention of her parents: they appear in Sonya's memory shortly before she dies. The first and second additions have technical motivation, whereas the third is a thematic addition, highlighting the murder of Jews by the Germans during World War II; thereby, the war is not limited to a defence of the country, but extended to a fight against the racial aggressor.

The production was originally divided into two parts, until, five days before the première, Lyubimov decided to merge the two parts in order to keep the audience involved rather than allow emotional relaxation in the interval.[6] The production was highly successful and much praised by the critics: Vitaly Shapovalov's acting as Vaskov was excellent, and the set design by David Borovsky ingenious. *Dawns* was considered a landmark in the history of the Soviet theatre,[7] and at the same time marked the beginning of a new phase of creativity at the Taganka theatre in relation to set design, acting and thematic treatment.

The set was simple, but complex in its links with the story; basic, but multifunctional; abstract, but precise, detailed, and exact. It consisted of several wooden boards, which at first form the body of a military truck (Figure 21). This body could fall apart, and the boards might form a shed in which the girls sleep, or a sauna with the boards elevated at 80 cm from the floor in horizontal position, under which the women's legs appeared in the steam of the sauna (Figure 22), or a marsh with the boards sloped at 15°–20°, or woods, with the boards in vertical position fixed to the upper bars (Figure 23).[8] The back wall of the stage and the entrances were covered with tarpaulin. Pistol shots and bombshells were conveyed by sound and light effects. The truck had the number plate IKh 16-06 painted on one board, drawing the audience's attention immediately to the superiority of the German numbers: "theirs" (*ikh*) were 16 – against 6 of "ours".

The audience was summoned into the auditorium by a war-time siren that Vaskov rang in the foyer, replacing the usual bell. The spectators were forced, upon entering, to touch and move aside a piece of military tarpaulin at the entrance doors, and the detachment of women soldiers entered via the aisle in the auditorium. These devices helped to break down the barrier between events on stage and the auditorium. The audience was integrated, rather than separated.

> The line of footlights is destroyed, the production draws its force from the merging of stage and audience, in complete reciprocity. "Dawns" – is not a spectacle for the calm and detached: the metaphors here are symbols of common feeling.[9]

Yet *Dawns* contained no explicit appeal to the audience, no quest for participation, but an address to the spectator's emotions. Thus the relationship to the audience was established more subtly than in earlier Taganka productions, with their open appeals to and overt integration of the audience. The spectators were challenged not intellectually, but emotionally. They were not invited to feel jubilation concerning victory in the war, but to weep for those who had lost their lives:

> The talent of the theatre lies in the awakening of the spectator's passions and his talent, of his soul and his imagination. The spectator becomes here, willy-nilly, creator, collaborator of the theatre...[10]

The designer helped this appeal to the spectator's imagination by providing an abstract set, which was, however, precise enough to create the atmosphere of certain times and circumstances. Woods and marshes may have been artificial, but by means of other specific objects, such as punting poles, number plates or food, they acquired a specific meaning and filled the set with atmosphere. This approach to set design was typical for the future collaboration between Borovsky and Lyubimov: the concrete and the abstract are combined as a synecdoche, in which the concrete is only a part of the abstract entity.

Lyubimov had until now always used the actor as a means to create a picture, as one element in an entity. *Dawns* was the first production notable for an outstanding performance from Vitaly Shapovalov as Vaskov; he has played this part since 1971 without an understudy, even during the years from 1984 to 1987, when Efros was the artistic director of the Taganka theatre, and Shapovalov had left, together with Borovsky, Filatov and Smekhov, for the Sovremennik theatre. His acting provided a profound psychological portrayal, but it was naturalistic rather than artificial:

> The people in the performance appeared to have been taken from the auditorium and placed onto the stage without previously completing a course at any theatre school.[11]

As in earlier productions, the actor was not asked to be somebody else, or pretend to be his character, but to bring as much of his personal experience as possible to the role.

The first part of the production dealt with the everyday life of the detachment under the command of sergeant Vaskov. Vaskov was engaged in woodcutting or absurd phone-calls to the major, while the women soldiers carried on with their lives in the shed, washed their

clothes and hung them out to dry on the boards, had a bath in the sauna
and sunbathed at the word of command on the extended boards of the
truck. They received letters from their friends, chatted about their lives,
and visited their children. This happy communal life was frequently
disturbed by raids of German warplanes, represented by means of sound
and flashing lights directed into the auditorium. At the dramatic peak of
the production, German soldiers physically threatened the detachment:
several parachutists descended on ropes from the flying bars and climbed
down behind the boards. At this point, the calm horizontal position of
the boards changed to a vertical one.[12] The boards no longer had a
protective and sheltering function, but became menacing: behind each
board, a German invader might be hiding. As the scene changed, Hitler's
voice sounded over the amplifier. The sergeant and five selected women
soldiers set off to search for the Germans, whom they believed to number
only two, first going through the marsh (represented by the slightly
sloped boards behind the light curtain, with the noise of bubbling water).
Vaskov enquired about the individual fates of his protégées in scenes
with each of them: for Vaskov and for the audience, they were no longer
merely soldiers fulfilling a duty, but had become individuals. This more
personal relationship was underlined when both superiors, Kiryanova
and Vaskov, asked to be called by their first names, as death was
impending. The deaths of the women were accompanied by a musical
"accent" consisting of a short, unconnected beat of the cymbal. They were
preceded by a short recollection of past happiness, a summary of hopes
and dreams they had for their lives, enacted on one side of the board; on
the other side, the killed person leaned as the board turned round. Their
deaths were followed by folk songs sung by the detachment, each with a
reference to the life of the person who had died.[13]

> The songs used in Dawns are either folk songs or songs that have effectively
> become part of contemporary folklore. ... In those songs there resounds the
> mournful and ennobling force of the people's lament, filled with the belief that life
> does not end in death.[14]

The music of the production drew largely on folk songs and music played
on the accordion or mouth organ by Vaskov. At the end, all the boards
remained empty, turning round to the accompaniment of a waltz, as
Vaskov remained alone on stage with his grief. The finale was composed
of another folk song sung by the women.[15]

Vaskov was first shown as a person who carried out his duty to
his country. Yet the death of those who would normally ensure future
generations of this country made him doubt and query the meaning of

the war. Times and circumstances that drive human beings, in this case women, into roles for which they are unsuited, such as killing, were made responsible for the tragic deaths.

Although with Boris Vasiliev's *But the Dawns Here are so Calm...* Lyubimov chose a piece of literature which may be classified as "Socialist Realist" in its portrayal of heroism and patriotism, this did not in itself help the production to pass the censorship. In fact, the authorities were about to stop the work on the scenic version, when Vasiliev was awarded the First Prize of the Political Administration of the Army for his story, which made a prohibition quite impossible.[16] The interpretation Lyubimov gave to the story is quite different from Socialist Realism: Lyubimov questioned the sense of such cruelty,[17] challenged the official attitude to war by pointing out how many *individual* lives it cost, and asked whether any aim justifies such deaths. This interpretation of war was not in line with Soviet ideology, which considered war only in terms of the heroism of Soviet soldiers and saw its aim as producing "heroic" rather than human individuals.[18]

> The production forces us to remember and think about those many many other uncompleted lives, which were the price of victory. It forces us to acknowledge the destructive cruelty of war and the transforming force of patriotism as the driving force of the heroes and heroines.[19]

The licence drawn up after the viewing on 26 December 1970 reflected the officials' objections to this reading in their recommendation "to exclude the motifs of sacrifice from the heroes' stories, and to emphasise the theme of a conscious heroic deed" accomplished by the detachment. Apart from this, the Main Administration merely required the removal of the song "On the hills of Manchuria" which, in their opinion, might have been associated with the Japanese ascendancy over Manchuria and the defeat of the Russian Army in the Russo-Japanese War of 1904/5; and the deletion of a repetition of Blok's line "We, the children of Russia's terrible years", expressing Blok's fear and anxiety for Russia's future after the Revolution.[20]

The production was unanimously praised by the critics because it offered great scope for interpretation: reviewers could claim that the production extolled the heroic deeds of the Great Patriotic War.[21] The representatives of the Main Administration and the Ministry interpreted the production in terms of its acknowledgement of Soviet heroism. Their critical remarks concerned the emphasis on the individual rather than the mass of the Soviet nation: the requiem for each of the women in the form of a folk song, the memorial with torches in the foyer.[22]

In the foyer, where the production ended, the audience was faced with five torches lit on the staircase: a memorial to five *individuals*, not an "unknown soldier" (Figure 24).

An innovation was made in this production by the set designer Borovsky who also produced the layout for the programme. Although symbols had occasionally been used,[23] the programme had never abandoned the standard form. The programme for *Dawns* underlined the theme of individuals by having the names of the heroines and the hero dominate (Figure 25).

Crossroads was another production about World War II, based on the Belorussian Vasil Bykov's stories *Kruglyansky Bridge* (1969) and *Sotnikov* (1970)[24] in his own adaptation; it was premièred on 6 October 1977. The adaptation juxtaposes and develops simultaneously the plots of the two stories. On stage, the places of action were differentiated by means of two bridges (one for each story), crossing the stage floor covered with barbed wire and panels of prohibitions in German and Russian to reflect the atmosphere of World War II (set design by David Borovsky).

Maslakov, Britvin, and Stepka, the protagonists of *Kruglyansky Bridge*, leave their partisan camp to set the bridge to Kruglyansk on fire, while Rybak and Sotnikov (of *Sotnikov*) try to procure food for their fellow partisans. Maslakov and Sotnikov are injured in a clash with the German occupiers; both escape with their companions, Stepka and Rybak; and both are helped by children: the boy Mitya assists Maslakov's transportation, and Demchikha and her children provide a shelter for Sotnikov. Meanwhile Britvin develops and executes a new plan: he blows up the bridge, sacrificing Mitya. Similarly, Rybak deliberately risks Demchikha's life when hiding Sotnikov in her hut. Thus, both Britvin and Rybak act ruthlessly against others; they survive. Maslakov, Stepka and Sotnikov act with respect for human life, and they all die: Maslakov dies of his injury; Sotnikov is hanged; and Stepka is imprisoned (for having fired at Britvin when learning that the latter deliberately sacrificed Mitya), waiting to confess to attempted murder, for which he will almost certainly be sentenced to death. Bykov's works imply that the incompetent people without humanist values survive.

However, the production was hardly reviewed and remained in repertoire for less than two years. Bykov's lack of distance from his protagonists made it impossible to portray on stage the thoughts and the mental world of the characters (e.g. through a commentator); this is, however, vital for an understanding of such characters as Sotnikov, Rybak and Stepka. Furthermore, the superimposing of the two stories had the effect of overloading the stage, to such an extent that *Kruglyansky Bridge* and *Sotnikov* finally weakened each other.[25]

It seems, then, that by 1977 the theme of World War II and its effect on life in the Soviet Union had been exhausted in terms of the theme of heroic versus individual qualities. Also, it must have been very difficult, if not impossible, for Lyubimov to create such a perfect production as *Dawns* about the same theme, and on the basis of an adaptation which was neither written for nor by him.

The individual isolated from society: *Hamlet*

At the end of the 1960s Lyubimov had wanted to mount a collage of Shakespeare's chronicle plays (*Richard II, Henry IV, V, VI*), but the project did not meet with the approval of the authorities.[26] To some extent, then, the Main Administration determined the choice of *Hamlet* (1971).

The adaptation *The Chronicle Plays* was written by Aleksandr Anikst.[27] It surveys the reigns of Richard II, Henry IV, Henry V, Henry VI and Edward IV on the basis of Shakespeare's *Richard II, Henry IV* (*Parts 1 and 2*), and *Henry VI* (*Parts 1–3*). The script adopts the figures "Herald" and "Rumour" from the prologue to *Henry IV* (*Part 2*) as commentators on the abridged history of England in the 15th century. Rumour comments on the motions of the wheel of fortune, on the rule of Henry V and Henry VI, and on the character of the queen of *Henry VI*; he also announces when it is time for the king to marry. Herald proclaims official changes of rule (Richard II to Henry IV), the death of Henry IV, the achievements of Henry V, and the dates of reigns. Rumour and Herald complement each other when Herald, about to announce the new king Richard III while Henry has not yet abdicated, is interrupted by Rumour. As Rumour announces Edward IV, Herald doubts the certainty of that statement. Rumour and Herald conclude the play with an outlook on the future: the death of Edward IV, the murder of Edward V, and the short reign of Richard III. Rumour and Herald serve to link the history of the plays; their comments on history are accompanied by mime.

The text of the six plays has, of course, been abridged. The adaptation concentrates on the struggle for power waged by the kings and nobles. The personality of the kings is emphasised: Bolingbroke is a fighter, exiled for truth, and returning for justice – and power; he detests the bloodshed of the murder of Richard II. Hal, the future Henry V, transforms from an adventurer to a victorious fighter and triumphant king. Henry IV appears as the peaceful king, who forgives easily, for example when Hal takes the crown believing his father dead.

The Chronicle Plays were set at a time of political unrest in England when, despite the peaceful intentions of the rulers, the nobility's claim for absolute power caused wars and bloodshed. Frequent allusions to the people overturning the règime were too topical for current Soviet politics and attracted the attention of the Main Administration. The adaptation showed history as a closed circle with no scope for change, whereas in Shakespeare's plays history was, according to the review commissioned by the Main Administration, shown as a dynamic process.[28] Moreover, veiled contemporary references could abound in such a montage and therefore the *Chronicles* were not cleared for inclusion in the repertoire.

Instead, Lyubimov decided to stage *Hamlet*. He had never planned to produce this tragedy, and only turned to it because Vladimir Vysotsky badly wanted to play the lead.[29] Then Lyubimov began to think about the play and developed a concept for a possible production.

The text for *Hamlet* was based on Pasternak's translation, but was adapted for the purposes of the theatre. The language was made more explicit and precise at times. Furthermore, the text was modified: scenes with the grave-diggers were inserted;[30] the characters Fortinbras and Voltemand did not appear at all; the appearances of Barnardo, Francesco and Marcellus were abridged, as were the scenes between Hamlet and the Ghost (I, 5), Hamlet and the Queen (III, 4), and Guildenstern's calling Hamlet to the Queen (III, 2). In IV, 6 only Hamlet's letter was read. Osric's conversation with Hamlet was shortened (V, 2). The dialogues between Horatio and Hamlet, and Horatio and Fortinbras at the end of the play (V, 2) were omitted. Act IV, Scene 4 was deleted entirely, but pieces of Hamlet's final speech in that scene were used at the end of the play. The scene in which Hamlet hesitates to kill the praying King (III, 3) was presented in the form of a dialogue, and the two monologues embodied reactions to one another. The interval occurred at the moment when Hamlet told his mother to seek remorse or repentance (III, 4).

In the 1960s Lyubimov had developed an approach which started off with an empty stage. Only essential objects were used as props, and they were of authentic or natural material, whereas the set design was essentially abstract. In *Hamlet*, this approach led to one of the finest examples of set design intrinsically linked with the production, an achievement which was the result of a collaboration between Lyubimov and his chief set designer, David Borovsky: a curtain could be moved across the bare stage in all directions. This now legendary curtain was woven from thick yarn of an earthen colour, and it was rough and patchy (Figure 26). When considering a production of *Hamlet*, Lyubimov and Borovsky had been thinking about the set for some time, and had remembered Brook's *King Lear*, where leather had been used for costumes as a historically authentic material. At the same time, it was not pompous or specific, which would make a "costume show" where the exterior conceals both thought and word. However, leather was an expensive and luxurious material in the Soviet Union, and *Hamlet* was intended to be staged in such a way that the costumes would be neutral and the audience would not remember them. The choice fell on rough, loosely knitted or woven wool. The curtain was made first; the costumes matched it in manner and were kept in their natural colours: white for King and Queen, brown for Polonius, Laertes and Ophelia, black for Hamlet.[31] The degree of whiteness of dress and the height of collar were indicative of rank.[32] The curtain dominated the stage with its heaviness, and played a dynamic role, fulfilling two functions. Firstly, it served as a theatrical curtain, being lifted for exits and entrances (e.g. the throne scene, where the curtain was lifted by the grave-diggers). Secondly, the curtain was a symbol – it was an active character in the performance, threatening and sweeping characters away, hiding spies and agents who overheard dialogues and the most intimate monologues: the space was public, not private. The metaphorical function of the curtain posed a riddle to most critics. Anikst called it an "enormous featureless force", to which Bachelis added "which is hostile to Hamlet", thereby coming closest to a definition of the curtain's symbolic function.[33] The curtain also created the atmosphere of a prison: it looked like a spider's web, in which characters became entangled, literally and symbolically, and it could be lit from below by the light curtain to give the impression of prison bars.[34]

At the front centre of the stage there was a square patch, filled with real earth and skulls, which represented a grave. Swords were displayed on the back wall and the front stage, and a coffin was used as a bench in several scenes. Chains of office for the King and Queen symbolised their position. Apart from these, no other props were used (Figure 27). This set allowed the play to be embedded in its historical context at the same time as bearing significance for the present.

Music played an active rather than illustrative part in the production. Hamlet was frequently accompanied by a buffoon playing Mozart tunes on a cornet, completing a phrase or setting a counterpoint to the spoken word. A bagpiper crossed the stage during some scenes. Ophelia sang a children's song to the Queen and the King, which was repeated in playback several times to accentuate her madness.

The play began with Vladimir Vysotsky, singer, bard and poet, crouched against the back wall, reciting Pasternak's poem "Hamlet"[35] and accompanying himself on the guitar (Figure 28). This song had the function of temporarily breaking the fourth wall with the auditorium: it expressed "the wish to be on 'ty' [informal, intimate terms] with the spectator",[36] and underlined that the audience was seeing not a prince, but an ordinary man from the street.

As the actors came on stage, they all put black ribbons upon their arms: they were mourning the death of Hamlet's father. They did not pretend to mourn, but illustrated the mourning of the figures they represented. The rules of the play enabled the actor to preserve his face rather than betray his identity.

> The actors are contemporary not because they wear sweaters, but in their personal rather than traditional attitude towards their roles.[37]

> They do not play, but . . . speak the truth, one truth, only one truth.[38]

This approach to acting, which brought out the implications of the events experienced by the protagonist for the personality of the actor, placed the audience face to face with the individual on stage, allowing them to identify with his thoughts, and making them aware of their incapacity to help: they were in the same desperate situation as Hamlet, faced with ultimate death.

Hamlet was alone physically in the opening scene, separate from the other actors, who entered after the grave-diggers and who were swept away again by the curtain. His solitude was an indication of his position in Lyubimov's production: he proved to be alone in an enemy world. All his dialogues, and even his monologues, were overheard by his enemies: "To be or not to be" was overheard by Claudius, Polonius, Rosencrantz and Guildenstern hiding behind the curtain, and each of them echoed the question in a different tone, implying a difference in meaning: what for Hamlet was a query of how to exist was to them a question about their career, power and ambitions. "The time is out of joint" was repeated by Claudius and Polonius. Polonius overheard – visible to the audience behind the curtain – the dialogue between Laertes and Ophelia before the departure of Laertes (I, 3). Polonius, of course, also overheard the scene between Hamlet and Gertrude (III, 4) and was killed by Hamlet through the curtain. Moreover, Hamlet was constantly followed by Rosencrantz and Guildenstern, the actual spies. Denmark was not just "a prison" as Hamlet expresses it (II, 2), but a police state, where words would be overheard and deeds watched.

From the very start, Lyubimov's Hamlet was aware of the events that had happened. He had already thought about everything, and merely needed to act. Even if the result of his action was doubtful, he was compelled to act according to his conscience. Hence Hamlet's "To be or not to be" was not a question so much as an exclamation; it was no philosophical reflection, but an expression for its own sake; finally, it was not concerned with his own self, but with the abstract concept of the meaning of human existence. His problem was existential; he pondered less on his actions, than on the way of making things happen; not the aims, but the means and ways to achieve them. Hamlet knew how much depended on the choice of the right way, and that this was much more important than the actual achievement of justice.

> Hamlet is not ... an aristocrat, a prince, but a simple young man, sometimes even unrefined in manners, a man of revolt who knows many things, but who – already instructed about the disastrous consequences of the "best intentions" – is very frightened to err.[39]

This made the performance by the hired actors unnecessary: Hamlet needed no further proof of Claudius's guilt, and hence the performance by the Court actors was reduced to a mime of grotesque manners, so crudely performed that Claudius might be seen as running away from the bad acting.[40]

Hamlet's father was not an apparition, but a figure resembling a twin brother of Claudius. He was perceived only by Hamlet, and hence it was clear that Hamlet saw him in his mind's eye: he was an embodiment of Hamlet's thought and memory. Gertrude was blinded in the scene with Hamlet: after putting cream on her face – she was ready to go to bed – she placed pads over her eyes and therefore both physically and symbolically she could not see the ghost.

All the characters shared one thing: they all faced death, and yet each of them was alone in that common destiny. Death was omnipresent in the production, not only in the form of the threatening curtain, but even more in the guise of the grave at the front centre stage, with the grave-diggers present from the start and appearing several times later between scenes: "All the action happens literally by the open grave. Long before death, each of the participants of the tragedy sees what awaits him".[41] Since all face death and know their destiny, Hamlet was compelled to act to ensure that his moral obligations should be fulfilled.

Ophelia's madness was reversible: she returned to the happiness of her childhood; she played in the sand, swayed with the curtain in the scene with Hamlet in remembrance of a happy past, hummed a children's song. Her only way to exist in the evil world that surrounds her was to escape from it mentally. Yet if this world is unhealthy, then her reactions must be seen as sane, not mad:

> It is as if the theatre says that there is more harmony and light in the benighted conscience of Ophelia, lapsing into childhood, than in the egoistic world that surrounds her, resembling a madhouse.[42]

Ophelia was instructed by and obedient to Polonius; she was a marionette, used as such, and Hamlet was aware of this function: "She does not play but is played with".[43]

> Hamlet, alone in a hostile world, was a tragic figure enraged against this world.

> Hamlet is not a *"nice prince"*, ... but a straightforward, biting fellow, akin to the "angry young men". In Lyubimov's interpretation of the tragedy ... there are none of Hamlet's doubts. The hero burns with rage against the world. ... A vigilant, not insane Hamlet–Vladimir Vysotsky, in solitude fighting against evil, personified by the King, murderer and tyrant, and against all who are with Claudius.[44]

Hamlet was an honest individual among people filled with evil. He had nobody he could trust or share his thoughts with. A sense of community had been lost; the individual was alone in his struggle against evil. The solidarity of *The Good Person of Szechwan* had given way to the solitude of *Hamlet*. "We" becomes "I". Yet even a man like Hamlet had the strength and power to combat evil:

> The conviction that a political mind operating the complex machinery of state power is under all circumstances stronger than the mind of a separate being – be it only an individual human being – not subdued to state mechanisms, has been dispersed like smoke.[45]

This interpretation of Hamlet as an individual with moral force against a ruling authority, and the function of the grave-diggers as representatives of the people's power, strongly displeased the representatives of the Main Administration. The role of the grave-diggers had been elaborated in the production: they not only made the frightening appear ridiculous, but Lyubimov also used them to represent the power of the people.

> With regards to the finale: perhaps it has not dawned on you yet and it seems to you that these grave-diggers are simply gossiping, that they are no personification of the people. But to us, this is not so. They contain the great health and strength of the people.[46]

The representatives of the Main Administration and the Ministry grasped the idea behind the production, reinforcing the personality of an individual being, and attacked not the idea, but all sorts of minor points to demolish the concept of the production.

Lyubimov had equipped Hamlet not with the attributes of a prince, but with those of a man of the people, an ordinary human being, an individual with the moral strength to resist superior forces. His choice of Vladimir Vysotsky for this part was therefore entirely logical: he described him with the attributes "earthy", "flesh of the flesh", "from the street". Vysotsky thus ideally suited his purpose of bringing the tragedy closer to the people. For the Main Administration, Hamlet had to remain the genius who *alone* could think of such phrases as "To be or not to be" and "The time is out of joint", which were therefore not to be repeated by Polonius and Claudius as Lyubimov had intended. Hamlet should be distanced from the people, a unique personality who *alone* is able to master the ethical dilemma he confronts. All the devices intended to bring the plot closer to the people, such as the insertion of elements of the popular or street theatre, were therefore subjected to criticism: the game with the three skulls in the scene between Hamlet, Rosenkrantz and Guildenstern, which was intended to show that the latter had lost their human face by their denunciations; the footwash for Polonius; Vysotsky's guitar accompaniment for his recital of Pasternak's unpublished poem "Hamlet"; the comic scene with the gravediggers based on Tom Stoppard's *Rosenkrantz and Guildenstern are Dead* which the drunken grave-diggers conclude with the question "Was this really a prince who talked with the people?"; and the omission of the epilogue with Fortinbras, which was irrelevant to Lyubimov's purpose.

Apart from these objections to the "popularization" of the tragedy, the representatives of the Main Administration and the Ministry undoubtedly felt some indignation at seeing Hamlet played by an actor who was a notorious drinker, who played the guitar, whose songs were circulated in *magnitizdat* (unofficial distribution of tape recordings) throughout the country, and who had been reprimanded both for his unofficial concerts and for his lack of discipline as a consequence of his alcohol addiction.[47]

Lyubimov continued to work on *Hamlet* after the Taganka version had taken shape. When he was invited to direct a production at the Lyric Theatre, Hammersmith in 1983, he initially talked about and signed contracts for *Hamlet*. The decision to direct *Crime and Punishment* instead was taken virtually at the last minute and not upon Lyubimov's initiative.[48] Furthermore, Lyubimov chose to teach an actors' and directors' seminar on *Hamlet* in (West) Berlin in the summer of 1988, presenting a concept which had seen further development since the 1971 Moscow production; he also staged the play at Leicester's Haymarket Theatre in September 1989, and the production subsequently toured seven countries.

The Hamlet emerging from the seminar in Berlin diverged in many points from the one presented by Vysotsky. The concept of the set design had not changed at all. The atmosphere described above, the overhearing of substantial monologues had not been modified. But the interpretation of the part of Hamlet himself had changed to an essentially Christian one. Lyubimov argued that this interpretation of Hamlet as a person in religious doubt had never been achieved in Vysotsky's interpretation of the part, since Vysotsky had never grasped the crux of that problem. Lyubimov gave some examples to illustrate Vysotsky's difficulties with the part: when Vysotsky was due to play Hamlet in Marseilles, he became so drunk that medical consent was refused for him to perform. But Vysotsky insisted, played the part, and in that condition best interpreted the problem of death for Hamlet. Moreover, during rehearsal, Vysotsky kept forgetting the omnipresence of death in the monologue "To be or not to be"; consequently, he was tied with a rubber band to the grave, so that he would be pulled back to the grave when physically moving too far away from it.

Lyubimov's Christian interpretation was based upon Hamlet's reflections on suicide.[49] In "To be or not to be" Hamlet is still concerned with existence, in paraphrase "to live or not to live"; but his soliloquy is threefold in structure: Hamlet first reflects upon death, then accuses himself of fearing the unknown,[50] then reproaches himself that his religious belief is not strong enough. The King could not pray, since he had committed a crime, but he made several attempts to do so. Then Hamlet emerged to kill Claudius, raised his sword to commit the murder, and at the last moment refrained and stepped back. In Lyubimov's version, Hamlet had, at the moment of changing his plans, caught a short glimpse of his father. This reminded him that his father had died without confession, i.e. in sin. If he were to kill Claudius now, in the moment of repentance and prayer, he would send his father's murderer to heaven.

When given the cup with the poisoned drink, Hamlet gargled with the liquid and then spat it out: he was aware that the drink might contain poison, but did not dare accuse anyone since he could not prove his suspicions. Hamlet was ever-careful not to err, and sought evidence before accusing or taking revenge.

Lyubimov sided with Pasternak in comparing Hamlet with Christ: when bearing the cross at Golgotha, Christ asked for help with his burden; so did Hamlet, who asked himself whether he was born to judge, to take revenge. Hamlet adhered completely, in all his words and acts, to a Christian morality, and yet he sincerely doubted the strength of his belief. In agreement with the new concept that Lyubimov applied to the text, he used different musics: no longer that of court players, the powerful music of a royal state, but liturgical, spiritual music composed by the Estonian Arvo Pärt. The interpretation moved the focus from the individual alone against the world to the individual preoccupied with religion. It was as if solidarity could not save society; mankind could not assist the individual; therefore only God can help the people to find a meaning in life. This religious approach might be considered unique to a play like *Hamlet*, but it manifested itself in other works of later years, such as *Boris Godunov*, *Jenufa* and *Rheingold*.

The loss of traditional values: *The Rush Hour*, *The Wooden Horses* and *The Exchange*

As society was stagnant and no longer represented a homogeneous group capable of generating changes, the individual was out of harmony with that society and withdrew into himself. At the same time, the individual began to develop negative features such as egoism and irresponsibility. Lyubimov perceived the reason for this degradation of human values in the loss of tradition, in the loss of humanism as opposed to materialism.

In 1969 the theatre had premièred *The Rush Hour*, based on the novel *Godzina szczytu* (1968) by the Polish writer Jerzy Stawinski.[51] The adaptation was prepared by Veniamin Smekhov, who played the role of the protagonist in the production. It was permitted after receiving severe and strict comments from the Main Administration and the Ministry of Culture, which asked for ten modifications at the viewings of 28 November 1969 and 2 December 1969.

The novel is about four days in the life of Krzysztof Maksymovicz, an untalented but successful bureaucrat. He leads a seemingly perfect life. An egoist, he is incapable of humane feelings, capable only of intrigues and treachery. At 42, he still feels like a young man, until Friday, 11 November 1966, when he meets Andrzej Bielecki, a resistance fighter, whom Krzysztof could have saved in the war from camp and prison, and his family from death, but failed to do so, instead saving his own life. When Krzysztof visits the doctor the next morning, he reads on the report the diagnosis "cancer". Thereupon, he starts to order his life and clear his conscience. But his mistress refuses to marry him, having long stopped loving him after realising how selfish he is. His daughter has turned into a cynic. Both his colleagues, Obúchowski and Radniewski, see through his intrigues. His wife Zosia, whom he no longer loves, has a relationship with Andrzej. Krzysztof is left with nobody to turn to, stripped of all the appearances that constituted for him a "successful" life. He then visits the widow of his friend, Elzbietka Borzecki; he refused to employ her because she was neither young nor pretty – and now saves her life by sending her to a health centre, performing the only honest and good deed in his entire life. After he has destroyed the illusions about his life, Krzysztof discovers after the operation that he had a hernia, not cancer. The novel is written from the stance of a first-person narrator taking the part of Krzysztof; he reconsiders the four days in question and his past life.

The play consists of two acts and an epilogue. The stance of a first-person narrative for Krzysztof has been adopted from the novel: Krzysztof leads the action, introduces the characters with dialogues and remarks, mingling comment and direct speech in accordance with the Brechtian devices of alienation. Krzysztof prompts re-enactments of the past, reviving in his memory characters, who turn into interlocutors (Andrzej, Borzecki). Few changes have been made for the adaptation. The information on some characters like Trzos, Bozena and Borzecka has been drawn together for the introduction to characterise their essential attitudes. The remembrance of the Madrasek-episode has been used as a prologue to the second part to display the "lottery" of life for Krzysztof: during the war he had been chosen by Madrasek out of a whole detachment for a special task. The account of Krzysztof transporting arms with Andrzej in the war, and his choice of action after Trusik's arrest – to save his life or that of Andrzej – have been left out, as well as Krzysztof's memory of causing his grandmother's heart attack by making the arm of the saint (to which she regularly prayed) move. Moreover, Krzysztof does not contemplate suicide in the play. The dramatic action remains restricted to the four days, omitting the operation, the blame put by Krzysztof on the doctor for not confirming his fatal illness, and Krzysztof's future plans. The result of the operation is only mentioned in the epilogue, as well as Trzos's divorce from his young wife.

The sequence of events has remained unchanged, with the exception of the introduction, which quotes later incidents, and the recalling of Borzecki and his wife as a parallel for the happiness Krzysztof sees in Andrzej and Zosia. Some minor changes had to be made in connection with censorship which insisted that there must be no analogies to Soviet life in such delicate issues as alcoholism and contraception, emigration and history: the censors demanded the replacement of the word "abortion" by "that" in the dialogue between Ewa and Krzysztof, the specification of location (Poland) in the utterance "It is idiocy to fight against vodka in our country" , the omission of "You are thinking of staying in Mexico", and "The black days of the Occupation, or rather the bright days of our heroic past...".[52]

The production was played on a bare stage. Elements of the set (designed by David Borovsky) included a horizontal lift filled with puppets, and a pendulum at the front centre stage. This pendulum was a symbol for time: Krzysztof was told by Radniewski that he led a life conforming to past principles. Krzysztof was an anachronism in the present, and not congruent with what he pretended to be. On the one hand, he was a very "modern" man as far as his ideas about his mistress go; on the other hand, his ideas about the behaviour of his wife or daughter were antiquated, corresponding to wartime rather than the present. He constantly insisted on his youth, even feeling too young to be the father of a teenage daughter. Krzysztof wanted time to go faster for his success and career, but slower for his age. Thus all the characters moved quickly in relation to the pace of the pendulum:

> The characters live faster than the time requires, but they do not surpass it: they live in the rhythm of a time invented by them, opposing themselves to humanity.[53]

Moreover, an essential element of the set design, similar to the use of the detachment of soldiers in *The Mother*, was the crowd of people. They were choreographed to form a parade at the beginning of each act: they walked, like mannequins in a fashion show, along the rectangle of the stage (Figure 29), revealing the labels of their dresses (in Krzysztof's coat is the emblem of the Taganka theatre).[54] Entrances and exits were choreographed as well. This device was not only an active element of the set design, but worked also as a symbol for the superficiality of life:

> The mannequin, stepping out onto the catwalk and completing twenty steps to and fro, leaves her life behind the even, polished panels. For the heroes of this satirical production, twenty steps have turned into life, since their life is also "for appearance" and requires certain norms of behaviour, as they understand them: make an impression, put others into the shade, and at the same time conform to the standard. They live ... thinking they control everywhere and everything, and yet controlling nowhere and nothing.[55]

People were reduced to façades, appearances, masks. If they were dropped, as in the conversation between Obúchowski, Radniewski and Krzysztof during the lunch, the show-life came to a halt, leaving no chance for return. The show-production was a demonstration of types of human behaviour: "[The mannequins] do not show fashion, but human types"[56] and types would continue to exist, especially types such as Krzysztof. In the adaptation, he was therefore deprived of his future plans, but continued to strive for a position in which he would rule time, by symbolically climbing onto the pendulum at the end.

It was the so-called "modern" or "contemporary" way of life led by Krzysztof, based on pretending and demonstrating, rather than existing, which was criticised both by Stawinski and Lyubimov. Yet Lyubimov took irony and cynicism a step further. The ironic theme of the tale was strengthened by the theatre: "There is no tragedy for the hero – instead of cancer he is derisively rewarded with a hernia".[57] The only contrast to the empty style of life led by Krzysztof and his acquaintances, was Borzecka, treated poetically in the production with musical accompaniment by Chopin. She was the only true and honest character.

In scenes of remembrance of the past, the visual approach was also poetic: candles were placed onto the pendulum, as if to create a memorial for those who had died.[58]

The novel was ideally suited for theatrical adaptation. The experience with *predstavlenie* enabled the theatre to use the first-person narrator simultaneously as both commentator and protagonist. The narrative stance allowed the Brechtian alienation effect to develop more than in a dramatic text or in an omniscient narrator's narrative. The commentator–actor function of the protagonist made it possible for him to be an egotist, but to step aside and criticise his own behaviour, to observe himself: "Krzysztof – V. Smekhov – is the accused, but at the same time he is judge, prosecutor, witness, attorney, public".[59]

All the characters made comments on the way in which they pronounce their remarks, thereby illustrating that they were aware of playing a part in Krzysztof's game, of wearing a mask in order to conform to what Krzysztof considered a modern style of life.

> All the characters understand perfectly well the core, the real value of their offences, commenting on them with intonations which leave no doubt.[60]

The theme of the novel, – egoism and selfishness instead of humane behaviour, appearance rather than existence, the wearing of a mask which, when dropped, leaves a non-personality, – was in line with the Taganka's current concerns and prefigured the problem of the loss of values and of honesty, which would later be analysed in the protagonists of Abramov and Trifonov. It was no longer the individual as the generator of social change, but the individual and his conscience who would form the centre of Lyubimov's attention. This protracted search for truth in the individual rather than in society would reach its climax in the 1970s. This production was a precursor.

Fedor Abramov's *The Wooden Horses* (1974) was, after *The Tough*, the second piece of village prose Lyubimov turned to. The adaptation was based on the short stories *The Wooden Horses* (1969), *Pelageya* (1967–69) and *Alka* (1971).[61] These works are about the lives of three women, Milentevna, Pelageya and Alka, in the rural community of a village during three different historical periods of the Soviet Union. In *The Wooden Horses*, Milentevna, aged 76, comes to visit her son Maksim. The story of her life bears the imprint of Stalin's agricultural policies of collectivisation in the 1930s: after Milentevna's initiative to cultivate the land and turn her husband's family (previously hunters) into farmers, her husband and father-in-law were arrested as *kulaks* (peasants owning substantial plots of land) during the purges of the forced collectivisation. Milentevna is a woman full of energy and inspiration despite her hard lot during the 1930s. In *Pelageya*, the heroine represents the next generation of peasant women. She is exposed to the effects of Stalin's agricultural policies of the 1940s: her baby son died of starvation, and Pelageya left the kolkhoz to establish a bakery in order to ensure proper nutrition for her daughter Alka. Alka represents the youngest generation of women in the rural society of the Soviet Union in the late 1960s: she eventually leaves the countryside to live in the city. Although the background against which the novels are set shows the development of Soviet agricultural policies over four decades, Abramov's prime concern is the destructive effect of these policies on human beings and on their moral values.

The production *The Wooden Horses*, however, dwells on the juxtaposition of two women of different generations (Milentevna and Pelageya) rather than on the evolution the attitudes to rural life over three generations. The contrast is between urban life, progress and the present and rural life, tradition and the past.

The dramatisation is divided into two parts; the first is based on *The Wooden Horses*, the second on *Pelageya* and *Alka*. The two parts are preceded by a prologue, in which the protagonists of all three stories are placed next to one another, and followed by an epilogue, which sees Alka after Pelageya's death. Although the story *The Wooden Horses* is relatively short, it occupies a third of the dramatisation. The story is told by a first-person narrator, who uses literary language and is obviously a stranger to rural life. The village people speak a local peasant dialect of Northern Russia, which even the narrator sometimes cannot follow. The adaptation effaces the narrator entirely, thus abandoning the exterior stance on rural life which he provides in the story. Instead, the dramatisation gives an inside view by making the village people the only participants in the conversation, thereby leaving the audience in the position of an outside observer. The village people take over the role of narrator when comparing urban and rural life. The only "objective" stance provided is a disembodied voice, asking for clarification when the dialect might leave the audience in doubt, or providing an answer when the villagers ask about things beyond their ken.[62]

Milentevna's past is rendered vividly in the dramatisation by a re-enactment of her marriage and the attitude of the Urvaevs to her with a re-animation of her late husband. Several dialogues have been added,[63] and an allusion to the Taganka is made when Mara reveals that an Urvaev holds an important post in Moscow, and the old woman replies that he works at the Taganka (square) as a traffic warden.[64] Other additional dialogues reveal rural attitudes to problems of science, politics or social progress, and provide thereby an ironic view of urban life viewed by an outsider, while at the same time underlining the ignorance of the village people. Thus, when Prokhor, Mara and Evgeniya discuss the medical profession in an attempt to assess what to do about Milentevna's cold, Mara and Evgeniya cannot even pronounce "hypertension", and Mara takes it to be an imported disease, using the occasion to repeat her daughter's comments on the influx of foreigners – all held to be potential spies – into the cities; Prokhor adds that imported medications are a device by which capitalism fights Soviet socialism. Mara recalls her daughter's account that Man has neglected his roots since conquering the moon,[65] which is, of course, a reference to contemporary achievements by the Soviet Union.

Dialogues on a variety of topics have been inserted at the end of the first act.[66] First, the conversation concerns the difference between rural and urban life, with urban people longing for the country and vice versa. Milentevna recalls that some girls from town stayed with her during several summer holidays to write down her stories, to study her dialect, and to collect items of the past. Here the narrator's passion for antique objects has been transferred to the student girls. Milentevna, who is far from glorifying the past, appreciates, however, the interest young people feel for the past and tradition. The attitudes of Mara and the old woman are juxtaposed to Milentevna's viewpoints. Mara has no opinions of her own, but notices the decline of the present generation: her daughter lives on social security. Icons, treasures of religious life in the village, have been turned into consumer goods by their transfer to urban museums. The old woman sees the younger generation in a negative way and despises it; it becomes clear from the repetitive monotony of her argument that she is prejudiced. Moreover, she appears herself as a fool in her accounts (she once talked to a statue and was infuriated when it did not reply), yet at the same time with this story she mocks the abundance of statues in towns. She is baffled when her grandchild draws a cow with six legs. This refers both to the strangeness of rural life for urban children, and also to her own failure to understand her grandchild, who perhaps wanted to show a cow in motion; she thereby represents an uneducated attitude to a more abstract form of art. Her function is twofold: she makes herself ridiculous as an uneducated woman, but at the same time she mocks the modern way of life and shows its disadvantages in comparison to the traditional way of life preserved in rural areas.

The second part of the dramatisation is based on *Pelageya* and *Alka*, both narrated in the original by an omniscient narrator. The dramatisation clearly places the emphasis on *Pelageya*, taking only minor episodes from *Alka*, such as the importance of dress materials for Pelageya, or the little buckets Pavel made for Pelageya and which he placed all along the rivers. Alka's conflict – her inability to decide whether to live in the country or in town, which is the main theme of *Alka* – has been neglected, and it might therefore be fairer to omit the short story *Alka* from the list of material used for the dramatisation. There is little verbal humour in this act, and it affects only Manya, who uses uneducated speech (*storan* for *restaurant*, *fitsyanka* for *ofitsyantka*, *penziya* for *pensiya*).

The set for *The Wooden Horses* was the result of David Borovsky's collection of authentic material in the region where the stories were set.[67] Harrows hung from the ceiling and served as kitchen shelves in the first act, with old spoons and saucepans on them; they were the shelves of shops in the second act, displaying loaves of bread and coats to represent the bakery and Oksya's shop respectively (Figure 30 and 31). Some benches (in the first act decorated with wooden horses), tables, and a wooden board (which serves as a bed), were the only props. The audience entered via the stage,[68] and spectators then took their seats in the auditorium, to observe other spectators entering the same way. This allowed the audience to come into close contact with the stage properties and helped to break down the separation of the stage action from the audience.

The costumes were folk dresses as worn in Northern Russian villages. Local dialect was spoken, and the protagonists Pelageya, Milentevna and Evgeniya (played by Zinaida Slavina, Alla Demidova and Tatyana Zhukova), seemed at home in that atmosphere. Folk music, composed and arranged by Nikolay Sidelnikov, differentiated between Milentevna, accompanied by choral songs, and Pelageya, accompanied by balalaika tunes;[69] furthermore, the neighing and galloping of horses underscored the rhythm of the production.

The action of the first act appeared very static. Evgeniya narrated Milentevna's life, while Milentevna sat and listened. The mood of this act was opposed to that of the second act, which was dominated by Pelageya's dynamism, her restlessness and constant talk, together with her inability to listen. Her extroverted character stood in sharp contrast to the introverted personality of Milentevna. Pelageya was obsessed with the materialistic side of life; she always desired more than others, obtaining a well, a bath and a bakery of her own before anyone else in the village. It was therefore no longer necessary to incorporate Alka's story in order to continue the line of three generations. On stage, the contrast between Milentevna and Pelageya was sharp enough to make clear that once the uprooting has started, there could be no return for Alka.

> Throughout the whole performance, Alka is tormented by thoughts of, and the
> search for, her identity, for those spiritual values on which life has to be built
> and which need to be maintained.[70]

Her empty glance into the audience at the end of the production
indicated resignation at her incapacity to return to her own roots and
traditions: "The theatre does not yet say what needs to be done, but
hastens to say what must not be forgotten".[71]

Humour and irony life were largely verbal in the first act, while
they dominated more overtly the physical actions of the second act.
Pelageya's reaction to Anisya's invitation was rendered in a humorous
way: Pelageya, already in bed, rose abruptly to talk to Anisya, and lay
down flat again when she finished talking to her sister-in-law. The two
Manyas looked comic when they arrived at Anisya's carrying two glasses
for their hoped-for drinks. Manya's behaviour when she visited Pelageya,
and her outfit when she returned from town looking like a "scarecrow"
(according to the novel) were exaggerated on stage. Whereas humour
was subtle and ambivalent in Milentevna's environment, it had become
coarse, with a tendency to slapstick, in Pelageya's world.

The two parties, at Anisya's and Petr Ivanovich's, were not
separated, as in the story, but ran parallel on the right and left side of the
stage, thus underlining their temporal coincidence; shifts of focus were
marked by shifting spotlights. This technique indicated that Pelageya
preferred not to be with her family but to gain some advantage for her
husband and daughter. One critic suggested that the production dwelt on
Pelageya's responsibility for her fate:[72] she chose to be with strangers
rather than the family, chose a lover rather than faithfulness to her
husband in order to secure the bakery for herself, and chose to devote her
life to material achievements rather than to the education of her daughter
along traditional lines.

Episodes could be enacted while they were narrated on stage, as
well as underlined by sound or the simple appearance of the person
concerned. Thus, a shot could be heard when Evgeniya remembered that
Milentevna's husband had fired at his wife; the arrest of the Urvaevs for
turning forest into field was demonstrated on stage; Pavel would sit on
stage to make the little buckets when Pelageya remembered him doing
this.

Fire and water played an important role in both parts of the
production. Orange light was used in two levels of intensity to capture
the heat emanating from Pelageya's oven, or the reflection of the wooden
horses as perceived by Milentevna in the sunset. Water was relevant for
both characters: Milentevna's health cannot be damaged by rainwater

(she comes back wet after a walk), and Pelageya needs water on the way to the bakery to satisfy her thirst.[73] But water also had a symbolic function:

> Pelageya has not thought about a meaning in life, and she has lived, perhaps, in vain, but does that mean that people do not need the "water of life" which Milentevna explained?[74]

Tradition and ritual always held great importance for the people in the village. Pavel's funeral, however, was ambivalent in combining old rituals (the relatives appear with candles) with modern funeral rites, in which rituals were replaced by official speeches praising the late person's social achievements, in this case delivered by the kolkhoz chairman. This juxtaposition, which made the latter look ridiculous and flat, reflected the stance of the Taganka theatre.

In each act, the actors were omnipresent on stage. In the first act, they sat on benches at the sides, in the second, they emerged from behind white curtains along both sides of the stage. The wooden horses on the benches and the material of the curtains symbolised the main attributes of the protagonists of the two acts: Milentevna's appreciation of the wooden horses, and Pelageya's obsession with dress materials, which she collected in a trunk and which, to her, were her very life. All the women, Pelageya, Milentevna and Alka, were present at the beginning of each act, together with the inhabitants of the village at the sides of the stage. Their omnipresence underlined the rural community, from which they all emerged and to which they duly returned. The calmness of the production, the depth of psychological portrayal, and the preoccupation with the theme of tradition and its relevance for modern society, made this production a forerunner of the folk tradition which characterises the productions of the 1980s. Yet the situation of a character such as Alka, for whom a return to her roots had become impossible, endowed the performance with a tragic note throughout, which stood in sharp contrast to the optimism of *The Tough*. *The Wooden Horses* dealt with the respective value systems of a civilized and a rural society, with the themes of tradition and progress, and thereby addressed ethical issues.

The representatives of the Main Administration were somewhat preoccupied by the theme of "de-kulakization" and its presentation on stage: as Milentevna remembered the past, the harrows which formed part of the set became prison bars, behind which stood the victims of "de-kulakization". Although this part of Soviet history was known, it was officially evaluated as a positive measure and therefore not meant to be presented on stage in its tragic implication for the individual. Furthermore, the excessive consumption of alcohol by the old women of the village and the guests at a party was rejected as not corresponding to reality.[75] Several textual passages concerning arrests in 1946, a reference to Ho Chi Min (rhyming with "vitamin"), society's lack of regard for peasant work, a remark associating dirt with the October Revolution ("Why is it so muddy, if our life is built on that mud") had to be omitted before the Main Administration agreed to send the play to *Glavlit* for approval.[76] The young girl Alka's idea of earning a living as a stewardess and using her sexual appeal to attract men (she does not speak a foreign language, "but all men understand one language...") was not considered an appropriate ending for the production, which should have concluded on a positive note affirming life in the countryside.

The press approached the Taganka theatre's production of Abramov's prose with a great deal of scepticism; it was unthinkable for critics such as Zalygin, Krymova or Chernichenko that Abramov's prose could find a successful interpretation on the stage of a theatre famous for its expressive and agitational productions. Nevertheless, the production met with great approval, and Abramov himself called it his favourite stage version.[77]

Yury Trifonov's *The Exchange* encountered few problems in reaching the stage of the Taganka theatre, where it was premièred on 20 April 1976 after a few comments by the authorities.[78] The adaptation was written by Trifonov himself and called "a story for the theatre". The technique of dramatising a prose text for the stage differs in this case from other adaptations offered at the Taganka, and therefore deserves special attention.

The story has two levels. On one level, it is about the engineer Dmitriev, who, pushed by his wife Lena, née Lukyanova, asks his fatally ill mother Ksenia to move in with them, so that, after her death, the Dmitrievs will be entitled to exchange two one-bedroom flats for a two-bedroom apartment. On another level, the play is about the exchange of humanist for materialist values.

It is noteworthy that a narrator-figure, or an author–commentator, added in other Taganka dramatisations, has not been inserted here. The story is a third-person narrative; its hero, Dmitriev, has been transformed into a narrator–commentator while at the same time playing his part and thus participating in the action. This demands, of course, that the actor should have a great deal of experience and familiarity with Brecht's techniques for the achievement of the alienation effect.[79] Dmitriev narrates his story, comments on the action, and some episodes are illustrated by characters (most of whom are ever-present on stage) in a re-enactment. This is the case with the arrival of the Lukyanovs at the dacha, Kseniya

Fedorovna's return from hospital, and Dmitriev's conversation with Snitkin at work.[80] Dmitriev analyses his situation, sharing his thoughts with the audience. The world on stage is that created in his mind and presented to the spectator. The adaptation does not, as McLain suggests, use an impressionistic method to achieve a "kaleidoscopic effect",[81] but is a carefully structured narrative, told by the protagonist, and animated by the characters of the novel and the protagonist himself. This means, however, a reduction of the psychological portrayal of all the characters except for the protagonist:

> Several characters remain without detailed attention from the director. They are drawn as sketches. ... All those characters are only functional, carriers of information, deprived of artistic or personal comprehension of character, psychology or fate.[82]

If the story and the dramatisation are compared, it becomes apparent that only a few minor changes have been made. The omissions and cuts affect Dmitriev's perception of the morning routine, of urban life and of nature. Moreover, the dramatisation ends with Kseniya Fedorovna's consent to the exchange, thus omitting both the outcome and consequences of the exchange for the Dmitrievs. A few passages of dialogue have been inserted, as in the discussion of the sewerage system at the dacha, or the revolutionary's speech at the funeral,[83] but they are merely illustrations of what is accounted for in the story by other images. Notable, however, is the introduction of a broker, who appears seven times to comment on the action and throw the events back at the audience by the use of direct address, thereby linking the stage events to the spectators.[84] Yet he also advertises flats for exchange, and reports on the progress of Dmitriev's exchange, in which, at the end, thirteen parties are involved.

Most revealing is a comparison of the structure of the story and the dramatisation. The story begins with the present situation in Dmitriev's family, living in one room, and Dmitriev's everyday problems; then it deals with the past before moving back to Dmitriev's current affairs: his journey to Perelygino and visit to his mother, followed by the story of the exchange of flats achieved shortly before his mother's death. The reader is presented with the character of Dmitriev, who is prompted by a problem in the present to think about the past and search there for the reasons for his situation, only to return to the present with his reflections making no impact upon his further action. The play *deliberately* restructures the story. The dramatisation may be divided into four parts.[85] The first deals with the past: Dmitriev remembers the initial conflicts over the dacha, the argument between the two families, and his love for Lena. The extracts taken from five different parts of the story are centred in circles around Dmitriev's appraisal of Lena's taste. In the first circle, he remembers the positive sides of his life with Lena (her love, their stay in Batum), and only in the second, more distant circle, he remembers the negative sides, their arguments. A summary of past conflicts is then made by Dmitriev's conclusion that it is impossible to bring his mother and wife together. The second part deals with the present: the exchange plans as proposed by Lena, Dmitriev's work and financial problems. This section adheres to the story in its sequence of events. The third part follows on the first of the dramatisation, although continuing the sequence of events in the narrative, dealing with the opposition of the worlds of the two families, the final argument between them, the Bubrik episode, and the dispute between Marina and Lena at the birthday party. The fourth part reverts to the present, when Dmitriev finally arrives at the dacha and a decision over the exchange is made by Kseniya Fedorovna's consent two days later. There is thus a movement in two sections in the dramatisation: from the distant past to the present (Parts I and II) and from the immediate past to the present, with a slight lapse of time (Parts III and IV). The borderline between the two sections is marked by Dmitriev's appeal to his father for help in a situation he cannot cope with, and with a problem he cannot resolve.[86]

> DMITRIEV What shall I do?
> FATHER Be careful, son. Don't rush things! [...] You must tell mother every-thing the way it is, frankly, that is the only way! [...] You see, son, the most difficult thing is to understand what you have to do in this world... Hardly anybody understands this...[87]

The set by David Borovsky consisted of pieces of furniture of different periods and styles, placed along the front of the stage in "arranged chaos". Two house entrances were located on the right and left forestages (Figure 32). The furniture not only rendered the interior of the Dmitrievs' room and the dacha; the space overloaded with furniture was an image of Dmitriev's mind. Certain areas and pieces of furniture were linked with certain characters, most of whom were omnipresent. On the far left was the world of the Lukyanovs, followed by the dacha where Lora and her mother lived; the Dmitrievs' room was slightly right of centre. Dmitriev sat here in front of the television. This space crammed with furniture was contrasted to the vast empty space upstage, which was lit at intervals for two skaters to perform there. They moved as if on an enlarged television screen, which would be switched on by Dmitriev.

McLain interpreted this contrast of spaces on the level of housing problems:

> The reality of the housing shortage in this country of vast spaces is schematically created by having the awkward, aggravating, claustrophobia of the jumbled furniture juxtaposed against a seemingly endless expanse of space.[88]

McLain also saw in the pair – dressed in red – the embodiment of the "Soviet dream". Yet their dresses changed; they were sometimes white, sometimes yellow and violet, sometimes blue, and they performed to old music. Therefore they should really be seen as the opposite of a "Soviet dream": the reminder of past traditions.

> The times of a certain way of life have gone ... the times – how sad – of tradition have gone: a style disappears with a way of life, traditions disappear with people ... The figure skaters of the production are a conservation of style: "Kalinka", Charleston, a waltz of the distant 20s.[89]

The skaters were, significantly, in motion whilst the action downstage was static.

Many items Dmitriev remembered were represented on stage, such as his childhood drawings, the keys for Kseniya Fedorovna's flat, grandfather's portrait, a card of the GINEGA (State Institute for Gas and Petrol), which hung on the washing line, and the number plate of the Opel car. Furthermore, some objects appeared from out of the empty space, such as the cognac and tomatoes Dmitriev was offered by Tanya. The most surprising element of the decoration was the tree in the middle of the centre aisle in the auditorium. A red ball, derived from grandfather's humorous story about Marya Petrovna, was caught in the tree, which at times threw its enlarged reflection onto the back wall. Furthermore, Lyubimov would usually sit in the auditorium at each performance and shake the tree each time it was referred to.[90] The time of the action determined where this action took place; events of the past, which were being recalled, unfolded in the auditorium, while events of the present occupied the actual stage.[91]

Ambulance lights accompanied by horns were frequently employed to enhance the urgency of the exchange due to Kseniya Fedorovna's illness. Warm light surrounded Kseniya Fedorovna, whereas other characters usually appeared in flashing spots. The recorded sound of a car was used to mark the arrival of the taxi.

The programme reminded the audience of the more evident meaning of "exchange", – the exchange of flats: it was an application form for a flat exchange, filled in as if the Taganka theatre were to change houses (Figure 33). The broker in the performance underlined this aspect, when he ended the seemingly endless enumeration of parties involved in the exchange with a move from the "Vakhtangov theatre" to the "Taganskii Tupik" [Cul-de-sac], which doubtlessly commented on the situation of the Taganka theatre – on the outskirts of the centre, in a building incapable of holding the increasing audience.

The production, however, concentrated on the second meaning of "exchange" explored in the story: the exchange of ideas, worlds, and philosophies. Dmitriev has exchanged his world, the tradition and moral code of his family for that of the Lukyanovs, who have no values other than their preoccupation with survival in the Soviet socialist system. In Lyubimov's interpretation, Dmitriev left the world of a Russian – intellectual – family for that of a Soviet – materialistic – one. Significantly, it was Kseniya Fedorovna who was bathed in warm light, and the grandfather who was accompanied by Glinka's classical music. Dmitriev, on the other hand, was hardly in contact with the shadow of the tree, since he merely remembered the past, not realising the grounds for the impossibility of uniting the two worlds of Russian and Soviet life. Dmitriev tried to find a middle way, but betrayed himself by doing so.

Although the audience was presented with Dmitriev's self-scrutiny, it was not asked to condemn him; for were not Dmitriev's problems also those of the audience, as the broker had just pointed out? The audience should consider the process of the *Lukyanovisation* of society, and through the sad portrayal of what was shown on stage the audience was asked whether it really desired the loss of all traditions, roots and moral values, which were ignored in the Soviet style of life.

The "Soviet" characters in the production were objects of satire: the drunken Kalugin tumbled against the tree in the auditorium when leaving the stage; the Lukyanovs were mocked by their speech; and the broker was a mere laughing-stock.

In his production Lyubimov dwelt on the link between past and present, emphasising the need to conserve moral values, traditions, and rituals. He was interested in the question of how an individual can abandon his roots and become "Soviet" without destroying his identity or troubling his conscience, since "even an insignificant concession by the conscience means spiritual death".[92] He was no longer concerned with society as a whole, but with individuality degenerating in the course of the Sovietisation of society. It had become clear to Lyubimov that a process of social change could only start from and with the individual, not from "above" or "outside". Evtushenko correctly remarked that "the progress of our society is impossible without an improvement in the quality of human relationships".[93]

It is along that line of interpretation that the imagery of the television screen with a magnifying glass in front of it and an enlarged version of the programme on the back stage has to be placed. Television dominates our lives and destroys communication. Phone calls were made from one end of the stage to the other, people did not look at each other when they spoke, the volume of music reduced words to gestures and pantomime (as in the scene between Dmitriev and Zherekhov). Communication had become impossible in the face of mass media and the "progress" of technology, and its most bitter consequence was the loss of tradition.

At the end of the production, rain came through a sprinkler system onto the downstage area. This rain was symbolic: it was a last remnant of the past, of nature, directed against "Soviet" people, who like the broker must be on constant watch – he always carried an umbrella. Then, a polythene cover was spread over the set and the characters. The image was frozen in the same manner as it had been animated at the beginning. The portrait had been completed, the glimpse into the past was over. At the same time, the skaters performed in their space: some traditions survived as the present stagnated. Pessimism and a tragic note dominated the performance, and the glimpse of hope at the end remained unattainable for the characters.

There was no appeal, no agitational element in this production. It was a portrait, an "elegy",[94] only interrupted at times by the broker's remarks to the audience. The problem was revealed by Dmitriev, and it was by means of thought and reflection on the events shown that the audience was asked to reconsider its own way of life.

In its preoccupation with conscience, *The Exchange* was a culminating point in the line of productions embracing *Dawns*, *Hamlet*, and *The Wooden Horses*, which all investigated the problems of human conscience faced with war, crime, and the traditional style of life respectively. In this production, the view of conscience acquired a pessimistic overtone: Dmitriev stepped over the borderline his conscience set him by "sacrificing" his mother for an easy and pleasant personal life.

The individual conscience: *Crime and Punishment* and *The House on the Embankment*

The opposition of the individual and society led to the isolation and withdrawal of the individual. *Crime and Punishment* was the logical conclusion of the investigation started by Hamlet, the individual, who had been rejected and expelled by society; the individual Raskolnikov would seek to separate himself from a society which he felt had rejected him. Lyubimov had become increasingly anxious at people's obsession with ideas, which could bring about such dangerous manifestations as the destruction of human beings. Moreover, having investigated the question of the individual's responsibility, Lyubimov had gradually expanded the notion of responsibility to include that of conscience; the individual was held responsible for his actions, even if they had been committed because of extraneous circumstances.

Crime and Punishment was Lyubimov's first staging of a work by Dostoevsky. It was also his first production of a dramatic adaptation not to open in Moscow but in Budapest (1978). This same version opened at the Taganka Theatre in February 1979, but it was closed under Anatoly Efros in 1984 and not revived until December 1989. It was staged by Lyubimov in London (1983), Vienna (1984), Bologna (1984) and Washington (1987). The adaptation of Dostoevsky's novel *Crime and Punishment* was written by Yury Karyakin.[95]

The six parts (subdivided into chapters) and epilogue of the novel have been converted into two acts (subdivided into scenes), with a prologue and finale. Karyakin's version begins with the murder. It is clear from the outset of the novel that Raskolnikov will commit the crime; thus, the act has already taken place when the play starts: the dead bodies of the pawnbroker Alena Ivanovna and her sister Lizaveta lie by a door on the stage floor (Figure 34). Hence, most chapters of the first part of the novel have been omitted, some events narrated there happen after the crime; and Raskolnikov's thoughts are summarised in the first act of the play. Apart from this change, the sequence of events has largely been kept in the adaptation. The only exception is the very beginning of the play: Raskolnikov's return to the place of the crime is transposed to the prologue, and the meeting with the police clerk Zametov follows shortly after. Thus, Raskolnikov first appears at a point when not only the crime has been committed, but moreover he has experienced the first desire to return to the scene of the crime to "feel the thrill again", when he embarks upon his provocative game with Zametov, and later with the investigator Porfiry.

The play concentrates on Raskolnikov, Porfiry, and Svidrigailov, who form a series of characters that reason about crime and present their ideas on the topic in several debates. Porfiry takes the position of a humanist moralist, who cannot accept any crime. Svidrigailov adopts a nihilist stance: any crime to him is permitted, hence the taking of his own life falls within his ethics. Finally, there is Raskolnikov, who promulgates his ideas of the Nietzschean superman, and assumes the right to kill others. The philosophies of Svidrigailov and Raskolnikov resemble each other, yet Svidrigailov has no motive, no theory, and no respect for his own life, which distinguishes him from Raskolnikov. The character of

Svidrigailov is inflated in the play as compared with the novel. A clear parallel has been drawn here between Raskolnikov's sister, Dunya, and the prostitute Sonya: whereas Sonya has destroyed her life, Dunya, who is in danger of doing the same, must be prevented from selling herself off in a marriage to Luzhin; hence Raskolnikov seizes Sonya, and Svidrigailov takes Dunya away from Luzhin in a scene in the play. The character of Lebezyatnikov is satirised as a political agitator, a socialist dreamer, even more sharply than is shown in the novel. Omissions affect Razumikhin and his relationship to Raskolnikov and his family; the characters of Zozimov and Ilya Petrovich; Sonya's role as the driving force behind Raskolnikov's surrender; his acceptance of life in prison, and his final turning to religion.

There are four dreams in the play. First, a boy (Raskolnikov as a child) moves out of a door on which Raskolnikov is beating. Nastasya flings a basin of blood at him (Figure 35). Second, the actors are blindfold victims while Porfiry, in the costume of Napoleon, orders Raskolnikov to kill Dunya, Sonya and his mother. Third, Svidrigailov sees Dunya half-naked on one side of the door. He plays a handclapping game with her and with several women who appear, of whom the last is a little girl. The final dream is a re-enactment of Raskolnikov's apocalyptic vision in prison: Napoleon, Sonya and Svidrigailov are its actors.

All these scenes represent the symbolic meaning of a dream rather than rendering the dream itself, and they reflect a state of mind. They are living images of Raskolnikov's (or Svidrigailov's) conscience, conveying the impact of events on their mind: the first dream stands for Raskolnikov's dream about the horse, in which he experienced and witnessed bloodshed for the first time in his life. In the last scene, Raskolnikov is in the prison church and sees the resurrection of the two women he killed. In the play, Raskolnikov experiences no conversion; it is the vision of the apocalypse which leads him to religion.

The production started in the foyer, where a schooldesk was displayed with copies of a school essay on *Crime and Punishment* scattered over it (Figure 36). The play had a finale without any source in the novel: the actor Aleksandr Trofimov, who played Raskolnikov, read an excerpt from a school essay on *Crime and Punishment*: "Raskolnikov was right to kill the old hag. Too bad he got caught".[96] This conclusion was the logical result of a Socialist Realist reading of the novel: Raskolnikov was right to revolt against the capitalist system as embodied by the pawnbroker Alena Ivanovna. The comment reflected the distortion of facts in order to make their interpretation fit in with current Soviet ideology, and the distortion of human morality by an ideology in order to make crime permissible for the achievement of higher ends. "The director concentrates on ... how an ideology manifests itself, in which murder is essential and crime is permitted."[97]

David Borovsky's set design (Figure 37) again departed from the empty stage. On the right side of the proscenium, Raskolnikov's poor room was depicted: it was simultaneouly the flat of the pawnbroker, and also Marmeladov's house. The bodies (puppets) of the murdered Alena Ivanovna and Lizaveta were placed there, papers were scattered across the floor, and a mirror and an icon were placed over a chest of drawers. Props included chairs, a bucket (Nastasya would constantly wipe the floor so that she could listen), and an axe, which was both a weapon and the means for Raskolnikov to draw the line which he transgressed. The main element of the décor was a set of doors with both symbolic and functional significance. One door, white and bloodstained after the first dream, moved autonomously across the stage; it was multifunctional. Another, glass, door was placed on the right side. Anatoly Smelyansky has provided an excellent analysis of the use of doors in this production:

> The production has many doors: the door of the auditorium, through which we had to enter; the door leading to the room of the murdered women; several doors, fixed on one axis, between which Raskolnikov hides, pressurised by the question whether he believes in the New Jerusalem; the door accompanies all the movements of the theme of Svidrigailov, right up to his last desperate gesture when a door is lifted up from the stage floor and he steps down slowly, into the void. The door is Sonya's accursed bed with a cushion, under which she hides the Gospels Lizaveta gave to her. The door is Marmeladov's coffin. The door is the place around which dreams swarm about childhood, visions of Napoleonic fame, and power over the quivering anthill. The bloodstain on the door is the image of redemption, of innocent suffering... The creators of the production caught here the most important leitmotif of *Crime and Punishment*. It is enough to say that the word "door" occurs more than two hundred times in the novel, and each time it is noted whether it is open or closed [as stated by V. Toporov].[98]

The entire cast was on stage throughout large parts of the production. Their virtual omnipresence stood in contrast to Raskolnikov's longing for solitude: all the actors appeared behind Raskolnikov as he uttered his wish to be alone. In other scenes, Raskolnikov was watched by a mass of people behind his chair. Raskolnikov's thoughts were made known to everybody in the first scene; his crime was spread by the newspapers, read by everybody simultaneously with him. Mikolka's attempted suicide and Marmeladov's death happened in public; Raskolnikov sent his family away in front of the whole cast; Marmeladov's declaration of his reliance on God's last Judgement was made in public; Raskolnikov admitted his belief in the resurrection of Lazarus in the face of everyone present on stage; Katerina Ivanovna died while all were in the room;

there was no privacy in the first scene between Raskolnikov and Sonya while they were discussing religion and belief in God; and Raskolnikov's arrest happened in public (II, 11), as did his conversion to religion in the final scene of the play. The space on stage was thus transformed into a *public* one, even for the most private scenes, such as dreams and confessions. Thoughts became known to everybody, minds were transparent. However, there was no external authority at work to achieve this transparency; conscience itself made every thought appear transparent and obvious to the common people. The audience saw Raskolnikov's mind and his conscience exposed before them. By means of a very simple theatrical device, the narrative stance employed in the novel (the narrator is omniscient concerning Raskolnikov) was successfully transposed to the stage.

In order to underline this transparency of conscience, many characters appeared in a spotlight or on a light path (*svetovaya doroga*)[99] when mentioned, or would illustrate scenes as if everything had happened in front of the mind's eye of the particular character. Thus, Lebezyatnikov distributed pamphlets when Marmeladov talked about the ideas he learned from him; Sonya was picked up by Luzhin, a customer, out of a line of prostitutes by the back wall when Marmeladov related her fate in the same scene; Luzhin appeared when Raskolnikov's mother read out her letter; Mikolka appeared with a rope around his neck, and again later in a spotlight; Lebezyatnikov wandered around the stage as Luzhin used his ideas in the conversation with Raskolnikov and Razumikhin; Liza and Alena Ivanovna appeared along with Dunya and Raskolnikov's mother, as if Raskolnikov were seeing his two victims instead of mother and sister; the Kobylyatnikovs appeared when mentioned by Lebezyatnikov.

The audience was not only addressed frequently, but was supposed to be an active participant in the production. In the very first scene, the spectators were placed in spotlights by Raskolnikov; several entrances and exits were made via the same doors in the auditorium that the audience had used for entering. When Zametov mentioned that crime has increased, he pointed into the auditorium. When prostitutes were mentioned in the text,[100] the audience was hinted at. Moreover, a woman from the audience was equated with the prostitutes on stage. These prostitutes attacked people such as Razumikhin. Katerina Ivanovna shouted insults at the audience. Lebezyatnikov walked into the auditorium to collect money for a memorial statue to Raskolnikov. At the end, Raskolnikov's now insane mother distributed among the audience strips of a torn-up newspaper with reports about her son. The money stolen by Raskolnikov was hidden under a chair – "the stone" – in the auditorium. When Raskolnikov's mother and Dunya searched their flat in St Petersburg, they did so among the front rows in the auditorium. The audience was not just invited, but actually challenged to participate, to take a stand concerning the events on stage and towards Raskolnikov. At the same time they were insulted and attacked: prostitutes were selected from their midst, blinding light was directed into their faces, they entered through the same door as the assassin Raskolnikov, and constantly saw themselves reflected in a mirror on the chest of drawers, above the scene of the crime. The suggestion was that murderers can be found among the audience. Moreover, Porfiry's challenge that "the world has to be changed, beginning with oneself" was directly addressed to the auditorium.

Light played a highly significant role. Raskolnikov turned a spot into the audience and into his own face at the very beginning, as if to see those to whom he was about to reveal his conscience. At times, the use of spotlight projectors became more aggressive: Zametov shone one into Raskolnikov's face as if to test whether he was telling the truth or not, alluding to the interrogation methods of police and secret service. Porfiry repeated the procedure, and several actors placed spotlights performing the same function. Light from a projector appeared as aggressive light. It could be distorted by means of a stroboscope to render the nightmarish atmosphere of Raskolnikov's dreams.

In contrast to electric light stood the candle-light introduced by Sonya in the first act. Svidrigailov also used a non-electric light-source, in his case a match, shortly before his suicide when Raskolnikov's shadow covered him. Svidrigailov placed a candle on the door when accusing Raskolnikov of murder. Raskolnikov's mother died by the light of a candle. Candle-light assumed a symbolic function in these instances: for Sonya, Svidrigailov and Raskolnikov's mother, candle-light indicated their closeness to religion or to God, or their being close to death. The identification of candle-light as a religious symbol was essential for understanding the final scene, in which Sonya appeared with candles in the prison church, and was first pushed back by Raskolnikov. Then the actors – prisoners in handcuffs – appeared, and a boy entered and handed candles to Raskolnikov. Raskolnikov lit a candle for his mother and the two murdered women, at which point they rose from the dead. Svidrigailov extinguished the candles and Raskolnikov extinguished his. If, symbolically speaking, the people appealed to Raskolnikov's conscience, conscience led Raskolnikov to religion, and this belief undid his crime through the resurrection of the three women, which, it was implied, took place in Raskolnikov's mind. People such as Svidrigailov, without conscience, kill others, and themselves; they can annul even the vision of resurrection. Svidrigailov personified that part of reality which destroyed the last vision or dream of Raskolnikov: his redemption. Not driven by Sonya, but faced with the apocalypse – embodied by people such as Svidrigailov and Napoleon and their theories in the last dream –, Raskolnikov turned to God.

Electric light became a symbol of truth when it was used to bring light into Raskolnikov's face, even if that was done by those who prosecuted him. Svidrigailov tried to keep this bright light off Raskolnikov. Electric light could also evoke another level of symbolism. Most importantly, it threw enlarged shadows of the actors onto the back wall to make their gestures even more precise: Porfiry formed an axe with his hands, which seemed to hang above Raskolnikov's shadow on the back wall. Porfiry was at this moment in a position to exercise power over Raskolnikov's life, since he knew enough about the crime to arrest him. A light path, representing a different sphere on stage, was used for both illustrations, and for the enactment of significant scenes that eventually led to God: here, Raskolnikov met Polina, Katerina Ivanovna died, the prisoner Raskolnikov found faith.

Allegorical aspects were incorporated into the image of Svidrigailov. At first, he combed his hair like Napoleon, then shaped his moustache like Hitler's. He was an allegory for all those historical figures who personified his or Raskolnikov's theories, in which human life has no value in itself, and led these theories to their logical conclusion: the murder of all "worthless" people, all "lice".

Comic and grotesque elements occurred rarely, and were merely illustrative in character: Marmeladov indicated the size of his children and fell over; Porfiry skipped with a rope, which Zametov caught in a folder; Porfiry tore up Raskolnikov's article and kicked the crumpled paper-balls across the stage; Amaliya Ludvigovna emphasised her name as "Ludvi*govno*" [*Govno*: "shit"]. This grotesque reality reflected Raskolnikov's perception of the world, and thereby illustrated what drove him to imagining himself a Nietzschean superman:

> The caricature world Lyubimov creates about him [Raskolnikov] is a projection of Raskolnikov's sense of reality: it is the one certain truth about himself and as such his indictment.[101]

Rather as Poprishchin and Gogol turned mad because of a corrupt society, Raskolnikov was driven into a fixed idea of being a Nietzschean superman by a grotesque reality that surrounded him, and then became a murderer.

The music in the production was arranged by Edison Denisov and emphasised recurrent leitmotifs. A cradle song sounded for scenes referring to childhood in general: the letter from Raskolnikov's mother, the school essay, the memories of Raskolnikov's mother before her death, and Katerina Ivanovna's retreat into childish behaviour in her madness.

Liturgical tunes were played for scenes relating to death: Marmeladov's conversation with Raskolnikov when he mentioned suicide and God's Last Judgement, Marmeladov's death, the priest's appeal to Katerina Ivanovna to forgive her husband, Marfa Petrovna's death, Svidrigailov's "voyage", Liza's death as related by Sonya, Katerina Ivanovna's death and the death of Raskolnikov's mother. Gypsy and waltz or tango music marked the place of action in the restaurants where Raskolnikov met Zametov and Marmeladov respectively. A guitar tune accompanied Svidrigailov (played in the 1979 Moscow production by Vysotsky) to his grave: when he left the stage to die, disappearing into a ditch in the stage floor, a door opened in the floor with a guitar attached to it. Sirens wailed when Svidrigailov expounded his theory, and for his scene with Dunya; tubular alarm bells (for gale warnings) accompanied Raskolnikov's theory of population, just as if these theories – similar both in content and musical accompani-ment – needed an alarm to sound each time they were described.

Smelyansky suggested that, for Lyubimov, Raskolnikov's charac-ter was not limited to the historical horizon of his author:

> The spiritual composition of Dostoevsky's hero is replaced by a complex of ideas suggested by historical and artistic experience, extending beyond Dostoevsky and his time... [The theatre] tries to relate the metaphysical experience of Raskolnikov to a new generation. The spiritual problem of man's self-determina-tion in the world is replaced by the more concrete theme of the "intelligent man with the axe". The axe is real, not metaphysical, real as the blood of the victims.[102]

This concrete dimension was reflected in the use of a minimum of authentic props, and in the introduction of a "Man with an Axe" who accompanied Raskolnikov on stage. Lyubimov addressed the classical novel to a contemporary audience, transferring Dostoevsky into our time. Raskolnikov was not portrayed psychologically, but the ideas which motivate him were shown to be a destructive force within his personality: it was a split personality after the crime. Even if he turned to religion at the end of the play, the resurrection happened in his imaginative vision only: "In Lyubimov's production, forgiveness, the union of hangman and victim, are possible only in a dream".[103] Raskolnikov's conscience can never be granted redemption for the crime. Like Dostoevsky, Lyubimov chose conscience as the main theme of his production, rather than the social or judicial analysis of Raskolnikov's crime. He maintained that no idea can justify crime, no means justify ends, no ideology justifies the condoning of Raskolnikov's crime, as the school essay did.

> The novel – and the play – thus are a debate about ends and means – a matter at the very core of the basic dilemma of a regime like the Soviet one which claims

to be based on the principle that means – however cruel and inhuman – justify the ends, if those ends are the ultimate progress of humanity.[104]

For Lyubimov, Raskolnikov is an unscrupulous murderer. He not only physically destroyed the pawnbroker and Lizaveta with her unborn child, but also verbally annihilated Marmeladov by depriving him of his last hope when he denies the existence of God. Raskolnikov is not an occasional, but a notorious murderer:

> Fedor Dostoevsky wrote a novel on the theme that one must not kill once (*ubit'*). Yury Lyubimov staged a production on the theme that one must not kill at all (*ubivat'*). Raskolnikov in the novel is a murderer (*ubivets*). Raskolnikov in the production is an assassin (*ubiitsa*).[105]

Raskolnikov spat on the floor when Sonya told him to kiss the soil in repentance; he was aggressive during the reading of the Lazarus story. He was "wrong" in committing the crime, he "erred" in his idea that he is a superman, but showed no remorse.

> Lyubimov's Raskolnikov is a repulsive type. He is driven by aggression, which resembles that of a Muscovite bus or queue. Aggression is one of the main features of our contemporaries shortly before the period of perestroika. And suddenly it appears that in the old Lyubimov production, the future was anticipated.[106]

The fact that the production attacked a state which condoned crime led to a broad official silence. Yet the production was successful with foreign critics and audiences. Lyubimov was invited to stage *Crime and Punishment* in London in September 1983. The London version was successful enough to attract the Burgtheater in Vienna to stage a repeat at their theatre; invitations to Bologna and Washington followed. All these productions were revivals of the original Moscow version, except that the theme of religion as a support for moral values was emphasised in the later productions in the West:

> An intensely religious man, Lyubimov apparently believes that history went sour the moment man determined that God was dead and humans could therefore create their own moral law: the victories of Napoleon led directly to the crimes of Stalin.[107]

The "crimes of Stalin" formed the background for *The House on the Embankment* (1980), adapted by Yury Trifonov from his own novel. This work sees the hero, Glebov, remembering his youth in the 1930s, when, as a schoolboy, he denounced his schoolmate; and his adolescence when he had an affair with Sonya Ganchuk, who lived with her parents in the House on the Embankment, and whom he used to advance his career: her father was his supervisor at university. When, however, Ganchuk fell out of favour, Glebov swiftly changed his line and denounced Ganchuk.

At first sight the novel seems unsuitable for dramatisation, for at least three reasons. First, the narrative is a recollection by the hero Glebov after an accidental meeting with his old friend Shulepa in 1972. The action takes place in Glebov's mind during the time preceding and following the war, from the late 1930s to the early 1950s, while the protagonist himself remains in the present. Second, the text of the narrative is filtered through Glebov's mind and would apparently need to be much more explicit in places in order to be clear on stage. Third, the narrative stance shifts in the novel from an omniscient, but subjec-tivised, third-person narrator for Glebov's story to a first-person narrator who completes the picture given by the Glebov narrator and provides an objective view of the protagonist. The first problem was solved by an ingenious set design that physically separated the past from the present. The second issue was resolved in the adaptation itself; Trifonov partly rewrote some dialogues for the theatre (some characters became more explicit in what they say). The third question necessitated the introduc-tion of a first-person narrator into the adaptation; he is named the "Stranger" (*Neizvestny*), and he does not stand apart, like the usual narrator–commentator in Taganka-dramatisations, but belongs instead, as in the novel, to those characters of the past at the same time as being a person of the present when resuming his commentator function. The Stranger introduces, for example, all the characters of the past when they express their attitude to Glebov after the Ganchuk affair. Glebov is juxtaposed to the Stranger as the narrator–commentator of his memories, also functioning simultaneously as commentator and participant. Glebov plays his role with many "asides", expressing his thoughts, summarising the action and commenting on it.[108] Other actors comment as well, and are able to initiate a re-enactment of what they remember or see before their mind's eye: episodes such as Glebov's remembrance of the lift, or the arrival of the Ganchuks at the dacha after he had started his affair with Sonya, are re-enacted at his prompting.[109] When Shulepa remem-bers being beaten up at school, the scene comes alive; the Narrator's introduction functions similarly; and characters can appear or come alive when mentioned, as is the case with Glebov's friend Anton.[110]

The structure of the novel underwent few changes in the process of its adaptation for the stage. The time pattern was not altered. Both in the novel and the adaptation, the action moves from the present (1972) to the past (1930s–1950s) and back to the present (1974), with the past proceeding chronologically from 1937 to 1949/50, except for the parts narrated by the Stranger in the novel, which remain in the pre-war period; they are inserted as the Stranger's flashbacks in the play, where they have the same function as in the novel.

Three scenes at the beginning were inserted to disrupt the flow of the present; the scene with the lift operators and their questioning of each visitor is repeated. The lift operators assume a special function in the play: they give the command for the action to start, and their control function is extended when they warn Ganchuk and help Shulepnikov senior with his interrogation of Glebov.[111] Two scenes are added in which the faculty board discusses of plans to "purge" the faculty; and a faculty board member, Druzyaev, urges Glebov to speak at the meeting. Here, a technique of mixing remarks and dialogues from the university meeting and Glebov's thoughts about Sonya has been employed to underline Glebov's situation: he is torn between two sides, unable to make up his mind, while both sides torture his mind by appearing in a sequence of short glimpses.

The character of Anton has been modified: he not only records all the conversations in his notebooks, but also foresees the war and the blockade of Leningrad as early as May 1941. This expansion of Anton's text – appearing only twice in the production – is relevant, since he is the opposite pole of Glebov: a character of sincerity and truth who cannot, however, survive.[112] Another minor change should be noted: when Shulepa calls Glebov, he mentions that Glebov was looking for a table in the furniture shop in order to enhance the latter's desire to "possess" things (expressed in the novel with regard to Sonya and the Ganchuk properties). During the production, this table is shifted at times behind the wall as if to emphasise Glebov's concern with material possessions.

Memory plays a significant role in both the play and the novel. The production makes it obvious that the action is initiated by Glebov and filtered through his eyes by his prompting of re-enactments and his comments; moreover, his role in the Ganchuk affair is made clear in the introduction by the Stranger, underlining that a guilty conscience has caused his sudden remembrance of the past. The meeting with Shulepa was merely an external trigger for his memory. Glebov suppresses his memories, in contrast to the other characters, and he even tries to efface the memory of denouncing Slavka and Manyunya to Shulepnikov:

> GLEBOV: ... of course, I did not name anyone.
> SHULEPNIKOV'S STEPFATHER: What do you mean, you did not name any-one? You did, you named them...[113]

The capacity to forget, the power of memory and the consciousness of past deeds form the focal points of this production. Many dialogues reveal

Glebov's attitude to the past by contrasting his viewpoint to that of others. This is the case with the Stranger, who recognises the power of memory:

> GLEBOV: All my life I have tried to forget about that, and I nearly succeeded. Almost everything has been forgotten.
> STRANGER: ... People would be happy if they knew how to forget...
> GLEBOV: Everything will be forgotten! I can't remember anything! I forgot everything! But no, I remember some things... I hate those times, because they were my childhood![114]

In the argument with Ganchuk, Glebov expresses most explicitly his view that existence depends on memory, while Ganchuk draws his attention to the philosophical trap into which he has fallen:

> GLEBOV: But if I don't remember – that means nothing happened! You understand, time only exists within us! And if one doesn't remember, it means, those times didn't exist! Nothing existed!
> GANCHUK: ... You are making the same mistake as Kant: he suggests that time is the pure form of sensation ... that it exists only in one's conscience ... and is expressed by the changing conditions of our conscience! ... But we materialists know very well that time is the form of the movement of matter. And there is only one direction of this movement in time – mark this well! – from the past to the future!...[115]

Even Shulepa, who would have good reason to blot out his memories of the past and make them responsible for his present decline, remembers very clearly:

> GLEBOV: All that has disappeared from memory has disappeared for good!... Memory must not be a poison which slowly spreads and poisons man's entire life...
> SHULEPA: No, brother, I remember everything![116]

Finally, Sonya remembers when she fell in love, but she realises that Glebov has no memory of that past: "I asked because I remember very well. But you might forget".[117]

Glebov's conscience is unclean. The Stranger provides an honest picture of Glebov. In the novel, Glebov reveals his thoughts about the Ganchuk affair in an inner monologue which he claims to base on the confession he made to his dying aunt. In the stage version the Stranger functions as Glebov's *alter ego*, who discusses with him the options for his actions in the meeting that will decide the Ganchuk affair and encourages him to weigh the alternatives.

Glebov suppresses his conscience and his memory of the past. He has made a career, but has done so to the detriment of others. He has not come to terms with the past, with his denunciation of the boys at school and his failure to stand in for Ganchuk. He needs to face up to the past in order to clear his conscience.

By having a member of the faculty board of the 1950s, Shireiko, travel with Glebov to the conference in Paris in 1974, the drama points out that the leaders of the literary élite may not always have been honest in the past, and even if there are no black marks in their "files", there might be on their conscience. Lyubimov has found in this novel a theme which is very important to his theatre: the past and its implications for the present, conscience and its effect on contemporary people.

The dramatisation satisfied the censors after a few, very specific, and minor changes.[118] The lift operators' talk about how many flats have been emptied on one day,[119] a reminder of the disappearances of people during the Stalinist purges, had to be omitted. In an ode by Dzhambul Dzhabaev ("Stalin's Singer"),[120] recited by the school class, the names of its "heroes" Stalin and Ezhov had to be left out: the actors paused so that the audience, understanding from the context who was meant, immediately realised that the pause was the work of the censors. The text of the song "Oh, how fine is life in the land of the Soviets" from the film *Red Tie*,[121] sung by the Pioneers, had to be omitted, but it was sufficiently well-known to be understood even without words. Finally, Druzyaev could not use the word *kosmopolit* to denounce Ganchuk, since that was associated in the Soviet context with the Jewish question.[122] However, most members of the production were surprised that it satisfied the censors after attracting relatively few critical remarks, especially in the year of the Olympic Games, when Moscow was "cleaned up" and prostitutes, beggars and cripples were expelled from the city centre.

The stage version contains few stage directions, since it is intricately linked to the set designed by David Borovsky. There were two projects for the set design apart from the existing version.[123] First, it was suggested that a set should be built following the pattern of *The Exchange*: it should occupy the same small space downstage, and the old furniture of the 1930s would be replaced by new modern furniture in wooden boxes, the sort of new, imported furniture of which all Muscovites dream. Since this created an atmosphere of materialism by dwelling on material achievements only, Trifonov rejected the idea outright. Second, the present version was developed out of Borovsky's preoccupation with the impossibility of representing on stage the gigantic construction of the House, and the desire to make it a protagonist in the theatre production. The House, with its dominant colour grey, reflects the atmosphere of suspicion prevalent throughout the 1930s and 1940s. Third, yet another version was suggested; when Glebov encounters Shulepa in the furniture shop, he stumbles over him, sleeping in a discarded furniture wrapping, himself rejected by society. Pieces of wrapping were to be blown repeatedly across the stage by the wind, and all the characters should emerge from the "rubbish" on stage. Both the second and third versions were tested on stage, before the second was adopted, preferred by both Lyubimov and Trifonov.

The final version of the set was at once simple and ingenious. It consisted of a "wall" of glass panels built in the constructivist style of the 1930s by analogy with the lift shafts (or *gradusniki*, as Borovsky calls glass constructions among masses of concrete) of the real House.[124] The grey mass of concrete was reflected in the layout of the programme (Figure 38). The glass wall was composed of numerous dirty, greasy windows rebuilt in life-size; the glass was nearly opaque, as if it had conserved all the dirt of the 1940s (constructivist buildings in Moscow have no facility for window cleaning). Slightly right of centre, a lift was integrated into the construction. The "wall" was placed along the front of the stage, leaving only a narrow path downstage for the actor to walk along (Figure 39). The ingenuity of this set lay in its double function: it not only revealed the atmosphere of the 1930s underlying the production, but also divided the space of the theatre (both the stage and the auditorium) into two worlds: behind the wall was the world of the past, of those characters who had lived in the house and may no longer be alive, or who belong to it by their attitude to life, such as Marina and Margosha, wife and daughter of Glebov; this world exists only because it is fixed in Glebov's memory. In front of the wall, in the auditorium, was the world of the present, where Glebov stood to remember the past, and where Glebov's family lived (they did not, after all, live in the House). The door of the lift was the only link between these two worlds (Figure 40), and not accidentally it was guarded by two lift operators who exercised a control function in the play by their voices, which were played over an amplifier.[125]

Behind the wall was a staircase, at the top of which a militiaman appeared, symbolic reminder of the permanent control in – not just – the Stalin era. Strips of black tape were fixed onto a window to recall the times of war, when this was done to prevent the glass from flying.[126] The lift was not only the link between the worlds, but the sound of the lift also recalled the fear of arrest felt at that noise during the Stalin period. A similar function was fulfilled by knocks on walls or windows. A shopping bag with empty bottles was carried by Ganchuk and the Stranger to define their non-allegiance to the élitist class of the House. Water was splashed from behind onto a window pane to represent the painting by Aivazovsky in Alina Fedorovna's house.[127] Red Pioneers' scarfs were worn by all the actors when Glebov remembered his childhood, also alluding to the function of Pioneer organisations to improve children's discipline in contemporary society.

The actors behind the wall held torches with which they lit their faces from below when mentioned by Glebov. Thereby the faces appeared like masks, deprived of their human features. The characters Glebov remembered had no psychological depth and were therefore not given a psychological portrayal by the actors; they appeared like ghosts whom Glebov perceived and animated, and who disappeared in the same manner.

The voices behind the wall were not the natural voices of the actors, but were unreal and amplified (the latter for technical reasons, since there was only one natural opening, a swing window, in the construction). Apart from the voices of the lift operators, Shulepa's voice during the nightly phone call also sounded over an amplifier; Glebov stood at that time in the aisle, holding the receiver.

The music reflected the atmosphere of the 1930s and 1940s, and well-known songs from that period were played in the production.[128] They were taken from films with music composed by Dunaevsky, and songs performed by Utesov. Verdi's *Aida* accompanied Anton, and the "triumphal march" was used in a cynical way in the scene where Shulepa called Shireiko to "help" Glebov, underlining that it is the "denouncer" himself whom the "denounced" has asked for help.[129] The only contemporary tune featured was Vysotsky's song "Save Our Souls" (*Spasite nashi dushi*), which sounded after Glebov had received Shulepa's call that triggered the transition to the past: the audience was reminded that Glebov's soul needs to be saved.

The portrayal of some characters was striking. The Glebov family was ridiculed by their warnings concerning Shulepa, and was thus depicted as perceived by Glebov in the novel: Nila threatened Glebov with her index finger after the argument with his father over Shulepa: her finger was bandaged with a huge bow. Druzyaev was characterised in another way: he sat in a wheelchair. This was not only an allusion to his fate (he would soon disappear), but also to his character: he is a mental cripple. Shireiko covered Druzyaev's head with a blanket and struck it while discussing which busts Ganchuk kept in his study, thereby making a kind of "bust" out of Druzyaev.[130] Vernet pointed out that an allusion was made here to Ezhov, who was small of stature.[131] Another memorable characterisation was that of Ganchuk, who delivered his speeches about literature to his shadow, which sometimes disappeared, much to his own annoyance; thus, he was shown to be living an illusory life, in a distant past.[132]

The character of Glebov deserves particular attention, since the production was centred around him as protagonist or "anti-hero". Glebov told his own story alongside that of the Stranger, sometimes moving back to the past to provide a different perspective. Whereas Glebov was a participant in the action of both novel and adaptation, the Stranger was made a participant, a member of the other world, in the production only. Demidov pointed out that the Stranger was conceived as a "double" or twin to Glebov, a function which according to Demidov has no foundation in the novel,[133] where an omniscient narrator tells Glebov's story; however, he adopts a stance very much on Glebov's side, and is thus biased. In the production, Glebov narrated his own story, recounting it as if it were not his own:

> "Illusion" is the basis of his [Glebov's] concept of life, its basic category, which allows him to exist in a certain vacuum of "dark days", in a condition of personal ... illusion, a shadow in relation to his self. ... He is a nobody, a man in the third person, a shade of his shadow, and a ghost even for himself.[134]

He renounced any existence unless it could be remembered, and thus disowned the past that was emerging on stage as not being that of his childhood. Glebov was in conflict with his memory, which he sought to suppress. Thus, for example, Glebov actually drove Kunik back into the lift, which represented the path to the past.

Glebov was not on stage, but in the auditorium throughout, addressing his account directly to the audience. Frequently, phrases from the actors of the past were addressed to the audience (Shireiko: "You must all remember!"). The novel's hero was portrayed in a neutral tone, he was not condemned by the author. Neither was the audience meant to condemn Glebov. Glebov's account challenged the audience to defend him: when he encountered Shulepa (behind the glass) at the furniture store, Shulepa spat into Glebov's face (in the novel he spat out a cigarette): he spat at the glass, the spittle ran down the window, and Glebov, standing in front of the window, wiped it off his face. Glebov was asking for compassion, inviting the audience to consider why he was being treated in such a manner. After all, he had done nothing to harm anyone, he had not deliberately denounced anybody according to his own perception of the past. He was naive in his belief in his own rightness, but both Valery Zolotukhin and Veniamin Smekhov, who played the part of Glebov, portrayed him in their distinctive way, with neither of them emphasising the feature of naivety. Zolotukhin gave Glebov an evil character, as though he had acted, or rather "not acted", deliberately in the past, whereas Smekhov played him as a raisonneur, arguing with himself about his own life, and yet hypocritical to himself at the same time.

Thus the production was in its genre a "story for the theatre" told by a narrating cast of characters; it included re-enactments of the past in the form of memories brought to life on stage, and was in that respect uncharacteristic of the Taganka theatre's repertoire. Typical, however, was the thematic preoccupation with conscience, the memory of the past, and the history of the people. Since the attitude of figures like Glebov, Glebovitis or *Glebovshchina*, embodies an element found in everyone, the utmost integration of the audience was a principle of this production. The audience was challenged to think about how they would have acted, or how they would act. Time not only influences man, but each individual in his turn makes his own time, creates history, as Anton correctly pointed out. Therefore his notebooks were not only shown at the windows, but the audience was invited to read these notebooks in the theatre.[135]

> Each man is a mirror of nature and a mirror of the faults and achievements of his time, which, incidentally, forms people and is itself formed under their influence.[136]

Hence each individual has a responsibility for history, for the events of the past and present, which should be borne with honesty.

> According to Lyubimov, oblivion is a catastrophe; time is made by people, by each person, and therefore, in Lyubimov's view, each individual bears responsibility for the future.[137]

Lyubimov's interest in *The House on the Embankment* was aroused by the theme of an honest view not only of the individual's past, but also of national history as composed of many individual memories. The production therefore contained an appeal to review history on a second layer of interpretation, which was over-emphasised in reviews in the Western press which mainly considered the theme of Stalinism. Its prime concern was the conscience of the individual, the way man views his past and blots out memories which cannot be accommodated in the present or are incompatible with his contemporary conscience.

> Man must not forget the history of his own country. A nation which forgets its history is no longer a great nation ... [*Glebovshchina*, a Glebov-like mentality], means to survive, to adapt to a path of never-ending compromises and to keep oneself "clean". Mimicry. Survive at all costs, simply survive ... at the expense of others.[138]

Lyubimov fought against this *Glebovshchina* with his productions and his theatre. By showing the audience the Glebov within them, he emphasised that each spectator might have "black spots" in the past or guilt on his conscience, and appealed for the adoption of an honest view towards mistakes of the past, in order to achieve a true picture of history.

The theme of human conscience was linked to the development of society: in *The House on the Embankment*, man was portrayed as creator or eraser of history, with his conscience and memory playing a vital role for his present sincerity. This idea of man as creator – or eraser – of history stems from an elaboration of the theme of man and his conscience, since individuals compose a nation. This development reached its climax in this production. Whereas in the first period, Lyubimov had analysed the function of society, he was now preoccupied with the individual and his conscience. He reached a synthesis of these two positions in the 1980s, when neither the individual nor society on their own would be investigated, but instead the people, composed of individuals, and not institutionalised as a society stood at the forefront of his attention. These productions prepared the way for Lyubimov to move on to a "folk" theatre, shifting the perspective not away from the individual, but enlarging the focus to include the effects of individual conscience on the people as a whole.

The creativity of the individual: homage to Pushkin, Ostrovsky, Gogol, Bulgakov

Throughout the 1970s, one of Lyubimov's main preoccupations was to pay homage to the great Russian writers of the nineteenth and twentieth centuries, continuing a tradition he had begun with *Listen! Mayakovsky!* The theatre also persisted with the theme of the conflict between the writer and his rulers.

In 1973, Lyubimov turned to Pushkin for the first time, creating a production about the poet's life entitled *Comrade, believe...* His approach was similar to that chosen for *Listen!*, which dealt with the life and works of Mayakovsky. *Comrade, believe...*, written by Yury Lyubimov and his then common-law wife Lyudmila Tselikovskaya, is based on documents, letters, poems and epigrams. The title was derived from a line in Pushkin's poem "To Chaadaev"(1818):

Tovarishch, ver': vzoidet ona,	Comrade, believe: the star of
zvezda plenitel'nogo schast'ya,	captivating happiness will ascend,
Rossiya vspryanet oto sna,	Russia will rouse from her sleep,
I na oblomkakh samovlast'ya	and our names will be written
Napishut nashi imena!	on the ruins of autocracy!

The title thereby not only reflects the hope for a revolution that will overthrow the Tsarist regime, but also foreshadows the brotherhood of man under communism by using the form of address "comrade".[139] The subtitle defines the production as a "poetic presentation... letters by Pushkin... to Pushkin... about Pushkin...".[140]

The play consists of two parts, in which Pushkin's life unfolds through letters, poems, epigrams and dramatic writings. It basically observes chronological order. The adaptation concentrates on Pushkin at the lyceé (in a flashback on the way to his Kishinev exile), his meeting with three Tsars,[141] the "Ode to Liberty" and first skirmishes with the authorities, his exile in Odessa, the use of satire as a means to oppose the government, his exile in Mikhailovskoe, Anna Kern, and his involvement with the Decembrists in the first act; the second act deals with the poet's depression, his marriage, his superstitiousness, Bulgarin's attack on *Eugene Onegin*, Pushkin as Gentleman of the Bedchamber, his financial problems, his reminiscences of lycée friends, and the provocation by D'Anthès and Heeckeren that leads to the duel. The production illustrates the development of Pushkin's ideas by means of quotation from his letters and poems.[142] Pushkin also initiates the enactment of "A Conversation between the Bookseller and the Poet" (1824) and the recital of scenes from *Boris Godunov*,[143] in which the people are the protagonists.

> The most important problem in the play is that of Pushkin and the people... The theme of the people in this piece is found above all in the fragments from *Boris Godunov*.[144]

Some stanzas from *Eugene Onegin* were also recited by a Pushkin-figure in the auditorium.[145] Natan Eidelman pointed out that the production drew even upon unpublished material, and provided alternative versions of poetic lines in order to reveal the process of creation of "The Upas-Tree". Pushkin was shown in the act of composing the poem before deciding on the final choice of word: "Pushkin's draft lines, being transformed on stage into the final version – this is a striking artistic innovation".[146]

The production neglected Pushkin the playboy, gambler and mischievous pupil, as well as his longing to travel to other countries (1824/25), the trip to the Caucasus and the editing of *Sovremennik*. The conflict between the Tsar and Pushkin was not emphasised, and indeed the Tsar was shown as protective, being prepared to prevent Bulgarin's attacks on Pushkin's works. The only inconsistencies in chronology were the flashbacks to the lyceé on the way into exile and before death respectively; and the beginning of the play which started with the duel: two shots were audible, between which Lermontov's "The Death of the Poet" (1837) was recited. At the end of the play, no duel took place; it was merely alluded to in the measuring of the distance between the duellists, while Pushkin's life passed by in glimpses. His death was symbolically represented when he borrowed a tail-coat from Nashchokin, which he subsequently wore when he was buried, putting on, at that moment, a white death mask.

Lyubimov used a "literary" and theatrically unconventional approach in having five actors represent Pushkin:

> The piece is played from the standpoint of literary theatre, without the representation of historical persons. The actors stand "for", "instead of" Pushkin...
> The role "of" Pushkin is given to five actors, each of whom according to the idea of the director must convey his own qualities. One actor plays Pushkin the "worldly man", "the idle playboy", the Mozartian in creation, the tender fiancé and husband; another actor plays the hussar-Decembrist principle that lives in Pushkin, his love of freedom; the third, Pushkin the friend; the fourth, Pushkin the creator and thinker; and finally, the fifth actor, with a slight allusion to Pushkin's outer appearance, the poet's passion.[147]

This directive was quite consistently applied: the first Pushkin has discussions with the Tsars (Alexander I and Nicholas I), is poet and writer of more poetical letters, is the poet–publisher, the poet who is given Natalya in marriage and who writes letters to her, the poet of *Eugene Onegin* attacked by Bulgarin; he was played by Valery Zolotukhin. The second Pushkin is the political opponent of Miloradovich, the man socialising with women, chased and hated by Vorontsov, the poet in Odessa, returning to Mikhailovskoe depressed, yet full of satirical spirit, the commentator on theatre conventions for *Eugene Onegin*, the admirer of Anna Kern, the Decembrist, the Tsar in fictitious conversations between the poet and the Tsar, the superstitious poet, the writer of letters to the Tsar which are intercepted, and the man in financial trouble; he was played by Ivan Dykhovichny. The third is the friend, corresponding with Vyazemsky, Pushchin, the presenter of *Boris Godunov*, the adult in conflict with his parents, the man in the duel; he was played by Boris Galkin or Valery Pogoreltsev. The fourth is Pushkin at school, the thinker and commentator, played by Leonid Filatov. The fifth alludes to the outer appearance of the poet: in tail-coat, with curly hair, small in stature, the Gentleman of the Bedchamber who feels so much out of place in this function; he was represented by Rasmi Dzhabrailov. Other characters were played by one actor each with the exception of Natalya Goncharova, who was played by two actresses: Natalya Saiko played the caring wife, Nina Shatskaya the flirtatious and worldly woman who frequented the court. Moreover, parts which represent one and the same force were played by one actor, thus V. Ivanov played the Tsar, D'Anthès and the courier. This device enabled critics hostile to the Taganka, such as Yury Zubkov, to launch yet another attack upon the quality of the acting:

> However, is this decision [to have five actors for the part of Pushkin] not born out of something else – the director's lack of confidence in the creative abilities of his actors? Or, to be more precise, the recognition of their unpreparedness for the solution of such a difficult creative task?[148]

The set consisted of two carriages, one golden, the other black, neither of which had any wheels (set design by David Borovsky: Figure 41). The golden carriage represented the official and worldly sphere, belonging to the Tsar. The carriage stood inflexibly on stage, and Pushkin visited it for encounters with the Tsar, the secret police, for theatre visits and his marriage. The other carriage was black and mobile, suspended on ropes. When in motion, the actors' hands imitated the turning of the wheels. This carriage was used by Pushkin for the composition of poems; but it was also the place where the hanging of the five Decembrists took place: all five actors playing Pushkin climbed into the carriage, a stool fell over on the frontstage, and the shadows of five hanged men appeared on the back wall. The opposition of immobile and mobile worlds for the Tsar and the poet defined Pushkin's ideas as progressive and contrasted them with the reactionary attitude represented by Tsarist rule. Pushkin's carriage was mobile for another reason, too: Pushkin travelled a great deal during his lifetime, he was never settled for very long. Streets and roads thus played an important part in Pushkin's life, and they were symbolised not only by the carriages, but also by means of light, which was beamed across the stage floor in the form of a light path, on which the measuring of the distance for the duel took place, on which the secret police crawled and onto which letters and sheets of paper with Pushkin's writings were dropped.

> This path is the place of pilgrimage, the path of the people... The whole of Pushkin's life is distilled in the image of the path.[149]

The motif of letters and writings scattered across the stage was also reflected in the programme: it was shaped in the form of a letter inserted in an envelope, which was sealed at the back with the emblem of the Taganka theatre.

Time was of prime importance to Pushkin; he possessed a silver watch, he was very much concerned with his age, feeling old enough to get married, too old for being a Gentleman of the Bedchamber, and always aware of his imminent death: "*Ya skoro ves' umru...*" (I will soon die completely...). He realised, however, that his work would survive, thereby creating his immortality. He believed in "the immortality of art, which always strives to entend man's physical capacity".[150] Hence the prologue of the production continued with the lines from "André Chénier" (1825).[151]

Net, ves' ya ne umru,	No, I won't die completely,
Ya skoro ves' umru,	I will soon die completely,
* no, ten' moyu lyubya,*	but, if you love my shade,
khranite rukopis',	keep my manuscripts,
* o drugi, dlya sebya.*	dear friends, for yourself.

In the foyer, the ticking of a clock could be heard,[152] and throughout the production, the rhythm reflected the passage of time:

> Time, the gnawing feeling of time flying past, determines the rhythm of the production. This rhythm is set by the rhythmical knock of the wooden rattle, breaking off one scene after the other, by the harsh sounds of the bell, concluding the more dramatic scenes, and, finally, the strokes of the insistent metronome, twice or thrice introduced in the course of the performance.[153]

This rhythm also created the musicality and harmony of the production. The composition carefully balanced excerpts of poetry and prose, text and music, to create a melody that corresponded to each facet of Pushkin. Music accompanied the text, including melodies from Mussorgsky's *Boris Godunov*, Chaliapin's interpretation of "The Wanderer", Mozart tunes for the composition of *Mozart and Salieri*, Denis Davydov's hussar songs presented by Dykhovichny, or even counterpoints set to contemporary music by Bulat Okudzhava ("You Cannot Turn Time Back") and Pushkin's poems sung by the actors to music composed by Yury Butsko and Grigory Pyatigorsky.

> [Lyubimov] entered the world of Pushkin's poetry, its structure, its atmosphere, its rhythm. He tried to play the music of Pushkin's life and the music of Pushkin's poems.[154]

Lyubimov's theatre had been attracted by poets and classic literature in the past, and the interest in Pushkin was therefore not surprising. The theatre presented the poet Pushkin in a lively manner, similar to Mayakovsky in *Listen!*, combining life and work. No attempt was made to put Pushkin on a pedestal, instead "the actors ... discover Pushkin as he appeared to his contemporaries".[155] In this case, the theatre included a substantial extract from *Boris Godunov*, a play which had hitherto never been fully or successfully shown on the Soviet or Russian stage.

The Main Administration of Culture and the Ministry of Culture attacked the production for its unorthodox historical view of Pushkin and for relating *Eugene Onegin* to the contemporary audience. The actors Rasmi Dzhabrailov (small in stature and with a physical resemblance to Pushkin) and Nina Shatskaya (in her height bearing a resemblance to Natalya Goncharova) parodied the actual size of the "great" Pushkin in comparison to his wife;[156] this was considered unseemly. Furthermore, several phrases were sharply attacked, since they could be taken to refer to the contemporary world. Thus, for example, a change of the words from Pushkin's correspondence "Where I feel fine, there is my homeland" into "I do not want any other homeland than Russia" was required;[157] the omission of such lines as "This is what the state security requires", "Each Ministry has up to three benefactors", or "I am tired of depending on this or that director in my struggle for food" (on *his* situation and *his* conflict with the authorities) was demanded.[158] This shows how sensitive the authorities still were with regard to censorship and bureaucracy, and how preoccupied they were with preventing Pushkin's lines from acquiring a meaning for the contemporary audience: "The comments... should protect the spectator from unnecessary and incorrect associations with the present in certain scenes, and are intended to stop 'bridges' being thrown into the auditorium which deprive the action of its historic precision".[159] *Comrade, believe...* was delayed for some years: the theatre had asked the Ministry to commission the play in December 1971, and yet the première did not take place until 1973.

The production further demonstrated the theatre's interest in the lives of writers and poets, as previously with Chernyshevsky, Molière, Mayakovsky, John Reed and Lermontov. The technique of montage reached a climax in this production, drawing on the entire oeuvre of a writer rather than merely on a smaller number of works, as before. Furthermore, the form of *predstavlenie* ("presentation" or "demonstration") was taken to the extreme by having actors stand "for" the character they were to represent.[160] It was thus very regrettable that such a significant achievement should become a victim of the policy to remove Lyubimov's productions from the repertoire as early as May 1984.

To mark the 150th anniversary of the birth of the playwright Aleksandr Ostrovsky (1823–1886), Lyubimov and the artists of the Taganka theatre staged *The Gala*, which was premièred on 7 July 1973. The programme reflected the concept of the production as a gala evening for Ostrovsky in having the actors' heads superimposed onto an old picture showing Ostrovsky in the centre of a group of actors of his time (Figure 42).

The Gala is a montage of three plays by Ostrovsky, *The Storm* (1860), *A Festive Dream before Lunch* (1859) and *The Diary of a Scoundrel* (1868).[161] The plays were shortened in the text of individual scenes, but creative characters, such as actors or writers, were emphasised in the montage.

Ostrovsky prompted, seated in an armchair centre stage, and commented on the reactions of his contemporaries to his characters, and on actors such as Mikhail Shchepkin; he read excerpts from other works and interfered into the action. All the actors and characters of Ostrovsky's plays are omnipresent on stage and function as a choir in the tradition of folk theatre:

> In the centre, never disappearing for a minute, different characters of Ostrovsky sit, stand, slumber, sing old songs, read the papers of those times, "accompanying" the emotions of the protagonists.[162]

The plots of the three plays develop simultaneously: *The Storm* upstage, *The Diary of a Scoundrel* mid-stage and *A Festive Dream* at the front. The choice of plays ranges from tragic to farcical, and they portray different social classes: merchants, bourgeoisie and aristocracy.[163] Furthermore, each protagonist throws a different light on the notion of love: for the Balzaminovs, love is irrelevant for a marriage, as long as some material profit can be made; Glumov represents a cynical attitude to marriage, fooling society with its own conventions; while only Katerina is capable of true and free love, for which she is prepared to die.

On the front of the stage was a ravine, or abyss, on the edge of which moved pairs of lovers. Zubkov condemned this device for its sexual implications, since certain characters descended into the ravine and then returned with unbuttoned shirts.[164]

Katerina's death occurred at the end of the performance, with *The Storm* forming a framework for the entire production. With the omnipresence of all the characters on stage, the production seemed to reprimand everybody for Katerina's death:

> Katerina has thrown herself into the water because of Kabanova, because of her fate, but literally those accused stand on stage: Glumov and Balzaminov – all are involved in the tragedy of man, all those who place career more highly than honesty, those who measure love with money.[165]

The concern with human values and truth made the general theme of the production conform to the Taganka's preoccupations of the time. Even if this theme of truth and honesty was not coherently developed or emphasised here (after all, it was a benefit for Ostrovsky), it opened new perspectives on Ostrovsky's writing by underlining not his irony and satire with regard to the merchant classes, but his interest in humanising social forms and conventions.

First entitled *Gogolian Evening, Inspectorate Fairy Tales* was premièred at the Taganka on 9 June 1978. The set was designed by Eduard Kochergin, who had been contracted for the production from the Bolshoi

Drama Theatre in Leningrad. The text was composed by Lyubimov and based on excerpts from Gogol's prose and plays.[166]

Lyubimov cast two actors for the part of Gogol (a device already used in *Comrade, believe...* and *Listen!*), looking like two different statues in Moscow: the statue created by Nikolay Andreev showing the sad, introverted Gogol, which was removed by Stalin and banished into the courtyard facing the house where the writer died; and the heroic statue created by N. Tomsky, located at the end of Gogol Boulevard. The discrepancy between the two portraits roused Lyubimov's interest in the image of Gogol: this image of a man heroic or sad, sane or insane, is investigated in the production. This preoccupation is also reflected in the programme, which has the form of a postcard with Gogol's sketched portrait.

The first part opens with a performance of the last act of *The Government Inspector*; comments by spectators, critics, the Tsar and Gogol follow, derived mainly from Gogol's *After the Play*. The basic plot of *The Overcoat* is again followed by comments taken from *After the Play*. The plot of *The Nose* then precedes remarks by Hoffmann and Schiller from *Nevsky Prospect*. In *The Portrait*, the artist introduces as his models the characters of *Dead Souls*, which, in its turn, is reduced to the sale of the souls, the conclusion of the contract, its celebration, and the party at the governor's with Chichikov's incipient downfall. At the end of the first act, the actors take off their masks and comment on the characters. The second part continues with comments on Gogol's characters from *After the Play*, and with the rumours about Chichikov spreading at the party. Then comes a scene from *The Gamblers*, followed by a comment made by Agafya Tikhonovna in *The Marriage*. The passage from *The Diary of a Madman* presents the insane Poprishchin; more and more characters from other plays are then drawn into the set of the lunatic asylum: Khlestakov and Zemlyanika visit the psychiatric hospital; Gogol makes some remarks, is shown ill and then dies in a psychiatric hospital, thus drawing a parallel with his character Poprishchin. By Gogol's deathbed, his characters pronounce the best-known phrases of their parts. The inspector of the second part of *Dead Souls* ends with his speech on the state of corruption in Russia, and the actors comment on the performance they have achieved, regretting that the author is not in the auditorium to share their fame.

As is clear from the range of works used for the production, Lyubimov's concern was not so much with the plot of Gogol's works, or indeed with a story-line for his productions, but with impressions and fragments of the entire oeuvre in order to reveal facets of Gogol's personality.[167]

The set consisted of a backdrop of brownish-grey overcoat material, with cuttings for faces to appear and be lit like portraits, as in the scene of *The Portrait* (Figure 43). Gigantic constructions of Gogolian overcoats could emerge from a ditch below stage, into which they could equally well vanish. These were like puppets, with the heads of actors peeping out at the top (Figure 44), and as such were reminiscent of Meyerhold's use of large mannequins to replace the performers in the final tableau of his 1926 production of *The Government Inspector*.[168] Furthermore, groups of actors appeared in greatcoats and hats reminiscent of Ku Klux Klan garments (Figure 45). This created a phantasmagoric atmosphere, into which Gogol was integrated. Characters emanated from an underground, evil world; only Chichikov was allowed an existence on the stage floor.

> The theatre unfolded the phantasmagoria of the dead... souls... In the middle of this nightmare, hardly distinguished from the crowd of phantom-characters, walk figures representing the writer himself in two guises.[169]

The production was sharply attacked in *Pravda* and the hostile *Teatralnaya zhizn*, which reproached Lyubimov for reducing the actor to a mere executor.[170]

> What perfection of the actor can there be! His task is to open his parachute at the right moment during the flight of the director's fantasy, nothing else concerns him.[171]

Yet Lyubimov merely used his usual approach to acting as *predstavlenie*, in order to reveal universal and timeless characteristics in the action and the protagonists. Smelyansky even defined this device as "hyper-typisation" of character: "... not a type, but a *hyper-type* is created, that which precedes a character, or, if you like, is above him."[172] This "hyper-typisation" served as a means of abstracting the character from historical circumstances.

The integration of the audience in the production was generally disliked by officials in the 1960s and 1970s, since the reaction of the audience could not be controlled and the direct address could aid the transposition of an issue into a different temporal or geographical context. The spectator was not only "degraded" to the level of the characters in the scenes set in the lunatic asylum through the use of lighting; he was also in actual danger:

> The "contact" with the auditorium in the production becomes extremely dangerous for ... the spectator. As they enter, run in and plunge into the action straight from the doors leading from the foyer into the auditorium, the characters, forcing their way through the narrow path between the stage and the front row, may trip over your feet, collapse in your lap, and might, getting up, lean unceremoniously on your shoulder.[173]

The same critic equally sternly rejected the use of crooked mirrors, placed in the foyer to distort the self-image of the spectators, as an "importunate and false approach which has no connection with art".[174]

This hostile reception was typical of the official attitude to the Taganka theatre at the end of the 1970s, while also showing the inflexibility of Soviet critics. Lyubimov tried to reveal a Gogol split into two halves (comic and tragic), a Gogol who was the victim of the society he criticised; at the same time, Gogol's criticism was removed from its historical context and could equally be applied to a contemporary Soviet context. Lyubimov's Gogol lacks the ideals of the "Russian soul" and thus diverges from the official Soviet interpretation.[175]

Gogol reversed the traditional concepts of "sanity" and "insanity": the mad Poprishchin was normal and sane, since he was free and expressed himself freely; the same could consequently apply to Gogol. Thus the perception of the world was turned upside down: the madman led a better life than man in society, who had no escape – apart from madness.

> [The tragedy of man in Gogol's world] lies above all in the fact that there is no way out, no hope of breaking free from this strange madhouse – Russia.[176]

In the first act of the production, man was criticised for not working for the good of society, but only for money and personal profit, corrupting the bureaucracy for his own advantage. In the second act, this world was turned upside down: Gogol and Poprishchin were in the madhouse, the stage was filled with the patients of a psychiatric clinic and their warders. The first act then was reality, the second the logical result of free thinking, of man facing up to social reality. The madman became more real than man as a social being. There was an obvious allusion to the present in showing Gogol in the psychiatric clinic; he represented the fate of many contemporary Soviet writers, who were committed to hospitals for divergence from the official views. The audience was thus told that those writers have a sound and genuine perception of the world, and that the crooked mirror through which they perceive the world is more real than a normal mirror.

Inspectorate Fairy Tales was a production paying homage to a writer. It also contemplated the notion of reality, challenging the assumption that literature is a straightforward reflection thereof, and promulgating the idea that a distortion may be more truthful than a reflection.

A production of Bulgakov's *The Master and Margarita* (written in 1940, and partly published in the USSR in 1966/67, although fully only in 1973) was planned for the celebration of the tenth anniversary of the Taganka theatre in 1974.[177] Attempts had been made since 1971 to gain permission from the Main Administration for a stage version of the novel.[178] When no consent had been given by 1976, an oral agreement was reached between Lyubimov and the Main Administration which allowed him at least to rehearse, even if no financial means were allocated by the Main Administration to the theatre for the actual production. When rehearsals had reached a final stage, the Main Administration gave its consent to the production without further reservations.[179] So it was not until 1977 that *The Master and Margarita* was premièred, for the thirteenth anniversary of the theatre.[180] Lyubimov had always had in mind to use "quotes" from other productions in the form of elements of sets, and it was his idea that the set could be an amalgam of parts from the sets of other productions.[181]

There were no reviews immediately after the première on 6 April 1977. At the end of May, Nikolay Potapov discussed the production in *Pravda*,[182] reproaching Lyubimov with "vulgarity" and "loss of taste" for his portrayal of Margarita and Natasha during their flight (Natasha rides on Nikolay Ivanovich, who is wearing his underwear and carrying his briefcase in his mouth) and for Margarita's nudity during the ball (she sits naked with her back to the audience). There were no further reviews of *The Master and Margarita*. Indeed, until 1981 hardly any reviews appeared of any Taganka production, and if they did, they tended to be hostile. *The Master and Margarita* was among those productions which were closed immediately after Lyubimov was forced into exile. Efros became artistic director of the theatre in March 1984, and the production was cancelled by May of that year, despite its success with the audience. In that same season of 1976/77, the Taganka theatre was due to fall victim to another press campaign against Lyubimov's project for *The Queen of Spades*, which was savagely attacked in *Pravda* by the conductor of the Bolshoi Theatre, Algis Juraitis.

One side effect of the production was that it brought about drastic changes in the theatre's audience.[183] The fact that it was the first production of *The Master and Margarita* on the Moscow stage (a long-awaited dream of both theatres and audiences) and that it was created in a festive atmosphere (the Taganka theatre's anniversary, even if delayed, was reflected in the enthusiasm of the actors), made it a "deficit" item all Muscovites longed for. The Taganka soon lost contact with its own audience, since the audience for the *The Master* was largely determined by the system of influence and connections, the so-called *blat*: actors needed medical care, food, rail tickets etc., and anyone supplying these received in return tickets for the theatre.[184] With this production, tickets became objects of barter. Even in 1990, many productions of *The Master* had all the tickets distributed and sold to theatre workers only, i.e. they were not open to the public.

The Master and Margarita juxtaposes events in contemporary Moscow relating to the master (a writer) with those at a temporal and geographical distance relating to Pilate and Yeshua. They are linked by the master's work: he has written a novel about Pilate's sentencing Yeshua to death despite better knowledge. The master's novel had been condemned by the writers' union (MASSOLIT), and the master was admitted to an asylum. The master is relieved from his sufferings by his beloved Margarita, who concludes a pact with Woland (a Faustian devil "der stets das Böse will und stets das Gute schafft") and is united with the master. The master in turn is united with his novel, which he had burnt: yet the truth contained in a work of art cannot be destroyed. The arrival of Woland is made known to the master by Bezdomny, a talentless writer who is one of the first victims of Woland's raids on Moscow's theatrical and artistic establishment.

Bulgakov's novel was adapted by V. Dyachin,[185] and divided into three acts. Dyachin bore in mind the stage design suggested by Lyubimov. An author-figure has been added to the dramatis personae to introduce characters, comment on the action, render thoughts and summarise.

The first act starts with Bezdomny's admission to the asylum, which is split into two episodes to frame Berlioz's and Bezdomny's encounter with Woland at the Patriarch's Ponds. Further episodes in the asylum have been omitted. Accounts which support Bezdomny's report of Woland's magical power have been omitted; this means that the audience is temporarily left in doubt concerning the veracity of Bezdomny's account. The variety performance has been deferred to the second act, whereas Poplavsky's visit to Moscow has been moved forward to the first act. The people of MASSOLIT are portrayed episodically. The second act covers the events from the variety performance and its aftermath to Margarita's flight over Moscow and Satan's rout, after which Woland returns the manuscripts. The third act sees the morning after the rout, further events in Jerusalem with Pilate, Judas, Arthanius and Matthew, the meeting of Matthew the Levite and Woland during which Matthew leaves the Master's and Margarita's fate in the hands of Woland, and finally the departure of Woland and his retinue and of the Master and Margarita from Moscow.

The murder and subsequent resurrection of the Master and Margarita has been replaced by Bezdomny's account of their deaths. Other occurrences have been shortened or omitted. These changes do not, however, affect the course of events; they concern episodes difficult to stage, either technically or because of the overall length of the performance.[186]

The structure of the dramatisation differs from that of the novel. Whereas the novel is divided into two books and an epilogue, the dramatisation consists of a prologue and three acts, with several scenes in each (I: 15, II: 6, III: 5). According to patterns of dramatic structure, the first act forms the exposition, presenting the situation by introducing the worlds of the asylum, as well as of Woland and Pilate, and by initiating the action. The second act comprises the variety performance, the story of the Master and Margarita, and the rout, in order to reveal the central problem: the impossibility of reuniting the Master with Margarita. The third act presents the dénouement of this problem: the Master and Margarita are saved by Woland, and Pilate is saved by Yeshua. The novel with its two books has two emphases: the Master (I) and Margarita (II), with the epilogue describing the effects of Woland's presence in order to rescue the Master and Margarita. In the novel, the Master and Margarita are the chief protagonists; they assemble around themselves certain episodes relating to their roles, and the story of Pilate relates in the first book to the Master, in the second to Margarita. The main protagonist of the production is at first sight Woland, who holds the threads of every event and stands at the centre of the action in all three acts, which reveal, as it were, his deeds, his craft and his power. Woland's role is also enhanced by the fact that, in the production, he occupied the central area of the stage, with the world of the Master and Margarita to his right and that of Pilate to his left. The only power also dominating the central area was his counterpart Yeshua, who together with Woland held the curtain when it was turned.

However, if one scrutinises the structure of the adaptation, it becomes apparent that it is not Woland who leads the first act, but the Master and Bezdomny: the act starts with the asylum. Although Woland presents the story of Pilate to Bezdomny and the Master, it is the conversation between Bezdomny and the Master (and not, as in the novel, between Berlioz and Bezdomny) that creates the opportunity for Woland to appear.

> The meeting with Woland at Patriarch's Ponds, the death of Mikhail Berlioz, the appearance of Ivan in the MASSOLIT in underpants and with a candle, all this is brought into the performance as a scenic realisation of the conceivable: as a memory and account by Ivan, and at the same time as the process of "recognition" of the latest Muscovite events linked to the visit of the devil – for the Master. [The episodes of the first act] are introduced into the action like the content of a spiritual conversation between Ivan and the Master, as the theme of their talks and subject of their mutual and alerted interest. But it is Ivan rather than the Master who brings the diversity of scenes and episodes together.[189]

If one looks at the dramatisation from the point of view of balance between the satiric-grotesque-phantasmagoric (Woland and his retinue), the philosophic-historical (Pilate) and the realistic (Master and Margarita), then the reasons for the structural changes become clear. The prologue introduces the characters with their key lines while they are all on stage simultaneously, thereby enhancing the carnival atmosphere fostered by Lyubimov in the distribution of several minor parts to the same actor (e.g. Gotlib Roninson played Bengalsky and Poplavsky). In the first act, after the threat of committal to an asylum for "unwanted" writers and the appearance of Woland, both presented in a humorous manner, come two scenes from another layer of time, between Pilate and Yeshua, and between Pilate and Caiaphas. Then Woland claims a first victim, so becoming a threat. Three episodes connected with accidents in the MASSOLIT restaurant follow as a kind of "divertissement". Then Woland captures three more victims: Stepa Likhodeev, Varenukha and Bosoy; Poplavsky, the fourth, is "merely" terrified by the macabre games of Azazello. The act ends with two scenes, one concerning the Master, the other dealing with the crucifixion. Again, the Master and Pilate themes run consecutively, as if to reinforce their connection.

The second act is constructed in a similar way. The performance and its aftermath entertain the theatre audience, this time integrated into the stage action. The Master episode is again followed by a short interlude between Yeshua and Pilate. Then Margarita is invited by Azazello, and she flies to the rout. The Margarita line is broken up by the episode relating to Sokov, since it would otherwise extend over three consecutive and lengthy scenes.

The third act sees the reunion of the Master and Margarita, after which comes an account of Pilate's plots in Jerusalem. Matthew is juxtaposed with Woland, and the fate of the Master and Margarita is decided.

The production was unusual in that its set design was taken from various previous Taganka productions because of financial difficulties and also Lyubimov's desire to create a theatrical fantasy (Figure 46). Two wooden bars formed a huge cross on the back wall, as in *Hamlet*, defining the space from which Yeshua comes and to which he goes. A golden frame, taken from *Tartuffe*, was placed on the right forestage where Pilate resided; this frame also served as a counter for the lemonade vendor in the scene at the Patriarch's Ponds. The pendulum from *The Rush Hour* hung on the centre front stage; it could sway into the audience and along the front line of the stage, act as a broom for Margarita's flight, and as a means of transport for characters such as Azazello, Behemoth and Varenukha. Likhodeev used it on his way to Yalta, and Bezdomny for his persecution of Koroviev after Berlioz's death. A lectern taken from *The Tough* on the left forestage served the author/commentator. The roof and façade of a house, also on the left forestage and in front of the proscenium doors taken from *The Exchange*, designated the asylum, where Bezdomny and the Master meet, and Berlioz's house, where Woland and his retinue would take up residence, with the number 302-bis fixed to the wall. The curtain and the coffin from which the dead rise at the ball were taken from *Hamlet*. The cubes forming the bench at the Patriarch's Ponds came from *Listen!* and were marked with the Russian letters "Kh" and "V", the abbreviation for *"KHristos Voskres"* (Christ has risen), as if to underline who is right in the debate between Berlioz and Bezdomny concerning the existence of Christ. Finally, the board with the letters "IKh 16-06" from *But the Dawns Here are so Calm...* was converted into the lorry that took Bezdomny to the asylum. The set was an amalgam of carefully chosen elements from old productions for the purpose of creating new meanings. Rzhevsky has pointed out that Lyubimov manifested in this production the relative referentiality of theatre signifiers and signs, operating like words and language respectively.[190] All the elements have not only one function; they also define the spaces of action for characters or a group of characters. Thus, the stage was divided into three major areas: left, the world of the Master and Bezdomny, and initially also of Margarita; the centre was dominated by Woland and his retinue; the right and back wall with the curtain along the right side of the stage formed the world of Yeshua and Pilate; the crowd emerged from and withdrew to the back in mass scenes. The pace and rhythm that determined the actions in these three different areas were adapted to the corresponding time and place. Whereas Pilate's world was rather slow, with the dialogues seeming lengthy and the action almost static, and lethargy emanated from the world of Bezdomny and the Master, all fast-moving action took place in Woland's world, since the pace of life accelerated after his arrival in Moscow.

> In Bulgakov's novel, the Gospel history and the contemporary plot develop not only in a different historical time, but also in entirely different, colourful, rhythmical forms.[191]

The curtain and the pendulum were symbolic as well as functional: the pendulum measured the rhythm of Woland's earthly adventures. It moved when he completed a deed, and was thus under his control.

> Whether the theatre intended this or not, the visual, even conceptual centre of the production turned out to be this devil of indifference: the world of legend and the world of the present are located by the right and left wings, Woland, however, is in the centre, either stopping the pendulum, disturbing its course or again pushing it on... And it is important for the theatre to force us to consider: what hand pushes the pendulum? A good one? An evil one? Or, possible and frightening vision, is it stopped by an indifferent hand?[192]

The curtain separated the spaces of Yeshua and Woland by covering the cross for Woland's scenes, but it also pushed Yeshua and the prisoners back to the cross after the verdict, and thereby reflected the opinion of the people who desire the crucifixion. Both the curtain and the pendulum enabled Margarita and Natasha to fly. The curtain was also used to highlight the fate of the Master's book in the MASSOLIT: many hands appeared through the curtain, passing the manuscript along. The legs of the dancers came through the curtain to perform the Charleston in the variety performance. At the mention of Latunsky's destructive article, papers were read by Margarita in the window to the right, and hands held the article through the curtain. The contract Likhodeev signed with Woland appeared from behind the curtain as mysteriously as the trolley with hot dishes for breakfast.

The characters were all boldly drawn, if not caricatured. Koroviev wore checked trousers just as described in the novel; Behemoth sported a velvet jacket with a price label, and boxing gloves for cat's paws to reveal his second face; Hella, the nude witch, had plastic breasts tied to her back and a mask on the back of her head, while she was dressed in black; Azazello was a fire-eater. Often, a character or object would appear when mentioned to highlight appearances out of nowhere and disappearances into nowhere, while Woland was exercising his powers over the citizens of Moscow: the *komsomolka* was placed under a spotlight in the window during the prologue; numerous handkerchiefs in the curtain underlined Frieda's obsession; a knife was placed in the frame when Matthew spoke of his intention to kill the person responsible for Yeshua's death. Annushka emerged with the bottles of sunflower oil and with the brooch she had picked up; Berlioz and Bezdomny started hiccuping on a prompt by the narrator.

The audience was integrated into the performance. The exits and entrances of Poplavsky and Bosoy were made through the centre aisle, down which the dog Banga was also led on and off stage for some of the Pilate scenes; in the prologue Bezdomny left with candle and icon along the centre aisle, and Koroviev passed with the singing Acoustics Commission the same way. Phrases such as Woland's "I simply wanted to see some Muscovites en masse and the easiest way to do so is in a theatre" or "Are we not all atheists?" and other pointed remarks were addressed to the audience. The audience was especially ivolved during the variety performance. The models for the variety performance "shopping" entered and left via the auditorium, first dressed, then wearing underwear; white slips of paper (the false banknotes) were dropped like vouchers from the ceiling onto the audience, and the (real!) administrator of the Taganka theatre confirmed from a side door their validity as a ticket for any performance; the Sempleyarovs sat in the auditorium and were lit in a spot for the episode. The audience thus played an active part in the divertissement section of the production. It was not an unspecified and anonymous audience, but the spectators of the variety performance – duped by the devil. These spectators were ridiculed by Woland, who used them for his own entertainment. They could even be excluded by being plunged into pitch darkness when no witnesses were wanted for the scene of Koroviev's corruption of Nikanor Ivanovich. The spectators were alienated by being referred to as the audience of the variety performance; at the same time, they were criticised:

> Their expected failure to respond was used as a challenge to the inertia of the modern theater spectator, and, in the Moscow context, it also denoted a long-standing social-political passivity. The helplessness of the typical spectator before such challenges to join in the creation of the theater text is directly related to the lack of courage and power felt by Soviet citizens in their social context... The single unanswered question "Do you not demand anything?" became an overt political remark about the silence of the Soviet population.[193]

The theatre here clearly departed from the old principles of appeal. The audience alienated from the performers, and criticised for being silent. The same would be true for *Boris Godunov*.

The mode of the production was extremely expressive, and Lyubimov has paid particular attention to the development of the phantasmagoric atmosphere emanating from Woland and his retinue in their scenes. The variety performance conducted by Woland and his friends included all the sections given in the novel: cabaret, acrobatic numbers by Hella and Koroviev, false banknotes/tickets dropped onto the audience, the trick with Bengalsky's head, the fashion store episode and the Sempleyarov incident. Other magical acts of the devil were illustrated: Likhodeev spat out spirit served to him by the devil and it caught fire on the trolley; the drinks served after the ball burned in the glasses; as Woland understood from Koroviev that Sokov hid money under the floor at home, the trough of the light curtain opened and was hastily shut down by the uncovered Sokov. Similarly, Poplavsky was subjected to much mockery: introduced as "one of the most intelligent people ... of Kiev", he was driven off by Behemoth. Behemoth then ate an artificial white mouse and put the remainder of the eaten one into the disgusted Poplavsky's mouth and a real one upon his bald head. At this juncture, Poplavsky ran off stage through the centre aisle, carefully balancing the mouse; Behemoth and Azazello commented on the method of eating mice (the text for these comments was added to the scene): "You don't eat the tail with these!"

In contrast to the perfect illusion of magical forces at work in the schemes of Woland and his retinue stood the combination of the abstract and the real in the scenes involving Pilate. When the centurion Mark Muribellum beat Yeshua, he crashed his whip onto the floor, while Yeshua was thrown into the curtain by the effect; Yeshua did not wear handcuffs, yet held his hands as if they were tied; when the centurion was told to cut him loose, he plunged a knife into the floor and Yeshua was able to move his hands. Pilate's thoughts of how pleasant it would be to be relieved of all one's earthly burdens were symbolised by a servant holding a tray with a red cup of poison and standing behind Pilate in several scenes.

The most memorable scene, aesthetically, was that of Satan's rout. Margarita was led to Woland in candlelight, the candles being placed for the entire scene on the pendulum. Then she was seated with her bare back to the audience on a throne limited at the sides by two axes (the block from *Pugachev*), while the curtain was lit with numerous candles and the guests emerged from the coffin lit in green by the back wall. The scene was accompanied by waltzes of Johann Strauss, and Sergey Prokofiev's *Romeo and Juliet*, to the music of which Koroviev introduced the guests of the rout, before monotonously repeating his "delight" (*voskhishchenie*), whereas the rout was actually quite the opposite for him.

Another important feature in the production was the motif of the arts, and its treatment on stage. The action associated with the Pilate line of action is merely the "story" told by the Master in his novel, drawing, however, a parallel between the suffering of Christ and that of the writer, who both suffer because of their persistence in telling the truth. The performance started with the committal of a poet to an asylum for what he had expressed, orally or in writing. This was an overt comment upon the treatment still applied to unwanted voices throughout the Brezhnev era. The situation for the inmate was without hope: even the telephone was under the doctor's control, since he held the other end of the line, and a nurse noted down every word he uttered (Figure 47). The MASSOLIT institute and its representatives were ridiculed: they were preoccupied with their flats rather than their work, they could not convince by argument but needed to shout, and they hastened to rescue the china rather than Bezdomny when he arrived at the Griboedov restaurant. The climax of the dramatic action and the central theme of the production, enhanced by the music of the Montagues and Capulets from Prokofiev's *Romeo and Juliet*, was Woland's confirmation that "Manuscripts do not burn";[194] at this point, the second act ended and the scene was continued at the beginning of the third.[195] The music by Prokofiev on both occasions served to illuminate the creativity involved in fantasy and writing.

The theme of the truth of the spoken word was highlighted by a method characteristic of the Taganka theatre: a "Freudian slip". When Pilate asked Arthanius about Judas's fate, Arthanius said "As you ordered" before correcting himself to "As you presupposed" (*kak vy prika ... zali/kak vy predpolagali*);[196] similarly, Koroviev made a slip when denouncing Nikanor Ivanovich to the police: he referred to Nikanor Ivanovich not as the person "mentioned above", but as the chairman already "taken in" by the police (*izlozhennogo/zalozhennogo*).[197] Into the same category of devices falls the mute repetition of the name "Ga Notsri" when Pilate had to pronounce the name of the prisoner to be released, Bar-Abba. In that respect, memory formed a relevant aspect of truth. Several people were said to have a bad memory: Nikanor Ivanovich when denying the possession of any papers about Woland's arrival; Sokov when complaining about the false money; and Annushka when refusing any knowledge of the brooch, i.e. when denying the possession of objects created by the devil, they were told "Citizens, what is wrong with your memory!". The truth of art was at the centre of Lyubimov's attention, truth which lies within a work regardless of what happens to its creator. This was, of course, also relevant for the author of *The Master and Margarita*, who expressed what he saw as the truth, knowing perfectly well that his novel would not be published in his lifetime.

> The individual's imperative role in the performance was expressed ... through various strategies ... which demonstrated individual creation and the power of the individual to initiate aesthetic language.[198]

Homage was paid to Bulgakov at the end of the production. Portraits of the writer were placed in a diagonal on stage, and a memorial flame was lit magically as the actors bowed to the audience (Figure 48).

One may note with some astonishment at this point the transformation of Lyubimov's style: the references to disappearances, corruption etc. which would probably have been central in his first agitational phase, were virtually neglected in 1977. *The Master and Margarita* belongs thematically to the tragic dimension prevailing at the Taganka theatre in the 1970s: both the Master and Bulgakov, speakers of truth, died without seeing their works published in their own lifetime. The individual in search of truth was destroyed by institutions like MASSOLIT, which the audience was made to laugh at. Formally, the production stood apart from other productions of this decade with its atmosphere of a festival of theatricality, expressiveness and fantasy.

4

INDIVIDUAL AND ARTIST IN CRISIS

Lyubimov had formally ended one period by amalgamating the elements of previous set designs in *The Master and Margarita*; he had also stopped expecting to exert any significant influence by his appeals to society and to the individual.

The late 1970s were defined by his search for a new theatre and experiments with various theatrical forms. A deeply pessimistic undercurrent pervaded these productions: sincerity and humanist values are destroyed by the system, the individual is crippled; intellect is subjected by totalitarian régimes; the militarisation of everyday life paralyses the individual and his creativity.

The search for form: *Work is Work, In Search of a Genre, Fasten Your Seat Belts*

Lyubimov had always permitted other directors to stage productions at the Taganka theatre, and continued to do so in this phase particularly. At the same time, he allowed himself and his actors to become even more experimental. As early as 1975 Lyubimov had invited Anatoly Efros to stage *The Cherry Orchard*; this was followed by Yury Medvedev's *Work is Work* (1976), and Sergey Artsybashev's production of *The Little Orchestra of Hope* (1980). Anatoly Vasiliev rehearsed *Boris Godunov* for Lyubimov, and later directed *Vassa Zheleznova* (1981) and *Cerceau* (1985); Efim Kucher staged *Five Tales by Isaac Babel* (1981) and Yury Pogrebnichko *Three Sisters* and *The Elder Son*. Lyubimov also supported those actors in the theatre who had started to write prose and poetry (Alla Demidova, Leonid Filatov, Valery Zolotukhin, etc.) by giving them the opportunity to demonstrate various talents in a so-called *tvorcheskii vecher* (creative evening).

Work is Work was premièred in April 1976. It was a mime presented by Aida Chernova and Yury Medvedev, accompanied by Dmitry Mezhevich on the guitar with songs by Bulat Okudzhava (the title "Work is Work" was drawn from one of his songs). Chernova and Medvedev had performed mime interludes in earlier Taganka productions, such as *Ten Days*. Work is Work consisted of a series of their mime numbers, assembled around the theme of the "triumph of life over death"[1] by Lyubimov, who – in spite of this role – did not appear in the programme as director. He devised the finale, in which a mirror is held up to the audience, thus making the audience protagonists (Figure 49), and choreographed the use of light. The idea of such an experimental production fitted in well with Lyubimov's interest in plasticity of movement and in mime as a theatrical art. The production was removed from the repertoire during Lyubimov's exile, but was revived almost immediately after his return in 1988/89 under the title *Daughter, Father and Guitarist*; this time it was performed by Yury Medvedev and his daughter Viktoriya. In many ways, this immediate revival was Lyubimov's way of expressing his gratitude to Yury Medvedev, who had openly protested after Efros took over the Taganka theatre and was subsequently dismissed.[2] A mobile cube served as the place where the mimes change or rest. The theme had changed to that of man and identity, pointing at the danger of becoming a marionette rather than a person: "The linking theme is the true Lyubimovian theme of the freedom or unfreedom of the human personality".[3]

A similar idea lay behind *In Search of a Genre* (1978), which was devised as a *tvorcheskii vecher*: several actors and artists recited poetry, read from their works, improvised, related anecdotes of theatrical life, or played the guitar. The intention was to give actors the opportunity to present their writing and work which had been created outside the theatre. The evenings varied, for there was no set text or programme. Vysotsky and Mezhevich used to play the guitar; Filatov, Demidova, Zolotukhin and Smekhov were involved in reading and recital. Initially, several actors participated each time; after Lyubimov's return, this form of presentation was revived, but could be managed by one solo actor, Filatov, Smekhov and Demidova taking turns. The production ran either as a second, late-night show at 10 p.m. after a shorter production or as a replacement when a production had to be cancelled for reasons of illness.

With *Fasten Your Seat Belts*, premièred on 2 January 1975 to mark the thirtieth anniversary of the victory in World War II, Lyubimov appeared for the first time as a co-writer: the play in two acts was composed by himself and the writer Grigory Baklanov.[4]

The action of the play takes place on an aircraft with a committee of construction site inspectors on board, as well as the director of the site, a television crew, a theatre director and an author, and the worker Podzolkin returning to Moscow. Via the playing of a recorded report, a flashback into the past is initiated, and the backgrounds of the passengers and the reasons for their journey gradually emerge: the television crew tries to film, record or photograph some scenes which might bring them success in their journalistic career; Podzolkin has divorced his wife in order to obtain a larger flat, and thus the once fictive divorce has become real: he is now returning to win back his wife; the author and the director (in the production called Motovilov and Goncharov), with obvious parallels in their lives to Baklanov and Lyubimov, visit the construction site to gather material for a play. They remember the war, reflect upon the difficulties of the construction site, and debate the role of art. The commission, under the presidency of Shcherbatov, visits the site and accuses the director, Prishchemikhin (called Vannikov in the archival version) of fulfilling only 86% of the plan, and of dealing instead with human problems, such as food supplies, nurseries, the conservation of nature, and the threat of the greenhouse effect, which, according to the plan, are not his business. The commission condemns his concern, as well as his attempt to build the bridge in a different manner in order to save money and time. At the end of the play, the pilot announces an emergency landing.

The theme of war runs parallel to the treatment of contemporary problems like housing, fulfilment of the plan, and the suppression of personal responsibility or initiative. This was reflected in the set (designed by David Borovsky), which consisted of an aircraft, with soldiers representing the war period on the left, and contemporary characters on the right, all entering via the aisle. This differentiation was musically reinforced: Puccini's *Tosca* accompanied the contemporary scenes, while a sad song of the soldier and Vysotsky's "We turn the earth" were sung in the aisle and reflected the past.[5] The theme of the war also emerged from conversations between the characters: the director and the author philosophised about the war; Shcherbatov used to be a high ranking military man in the war, and served heroically with Prishchemikhin; the latter adopted a child whose mother was shot during the war. The characters meditate upon the changing morality of war and peace. All these men have been honest and sincere in the war, but not all of them have managed to remain sincere in the present. Only Prishchemikhin preserved his sincerity and honesty.

> The juxtaposition of two epochs in the production inevitably draws a conclusion on the transformation of Soviet man in the postwar years as something for worse than a typical effect, on the fragmentation and vulgarisation of his interests, on the tendency for compromise, insincerity and time-serving to triumph in him.[6]

Corruption prevailed: Andrey, Prishchemikhin's adopted son, advocated the principle of falling ill at the right moment to avoid decision-making. Tomchin, the site engineer, appeared to be happy to seize Prishchemikhin's post, and showed no concern for human problems. Shcherbatov understood Prishchemikhin's politics, but feared losing his job, and would only speak up after retirement. Prishchemikhin would have to appear before an assessment committee in Moscow, and his future would remain unclear, since the aircraft was forced to perform an emergency landing, after losing its way. The symbolism of this setting was obvious: the economic plan had failed, and the state had lost direction. The satire on Soviet society, on economic plans and mismanagement could hardly be missed.

But more important was the theme of man educated to lie, cheat and dissemble by a system which regarded truth as conflicting with the requirements of the plan. Since the play was considered to lack optimism for the future of society, the press launched a campaign against it. *Teatralnaya zhizn* invited several critics to express their – negative – views on the play.[7] The point was made that no foundation was given for the metamorphoses (loss of heroic qualities) of some characters (especially Shcherbatov) after the war and that heroes of the war would be heroes (and therefore honest) forever.

> Then, in the war, … people were genuine, fought honestly and displayed heroism. Some of them continue now to live honestly, and work conscientiously, while others have undergone some incomprehensible metamorphoses.[8]

The play was also considered to challenge communism in its representation of that metamorphosis which undermined "the holy ideals of communism for whose triumph twenty million people have given their lives".[9]

The play indeed criticised the system, but for turning humanist values and traditions upside down. Prishchemikhin was the mouthpiece of such criticism:

> Strong is the man who has character enough not to abuse power. Death from cancer – we are not amazed. Run over by a car – common thing. But if conscience killed a man, we cannot understand that. Dying as a man also doesn't mean a great deal.[10]

In the text, there were a great deal of verbal satire against the socialist system, such as references to the transformation of m^3 into cm^3 and megawatt into kilowatt so that they sound more, to ficticious divorce as a solution to housing problems, to the uniformity of book and film titles, and to denunciations. The preoccupation with human sincerity and honesty, however, revealed Lyubimov's style and his authorial voice, encouraging people to speak out:

> The connection between cause and effect has not been analysed; it is as if it were not there. In life, we often do not want to see the obvious. No, look, have courage. We turn away. We are afraid. And then the inevitable happens. And we start to make a fuss.[11]

Left in the air: *Turandot* and *Theatrical Novel*

Towards the beginning of the 1980s, Lyubimov appeared unable to tie loose ends together: he staged an uncompleted play by Brecht, which failed; he rehearsed Bulgakov's *Theatrical Novel* and left the production unfinished. It seems that, having pursued all the devices he had discovered in the initial years of the Taganka, he had – through the inertia of his audience and the hostility of censors – explored these new paths to their limit, and was now looking for other means of expression; these, he would later find through music.

Turandot is Brecht's last play, which survives only as a typescript dated 10 August 1954, ready for production, but without the final corrections which would have been accomplished during rehearsals.[12] Brecht had started to write a play about Princess Turandot in the 1930s, yet had abandoned the project for work on a novel about what he called the "TUI"'s (*Tellect-Ual-In*), intellectuals who whitewash events and create slogans for money.

The play is set in China, where the empire is on the verge of bankruptcy, since the price of cotton has fallen. The emperor is a puppet of his brother, who owns the monopoly on cotton and tries to burn the stock to make prices rise. The TUIs think not only for the emperor; they make opinions and offer them for sale (a form of prostitution). The emperor's daughter, Turandot, is attracted by intellect; although she is good-natured, she is also very naive, thoughtless, and fashion-conscious. Gogher Gogh is a mafioso, who is too stupid to pass the elementary entrance exam to become a TUI. A congress of the TUIs is called to explain the disappearance of the cotton and to calm the nation. Turandot and an old manchu coat, symbol of everlasting imperial power, are the reward for whoever rescues the empire's reputation. Several speakers fail to give a satisfactory explanation and are decapitated. The emperor threatens to abdicate, but Gogher rescues him, prohibiting questions of all kinds and creating a police force out of robbers and thieves; they burn the cotton, accusing the TUIs of the deed and threatening massive arrests, upon which the TUIs are forced to renounce their allegiance (their outer characteristic is a hat). As books are being destroyed for containing dangerous ideas, Sen, an old peasant who came from the provinces with his grandson Eh Feh, buys a book by the revolutionary Kai Ho and finally joins his forces. Gogher becomes "chancellor", having managed to burn the cotton stocks and boost the price. At this point, Turandot refuses to marry him and the theft of the coat is discovered. The field is clear for Kai Ho to arrive.

The play is an allegory on political issues: on a very basic level, it is a critique of intellectuals who sell knowledge to others, especially to political powers (the emperor and trade unions); it reveals the dangers implied in a commercialisation of intellect. Second, and evidently intended by Brecht, comes an allegory of the Third Reich: Gogher is a "chancellor", the TUIs are persecuted like the Jews, art and culture are attacked if they are not what the ruler desires, as happened under Hitler. On a third layer of interpretation, the play refers to the cultural revolution in China.

Since the play was left unfinished, it contained no songs, which were, however, a vital element for the alienation effect desired by both Brecht and Lyubimov. Lyubimov therefore used songs by Boris Slutsky, which were played already in the foyer before the performance began. The representatives of the Main Administration were uncertain about the legitimacy of such an interpolation. The set (by David Borovsky) was made from bamboo: it was a construction of a huge wheel flat on the stage, turned for one purpose only: to activate the emperor's fan, placed under a green umbrella and surrounded by a brass orchestra on an upper section of the set (Figure 50). This wheel provided fresh air for the emperor, at the same time functioning as a symbol of the state apparatus in which the emperor thinks merely of his own ease and benefit, exploiting the people. The set reflected the fact that not only was such exploitation the sole link between emperor and people, but also that the people were ruled by "something similar to the beating of a drum".[13]

The actors wore raincoats and white swimming caps. The TUIs were characterised not by hats, as in Brecht's original, but by the glasses. At the beginning and end, Sen and Eh Feh walked in a circle to turn the wheel, as the sun rose and set in the background:[14] they were searching for truth. The TUIs were called "TUALY" in the Russian version of the play. On the one hand, this is an abbreviated form of "intellek*tual*"; on the other, it constitutes the first syllable of the Russian word for "toilet" ("*tua*let"). Toilet paper was thus used for the posters in the demonstration, and rolls of toilet paper were displayed on stage. The TUIs were thus placed on an inferior, if not slanderous level in the allusion to toilets, which matched their portrayal as narrow-minded people: they enjoyed turning the wheels to make fresh air, i.e. they longed for monotony and agreed to the disciplined behaviour demanded by the figure of authority (the dictator Gogher).

The production was pessimistic in its outlook: reason and intellect were thoroughly corrupted, becoming a destructive force for an entire state, which longed for routine and mindless work. *Turandot* stood thus in sharp contrast to the two Brecht plays shown previously by the Taganka. Mankind was ruled by dullness: man strove for submission to totalitarianism. Mass scenes were frequent, very few actors performed solos: any form of individuality was lost, which helped the totalitarian system.

> With this production the theatre continues the theme of the contemporary anti-hero. Man loses his individuality and acquires so many masks that he becomes diverse, in essence nobody. This anti-hero does not gain a foothold in the world, but adapts himself to it. ... In *Turandot* Lyubimov tries to speak about the universality ... of this phenomenon.[15]

The production had been under pressure from the Main Administration and was removed from the repertoire in April 1981 at the theatre's initiative.[16] A crucial problem was posed by the allusions to China. As early as 1974, Lyubimov and Dupak wrote a letter to Demichev,[17] stressing that they saw no parallel between Kai Eh and Mao: "Kai Eh is not a revolutionary leader, or a popular liberator, but one of the pretenders in the power-struggle ... in the contemporary Chinese political wheel". They emphasized that the theatre would embed the play in a modern, anti-Maoist China and portray the features of Maoism, such as the cultural revolution, satirically. However, the start of rehearsals was delayed and the production did not open until December 1979.

The licence[18] required detailed changes, such as the omission of the line "what rules the people is what makes a noise" and of the (Soviet) term "comrade" to exclude any confusion of the Soviet and the Chinese systems; it also stipulated that there should be no improvisation on the text and no direct address to the audience.

Before the summer break of 1983, Lyubimov held a dress rehearsal of the first part of his and Grigory Faiman's adaptation of Bulgakov's *Theatrical Novel* (known in English translation as *Black Snow*), subtitled "Memoirs of a Dead Man".[19] In September 1983, Lyubimov left for London, was exiled and did not return to Moscow for five years. When he did eventually return, the possibility of completing *Theatrical Novel* was discussed, but rejected in favour of other projects.

Bulgakov's *Theatrical Novel* was written in the 1930s, but not published until the 1960s. It was a parody of the atmosphere and the ensemble of Stanislavsky's Moscow Arts Theatre, where Bulgakov had worked as a literary adviser. The adaptation draws largely on material from the novel, but also on other prose and dramatic works by Bulgakov: the author M. A., portrayed on the basis of *Notes on the Cuffs*,[20] emerges as a counterpart and commentator, an *alter ego* with whom Maksudov speaks. Instead of Rudolfi's diabolic appearance when Maksudov is about to commit suicide, the "devil" appears in person: the character of

Dymok/Angst, added to the plot, is a personification of Stalin. In the adaptation he is addressed as "Iosif Vissarionovich", thus adopting the role Stalin played in Bulgakov's life: Dymok sets the play into the theatre repertoire (in Bulgakov's life, this happened much later, in 1932, with *The Days of the Turbins*) and he terrifies the author in dreams. Another addition to the plot is the insertion of motifs from *Treatise on Housing* for scenes which reflect the atmosphere of terror at the time *Theatrical Novel* was written.

The author's imagination is lively, and reality and fantasy merge. As he reads *The White Guard*, the characters of the play *The Days of the Turbins* come to life as real people; while awaiting a decision from the theatre, Bulgakov's protagonists appear so that a parallel can be drawn to him.[21] In the epilogue, the character of Elena is seen. A figure from *The Days of the Turbins*, she is at the same time his third wife, and "Margo", echoing her counterpart Margarita (*The Master and Margarita*), who was modelled on Elena Sergeevna. Thus parts from Bulgakov's biography are intermingled with his animated fantasy and the plot of the *Theatrical Novel*.

The adaptation consists of three acts and an epilogue. In the first act, the added figure of the author, M. A., comments on the origin of the notes for *Theatrical Novel*. The protagonist Maksudov appears first still working for the newspaper, then writing a novel, which he reads to his friends. The writer suffers from financial problems: he cannot find a publisher for the novel, and is advised to write a play. Thus Maksudov becomes acquainted with the theatre. In the second act, arrests and interventions of the militia occur around the writer. Maksudov reads his play to Ivan Vasilievich, who is not content, since there are no parts for the older generation of actors. He rejects the play. The actor Bombardov explains technicalities of the theatre to Maksudov. In the third act, M. A. is at home, desperate, and contemplating suicide, when the additional character Dymok urges him to live. The director Strizh produces the play, and it becomes obvious that Maksudov has a protector (Dymok). In the epilogue, both Maksudov and M. A. die.

Again, one sees here a concern with the theme of the writer and authority and with the creative act of the artist. However, these themes had been superseded by the time Lyubimov was able to return to *Theatrical Novel*. Both in *Turandot*, and in *Theatrical Novel*, he had been compelled by external circumstances to abandon the projects. Yet he no longer had the wish to fight. The death of his leading actor Vladimir Vysotsky and the unsatisfactory space of the new stage were to intensify the crisis into which both the artist and the individual were gradually drawn.

Homage to *Vladimir Vysotsky*

The death in 1980 of Vladimir Vysotsky, the star of the theatre and most certainly a major driving force, marked one of the greatest losses the Taganka and Lyubimov had to cope with.

The production in homage to Vysotsky must be linked to the stream of productions honouring writers such as Pushkin, Ostrovsky, Gogol, Mayakovsky, and Bulgakov. Lyubimov intended to place Vysotsky in line with those writers when choosing the genre of his production:

> There is a point in creating a poetic performance in memory of Vysotsky. ...Vysotsky grew up and was formed as a poet in this theatre, and therefore we are morally obliged to create such a performance for him.[22]

Vysotsky is perceived as an individual in constant contact with his social environment, as an artist integrated in an ensemble omnipresent on stage. Vysotsky's songs belong to a modern urban folk tradition, with their juxtaposition of "conventional folk phraseology" and "vulgar urban slang".[23]

> The idea of creating a production came up shortly after Vysotsky's death. At the Artistic Council meeting of 1 August 1980 Lyubimov already expressed clear ideas about the production, such as the use of a set from Hamlet, the silences and absences of Vysotsky, improvisations on Shakespeare, and the role of Hamlet as a leitmotif. Lyubimov deliberately chose the ritual form of a funeral wake for the production. Why did I choose the traditional form of a wake? Because the wakes which took place at his home and in the theatre, on the actors' initiative, have stirred up my soul. This ritual form combined with the role he played all his life, and which influenced him: Hamlet.[24]

The text for the production is made up of poems and songs by Vysotsky, actors' comments, accounts and transitional passages, and excerpts from *Hamlet*, sometimes creating a parody of the text, as with the grave-diggers and actors. It is as if the actors were conducting a dialogue with the absent poet, enhancing thereby the tragic nature of his absence: "The poet has not left, he replies with words from the production, with his songs – this is his mortal role".[25]

Vysotsky consists of seven sections.[26] The first places Vysotsky within the context of Soviet culture. This section comprises recorded songs and recited poems.[27] It also quotes scenes from *Hamlet*, between Ophelia and Laertes, Hamlet and Queen Gertrude, and an improvised dialogue between the grave-diggers and Horatio illustrating the theme of rumour and truth. The section ends with a recording of Okudzhava's song "About Volodya Vysotsky". The second part consists of "street" and "criminal" songs. It is governed by the four couplets of the recorded version of "I Have a Guitar", interrupted by songs.[28] The third section is composed of "war" songs and poems and concludes with a questionnaire of 1970 in which Vysotsky, along with all the other actors of the Taganka theatre, answered questions concerning his favourite colour, flower, poet, etc.[29] The fourth section deals with the theme of imagination, "fairy tales"[30] and ends with a dialogue between the visiting actors in *Hamlet*. The fifth section quotes examples to illustrate Soviet life, taken from Vysotsky's songs: the genuine man of the people as represented by the puppet of the Taganka theatre's caretaker "Uncle Volodya", who performs in "Journey to Town"; television in "Dialogue in front of the TV"; alcoholism in "Militia Report"; newspapers in "Tender Truth"; difficulties of travelling abroad, "Instructions before a Journey"; overcrowded transport in "Citizens, Don't Shove". The sixth part concerns Vysotsky-Hamlet and the poet-creator: it has several extracts from Hamlet, and the poem "Cupolas" recited with modifications that refer to the Taganka production. It includes the song "The Smokeless Bath-House" with Zolotukhin commenting on the process of its creation, and finally a recital of "The Black Man". The last section deals with the poet's premonitions of death.[31] Recordings of Lyubimov's favourite songs "The Wolf Hunt" and "Unruly Horses" finish off the production.

The interpretations of the texts varied: recordings of Vysotsky's songs were played over an amplifier, sometimes with refrains sung by the actors. Certain songs or poems were interpreted by one actor, or several actors in the form of a dialogue. Passages of *Hamlet* were performed, or parodied in improvisation to make them suitable for the production, in which they were used for commentary. The text was thus recited, sung, recorded, or enacted. Moreover, irrespective of the mode of interpretation, the text was illustrated with gesture and images: "There is an enactment of songs, the words are commented upon by gestures".[32] Thus, leaflets were dropped when Vysotsky replied to the questionnaire (III). The words "hot blood" (*goryachaya krov'*) in the "Sad Romance"[33] were emphasised by pointing at a red shirt. In the scene about drunkenness (V), a liquid in a glass symbolised Vysotsky's passion for alcohol. To accompany the recital of "Tender Truth", actors held the paper *Sovetskaya Rossiya*.[34] The scene of "The Smokeless Bath-House" was set in the atmosphere of the Siberian hut where Zolotukhin and Vysotsky lived during filming: a light bulb was lowered onto the stage. The section about war was set behind the light curtain, and introduced by the sound of explosions created by the seats on the set flapping down. The poem "The Sea-Cove's Gone for Good"[35] was staged as a shadow-play with a poet, who resembles Pushkin.

The set was a rectangular block of seats from a theatre auditorium, which could be moved into various positions: vertical, horizontal, it could swing like the *Hamlet* curtain, only more slowly; the seats could, when upright, form windows for the actors. The block could be lowered to stage floor level, or raised to head heights; it could also be sloped. The seats could be covered with a white cloth, partially or fully, to resemble a coffin carried by the actors on stage (Figure 51).

The actors wore costumes from *Hamlet*. Puppets representing the actors, Vysotsky, and Lyubimov appeared in the rows of seats. Lyubimov's rehearsal desk in the auditorium was installed and lit up to underline the work in progress, the uncompleted nature of the production. Vysotsky and Lyubimov were both addressed, it seems, at least in the 1988 version: the theatre had indeed at that point lost both of them.

Some scenes were added by Nikolay Gubenko in the 1988 revival, which did not earn Lyubimov's approval.[36] Gubenko had Pioneers appear with a song sung at a very high pitch in the section about alcoholism (Figure 52): they even went up to a drunkard who had collapsed and lifted his arm, to no effect. This scene was evidently copied from *The House on the Embankment* where Pioneers appeared, and from *Listen!* where the recital by the schoolchildren caused great amusement. Furthermore, white busts of Vysotsky were carried on stage before "The Wolf Hunt". This was another allusion to *Listen!* where the idea of elevating Mayakovsky to the level of the gods had been rejected, but here it seemed to imply that Vysotsky belonged to the select group of "great" poets.

Documents concerning the closure in 1981 of *Vladimir Vysotsky* have been widely published.[37] As in the arguments over many other Taganka productions, the key issue was the conflict between the artist and the régime. The Main Administration of Culture made the point that "the basic idea of the poetic performance ... is the conflict between the poet and society".[38] In a report to the Central Committee, the Ministry of Culture pointed to a recurrent theme of Lyubimov's work: "The composition proves the hypotheses concerning the persecution of the poet, and his conflict with our society".[39] The theme of the conflict between the artist and the state had frequently emerged in Lyubimov's earlier productions and the press had reproached him with an obsession with this subject.[40] According to Demichev, Vysotsky was seen too much in terms of a dissident, and Zimyanin wrote in November 1981 to Chernenko that "the play is anti-Soviet and cannot be staged".[41] The Main Administration rejected most of the songs included in the production, since their themes were incompatible with Socialist art: alcoholism, death, Stalinism. The Main Administration firmly prohibited rehearsals on 17 July 1981.

Thanks to Andropov's intervention, a viewing with representatives of the Ministry of Culture was arranged for 18 July, after which the performance was allowed to be shown for the anniversary of Vysotsky's death, to a select audience on 25 July. Subsequently, the text was sent to the Main Administration for approval, but there was no possibility of any further discussion since the Main Administration abstained from two further viewings on 13 and 31 October 1981. This made the "official" attitude to Vladimir Vysotsky obvious: he had not been recognised as a poet during his lifetime, very few of his poems and songs had been published, and most had circulated on private tapes. His songs about the authentic life, about people and their problems, were adored by the people (*narod*). It is this attitude that the theatre expresses:

> His words reach the soul of everyone, they force the listener to look at himself. Addressing the alcoholic, the demagogue, the idler, the bureaucrat, he does not brand him, humiliate him, destroy him, but shows him his soul, shows what is happening within him, and what can happen in the future. The desire to depict man when evil emerges inside him is most important. Often the evil comes from the inability to recognise it on the part of the evil-doer; it is an evil of carelessness, of indifference.[42]

As with *Listen!* or *Comrade, believe...*, the image of the poet given in *Vladimir Vysotsky* was deemed unorthodox and unrepresentative of "Soviet Culture". The production was stigmatised as much as the poet himself, as much as the news about his death and funeral (neither had been widely reported).

Lyubimov threatened to leave the theatre when he realised the uncompromising stance of the Main Administration. He had to pay homage to Vysotsky in his own language, that of the theatre. The Taganka had to honour and create a memorial to its actor, poet and friend.

> I would be hypocritical if I said that I leave these walls easily. But I have definitively decided for myself: if this production does not take place, I consider it impossible to come to the theatre and begin rehearsals for another production.[43]

After the ban on *Vladimir Vysotsky*,[44] no other production could be premièred by Lyubimov before he was expelled in 1984. The authorities had started to silence Lyubimov.

> I created a number of works and I consider them to be extremely important to myself and to the theatre, because they are a new stage of creation for me both in the moral and aesthetic sense. Those works are closed. I cannot accept this... Neither I nor the theatre can imagine continuing our work without those three productions: [*Vysotsky, Kuzkin* and *Boris Godunov*].[45]

A new stage: *Three Sisters*

By 1981 a new stage had been built in order to accommodate the increasing number of spectators and to improve the technical equipment of the theatre. The premises of the Taganka theatre are located on a nineteenth century house of flour-tradesmen. In 1912, the cinema "Vulkan" opened in the building on Chkalov Street. From 1918 to 1920, the cinema served for meetings and concerts, and on 13 May 1920 Lenin delivered a speech there. In the 1920s, the building acted as a studio, later a branch of the Maly Theatre, until A. K. Plotnikov took over the theatre in 1945; at that point the corner building was acquired for the entrance, foyer and buffet of the Theatre of Drama and Comedy (Figure 53).[46]

Six hundred and fifty seats were crammed into the small auditorium of the theatre and technical installations were added for the productions. The Taganka also acquired other buildings in the area: a garage for storage, and a house with a small stage for rehearsals. The construction of the new stage started in 1972, and was designed to create an entirely new theatre complex on the corner of the Garden Ring and Upper Radishchev Street, integrating the seventeenth-century church of Nikola-on-Bolvan as a concert hall, and turning the street into a pedestrian zone for street performances.[47] The team of architects Gnedovsky, Tarantsov and Anisimov conceived the theatre's function as a linking element between urban life and performance, and aimed to create a new building which would conform in style to the innovative and avantgarde productions of the Taganka theatre.[48] The plan included the demolition of the old building after construction of the new stage to achieve a unity of style for façade and interior, both made of red brick and white limestone, and the use of triangular oriels conforming with the shape of the premises at the theatre's disposal. This plan was never realised: the pedestrian zone and the church as concert hall were never accomplished, and the church has recently been restored for religious functions. The resulting building, the only theatre constructed especially for a director since Meyerhold's theatre, was unsatisfactory upon completion in 1983.[49] The old stage was eventually not demolished, but restored. The new stage is equipped with a flexible stage which, as yet, has never been fully used (Figure 54). It has a larger auditorium, and the space on stage is vast and open, in contrast to the intimate atmosphere of the old stage. A red brick wall containing three rows of windows and doors constitutes the back of the new stage (Figure 55); the side walls of the auditorium and the balcony are of the same material. However, Lyubimov and Borovsky wanted a white wall, preferably the original wall of an old building located on the premises, as on the old stage (Figure 56).

The Taganka now has three stages: the old stage, the new stage, and the small stage, with 518, 773, and 80–150 seats respectively; the three stages can be used simultaneously (Figure 57).

Lyubimov had difficulties in becoming accustomed to the open and virtually unlimited space of the new stage, and only gradually tried to transfer to it some of the older productions, such as *Ten Days*, *The Good Person of Szechwan*, *Tartuffe*, and *The Fallen and the Living*. Many productions had to remain on the old stage for purely technical reasons, such as *The Master and Margarita*, *The House on the Embankment* and *Vladimir Vysotsky* with their heavy sets. *The Wooden Horses* and *But the Dawns here are so Calm. . .* were transferred, but moved back to the old stage by 1990 for aesthetic reasons: they were designed for a much more intimate setting than was spatially available on the new stage.

The first play produced on the new stage was *Three Sisters*, which opened in May 1981, when access to the new stage was still through the old foyer. The official inauguration of the new stage with the new foyer did not take place until 23 April 1983.

Three Sisters had already been rehearsed by Yury Pogrebnichko for about a year[50] when it became clear to Lyubimov that the rehearsals were not making progress and he intervened to complete the production. Thus, any study of *Three Sisters* should bear in mind that it was not a production where the entire concept was worked out by Lyubimov.[51] Hence, even if many features were characteristic of Lyubimov's style, they may not have been coherently applied here.

The décor was designed by Pogrebnichko's associate Yury Kononenko. The set was abstract, yet charged with symbols, and as such uncharacteristic of Lyubimov's approach. The set limited the open and vast space of the new stage by means of metallic panels the same height as the stage. These were painted with frescoes so that the figures remained imprecise and only faintly visible, somewhat reminiscent of icons. On the sides of these panels were taps, each with a mirror above and a bucket beneath. On the left side were three beds, such as those found in military barracks, one filled with stones, one empty, and the other properly made up with pillows. In the centre was a small wooden stage, elevated above the rest of the playing-area (the 'wooden stage') with two lines of Viennese chairs in front of it. To the right stood three chairs with dustcovers and a piano with candles, flowers and a photograph on too. Further to the right was a small forestage, backed by four panels of mirrors, in which the audience was reflected. The stage was encircled by light bulbs (Figure 58).

First, the set allocated from the outset certain areas of the stage to certain characters: the right forestage was Masha's world, and, at times,

Vershinin's; the three chairs in covers and the piano were the space for the other sisters and Andrey; the left of the stage with the beds represented the world of the soldiers; the centre was the point of intersection for the two worlds, where people meet and part (here, Irina and Masha say farewell to Tuzenbakh and Vershinin respectively). This clear separation of spaces of action was typical of Lyubimov and was largely introduced by him into the production.

The wooden stage had a metatheatrical function.[52] It was used for actors to re-enact for the benefit of other characters episodes relating to their past, or to demonstrate and emphasise the most decisive moments. Karaulov compared the wooden stage to a place of execution:

> For Lyubimov, this little theatre is like a place of execution. Vershinin's words about 'how everything has its end' sound here [like] a last confession. Irina rejects Soleny – and from here Chebutykin leads the duellists 'into their positions'. A little later ... Soleny crosses the stage, visible to the audience, and stands for a long time washing the blood from his hands ... And Tuzenbakh, as if preparing for death, suddenly starts a convulsive folk dance.[53]

The chairs placed in front of the wooden stage would frequently be occupied by the soldiers, not in order to view the action on the wooden stage, but to contemplate the audience in the auditorium. In that respect, the metatheatrical function of the wooden stage was reversed: the action on stage was not observed by the actors, and instead the auditorium was put in its place. The theatre thus commented not on itself, but on the audience.

The relationship with the audience was thereby unusual. The auditorium was illuminated by dim or bright light for much of the production. Moreover, it was challenged not only by the penetrating looks of the soldiers – pseudo-spectators of the events on the wooden stage –, but also by being used as a replacement for the actors: when the photograph was taken in the first act, the actors sat on the two lines of chairs and turned to the audience to photograph it. The challenge to the audience was taken a step further by the use of the mirror: the spectators were constantly faced with their own reflection in the huge mirror to the right (Figure 59). They were thus permanently reminded that they were in a theatre, and that they themselves should really be on stage, as the subject and main protagonist of the play. This was enhanced by the actors' pointing at the mirror when they bowed at the end of the performance.

The use of masks was noteworthy. The mummers, who were wearing masks, were excluded; ritual was banned by Natasha, the figure in the play who seems to prefigure the "Soviet" character, always looking into a "purposeful" future. However, white paper masks were worn by all the actors instead for the scene. Yet these masks were not ritualistic, but symbolic in indicating uniformity and the loss of individuality.

> Something happened to mankind, people forgot, lost the habit of a free life...
> And therefore the destinies of Chekhov's heroes are so similar. They are
> depersonalised, their faces have turned to blank masks...[54]

The masks enabled the actors to admit that they were pretending, that reality was far removed from their dream. The fire became a symbol of truth: it ended all the games with the masks, and was represented on stage by red light projected into the side mirror.

Most of the men were in military greatcoats, and the presence of military personnel on stage was emphasised. As prescribed by Chekhov, Masha and Irina were in black and white. Only Olga's dark blue dress had been replaced by a khaki uniform, reminiscent of army uniforms in modern Soviet Russia. The military style of costumes and the persistent use of military music emphasised this theme. Olga had something of a military manner, not only in the way she addressed her sisters, but even her final monologue was pronounced like a dictation she might be giving to her pupils.[55] Olga herself was submissive to regulations: she had become a schoolmistress against her own volition. In the last act, she tore Masha away from Vershinin rather than comforting her. Yet the military aspect dominated the production in another way, too. The military régime made all decisions superfluous, robbed characters of their initiative and energy, and left them in the grip of a destiny which they knew they could not change (Irina and Tuzenbakh). Only Masha retained hope and energy, and she was therefore set apart from the others until her hopes disappeared with the departure of Vershinin, when she joined the world of her sisters spatially on stage.

Striking images pervaded the production. Natasha wound wool from the pram when talking to Andrey about their son taking over Irina's room; she entangled him with the yarn, making it impossible for him to move. Oranges, as a symbol for the Muscovite style of life, were carried on stage at one time, but this episode no longer remains in the production.[56] Anfisa, condemned to eternal servitude by Natasha, rendered this inhuman and absurd order by constant movement similar to that of a *vanka-vstanka*.[57] Kulygin's book was not something special he was about to give to Irina; all the characters had a copy which they brandished when it was offered in order to reveal Kulygin's ridiculous obsession with his school. Kulygin was also engaged in a comically constant pursuit of Masha, his love, or the illusion of love.[58]

The play underwent few changes. Often, omissions were confined to minor details; yet there was systematic omission as far as the following aspects were concerned. The theme of work for Irina was effaced completely; Tuzenbakh did not discuss with Irina his quitting of the military service, nor was there ever any mention of the possibility that Irina might also work. Furthermore, Andrey was not shown as a gambler. Natasha was preoccupied with her children only as long as there was nothing more interesting for her to do; she abruptly stopped talking about the change of rooms when Protopopov arrived, and instantly abandoned her boasting about the children in order to attend to the chopping down of the trees. The regimented, Soviet style of life as led by Natasha was interpreted in a negative manner; she was a negligent mother.

As usual, Lyubimov was accused of failing to provide a psychological portrayal of the characters and of using a purely formal approach which prevented the layers of Chekhov's subtext from emerging.[59] Yet it was the very discrepancy between the word and the situation and action which created the tension of the play. This gave Lyubimov the justification for staging it as a condensation of Chekhovian philosophy.

> In *Three Sisters* Lyubimov ... stages the whole of Chekhov. More precisely, a synopsis of the complete Chekhov. He reduces Chekhov to a system of signs.[60]

For Lyubimov, not only the dramatic text had importance as a basis of the production, but also the fact that the traditional Chekhovian interpretation on stage was no longer valid for the contemporary theatre. What for Chekhov was the future, a bright future, was the time the contemporary audience lived in.

> The director drastically reconsiders the common stereotype of Chekhovian theatre, linked to the motif of 'hope in the bright future'. How often has mankind deceived itself with unrealisable illusions! Lyubimov's view is commonsensical and categorical: it is time, at last, to liberate oneself from the habit of writing everything off and adjourning for the future, ... of justifying – in the name of the future – any sacrifices and privations, and of shifting our problems onto the shoulders of the next generation.[61]

There was no relief in the future, no hope, no optimism; hence the production dwelt on the present, in which problems needed to be resolved and questions answered: "You must not hope in the future. All questions must be answered now! And if nothing comes of it, the future will not help either".[62] The Chekhovian future has become the present. But what we, the audience, have made of what used to be our common future was the question permanently confronting the audience. The spectators were challenged, almost reproached for the situation, and thereby reminded of their power to produce change in the present. The spectators were not only continually faced with their own reflection, as the creator of this present. They were also reminded of what Chekhov's play sounded like in former times, when Chekhov's future had not yet reached the contemporary era, by recordings of the voices of Vasily Kachalov and Sergey Yursky with Emma Popova.[63] Music enhanced the opposition between past and present: military music and marches were contrasted with nostalgic music by Tchaikovsky and Vivaldi.

The most important reminder, however, that the audience was faced with a text whose future had become present, and whose dreams had been replaced by grim realities, was the initial and final image of the production. The mirror panels at the side of the stage were lowered to open the view onto the streets of the contemporary dull or bright, sunny or snowy streets of Moscow, the Garden Ring[64] and a brass band stood on a balcony playing an old military march (Figure 60). This image framed the production, established the military leitmotif and made unmiskatably clear that the Moscow the sisters are longing for is there outside, before the audience's eyes. The sisters even knocked at the mirrors when speaking of their desire to go to Moscow, as if asking to be let out onto the streets. The audience was sent out at the end of the production into that very same Moscow the sisters had been yearning for. The present is there outside, and that is what we have made of our past dreams. It is a result of the people's inertia. Therefore the people was called upon to think not about the future, but about the present.

> This *Three Sisters* has been staged not about the intelligentsia, nor about the fate of culture, but rather about the fate of the people.[65]

Lyubimov was already working towards a theatre in which the people would become the protagonist.

Chekhov's characters were deprived of hope in the future. There is no future, there is only the bleak present. This pessimism is typical of Lyubimov in the early 1980s. Submission to military orders leads to inertia, passivity and lethargy, depriving people of hope. However, people do not have to succumb to regulations; they can take the initiative and capture, like Masha, some minutes of hope that might last for lifetime:

> Demidova's Masha rightly becomes the heroine of the production. Such people are precious to Lyubimov's theatre, his hopes rest on them, even if he realises their exceptional nature.[66]

Hence the emphasis was on the individual, not on the community of society. But it was also significant that Masha pronounced her second-act speech as an epigraph to the performance:

> I think a human being has got to have some faith, or at least he's got to seek faith. Otherwise his life will be empty, empty.[67]

This emphasis on faith to help to find a meaning in life, and the right attitude to life, already pointed towards Lyubimov's subsequent concern with the theme of religion. The idea of an omnipotent *narod* (people) foretold his transition towards ritual and folk theatre in *Boris Godunov*. Although both religion and folk theatre were only emerging in this production of *Three Sisters*, they certainly anticipated Lyubimov's later style.

In these productions which perceived the individual in crisis, the audience was attacked and condemned as the director's dissatisfaction grew. The audience was the protagonist in *Work is Work*, challenged to act. The spectators were placed in the spotlight, on the stage, and scrutinised in *Three Sisters*, challenged to look at what they had made of the present.

The creation of a common bond with the audience, and the role of the spectator as the virtual protagonist in the production, did not activate any reactions – either literally or figuratively – from the audience. Moreover, the theatre was losing its audience: more and more tickets were distributed through inside connections (especially concerning *The Master and Margarita*), and people who did not really need the theatre were sitting in the audience, making it even more difficult for the actors to play to them.[68] Anatoly Gorelov commented sharply on the paradoxical situation in which the Taganka theatre and its audience found themselves at the beginning of the 1980s:

> We use the theatre to discover truth, which we cannot find in any other way... How strange that those who organise untruth also need truth.[69]

Figure 21 *But the Dawns here are so Calm...*, arrival of the detachment in the truck, Vaskov: Shapovalov.

Figure 22 *But the Dawns ...*, sauna scene.

Figure 23 *But the Dawns ...*, woods.

Figure 24 *But the Dawns ...*, the staircase in the foyer after the performance.

Главное управление культуры исполкома Моссовета

Б. ВАСИЛЬЕВ

А ЗОРИ ЗДЕСЬ ТИХИЕ...

ДЕЙСТВУЮЩИЕ ЛИЦА и ИСПОЛНИТЕЛИ:

СТАРШИНА ВАСКОВ

заслуженный артист РСФСР
— В. Шаповалов

Зенитчицы

Кирьянова — В. Радунская
Майор — И. Бортник
Ю. Беляев.
Ю. Осипов
Катенька — О. Гулынская
Е. Граббе·
Хозяйка — И. Ульянова
О. Мулина
Соседка — Т. Лукьянова

— Л. Бойко, Е. Габец, Т. Груднева, Н. Ковалева,
И. Кулевская, Н. Маркина, О. Мулина

ГАЛЯ ЧЕТВЕРТАК

— Л. Комаровская
И. Фролова

СОНЯ ГУРВИЧ

— Н. Сайко
О. Гулынская
заслуженный артист РСФСР

Отец Сони Гурвич — Г. Ронинсон
С. Фарада·
заслуженная артистка РСФСР

Мать Сони Гурвич — Г. Власова
заслуженная артистка РСФСР
Т. Махова

ЖЕНЯ КОМЕЛЬКОВА

— Н. Шацкая
Т. Иваненко
Мать
Жени Комельковой — И. Ульянова
О. Мулина

ЛИЗА БРИЧКИНА

— М. Полицеймако
Е. Корнилова

Отец Лизы Бричкиной — Ю. Смирнов
В. Штернберг

Гость в доме Бричкиной — К. Желдин
Н. Прозоровский

РИТА ОСЯНИНА

— Н. Кузнецова
Осянин — В. Матюхин
Л. Власов

Немецкие солдаты — В. Бохон, Л. Власов, А. Граббе, А. Давыдов,
Н. Матюхин, Д. Певцов, С. Савченко, В. Штернберг,
И. Штернберг, В. Шуляковский, С. Холмогоров,
А. Фурсенко, В. Черняев

Цена 6 коп.

Зак. 7630 ПО «Периодика» УИМ, 1985 г. Тир. 5000

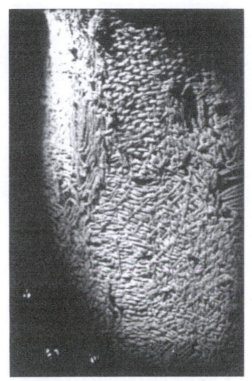

Figure 26 *Hamlet*, close-up of curtain.

Figure 27 *Hamlet*, set design.

Figure 28 *Hamlet*, Hamlet: Vysotsky.

Figure 29 *The Rush Hour.*

Figure 30 *The Wooden Horses*, Milentevna: Alla Demidova (Act I).

Figure 31 *The Wooden Horses*, Pelageya: Zinaida Slavina (Act II).

Figure 32 *The Exchange.*

обмена жилых помещений Управления
учета и распределения жилплощади
Мосгорисполкома

Группа *Ждановского* р-на

Входящий № *25* от *3 апреля*

З А Я В Л Е Н И Е

об обмене жилой площади

Я, ответственный съемщик, гр. *Московский театр драмы и комедии на Таганке*

(фамилия, имя, отчество)

проживающий по адресу: гор. *Москва* ул., пер. пр. *Чкалова*

дом № *76* кв. — корп. телефон домашн. *272-62-40* служебн. *272-63-00*

Дом находится в ведении *Главного управления культуры Мосгорисполкома*

(указать номер ЖЭК, район, название ведомства или предприятия, ЖСК)

ПРЕДЛАГАЮ К ОБМЕНУ: *«Обмен» по повести Ю.В. Трифонова*

(указать отд. кв. или комнаты, метраж, смеж. или изолиров.)

на *I* эт *2-х* эт. дома *кирпичного*

(кирп. дер. смешан. панельный блочный)

имеющего: *15 городских и 40 внутренних телефонов, горячую воду*

(перечислить удобства)

кухня, размер *5* кв. м., санузел совмещ. *12*, раздельн. *2*

(совмещ. или раздельн.)

в кварт. еще комнат _____ семей _____ человек *171*

Из проживающих в семье и в квартире состоит ли кто на учете в диспансерах психоневрологическом или туберкулезном *да*

На указанной жилой площади я, отв. съемщик *Любимов Юрий Петрович*, проживаю

с *23 апреля* 19*64* г. на основании ордера № *82*, выданного *МК РСФСР*

5 февраля 19*64* г. на *60* чел. Указанную жилплощадь получил *по улучшению жилищных условий*

(как очередник, по улучш. жил. услов., по реконструкции, сносу, обмену, если по обмену, указать адрес, по которому проживал до обмена, и размер жилой площади)

(если вступил в ЖСК то куда сдана площадь, или кто остался в ней проживать, подлежит ли уплотнению)

На указанной жилой площади в настоящее время проживает, включая съемщик

№№ п.п	Фамилия, имя, отчество	Год рожд.	Родств. отношения	С какого года проживает в Москве	Откуда и когда прибыл на эту площадь	Место работы и должность
	Дмитриев В.Г.		муж		В. Вилькин, Л. Филатов	
	Ксения Федоровна		его мать		А. Богина	
	Дмитриев Г.Ч.		его отец		А. Пороховщиков	
	Дмитриев Ф.Н.		его дед		В. Соболев	
	Лена		его жена		И. Ульянова, з.а. РСФСР И. Демидова, Е. Корнилова	
	Наташка		его дочь		Люба Каржавина	
	Лукьянова В.П.		мать Лены		Г. Власова	
	Лукьянов И.В.		отец Лены		Л. Штейнрах	
	Лора		сестра Дмитриева		И.В. Раевская, з.а. РСФСР З. Славина, А. Бойко	
	Марина		двоюродная сестра		И. Лукьянова, Т. Додина	
	Феликс		муж Лоры		Ю. Беляев	
	тетя Женя		тетка Дмитриева		з.а. РСФСР Т. Махова	
	Дядя Вася				В. Черняев	
	Дядя Коля				Ю. Беляев	
	Таня				И. Кузнецова, Л. Савченко, Е. Поплавская	
	Алик		сын Тани		А. Вешняк Кольцов	
	Витя		муж Тани		В. Подколзин	
	Белка Бубрик, родственник Дмитриевых		его жена		А. Семенов, С. Фарада	
	Инночка				В. Глаголин, Л. Давыдова	
	Такель				В. Петров, з.а. РСФСР Г. Ронинсон, С. Холмогоров, А. Сабинин	
	Гикега				Р. Джабраилов	
	слесарь на даче				С. Подколзин, О. Гудзиков, Л. Давыдова	
	соседи Дмитриевых				В. Черняев, С. Подколзин	
	шахматисты Гикега					
	старая революционерка				И. Фролова	

из них: в Советской Армии и в командировках по бронь

Проживают без права на площадь

Артисты Марина и Виктор Свидерские				

Сведения о лицах, ранее значившихся в ордере и выбывших с площади:

№№ п/п	Фамилия, имя, отчество	Год рожд.	Родств. отношения	Когда и куда выбыл
	Губенко			_Мосфильм_
	Эйбоженко			_Малый театр_
	Калягин			_МХАТ_
	Любшин			_Театр им. Ермоловой_
	Фоменко			_в неизвестном направлении_

Причины обмена: _____

Я, ответственный съемщик, _Любимов Ю.П._ и все совершеннолетн. члены семьи желаем произвести обмен с гражд. _Трифоновым Ю.В._, проживающим (ей) по адресу: г. _Москва_, ул., пер., пр. _Георгию Дех_ дом № ____ кв. ____ корп. ____ на площадь, состоящую из _I пьесы «Обмен»_ общим метражом _____ кв. м.

ПРИ РАЗЪЕЗДЕ укажите, куда и на какую пл. переезжают остальные члены семьи

1. _Д.Л. Боровский - художник_
2. _Э.В. Денисов - композитор_
3. _Е.М. Кучер - режиссер, В. Александров - режиссер-стажер_

Указанная жилая площадь нами осмотрена и никаких претензий к Бюро обмена или к отделу учета и распред. жилплощади _Ждановского_ района г. Москвы, а также к гражданам иметь не будем.

отв. съемщик _(подпись)_

ПОДПИСИ:—

совершеннолетние члены семьи _Д.Л. Боровский, Э.В. Денисов, Е.М. Кучер_

Подлежит ли дом сносу или капитальному ремонту: _подлежит реконструкции_ (указать, когда)

За указание неправильных сведений подписавшие анкету несут ответственность по закону.

М. П. Начальник ЖЭК № _(подпись)_ района _____ (подпись)

Бухгалтер _(подпись)_ (подпись)

На где, как подобран обмен (по картотеке, бюллетеню, группой, самостоятельно).

Состоит ли на учете по обмену жилой площади: _да_ _____ (указать: да, нет)

Представлены документы, подтверждающие родственные отношения при съезде и другие дополнительные документы

1. _Гос. академический театр им. Евг. Вахтангова_
2. _Театральное училище им. Б.В. Щукина_
3. _____
4. _____

Подпись инспектора Бюро обмена _(подпись)_

373

35

The Exchange, reverse side of programme.

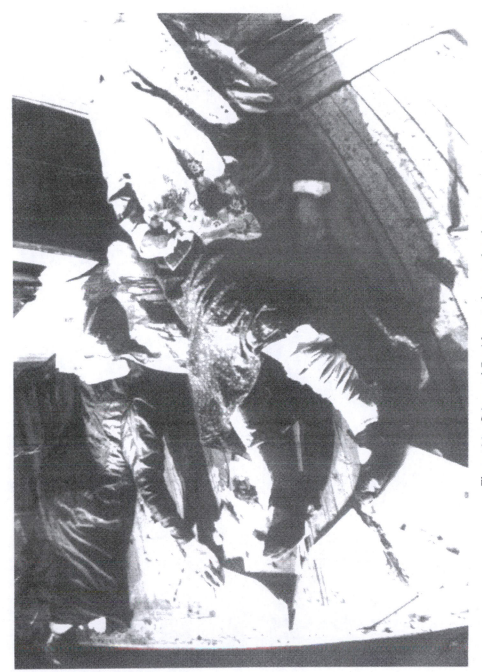

Figure 34 *Crime and Punishment,* the murdered women.

Figure 35 *Crime and Punishement*, dream sequence.

Figure 36 *Crime and Punishment*, foyer.

Figure 37 *Crime and Punishment*, set design.

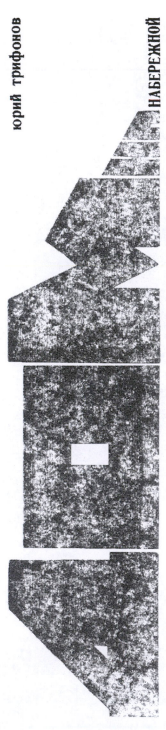

Figure 38 *The House on the Embankment*, programme.

Figure 39 ·*The House on the Embankment*, set design.

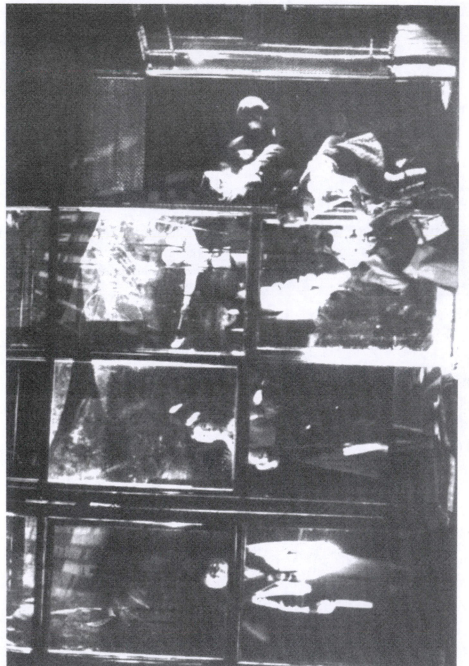

Figure 40 *The House on the Embankment.*

Figure 41 *Comrade, believe ...*

Figure 42 *The Gala*, programme.

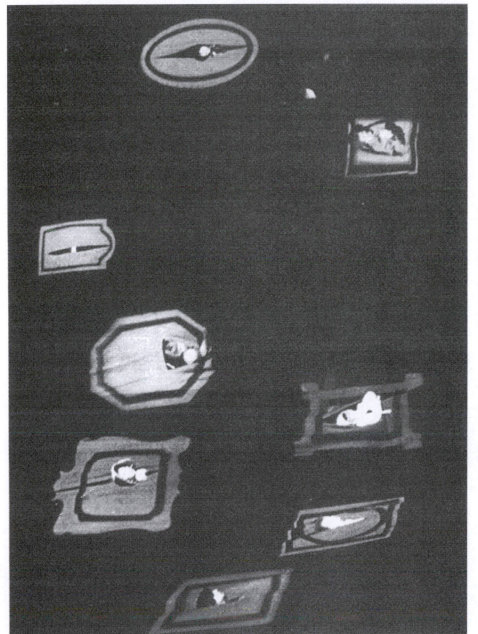

Figure 43 *Inspectorate Fairy Tales: The Portrait.*

Figure 44 *Inspectorate Fairy Tales.*

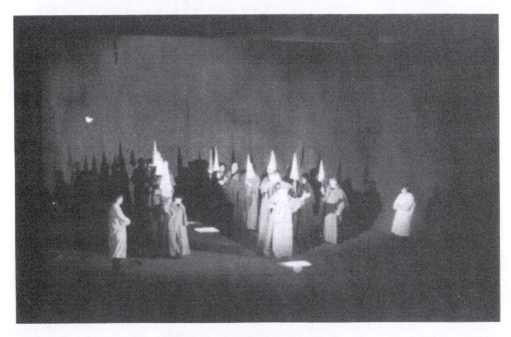

Figure 45 *Inspectorate Fairy Tales.*

Figure 46 *The Master and Margarita.*

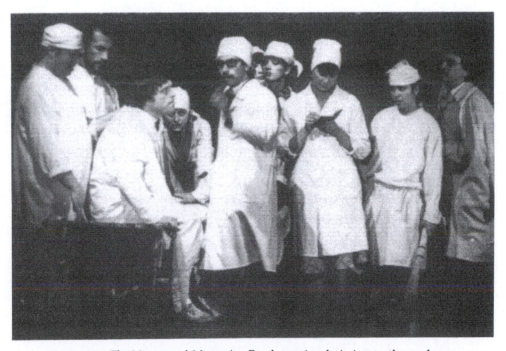

Figure 47 *The Master and Margarita,* Bezdomny's admission to the asylum.

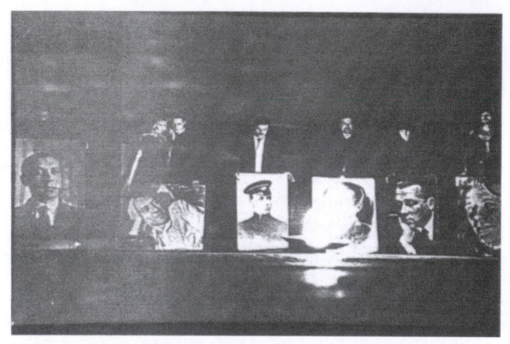

Figure 48 *The Master and Margarita*, finale: homage to Bulgakov.

Figure 49 *Work is Work (Daughter, Father and Guitarist)*, finale: Viktoriya Medvedeva, Dmitry Mezhevich and Yury Medvedev.

Figure 50 *Turandot.*

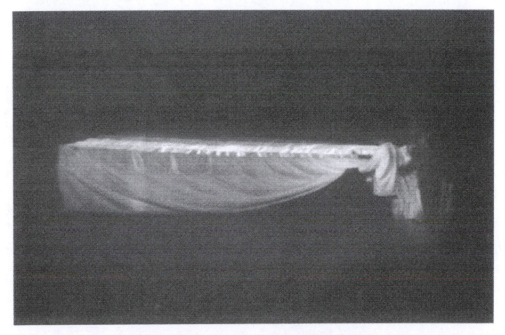

Figure 51 *Vladimir Vysotsky,* funeral scene.

Figure 52 *Vladimir Vysotsky, Pioneer scene.*

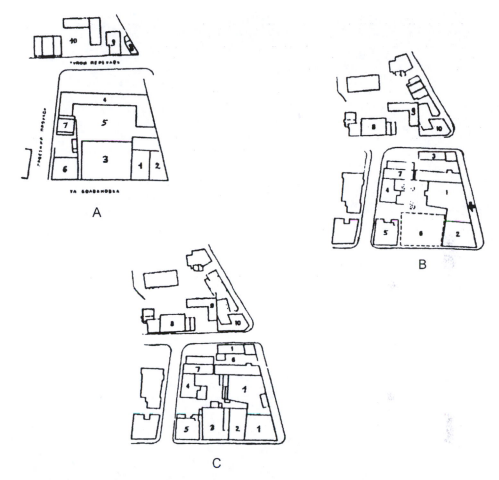

Figure 53 The premises of the Taganka Theatre.

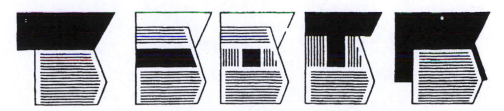

Figure 54 Variations of transformation of the new Taganka stage.

Figure 55   The New Stage.

Figure 56   The Old Stage.

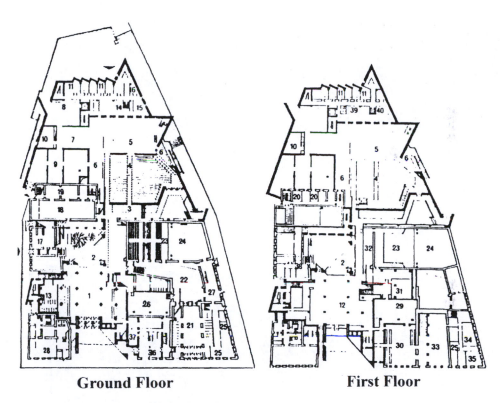

Ground Floor **First Floor**

Figure 57 Plan of the ground and the first floor of the new Taganka theatre.

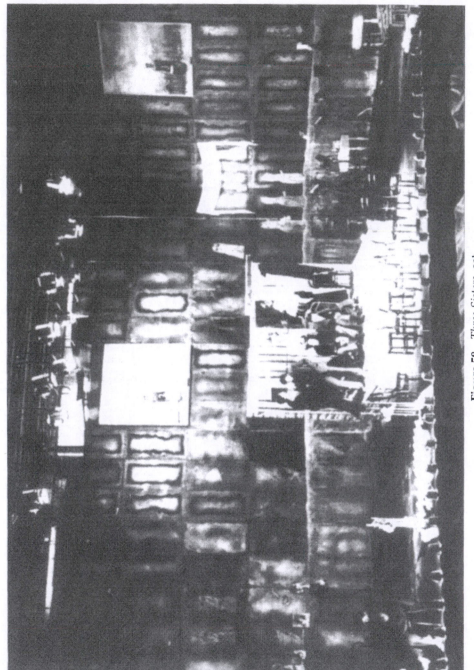

Figure 58 *Three Sisters,* set.

Figure 59 *Three Sisters*, audience and auditorium in side mirrors.

Figure 60 *Three Sisters*, open-side stage with brass band.

PART III
THE 1980s IN THE WEST

5

IN EXILE

Lyubimov's "Crime" and "Punishment"

In the 1960s the Taganka Theatre had established a special relationship with the state and Party organs. The behaviour of the representatives of the Ministry and the Main Administration was dominated by three features. First, the officials had to be prepared to justify their action at any given moment to higher organs, i.e. the Central Committee. Therefore they had to safeguard themselves by expressing ideological reservations and objections in the discussions or in the licence, even if they were willing to tolerate draft rehearsals (*chernovye repetitsii*) before official approval was given. Second, the representatives soon became both intrigued and challenged by Lyubimov's readiness to defend himself, and his energy in fighting for his work. Third, all the representatives thought of themselves not only as competent, but also as artistically creative in their own right, and therefore intervened in the director's work with their own suggestions. In a conversation in 1991, a former representative of the Main Administration expressed the sincere conviction that these discussions had helped the director to improve his work artistically. Yet, in essence, the representatives were mere puppets, and could be replaced by any other official at any time.[1]

Lyubimov's attitude throughout was that of a creative artist ready to defend his work through thick and thin; that of a Communist Party member who refused to accept a hard ideological line or the state and Party bureaucracy, and who addressed officials on an equal footing; that of a citizen who acted for the benefit of his fellow-countrymen, trying to equip them with moral values in times when the "system" had forgotten all about ethics. If necessary he would use all possible connections with the Central Committee and other organs to gain support. On three occasions he addressed letters to Brezhnev: in 1968, when Brezhnev confirmed him as the head of the Taganka theatre; in 1978, when he was exposed to a libellous press campaign in *Pravda*; and in 1981, when he made a final attempt to obtain permission to stage *Vysotsky*.

For an assessment of the extent to which the repertoire of the Taganka theatre was affected by cultural politics, bare statistics might provide only a one-sided and superficial picture. Between 1964 and 1983, four completed productions were banned (*The Tough, Protect Your Faces,*

Vysotsky, and *Boris Godunov*); the choice of plays had often depended on the controlling bodies, while other projects did not even receive permission for rehearsal, such as Erdman's *The Suicide* or Dostoevsky's *The Possessed*. However, numbers are less revealing than the manner in which the state and Party apparatus related to the theatre. The tone of the state officials in discussions after 1966/67 was invariably hostile; these representatives always dwelt on their authority (reflected in their position rather than their competence). Lyubimov objected particularly to their pseudo-competence in artistic matters: he refused to be told how to create *his* productions by officials, office workers, bureaucrats who were frequently uneducated.

The artistic quality of certain productions undoubtedly suffered from the changes required. The system of control necessitated a constant struggle against suggestions made by artistically unqualified people. In the long run this incessant conflict could provide no source of artistic or creative inspiration, but merely reinforced the "artistic individuality" of the director against the "unartistic collectivity" of the state officials. The debates may well have prompted the Artistic Council's united opposition against the state officials, and the ensemble's solidarity in defending its work. Yet ultimately, the individual, the director, the artist, was alone in defending his own creation: "Art is different in that it cannot be resolved collectively, but can come alive only on an individual basis".[2]

Lyubimov was steadfast in his opposition to any form of authoritarianism and any suppression of individuality. Even if bureaucratic control had now ceased to exist, the individual (his actions, conscience and responsibility) remained at the forefront of Lyubimov's attention. It made little difference to Lyubimov whether this individual was threatened by a régime, a system, a bureaucracy, by materialism or corruption: he was firm in his opposition to *any* system.

In the early 1980s more and more frequently Lyubimov was invited and permitted to stage operas in the West, leaving younger directors to rehearse at the Taganka theatre.

In the summer of 1983 at the end of the season Lyubimov left for London, where he had been invited by the director of the Lyric Theatre, Peter James, to present Dostoevsky's *Crime and Punishment*. At this time official pressure on the Taganka theatre had increased to such an extent that any further development of the repertoire was paralysed. In November 1982 Andropov, the former head of the KGB, who had held a protective hand over the theatre on more than one occasion (Lyubimov had allegedly discouraged Andropov's children from taking up a stage-career), had become General Secretary of the Communist Party. There was the possibility of liberalisation, of the removal of hardliners from key positions in the cultural sectors of the Party and state apparatus. Before leaving for London, Lyubimov had written a letter to Andropov, pointing out the harm exerted by Zimyanin and Demichev upon the cultural life of the Soviet Union.[3] Lyubimov's interview with *The Times* correspondent Bryan Appleyard must therefore be seen as a statement that might play into Andropov's hands: it would expose – in the West – the rigidity of the state and Party apparatus in the artistic world and thereby enable Andropov to depose hardliners such as Demichev or Zimyanin.[4] However, by the time the interview was published on 5 September 1983, Andropov had already fallen seriously ill and the hardliners themselves were in control. Lyubimov's letter fell into the hands of his enemies, and the publication coincided – tragically – with the shooting down of the Korean airliner, thus exposing the Soviet Union to Western criticism on two fronts at once, and leaving Lyubimov in an extremely delicate position.

Prior to his departure from the Soviet Union Lyubimov had been harrassed with anonymous letters[5] and he was further intimidated by Mr. Filatov of the Soviet Embassy in London; he was told that "the crime was obvious and the punishment would follow".[6] Lyubimov had his visa for Britain extended by one month on health grounds; and then he proceeded directly to Bologna, where he was due to direct *Tristan and Isolde* which opened in December 1983. In January 1984 he received the *London Evening Standard* Award for the best production of 1983. On 9 February 1984, Andropov died. A month later Valery Shchadrin, head of the Main Administration, dismissed Lyubimov as Artistic Director of the Taganka theatre because of his "lengthy absence from work" and appointed Efros to the post. Lyubimov was expelled from the Party (he had been a member since 1953) for not paying the annual membership fees, and on 26 July 1984 he was stripped of his Soviet citizenship. The régime had triumphed.

The Possessed

Lyubimov's production of *Crime and Punishment* had proved so successful that he was invited to direct another Dostoevsky adaptation in London. The choice fell on *The Possessed* which he had tried to stage in Moscow at the Taganka theatre, but the production had been banned by the authorities after six weeks of rehearsal in 1982. These prohibitions were not, however, merely a result of his particular reading of the text; no Moscow theatre was allowed to produce an adaptation of *The Possessed* at any time from the foundation of the Soviet Union until the beginning of Gorbachev's *glasnost* and *perestroika*.

Lyubimov identified a thematic connection of the two novels in the parallel between Raskolnikov's idea of power and Shigalev's theory of the despotic rule of a tenth of mankind over the remaining nine-tenths:

> *The Possessed* is a new chapter of *Crime and Punishment*. Raskolnikov foresees in his dream at the end of the novel the same apocalyptic future of a desperate and furious mankind possessed by a delirium of self-destruction.[7]

Although there are several well-known adaptations of *The Possessed*, such as those by Albert Camus and Nemirovich-Danchenko, Lyubimov chose none of these. Indeed, in 1973 Vladimir Maksimov had written an adaptation for Lyubimov, subtitled "scenic montage ... based on the concept of the director Yury Lyubimov",[8] but it was never staged by Lyubimov. Later, Yury Karyakin, author of the adaptation of *Crime and Punishment*, wrote a version, which Lyubimov used in Moscow at the beginning of the 1980s.[9] Finally, Lyubimov composed his own version, translated into English by Richard Crane.[10] All three versions adhere to the novel in the overall sequence of events. However, the emphasis on particular characters and events varies in each adaptation.

Maksimov's text is in two acts of four scenes each, preceded by a prologue, which introduces the protagonists in their typical social setting. Maksimov concentrates on Maria Lebyadkina's visit to Varvara Petrovna's, the relationship between Petr Verkhovensky and von Lembke, Stavrogin's behaviour in the past and the present, and the prophet Semen Yakovlevich; on Stepan Trofimovich's friends and the political group around Petr Verkhovensky, the literary matinée and the ball, followed by the fire, the relationship between Liza and Stavrogin, and Shatov's murder followed by Kirillov's suicide as components of Verkhovensky's plot; the finale consists of the voice of a "grand inquisitor" commenting on the burning crucifix. Maksimov omits Dasha and Tikhon entirely; in his version, the chronicler is an "author" who participates in the events rather than commenting upon them.

Karyakin's version contains three acts, with a prologue and epilogue. The prologue consists of an episode between Maria Lebyadkina and Shatov; the first act considers Stepan Trofimovich's relationships with other characters, especially Dasha and Varvara Petrovna; Maria's visit to Varvara Petrovna's; Stavrogin's relationship to Liza, Dasha, Shatov, Kirillov and the Lebyadkins; Verkhovensky's political and social activity; and Stavrogin's visit to Tikhon, with the confession read out by the chronicler. The second act comprises the relationship between Verkhovensky and the von Lembkes, the ball, the final meeting between Liza and Stavrogin, and the chronicler's report on Stavrogin's death. The third act deals with the return of Shatov's wife, Verkhovensky's plan concerning Shatov's murder and Kirilov's suicide, followed by his departure, and Stepan Trofimovich's death.

Lyubimov's version is in two acts with four and thirty-one scenes respectively, together with a prologue and epilogue. The prologue consists of songs based on the two epigraphs to the novel (from Pushkin and St. Luke). The first act introduces the protagonists, before the scene of Maria's visit to Varvara Petrovna's is developed. Then, Stavrogin visits Shatov and upon his recommendation goes to Tikhon; at this point, the play is interrupted for the interval, during which Stavrogin's confession is distributed to the audience. The second act opens with Tikhon's reaction to the confession; then, Stavrogin's relationship with Gaganov, Kirillov, the Lebyadkins, and Dasha, as well as Verkhovensky's links with Stepan Trofimovich, Shatov, Stavrogin, von Lembke, Our Group, and Karmazinov are illustrated in short scenes; next come the fête and the fire, with the discovery of the murder of the Lebyadkins; Stavrogin commits suicide and Stepan Trofimovich dies. In the epilogue, Tikhon is seen praying.

Lyubimov's adaptation reveals, especially when contrasted with the two rejected versions, first and foremost an emphasis on religion: the figure of Tikhon is preferred to that of Semen; the confession is emphasised by being placed at the end of an act; and Tikhon speaks a final prayer in Lyubimov's version. The kaleidoscopic introduction of characters is derived from Maksimov; the speed of action in the second act (with 31 scenes) is in reminiscent of Karyakin, as is the arrangement of scenes around the characters of Verkhovensky and Stavrogin. Finally, the chronicler as commentator, speaking "aside" rather than being integrated into the action, is also a principle adopted from Karyakin's version.

The Possessed was produced at the Almeida Theatre in 1985, with a set designed by Stefanos Lazaridis. This set consisted of three sides or "walls" of black elasticated vertical blinds, each approximately 15 cm wide, capable of being stretched for exits and entrances; of being loosened individually from the bar securing them to the floor and lifted to form visible entrances, porches or ceilings; finally, of being pulled across the stage. The set allowed flexibility of location in its abstract aspect, and served the purpose of moving away from a specific historical context to a more abstract one. At the same time, it fulfilled symbolic functions in its more "active" role: characters became ensnared in the black straps, as when Lebyadkin dreamed about Liza and an unrealisable union with her, or Varvara Petrovna's umbrella became entangled in the blinds while she was going "straight to see Stepan".[11] Characters, or at least their arms or heads, appeared momentarily through the elastic blinds and disappeared again, for instance when they were mentioned in a conversation on stage. This effect was enhanced by ghostly spotlighting.

Props consisted of a piano – used multifunctionally as piano, desk or sideboard – candles, torches, masks, and, above all, placards, banners and posters with the chapter headings of the novel, a technique highly reminiscent of Brecht. Placards were carried by individual actors or used by them. They formed obstacles, as for Varvara Petrovna, who stumbled over one at the mention of the scandal (I, 2) or served as props: "All in expectation" was used as a dressing table for Maria Lebyadkina, and "Our Group" formed a tablecloth at the meeting (I, 1 and II, 3); "The Cripple" was a crutch for the lame Maria; "S. T. Verkhovensky's Final Pilgrimage" formed a lectern for speakers; "Prince Hal" provided a hammock upon which Stavrogin was carried on stage at the beginning. Verkhovensky covered his face in shame with "The Wise Serpent" at Lebyadkin's words defending his deeds in front of Varvara Petrovna (II, 2); Shatov became caught up in "The Wise Serpent" when conversing with Stavrogin (II, 3); "Prince Hal" marked the limits of a room, and Lebyadkin was tangled up in "The Wise Serpent" in the scene with Marya (II, 8). S. T. Verkhovensky used his placard to disperse the "mists of autumn" he had just mentioned.[12] Moreover, placards which characterise individuals could stand instead of them: the stabbing of Maria was indicated by the stabbing of her placard "The Cripple"; Stavrogin used the banner of "The Wise Serpent" to strangle himself, and was covered by the same banner for his funeral. In this respect, "The Wise Serpent" was "his" banner, but in a more active way than was the case with other characters. When talking to Tikhon at the end of the first act, Stavrogin first hid his face in shame in the banner, and then threw it away. This echoed God's warning in paradise, which also was ignored and rejected, and which brought evil into Man's life: Stavrogin rejected the advice of the representative of God, and it was therefore only appropriate that the serpent should bring about his death.

Leaflets with Stavrogin's confession were distributed before the interval, and his announcement to make his confession publicly known actually happened. Thus, "just for once the interval served a useful purpose" to a director who dislikes intervals.[13]

Lighting effects were produced not only by the usual equipment, but also by means of props. Torches could light up faces. For instance, when Shatov and Stavrogin met at night (I, 3), torchlight allowed mutual recognition and enhanced the secrecy of their meeting. Torchlight likewise underlined secrecy in connection with the activities of the Group when identifying Fedka (II, 28). Candles emphasised the insanity of Kirillov and Maria, though their madness is of a fundamentally different origin: Kirillov is pursued by his philosophical ideas and their logical conclusion while Maria is mentally and physically ill.

Light and sound were to a certain extent interchangeable: the sound of a gun was replaced by a flash of light to mark the murder in the final scenes of the second act. On the one hand, music could synchronise movement – but it also frequently formed a counterpoint to the text.

In *The Possessed* movement often took precedence over word: attitudes to religion were expressed by gesture alone. When the actors formed a line and indicated their reactions to Tikhon's recital of the chapter from St Luke in the prologue, they held their hands behind their ears, as though to reinforce the attention they were paying to the speech, or they stopped their ears and were indifferent, glancing into the void. Movement was blatantly choreographed by the director, who in his turn reduced the actors to puppets, since precision and discipline are imperatives in choreography. Meyerhold had already been taxed with "reducing the artist to a mere puppet"[14] and Paola Dionisotti pointed out that Lyubimov indeed "sees himself sometimes as a choreographer, and us as dancers, his job to teach us the steps, ours to memorise them".[15] Gesture acquired even greater relevance since the characters had little depth: they did not act independently (frequently doing no more than act out what the narrator announced, like puppets). The device of a chronicler was used to narrate and to introduce the characters. This narrator-figure occasionally stepped in to comment, but also participated actively in the play. Roles were performed in conformity with his account; the characteristics of the people were defined, illustrated and labelled (I, 1): a self-adhesive label was actually placed on their mouth, back, forehead or shoulder. However, the narrator's account was often at odds with the event, which might be held up to ridicule through dance-like movement or formalised gesture; thus, for instance, the choreographed movement of fainting at the end of the Devil's song in the prologue, or Liputina's fainting (I, 1) subjected the act of fainting itself to ridicule. Stavrogin even became the chronicler's puppet when he enacted the striking of Shatov.[16] This device of enactment to a chronicler's narrative allowed portrayal of the "typical demeanour" of human beings in society: "Language contains gesture if it is based on demeanour, if it reflects certain attitudes of the speaker towards other people".[17]

Yuliya von Lembke led an imaginary dog on a real leash (I, 1); Liza and S. T. embraced and kissed each other while performing their actions in the empty air; riding on horseback or in a carriage was indicated by the rocking movements of the travellers. Such features not only identified the characters' social demeanour in the Brechtian sense, but went beyond that in presenting a caricature of their social habits. Maurice's mask fulfilled much the same function, reducing this figure to a mere puppet. He had no depth or function apart from doing as he is told, and was therefore given a stage-mask. Since he generally had no expression and nothing to express, it was only when he found something to say that he would take off the mask.[18] Other characters were caricatured; the most striking example was Petr Verkhovensky, who, in appearance, behaviour and gesture was a parody of Lenin – but such caricatures are also seen in the novel, where Verkhovensky is a parody of Nechaev.

The grotesque was an important device, forming a central element in both the novel and the production. The grotesque was achieved both by verbal contradiction and incongruity. Incongruity lay in the juxtaposition of the philosophical attitudes by which people were possessed and their appearance, facial expression and behaviour: Stavrogin was outwardly characterised as a dandy, but both this and his calmness failed to correspond with his political attitudes and his function in the Group: Verkhovensky pursued Stavrogin, who was impassive (II, 15); Stavrogin remained seated in his chair while Verkhovensky formulated the ideas of the Group (II, 3); he showed the same immobility in a conversation with Shatov (I, 3). However, in a scene in which he was confronted with calmness, he became restless. Maria sat placidly during the entire scene between Lebyadkin and Stavrogin (II, 8). Significantly, she was the only "authentic" character, in that she alone was able to face a mirror and hold it up to the audience (I, 1). She had an identity – even if the image attributed to her was that of a naive and mentally disturbed girl. Stavrogin emerged from the production as a revolutionary who does not want or is unable to act, and thus was in himself grotesque. His exaggerated apology (I, 1) seemed grotesquely incongruous with his elegant appearance, and he reduced the seriousness of a duel to the level of the absurd when shooting a pheasant (II, 5), which Maria then brought on stage. The grotesque found expression also in the contrast between act and word, as for example when Stavrogin led old Gaganov by the nose, after he had just said, "No one leads me by the nose, I tell you. Not me. Not by the nose. Oh no. I won't be led by the nose, not by anyone – !";[19] in Liputin's static position in the committee alongside his exclamation of enthusiasm for Shigalevism ("Brilliant!"),[20] in Dasha's having a label stuck over her mouth when Varvara Petrovna wants "a word" with her.[21] The entire scene between Karmazinov and Verkhovensky (II, 21) appeared full of grotesque, since Verkhovensky deliberately pretended not to know how to behave in order to offend the writer.

Verbal grotesque went hand in hand with incongruity: Tikhon's feigned concern with the style of Stavrogin's confession; Lebyadkin's "philosophical" answer to Varvara Petrovna's practical enquiry as to why Maria accepts money only from her, in which the philosophy consists of a recital of the poem "The Cockroach"; or Varvara Petrovna's statement that she has "come to fling everything wide open! Shut the door!"[22]

Bureaucracy was a major target of both physical and verbal grotesque: the Governor von Lembke and his family were exposed to ridicule, and on a purely verbal level such lines as "bureaucrats [have] smartly organised mutual support systems and wives with ideas", or "that's the official version. The truth is...", or "I'm a journalist. Only we're not allowed to print. So I do it by word of mouth"[23] reflected problems of both Dostoevsky's and contemporary society.

The grotesque formed part of a carnivalistic atmosphere which characterised not only the stage production, but also Dostoevsky's work. It was one of the means devised to convey the novel's complex structure, resulting from the tension between its two main protagonists, Verkhovensky and Stavrogin. Lyubimov claims that:

> Dostoevsky's heroes cannot be presented on stage as real characters. In the *"polyphonic"* structure of the novel, – to use Bakhtin's terminology – each character embodies a philosophical option of the author's, a fragment of his personality.[24]

Characters were thus reduced to representing existential alternatives; therefore it was not the political vision of *The Possessed* that should interest and matter to us, but its philosophy:

> *The Possessed* is not a political pamphlet. I would rather call it a tragic farce. The ideological opposition is neither the most important aspect of the novel nor what renders it so crucial and topical today. Dostoevsky mocks the Slavophiles, the Westerners, and the quarrel that opposes them.[25]

It is the destiny of Russia, in thrall to the ideas of Slavophiles and Westerners, that matters to Dostoevsky; but it was the impact of those ideas on people which lay at the core of Lyubimov's production. Ideas enslave people, 'possessing' them to the extent of distorting their very appearance, turning them into puppets.

The pace of the production varied, movements were performed in a dance-like way, the rhythm of the performance was accelerated to a degree that transformed it frequently into grotesque. Scenes grew shorter and shorter towards the end, the chaos on stage increased, the music became ever more agitated, and ideas developed too quickly to take real shape or acquire any depth. Thus even the scene in which Stavrogin and S. T. Verkhovensky enacted a discussion of their ideas was staged in an accelerated tempo; Karmazinov's reactionary poem, on the other hand, was recited slowly, and his voice sounded like a record player at the wrong speed. The audience was invited to laugh at a production which seemed exaggerated and bizarre. Yet even as they laughed, they were themselves parodied and mocked as Dostoevsky's characters engaged in political combat and mutual destruction for the sake of ideas, because by the time those ideas had been realised, the ideas were distorted and man was destroyed; human struggle was exposed as a vain masquerade of the absurd; all acts were absurd, ridiculous; social conventions such as politeness, enthusiasm and apology were taken to their extremes, and the void appeared from behind the mask. At the end of the production, the living were left to cradle the dead: "The Dead descend on the living, who cradle them in their arms and rock them like their own souls".[26]

This production should be appreciated for its theatricality; the adaptation of a Dostoevsky classic for contemporary society was achieved by using an abstract and symbolic set, by accelerating the speed of the performance and by making people and their deeds and words subject to the grotesque and absurd. The form of the production turned out to be as chaotic as the profusion of ideas, and the actor was reduced to a puppet in the same way that man is obsessed by political ideology.

However, both audience and press in Britain reacted with little comprehension and great astonishment to the "sheer profusion of theatrical devices".[27] According to the newspapers, the production "cannot hope to provoke anything but admiration for its technique",[28] the "very theatricality of the piece precludes dramatic involvement",[29] and Lyubimov's role was reduced to that of a "puppeteer", directing a "disciplined team of puppets".[30] In failing to relate Lyubimov's approach to Continental and Russian traditions of theatre, the press and audience certainly did not find in the production what they seem to have been looking for: a substitute for reading Dostoevsky's novel. Lyubimov's first attempt to direct a new theatrical production in the West had thus failed, at least in the eyes of the audience and the critics.

6

LYUBIMOV AT THE OPERA

A development in three stages may be discerned in Lyubimov's work in the opera, although these temporal divisions may not be as clear-cut as in the theatre, since operatic contracts often depended on external circumstances. In the first phase (1974–1983), Lyubimov attacked opera traditions and conventions. The second period (1982–1988) witnessed a preoccupation with the theme of society versus the individual, showing the individual as a victim of social conventions. In the last stage (1985–1990), faith and religion were the main concerns, both offering solace for the individual.

Towards a new opera (1974–1983)

While artistic director of the Taganka, Lyubimov had produced several operas in the West, mostly at La Scala, where both Luigi Nono and Claudio Abbado appreciated his creative innovations.

Lyubimov had staged his first non-theatrical production and his first production outside the Taganka theatre in 1974, when he directed Boris Tishchenko's "choreographic meditations" *Yaroslavna*, based on the epic tale of Prince Igor, at Leningrad's Maly Theatre of Opera and Ballet.

In April 1975, he achieved his first production in the West, at La Scala in Milan: *Al gran sole carico d'amore*, a "scenic action" by Luigi Nono.[1] Nono's libretto was co-written by Lyubimov and Borovsky, drawing on material by Bert Brecht, Che Guevara, Maksim Gorky's *The Mother*, Lenin, Marx, Arthur Rimbaud, Cesare Pavese, the Cuban revolutionaries Celia Sanchez and Haydée Santamaria, the Bolivian guerrilla Tania Bunke and the anarchist and the Paris Communard Louise Michel. The theme of the opera is the role of women in rebellions, from the Paris Commune through the Russian and Cuban revolutions, to the Italian Resistance. Women emerge as a consciousness-raising force; the title of the piece is drawn from a poem by Rimbaud about the Paris Commune. The opera offers no chronological account of the rebellions, but aims at evoking associations via analogies, and is thus poetic in its structure. This corresponds to Lyubimov's work in the theatre during his first years at the Taganka, when the project was started: textual montage, poetic structure, and a clear political stance dominated both the opera and Lyubimov's theatre productions.

In 1977/78, Lyubimov was invited to stage Tchaikovsky's *The Queen of Spades*, which was due to be premièred at the Palais Garnier in Paris in July 1978 in a new, modernised version created by Lyubimov himself and Alfred Schnittke. The project ended with one of the greatest scandals in the history of French–Soviet cultural relations: in an interview published in *L'Humanité* during a visit to France in November 1977, Lyubimov had expressed his criticism of Soviet cultural politics with regard to state subsidies for his theatre. *Literaturnaya gazeta* subsequently attacked the "false" statements made there,[2] and defended itself against a counter-attack launched by Lyubimov, in which he pointed out inaccuracies in the translation of an interview printed in *L'Unità*.[3] Algis Juraitis, conductor of the Bolshoi Theatre, managed – without the permission of the director of the Paris Opéra, Rolf Liebermann – to see the project at the Opéra in Paris, and published an article in *Pravda*, attacking Lyubimov and Schnittke for "the destruction of the great heritage of Russian culture" by turning the opera into an "Americanised musical", of "immorality in dealing with Russian classics" and "mockery of a masterpiece of Russian opera", and of using a "pseudo-pretence of 'contemporisation' of the classics to torture and mutilate this great music..."[4] Accusing them of insincerity and lack of originality (only a copy, not the original, of the letter had been sent), the chief editor of *Pravda* refused to publish a reply from the three accused, Lyubimov, Schnittke and the conductor Gennady Rozhdestvensky; this reply then appeared in *Le Monde*.[5] In their letter the authors enumerated errors in Juraitis's article and justified the changes in *The Queen of Spades* with references to Tchaikovsky's correspondence. However, the Ministry of Culture cancelled the contract with the Opéra (which had already advertised the première, ordered the set design and contracted the participants and which subsequently made a loss of four million francs).[6]

The changes made in *The Queen of Spades* for the Parisian project concerned the libretto, and were designed to bring the romanticised version by Modest Tchaikovsky back to Pushkin's story: the death of Hermann and Liza were omitted; instead, Hermann became insane, and Liza sought refuge in an arranged marriage. The love-motive was neglected in the relationship between Hermann and Liza, as was the motive of revenge for Eletsky. The choruses in the Garden scene were cut, as well as Eletsky's and Tomsky's major arias. Harpsichord music accompanied the additional comments on the action. This first attempt to renew a classical opera was thwarted by the Soviet authorities.

In the following years, Lyubimov staged *Boris Godunov* at La Scala, not in the widely used version by Rimsky-Korsakov, but in the reconstructed original version by Paul Lamm. The stage was dominated by an icon of the Virgin Mary, underlining the religious motif and reducing man to a small creature in comparison to Mary. Similarly, in Mussorgsky's *Khovanshchina*, Lyubimov rejected the Rimsky-Korsakov version in favour of Shostakovich's, adhering more closely to Mussorgsky's original.

After restoring original versions of Mussorgsky's operas, Lyubimov's experimentation now extended to operatic form. In May 1982, he directed Mozart's *Don Giovanni* in Budapest. This time, he broke with opera convention by placing the orchestra on stage, setting Leporello as a violinist in their midst, and turning the orchestra pit into a hell, from which Don Giovanni emerged and later disappeared.

In the following year, Lyubimov staged his first Wagner opera, *Tristan and Isolde*, in Bologna. For the first time, he made a substantial change in an opera itself: he integrated into the plot the personal and biographical background of the composer. Wagner's friends, the Wesendoncks, were not only referred to in the foyer, where their names were placed together with Wagner's on a table reservation, but they appeared together with Wagner in a prologue and epilogue; Wagner turned into Tristan, Otto Wesendonck into King Marke, and Mathilde Wesendonck into Isolde for the performance. The set, built by Stefanos Lazaridis, was an abstract, wooden construction, representing a frame with mirrors, broken up by openings that looked like zoom lenses: here flashbacks or journeys into the mind took place.

With *Salammbô* (Naples and Paris), Lyubimov returned to the re-creation of original versions. The opera, unfinished by Mussorgsky, was performed here for the first time in a reconstruction by Zoltan Pesko, who managed to preserve its fragmentary nature. As with *Tristan and Isolde*, the composer appeared in the production in a dialogue with Flaubert during the prologue and epilogue. Borovsky's set consisted of nine panels with a sand-colour material and a matching backdrop to represent Carthage.

Thus, in his first opera productions, Lyubimov experimented with form: in *Al gran sole carico d'amore* with that of the text, in *Don Giovanni*, *Tristan and Isolde*, *Salammbô*, with that of the music.

Social conventions versus the individual (1982–1988)

While striving for formal innovations in the opera, Lyubimov centred his productions around the theme of the individual versus society, which had been his preoccupation at the Taganka throughout the 1970s.

In April 1982, *I Quattro Rusteghi* was premièred in Munich. The choice depended not on Lyubimov, who wanted to stage Verdi's *Nabucco* or *Macbeth*, but resulted from internal difficulties with choirs at the

Bavarian Opera House. The 'opera buffa' was staged with elements of slapstick and commedia dell'arte. Set in the eighteenth-century Venice of Goldoni, the production reduced man to the level of a puppet, performing doll-like movements, and often corrected by the additional figure of a harlequin: man was subject to, and victim of, conventions.

Berg's *Lulu* (1983) was staged in Turin with a set by David Borovsky, which reflected the 1930s, when the opera was composed. The atmosphere is one of military power, dominated by the colour grey, and backed by a metallic construction, behind which only a few flowers were visible, representing a dehumanised world. Lattices covered the orchestra pit, and rose to form the cage for animals in the prologue, or the prison for Lulu after her murder of Schön. A pierrot followed Lulu as her double, and the heroine was seen as a prisoner of convention: she was a poineer of sensuality, a sensuality destroyed by social conventions. Society was perceived as destructive, since it drove Lulu to commit crime. She thus became a victim of society, trapped in a prison of social conventions and her own criminality, from which she could escape only after death.

Under the impact of the loss of his theatre, and faced with the impossibility of returning, Lyubimov staged Verdi's *Rigoletto* for the Florence May Festival (Maggio Musicale) in 1984. The production caused a scandal in the press, since several singers and the conductor left owing to the intolerance of the soprano Edita Gruberova, whilst the press attributed these conflicts to excessive demands from the director. Lyubimov returned to Verdi in making the plot a-historic, in abolishing the temporal distance which had been used by Verdi and Hugo to satisfy the censors. Puppets of seducers and historical dictators were suspended in a semicircle and formed the set, including a puppet theatre at the back, and three black figures embodying Monterone's curse. Gilda sat on a swing to "follow" the duke, where she should also sing her final aria, but Gruberova refused to do so; this device was meant to underline Gilda's naïvety in her firm belief in Mantua's love. The assumption that "clothes make man" was challenged: both Rigoletto, leaving his jester costume in front of his house, and the duke disguising himself as a student were unable to change character with costume: Rigoletto remained the jester, hired by the aristocracy, and Mantua remained a seducer. The aristocracy was shown as lacking human feeling. Verdi's scepticism and depressive and negative view were taken up by Lyubimov: he refused to accept the deceptively utopian tone of the opera.

Fidelio was premièred on 28 November 1985 in Stuttgart. Contemporary directors have met with difficulties in convincingly presenting Beethoven's utopian vision, according to which all the prisoners would be liberated at the end thanks to the personal initiative of Leonore. The synecdoche of "love to free one person" for "solidarity to free all prisoners" was rejected by Lyubimov in this production. He challenged the utopian ending, replacing it by the release of Florestan only, a Florestan mentally crippled by the conditions of his imprisonment: "A political faux-pas is being corrected. Nothing changes in the system based on military power".[7]

The stage was transformed into a prison, framed by metallic lattices, and with a pit crossed by a bridge representing the prison from which the prisoners were led. The tyrant Pizarro, dressed as a general, resumed his position as supervisor of the events on the central balcony, normally reserved for the Minister President, before entering via the auditorium. Meanwhile, the audience was surveyed from all the doors in the auditorium by men wearing trenchcoats and bowlers, reminiscent of KGB agents, who "released" the audience for the interval. The system represented was universal, as was the theme of the imprisonment of innocent people. The audience was reminded of this universality by a programme composed largely of reports from Amnesty International. The hope Beethoven sought with his utopian ending had disappeared: reality and history taught a different lesson. The production concluded with a requiem to those remaining in prison: candles were placed along the metal lattices of the prison, to which pictures were attached of those missing or still imprisoned. Lyubimov's *Fidelio* did not end on the triumphant finale, but on the initial adagio tune of the *Leonore* overture No. 3, halted before the triumphant allegro. Again, the director returned to the composer's original version.

Lyubimov's production of *The Master and Margarita*, the opera by the exiled East-German composer Rainer Kunad, was a copy of his Moscow production. However, Berlin Wall graffiti covered the back and side walls, emphasising that Kunad shared Lyubimov's fate of exile.

Eugene Onegin was produced in Bonn in 1987. It ended in a scandal: Lyubimov refused to attend the première, since he expected it to be a technical failure. On the opening night, stage hands could be seen crossing the stage to overcome defects. *Literaturnaya gazeta* used this debacle to demonstrate the "failures" of Lyubimov's work as a whole, and to attack his "profanation" of the classics.[8]

Although Pushkin's signature was projected onto the curtain before the start and during the intervals, no attempt was made to get closer to Pushkin's irony and away from Tchaikovsky's sentimentality. The set was composed of Petersburg iron gates, which opened and closed, and a set of screens at the back which were used for projections and shadow play. The shadows reflected and anticipated events, and revealed the psychology of the characters, especially of Tatyana:[9] as she composed her letter to Onegin, Onegin's enlarged shadow appeared and grew incessantly, while letters were dropped from the ceiling. Tatyana's conscience played a central role; everything was perceived through her mind.[10] The fences served to segregate parts of society: peasants were excluded, high society stood on a bridge formed by the railings. The fences symbolised the prison of convention, which Tatyana could leave only in her dreams.[11] In spite of the interesting concept of Tatyana's psyche exposed in visionary images on screens, and of her mind imprisoning her, this central image remained technically undeveloped. Nevertheless, Lyubimov's concern with the human mind and conscience could be recognised as a central feature of this production.

Tannhäuser, staged in Stuttgart in 1988 in the Parisian version, detached the plot from its historical background: contemporary costumes were used, with Duke Hermann appearing in the costume of Wilhelm II, on the balcony of the Minister President. The stage floor was covered by the pattern of a labyrinth; screens and shutters were placed in a semicircle around the stage and opened to reveal images of nature or the figure of the Pope in the background. The theme of the conflict of the bards was perceived as an attack on the individual's right to exist: Tannhäuser was banished, sent to Rome, because he had broken sexual conventions in admitting his enjoyment of Venus's seduction. Unconventionally, Venus died with Elisabeth and Tannhäuser at the end: Venus and Elisabeth, erotic and spiritual love, complemented each other. After their death, a little girl with a "Venus doll" appeared next to them: continuity was ensured.

In these works, Lyubimov focused on the individual in conflict with social conventions. On the one hand, society was perceived as having a crippling effect on individuals such as Lulu and Tannhäuser by its imposition of sexual taboos; the social and political system crippled the individual in *Fidelio*. On the other hand, the individual imposed self-censorship on his mind and thereby crippled himself, as did Tatyana in *Eugene Onegin*; man allowed himself to be reduced to a puppet, a marionette used by those in superior social positions in *I Quattro Rusteghi* and *Rigoletto*.

Religion as refuge? (1985–1990)

In exile, Lyubimov's view on the individual in the grip of social conventions became pessimistic and negative. Faith appeared to be man's only refuge.

In the production of Bach's *St Matthew Passion* in the church of San Marco (Milan), a cross of melting ice was used as the central symbol: it was weeping, dissolving itself, vanishing, as was belief in God. This was a vision of the apocalypse of religion.

Jenufa, staged in Zurich and London in 1986, pursued this religious aspect. The set (by Paul Hernon) consisted of an empty stage, the boards of which could be lifted to form houses, walls, a well (where the child was found), or trunks (to reveal the dowry shown to the guests before the wedding). The changes of the seasons (autumn, winter and spring) were symbolically announced by groups of people scattering leaves. Revolving side panels, black on one side, white on the other, reflected the positive or negative turn of the stage events. The slashing of Jenufa's cheek was marked by red cloths appearing on the rotating side panels. The grave of the murdered child was at stage front from the start: Kostelnicka stood there as Steva rejected Jenufa in favour of Karolka; the grave and the cross on it had their shadows enlarged on the back wall: there, Kostelnicka took the child to be murdered, and there, to the reflection of the cross, she withdrew after Jenufa had forgiven her. Laca and Jenufa, on the other hand, were united by the real grave. The loss of the child was what mattered to Jenufa, whereas Kostelnicka was concerned with the observation of conventions, appearances and reflections (she could not face the shame of Jenufa having an illegitimate child). A distinction was made between ideal and real loss. But for both Jenufa and Kostelnicka, the way led to the cross, to religion. Social conventions ruined their lives, and only religion offered hope and consolation.

Rheingold was premièred on 29 September 1988 as the preliminary evening of the Ring cycle planned (for 1988–1991) at the Covent Garden Royal Opera House as a collaboration between Haitink and Lyubimov. Lyubimov withdrew from the contract in December 1988 after disagreements between Paul Hernon, Bernard Haitink and himself.

The set consisted of a disc 10 feet in diameter, which could be turned round, moved up and down, or sloped. It served as the base where the Rhinemaidens play with Alberich. Loge emerged from the hole in the centre of the disc, with little flames around him, and Wotan and Loge descended into Nibelheim by the same route. Screens at the back wall opened and closed like lenses, as if the images appearing there were visions. A green cloth covered the stage for the entrance of Wotan and Fricka, replacing the garden where they awake. A white cloth was used for Alberich becoming invisible: a Disney-like snake and toad crawled out to represent his transformations.[12] Wotan's spear symbolised power: it was placed in a beam of light when Wotan's authority was in question.

The giants Fafner and Fasolt walked on stilts, wearing greatcoats. Loge was schizophrenic, dressed in a half-black, half-red tail suit. The Nibelungs were reduced to shades which became manifest in the opening of the back wall, lit in red, as a bevy of blacksmiths. The figure of Justice, a woman in black carrying scales, was added to the plot: she gave the spear to Wotan, when the giants captured Freia, when Wotan took the ring from Alberich, when Wotan handed the ring to the giants, and when Fafner and Fasolt fought over the gold. At the end, Loge removed the centrepiece of her scales, which had the form of a cross, and presented it to Wotan. Wotan was perceived as a just ruler, with Justice weighing his deeds. Northcott perceived here a Christian interpretation.[13]

The cycle was never completed, and it is therefore difficult to assess the overall concept for the *Ring*, although Lyubimov has referred to his treatment of *Rheingold* as an 'opera buffa', whereas he would perceive *Walküre* as tragedy, *Siegfried* as fairy tale, and *Götterdämmerung* as modern opera. The concept he would try to pursue was defined thus: "I'd like these operas to take us through the range of operatic art. At the point where the genres merge, something new occurs".[14]

The Queen of Spades was finally staged in Karlsruhe in November 1990 in the version elaborated for the Parisian opera. The design, created by Borovsky, turned the stage into a terraced construction, with the lower terraces occupied by the orchestra, and the upper forming a roulette table, the central section of which could be lowered to allow for exits and entrances. Thus, the stage was a casino, with the orchestra playing for both the audience and the gamblers. The predominance of the gambling motif was in line with the concept of the opera, which dwelt on Hermann's obsession with gambling. As this obsession grew, the action was increasingly perceived as if through Hermann's mind, such as the ball scene, in which the Countess, Liza and Eletsky dance around Hermann, sitting on his bed; they represented hallucination rather than reality. Similarly, the Countess appeared in her bedroom, located in a ditch formed by the converted table-panels now in vertical position and functioning as mirrors; she saw Hermann only in the mirror, hence his threat with the pistol was for her merely a reflection – and an illusion. The roulette tables turned to vertical position and became mirrors again at the end, blurring once more the line between illusion and reality. Dozens of actors appeared as the Countess's doubles when Hermann lost the game: he was now suffering from paranoia.

Symbolic use was made of the colour red to signal danger: the three light bulbs over the tables indicated the 3, 7, ace when Hermann gambled; Tomsky pulled out a red kerchief when about to tell the Countess's story; a red chair stood by the table for Hermann when he was attracted to the dangerous game; a red cross, and later the face of Christ were projected onto the golden backdrop when the theme of belief was concerned: Hermann has no real belief, but merely superstition; such "belief" is dangerous. Gambling to Hermann is the only hope, the only belief in an ideal: cards were scattered on a lightpath before the death of the Countess and before the game. Hermann became insane at the end, maniacally repeating "3, 7, ace . . .".

The production shifted the emphasis onto the theme of illusion and reality within the insane mind of a gambler. Lyubimov's *The Queen of Spades* pointed out that Hermann was obsessed from the start, hallucinating, perceiving reality as illusion and illusion as reality. The destructive effect on an individual of an obsession, here gambling, was analysed: obsession not only destroyed the individual, but turned his belief into mere superstition. *The Queen of Spades* thus combined the twin themes of obsession and belief, blending the two lines Lyubimov had pursued in the West in his productions of *The Possessed* and *Jenufa*.

Although Lyubimov was able to continue his artistic work while in exile, he was largely deprived of his native roots and traditions. He faced a new dilemma in the West: whereas censorship had destroyed his productions in Moscow, where man was oppressed by the absence of truth in society, materialism may destroy both man and the arts in the West.

Lyubimov's work at the Taganka theatre and in opera reveals a parallel development. First, he broke with conventions, striving for formal innovation. Having opened new ways in his formal approach, he proceeded to the theme of society as an oppressive and destructive force exerted against the individual. Finally, there could be no refuge, no salvation for the individual apart from religion. However, faith was prey to deformation (superstition) and destruction (atheism). The apocalypse, a total loss of moral and human values, spiritual impoverishment, and the reduction of man to an empty shell were the impressions Lyubimov took back to Moscow from his experience in the West, when he returned to Russia to direct *The Feast during the Plague*.

However, a new theme emerged from his work in the opera: at that point where religion is, in its distortion, no longer able to provide a refuge for the human soul, the aesthetic principle in art becomes a new value in itself. This was the idea Lyubimov had intended to develop in the unrealised *Ring*.

Figure 61 *Boris Godunov*, riding scene.

Figure 62 *Boris Godunov*, the pretender (Zolotukhin) by the fountain.

Figure 63 *Boris Godunov*, Vorotynsky and Shuisky.

Figure 64 *Boris Godunov*, finale: Yury Belyaev, Elena Gabets, Yury Lyubimov, Nikolay Gubenko, Feliks Antipov, Rasmi Dzhabrailov.

Figure 65 *The Feast during the Plague*, Dona Anna: Alla Demidova and Don Juan: Valery Zolotukhin.

Figure 66 *Elektra*, Elektra: Alla Demidova.

Figure 67 *Zhivago*, Zhivago: Valery Zolotukhin and Tonya: Lyubov Selyutina.

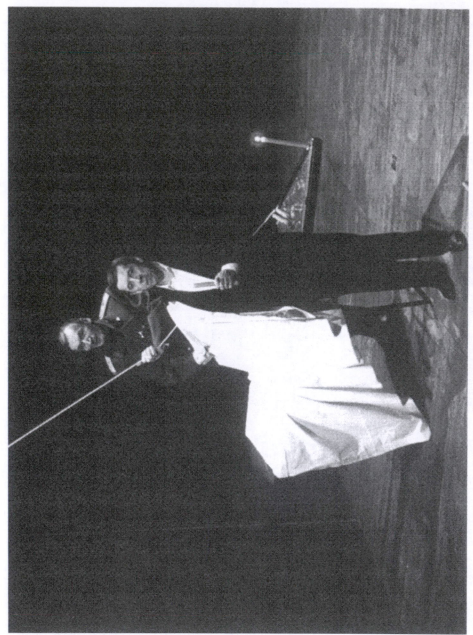

Figure 68 *Zhivago*, Strelnikov: Aleksandr Trofimov and Zhivago: Valery Zolotukhin.

Figure 69 *Zhivago.*

PART IV
MUSICAL VISIONS FOR THE 1990s

7

THE RETURN OF THE "MASTER"

Ever since Lyubimov's exile in 1984, the Taganka theatre had been under the direction of Anatoly Efros.[1] Much has been said and written about the three years Efros worked at the Taganka theatre; very little is factual, and most articles are charged with emotion, initially with anger, later with remorse.[2] Efros was not accepted by a large part of the ensemble, since he had taken the post without the consent of the theatre or Lyubimov. The collaboration between Efros and the Taganka ensemble therefore turned out to be a continuous struggle: Efros attempted to create a repertoire bearing his own aesthetic stamp with Lyubimov's actors, who tended to reject this concept since they had been trained in a different tradition, and only partly accepted Efros's style. The result was five new productions in the three years Efros headed the theatre. It must be said that Efros tried to preserve Lyubimov's repertoire, yet he had to capitulate *vis-à-vis* the Authors' Rights Agency (VAAP), which insisted that no adaptation written by Lyubimov could be played in order to avoid having to pay him royalties;[3] this, unfortunately, meant the removal of a substantial number of productions.[4] Nevertheless, Efros found himself accused in the Western press of deliberately ruining Lyubimov's repertoire. Similarly, rumours were spread that Efros had Lyubimov's office re-painted, thus destroying all the signatures and dedications on the walls; however, this painting work had only affected the walls in the auditorium of the old stage, which used to be black and had now been painted white, limiting thereby the effect of the "light curtain". The accusation itself shows that every opportunity was taken to defame Efros.[5] Efros died of a heart attack on 13 January 1987.

After his death, Nikolay Gubenko, an actor in Lyubimov's ensemble, who had in his career as a stage actor alternated with Vysotsky, took over the direction of the Taganka theatre, with the consent of the Taganka ensemble. Gubenko abandoned his activity as a film director and set himself the task of bringing Lyubimov back to Moscow. His attempts suffered a severe blow in March 1987, when a letter signed by ten leading émigré dissidents and expressing their doubt in the sincerity of Gorbachev's reforms was published in *Le Figaro*.[6] At the same time Gubenko, who had no experience in directing for the theatre, was hesitant about staging a production at the Taganka. From about April

1987 to the autumn of 1988 he revived: *The Master and Margarita; Listen!*; the "author's evening" *In Search of a Genre*; and finally *The Mother*, a production which was invited to Madrid in March 1988, marking the first invitation to the West of a Lyubimov production and the first meeting of the ensemble with Lyubimov after his exile. Moreover, Gubenko started to rehearse *Vladimir Vysotsky* and *Boris Godunov*, and had both productions ready for Lyubimov to review and rehearse in May 1988, when he came to Moscow for ten days on a private invitation by Gubenko. Both *Vladimir Vysotsky* and *Boris Godunov* were premièred during or shortly after Lyubimov's visit.

However, the Taganka saw only one première of a play not previously in the repertoire: Marina Tsvetaeva's *Phaedra*, directed by Roman Viktyuk. Gubenko's policy of reviving old productions was severely criticised in a press campaign in the Moscow newspapers in the autumn of 1988; the attacks were launched by a letter to *Moskovskaya pravda* from the actor Dmitry Pevtsov, who had joined the Taganka under Efros. Gubenko was reproached for reviving only old productions and removing most of Efros's works from the repertoire. Some theatre critics agreed with Pevtsov's attack, while others defended Gubenko's role at the Taganka.[7] Even if Gubenko's activities restored some of the history of the Taganka theatre by reviving its "lost" productions, he himself could not contribute to a further development of the aesthetics of the theatre. Thus, Gubenko's situation as director of the Taganka theatre was delicate, and although he acted with the support of many actors, critics and spectators, he was also subjected to severe attacks, which were to some extent justified and understandable. The Taganka theatre therefore needed a new production, if only to justify Gubenko. It can be argued for Gubenko that, along with the revival of old productions, he had managed to include in the repertoire those productions which had fallen victim to the cultural policy exercised by the authorities during the Brezhnev era, such as *Boris Godunov* (closed in 1982) and *Vladimir Vysotsky* (banned in 1981). This had become possible due to vast changes in the cultural politics of the Soviet Union. Within a year in office, Gorbachev had replaced all the hardliners occupying key positions in the cultural sectors: Vasily Zakharov was appointed Minister of Culture (succeeding Demichev); Boris Eltsin took over the Moscow City Committee from Viktor Grishin; on the Central Committee level, Egor Ligachev became responsible for ideology in the Secretariat (succeeding Zimyanin), Aleksandr Yakovlev was put in charge of the Department of Agitprop, and the editor and poet Yury Voronov became head of the Department of Culture (succeeding Shauro).[8] The subordination of theatres to Mossovet's Main Administration of Culture was formally abolished in 1987, when artistic and economic freedom was granted to those theatres taking part in an administrative experiment. The Taganka theatre participated in this experiment which was designed to create a period of transition towards self-management and self-financing, and which was introduced with the new law on theatres in 1991.[9] Theatres were still subsidised by Mossovet, but control was initially referred to the newly founded Union of Theatre Workers, and later abolished entirely. Thus, theatre censorship in the form in which it had existed under Brezhnev had ceased.

Hence, both the Taganka theatre itself (with its new director and the ensemble) and Lyubimov (speaking more and more frequently of his desire to return to his theatre) were ready for a return of the "master". In January 1989 Lyubimov was back in Moscow, and in December 1989 his Soviet citizenship was restored and he regained the artistic directorship of the theatre after Gubenko had been appointed USSR Minister of Culture. During the 1988/89 and 1989/90 seasons Lyubimov prepared the première of *The Tough* (23 February 1989), directed *The Feast during the Plague* (30 May 1989), revived *Crime and Punishment* (December 1989) and released *The Suicide* (24 July 1990), while still fulfilling his contracts abroad (*Hamlet* for the Haymarket Theatre, Leicester and *Lady Macbeth of Mtsensk* for the State Opera House, Hamburg).

By the time of the 1990/91 season, theatres were undergoing major reforms to facilitate their transition to market structures: sponsoring became possible and necessary in view of insufficient subsidies from Mossovet to pay for sets and costumes, premises could be let to secure extra income, and the contract system was encouraged. Lyubimov was quick to understand the need to run the theatre more efficiently – not least thanks to his experience in the West. On 8 December 1991, virtually on the eve of the collapse of the Soviet Union, Lyubimov signed a contract with the mayor of Moscow, Gavriil Popov, which was intended to introduce a contract system for the company members and give Lyubimov first refusal to buy the theatre should it be privatised.

Gubenko, having lost both his post at the Taganka and his ministerial appointment with Gorbachev's resignation in December 1991, attacked Lyubimov for not staging enough productions (to keep everybody on the payroll busy and thereby create a pretext for not sacking any members of the ensemble).[10] In the same month, Gubenko formed the "Fellowship of Taganka Actors" which was joined by those who felt dissatisfied both with the power Lyubimov had acquired through this contract and with his long absences for productions in the West.[11] The Fellowship asked Yury Luzhkov, Premier of the Moscow Government, to divide the theatre, but no action was taken.

In September 1992 the Fellowship appealed to Eltsin to agree to a division of the theatre; Eltsin insisted that a vote be taken. In October the vote went in favour of a division, which was confirmed by Mossovet on 28 April 1993. The matter was referred to the Moscow Arbitration Court, which confirmed Mossovet's decision. In July 1993 Gubenko occupied the new stage of the theatre with the support of a special militia unit and people's deputies, shutting off all connecting doors or corridors between the old and the new stage.

At the opening of the thirtieth season on 8 September 1993 the Taganka actors read a letter by Lyubimov in which he declared the theatre closed until its full use was restored, since he would be unable to perform a number of productions designed exclusively for the new stage. In the same month the Appeals Court annulled the earlier decision in favour of Gubenko and returned the theatre to Lyubimov, although the theatre remained "occupied" by the Fellowship. In December 1993 the Higher Arbitration Court reviewed the matter and decided in favour of Gubenko. On 28 April 1994 Yury Luzhkov reversed Mossovet's initial decision and passed the entire building into the hands of the Taganka company, arguing that the premises were designed for use by one company only; this decision was reversed by the Arbitration Court on 26 May 1994. The Appeals Court again decided in favour of Lyubimov, but the Higher Arbitration Court on 12 September 1994 urged the two parties to try to reach a settlement outside court. This proved impossible, and on 14 October 1994 the Taganka company was asked to remove all its property from the premises of the new building. The new building comprises 9146 square metres, the old building 2006 square metres. The theatre complex is not designed to be divided; there is an essential unity in the arrangement of administration, wardrobes and storage areas.

Soviet censorship seems to have been replaced by a Russian struggle for power between the Arbitration and Higher Arbitration Courts and the Appeals Court, between Mossovet organs and the Moscow government, between the Federal Government and the President.

In January 1995 Nikolay Gubenko was elected to the presidium of the Russian Communist Party led by Gennady Zyuganov while Yury Lyubimov arrived in Moscow to rehearse *Medea* for a co-production with Athens.

8

MUSICAL HARMONY
AND THE DOOMED INDIVIDUAL

As early as the 1960s Lyubimov had already used elements of the carnivalesque to enhance the democratic picture of society; Brecht's notion of street theatre further developed this notion of democratic participation by the audience. Elements of folk theatre emerged naturally in the attempt to return the theatre to past traditions: folk songs and the *chastushka* were frequently employed; the people (*narod*) became omnipresent on stage. It was therefore a logical and consistent step for Lyubimov to turn directly to elements of ritual and to the tradition of folk theatre in *Boris Godunov.*

Boris Godunov and conscience

Lyubimov's last production for the Taganka theatre before his exile, Pushkin's *Boris Godunov*, was banned in December 1982 before its première could take place. According to Lyubimov, *Boris Godunov* was stopped because the Main Administration saw a parallel between Andropov (who had come to power on 12 November 1982, shortly before the première) and the pretender (*samozvanets*).[1] The Western press attributed its closure to the fact that the production promoted the view that governments change at high speed, and yet the people continue to suffer, no matter who rules.[2] However, Lyubimov had rehearsed *Boris Godunov* throughout 1982, *before* Brezhnev's death and Andropov's accession. This did not prevent the Main Administration from closing the production before its scheduled première on much more trivial grounds, such as Zolotukhin's interpretation of the role of Dmitry, the finale with the Russian orthodox chant "Eternal Memory", and the Soviet Navy shirt worn by Dmitry; the officials also complained about the absence of costumes and about the programme, which did not assign actors to specific parts and permitted the doubling of actors for various roles.[3] The discussions took on a sharp tone when V. Seleznev, head of the Theatre Administration in the Main Administration of Culture, claimed that Lyubimov's office was state property and that Lyubimov had no *right* to be there. Lyubimov left the office in a fury and complained to Chernenko (General Department of the Central Committee) who angrily referred him to Zimyanin (Secretariat of the Central Committee). The latter threatened Lyubimov with expulsion from the Party (which would almost certainly have implied a removal from office).[4]

At this point, Lyubimov saw his repertoire crushed: *Vysotsky* and *Godunov* had been banned; permission for rehearsals of Erdman's *The Suicide* and Dostoevsky's *The Possessed* was refused.[5] It was not the number of petty interventions, but the accumulation of outright bans which put a halt to the development of Lyubimov's aesthetics.

Pushkin's *Boris Godunov* had remained unstaged for many years after its composition, and was regarded as a play for reading rather than staging. There had been only a few – and mainly unsuccessful – productions of *Boris Godunov*.[6] The reasons for this were numerous: the drama was written in blank verse, its episodic structure encompassed twenty different locations in twenty-three scenes, and the integration of mass and folk scenes posed a further problem for the stage. Yet Lyubimov overcame these difficulties by using a variety of theatrical devices and presented a successful stage version of *Boris Godunov* which remains a landmark in Soviet theatre history, even though it was not officially premièred until six years after the final dress rehearsal.

Boris Godunov was set on a bare stage, bounded at the back by the natural border to the scene, the red brick wall with windows and doors for exits and entrances (see Figure 55). The props were few and multifunctional: two chairs were removed from the stalls and placed on stage at either side; there was a wooden board, a crozier, a signpost and a bucket of water. The signpost, placed front centre, indicated "Asia" and "Europe" to either side of the stage; it stood not only for the different origins of Dmitry and Boris – Dmitry is of Polish-Lithuanian, Boris of Tartar origin – it also referred to the historical and geographical division of Russia, past and present, or even legend and truth.[7] The crozier was a symbol of power: Boris thrust it to the front centre stage, and both Dmitry and Boris laid their hands on it, physically announcing their claim to the throne. The plank or board could be placed across the chairs to represent the inn near the Lithuanian border where Varlaam and Misail get drunk and meet Grishka (the false Dmitry) during his flight. They placed imaginary glasses and a real cabbage on the board before crawling under it when the soldiers came searching for Grishka and – underlining their power – stepped onto the board. In the scene "The Lithuanian Frontier", the false Dmitry and Kurbsky rode horses: both imitated the movement of riding on the swaying plank (Figure 61). Basmanov used the board as a see-saw when trying to decide which side to take after Godunov's death and the rise of the usurper. Godunov leaned on it when talking to his son before his death: it was held up like one bar of a cross. He was then placed on the board, lying on his back: it now formed his death bed. When Kseniya and Fedor were killed, this too was done on the board: two swords were driven into the plank placed above the two, before Dmitry stepped on it to declare that they had poisoned themselves. The visual contradicts the verbal, and reveals the lie.

The bucket contained water, which was tipped onto Grishka's face when he awoke from his dream, while still in the monastery. It was filled with golden coins which were poured over Godunov for the ritual of his coronation. To Mniszech, the bucket represented a bottle of old Hungarian wine. But the bucket's most unusual function was at the fountain: the old, corrugated, dented bucket had a leak, through which a thin stream of water trickled as Dmitry said: "And there is the fountain", as he pointed to the bucket (Figure 62). The costumes were not specific; they were drawn from all periods of Russian history. Godunov wore a *khalat*, an oriental robe, a sign of his Tartar origin; Dmitry originally sported a Soviet sailor's shirt (Figure 62), although a parallel to the Revolution was soon feared:

> Dmitry played out his role of rebel and adventurer in a striped sailor's blouse – until a request from government officials to mute revolutionary associations induced Lyubimov to discard it.[8]

It was replaced by a shirt with a "D" embroidered on it – initial of the pretender and emblem of the Moscow "Dinamo" football club, which was founded by Dzerzhinsky for workers of the internal security forces (militia and KGB). Shuisky wore a leather coat reminiscent of those worn by the Cheka at the time of Dzerzhinsky; a *shinel*, a Gogolian overcoat, was worn by Vorotynsky (Figure 63); the patriarch was all in white. This mixture of costume and the unspecified distribution of roles created a carnivalesque atmosphere:

> The absence of props, by throwing the actors back on basic skills of their craft, complemented costuming and music in creating a free carnival atmosphere. Lyubimov's reference to Bakhtin was deliberate and particularly crucial to the performance in formulating theatrical communication. The carnival modality eliminated barriers between actors and audience by suggesting a common shared space and aesthetic time unbroken by conventions; theatrical and socio-political constraints were ignored in this small universe in favor of open address. The last spoken lines were typical; the participation in political expediency and political hopelessness before changes in the government, thus, became a personal rather than a historical issue for the audience.[9]

Pushkin's text was used almost in its entirety in Lyubimov's production; only a few cuts were effected in the scenes "Sevsk" and "A Forest", while

"A Plain near Novgorod-Seversk", largely written in French and German, was omitted. Special emphasis was laid by Lyubimov on the rhythm of the text: it should not be declamatory, but pronounced in a natural manner and addressed to the audience.

The spectators were integrated into the production: the auditorium was frequently flooded with light, for example when Boris Godunov doubted the pretender's identity. But more importantly, the text carried contemporary connotations for the actors, which they communicated to the audience. Indeed, Lyubimov persistently dwells on the contemporary and concrete significance that classic texts may carry:

> The word in Lyubimov's productions is perceived as if it literally belonged to the character, the actor and the author at the same time... The director and the performers are able to identify contemporary intonations in the speech of the past.[10]

The structure of *Boris Godunov* is episodic, and this might account for Lyubimov's special interest in it; the Taganka was familiar with a fragmentary structure thanks to its numerous adaptations of literature. The episodes were linked by a chorus – a device reminiscent of Greek theatre. However, this chorus provided more than a musical unity and comment. All the characters emerged from it and returned to it; Godunov walked round it at the very beginning to hear how it was tuned, i.e. to listen to the people's opinion about him taking the throne. The chorus *was* the omnipresent people, the *narod*. Not for one moment was an actor alone on stage: Dmitry listened to Godunov's monologues as much as Godunov listened to those of the false Dmitry; they even met physically on stage, although in Pushkin's original text they never talk to each other. They sat on chairs opposite one another, and both tried to lay their hands on the sword, image of power. The *narod* was the true protagonist, who decided who should gain power: by their physical presence the people tipped the balance as to who would reign. One after another, they turned away from Boris's son Fedor, appearing at the same window as Kseniya, only to run to the next, where they joined Dmitry and Marina. It was the opinion of the people which made Dmitry stronger than Basmanov and his army. At the same time, the chorus underlined the equality of the characters: they came from and returned to the crowd. Therefore the programme made no distinction between the actors and their parts, and the actors frequently played more than one role, often representing similar attitudes.

Folkloric tradition and ritual were used as a formal means to unite the thirty actors permanently on stage. At the same time, the singing (*raspevka*) was a rehearsal and training technique for actors. Thus, theatre presented itself on stage in the form of folk singing and choral rehearsal.

As a metatheatrical statement including rehearsal practices, finally, the opening reminded the audience that aesthetic generalization and communication, in this instance, were shaped in the specific verbal and kinetic procedures of the theatre.[11]

The dominant feature in the portrayal of Boris Godunov was his conscience; on various occasions he stopped his ears and closed his eyes to the utterances of the people when they referred to his crime. A boy in white appeared several times in the production: when the murdered Dmitry was mentioned, when Pimen talked about him, and when Godunov dreamt about the murdered child before he died. The boy does not exist in Pushkin's text; he is a vision of the boy Dmitry appearing in front of Godunov, who cannot efface the murder from his tormented conscience. Symbolically, the child would sit on Godunov's chair before he did.

Boris Godunov was shown as a wise politician rather than an unscrupulous murderer. His conscience was guilty and this made him hesitate to rule; he was haunted by the vision of the boy.

> Boris's tragic flaw ... is his inability to recognize that politically necessary acts such as murder neglect the religious-moral code of his culture which shapes conscience.[12]

> The idea of the production is to mobilise the conscience of every man alive. The only thing that can save us is our conscience.[13]

On his deathbed, Godunov was visited by the Patriarch, who – according to the ritual of the Russian Orthodox Church – performed the tonsure of the dying Tsar; he threw scissors thrice across Godunov, who had to pick them up and hand them back to the Patriarch. At this point, the boy in white held the candle, the sole source of light in the scene. Only the confession of the murder can bring atonement, only repentance can lead to the light.

Dmitry, on the other hand, was ridiculed. When woken up with cold water in the monastery, he left the bucket over his head for several moments. In the scene with Marina, laurels – symbol of power and victory – were tipped over his head; they came from a sachet. Moreover, in the scene at the fountain, Dmitry met the power-hungry Marina Mniszech, while he was obsessed with the woman Marina. The scene showed a struggle for power, waged first by Marina, then by Dmitry. He was humiliated by Marina, before he in turn humiliated her by depriving her of all the accessories of her beauty: wig, fur, belt and jewels were taken off her until Dmitry regained the power he had given away by revealing his devoted love and confessing to being the "False" Dmitry in front of her. He was also mocked by Varlaam, Misail and the police when his description (given in the arrest warrant) was compared to his real appearance in the scene at the Lithuanian border.

The finale accomplished the integration of the audience into the production. Nikolay Gubenko, the actor who had played the part of Boris Godunov, entered via the centre aisle onto the stage, dressed now in a suit. He placed flowers on the board, where the murders of Kseniya and Fedor had been committed, and where the usurper had taken up position; then he turned to the audience, pronouncing the words originally spoken by Mosalsky: "Why are you silent? Shout: Welcome Tsar Dmitry Ivanovich!" (Figure 64). The chorus sang a chant from the Russian Orthodox liturgy ("Eternal Memory"), while full light was directed into the auditorium. The audience was thus told that the people have the power to choose their rulers. Yet if we, the audience, know that the new Tsar is the false Dmitry, then why are we silent? Yet the silence does not stand for mere "voicelessness", but for moral silence:

> The theatre does not talk about the silence of the people, but when its conscience is silent, it is transformed into a dumb conformist, a mass of philistines, and on its millions of shoulders pretenders climb, one after the other, to power.[14]

By their presence, the people have the power to vote for their rulers; they have the duty to make sure that they are not ruled by a pretender. There is a move away from the tragic tone of *Hamlet* back to the optimism of *The Good Person of Szechwan*. However, several devices indicated a move in a new direction: the preoccupation with Godunov's visions and the tortment he inflicts upon his conscience; the use of ritual and religious music; Grishka's renunciation of his clerical origin (by wearing sailor's clothes); and finally, the homage paid to Godunov's murdered children at the end of the production. All these features revealed an emphasis on ritual and religious elements.

These religious aspects were drawn to a conclusion in the funeral chant for Godunov's children; they have been murdered by the people's silence concerning the pretender's rise to the throne.

> "Eternal Memory" ... tells of the impossibility of detaching either politics as a whole or a single human act from morality, the impossibility of exempting from examination the only objective criteria that humanity has worked out for its history – criteria of morality, as concisely and exhaustively expressed in the Christian Ten Commandments.[15]

There was no appeal at the end, as in *The Good Person of Szechwan*, but a reproachful challenge: Why do you, knowing the truth, not act, but remain silent? Why does your *conscience* not revolt? The audience applauded – at its own silence. The spectators in the theatre had seen a memorable production; in the contemporary social setting, they could speak up without getting into trouble.

> The audience is now different, it is silent only in the theatre, but on the whole, it has become more daring and says what it thinks. But to remind them once more of those times when all held their tongues is indeed worthwhile.[16]

The production had made theatrical contact with the audience, but the theatre had now lost the spectators' understanding with the changed social context; this production of *Boris Godunov* had clearly originated in the so-called "period of stagnation". The audience had changed along with the liberalisation under Gorbachev. The theme of the change of rulers at the expense of the people was relevant in 1982, but not for the spectator of 1988. Similarly, the religious note was certainly unusual and daring in 1982, but by 1988 this was no longer the case, and several critics commented on the obsolete style of the production.

> The favourite theatrical means of the director – illuminating the auditorium for those phrases which he considers essential to accentuate – seem unnecessary and archaic today. Formerly, every word was literally marked in italics. The religious motifs of the production, which five years ago seemed propagandistic of an alien concept of the world – today, in the millenium of the Christianisation of Russia, seem merely a modest tribute to the great historic jubilee.[17]

Reference to religion, which had once been daring to talk about, was now almost a commonplace. The production had, by the time of its première, already lost that relevance to contemporary problems for which productions at the Taganka were so well known. Yet the production retained some meaning for the contemporary spectator in its appeal to permanent moral values and to the human conscience. It was certainly a landmark in theatrical history for successfully bringing Pushkin's "armchair" drama (written for reading rather than staging) to the stage.

However, the move towards folklore and ritual helped the production to preserve some of its former topicality: at a time when the audience was no longer in need for solidarity or appeals, it was directed to its roots and common origin, to its unity. Moreover, the theatre spoke directly to the audience's conscience on a philosophical and moral rather than a politically explicit level. But to what extent communication on such a level was possible and even desired by the audience remained questionable. Here Lyubimov moved distinctly away from a theatre rooted in political reality towards a theatre of ritual:

> *Boris Godunov* is staged as a ritual, and the musical elements are also ritual: the
> lamenting, singing and praying. Ritual theatre is the strongest and most
> profound form. It takes away the superficiality of everyday theatre and looks for
> the utmost intensification. The ritual has to be known; it has deep roots, and the
> sources have to be understood, they are very important.[18]

People are urged not to forget traditions, roots and rituals, and above all
not to forget the belief in God, for these unite people even at times of
political upheaval: "[The Taganka] was the only theatre where people
went as if to church – to clear themselves of the lies that pervade our life,
and to communicate with the living word of truth and art".[19]

The Feast during the Plague and death

Lyubimov recognised the need to address the audience in a different way
and with different issues; yet he was to refuse to cater for the audience's
taste in employing all the devices formerly frowned upon or the texts
banned from Moscow repertoires. His concern was no longer with
political change but with ethical and aesthetic issues.

Pushkin's *Little Tragedies* was premièred on 30 May 1989.
Although it was the first new production after a series of revivals at the
Taganka, Lyubimov had already staged *Little Tragedies* in Stockholm in
1986 with a slightly different set design, based on the contrast between
black and white.[20] The Moscow version was performed on the new rather
than his favourite old stage; and the cast drew together the leading actors
of the ensemble: Alla Demidova, Leonid Filatov, Valery Zolotukhin, Nina
Shatskaya, Natalya Saiko, Feliks Antipov and Ivan Bortnik. The production bore the title of one of the tragedies, *The Feast during the Plague*, which
is justified both by the textual and theatrical interpretation.

Pushkin's text was restructured, expanded, cut, and mingled with
other texts; in short, Lyubimov did everything he could to give more
conservative critics good reason to attack his treatment of a classic work.
The Taganka version consists of twelve scenes, of which the first and last
form a prologue and epilogue respectively. The sequence of the *Little
Tragedies* has been changed: *The Covetous Knight* is followed by *The Stone
Guest*, which is broken up after the third scene (ending with the statue
moving after Don Juan's invitation) for the interval, after which it
is continued, followed by the major part of *The Feast during the Plague*,
and by *Mozart and Salieri*. Extracts from *The Feast* also occur as an
introduction and transition between the other tragedies. The production

concludes with an epilogue, Pushkin's *Scene from Faust* (1825). The texts of the tragedies have remained largely unchanged.[21]

The character of Clothilda has been created from Albert's mention of her in *The Covetous Knight*, but she plays a more comprehensive role, which will be discussed later. Some verses have been added for the characters of Dona Anna, Don Juan, Mozart and Margareta, together with some songs for the interludes and a recital by Laura in *The Stone Guest* of Marina Mniszech's monologue from *Boris Godunov*. Apart from the fact that *The Feast* is used as a structural link between the tragedies, the individual plays are themselves broken up when the scenes change: they are introduced and concluded by the female characters Mary, Louisa and Clothilda.

Thus, the textual base for the production has seen three major changes: first, *The Feast* is used as a theme for all the tragedies, as a point from which they start and to which they return; second, the addition of *Faust* for the epilogue, and third, the insertion of songs and verse in the interludes and the introduction. The last of these compositional devices, the recital of verse, helps to create a rehearsal atmosphere, from which the production begins. The introductory scene, or the prologue, thereby creates a statement about the function of theatre in underlining that the action to follow is a result of rehearsals, a product created from a situation of improvisation and recital, thereby emphasising its theatricality.

"[*The Feast during the Plague*] is, on the whole, a production about life and death. In different types, we see different figures. We see immortals, like Mozart, and mortals, like ourselves".[22] Formally, the motif of death determined the set design. The set was created by starting off from the bare stage, with its large space unlimited. The sides consisted of a metal network covering the theatre equipment; at the back was the red brick wall of the new stage, partly covered in the centre with some white panels. The decoration occupied a mere tenth of the space: a table stretched along the front edge of the stage. This table, covered with a black cloth, was multi-functional: the table itself represented the grave of the Commandant in *The Stone Guest*; it served as a bed in the scene between Laura and Don Juan in *The Stone Guest*; and it turned into a trunk (with the treasures) in *The Covetous Knight*. When the tablecloth was held up at either end and people stamped to the rhythm of horse-riding, it became part of a carriage; it denoted several horses in the scene of the Duke's arrival in *The Covetous Knight* or Don Juan's arrival at the monastery after exile and later in Madrid in *The Stone Guest*. The set design was dominated by the non-colours black and white. The characters were all dressed in black costumes. They were seated around the table in chairs on casters, on which they could roll to the back and return to the front, but they hardly ever moved independently from their chairs (only for exits and entrances). The table was laid for the feast, with glasses, wine, artificial fruit decoratively displayed in a bowl, and little glasses of spirit, which was burnt at the start of the banquet and to commence the major scene of *The Feast*.

White lilies, a black rose (both artificial), a magnifying glass, a tray, coins and a little devil puppet were the only props. Moreover, masks made out of white plaster, which looked as if they had been cast from the faces of the actors who wore them, portrayed the characters in a condition close to death. They were worn by all the actors at the beginning, when the Young Man mentions the plague,[23] when death glances at Don Juan after his challenge to the Commandant and the latter's appearance, with all the actors standing by the windows at the back wearing their masks, ready to leave before or enter after the interval. The masks were also held to the actors' faces at the end. Moreover, Shatskaya always held a mask in front of her face for the lines she spoke as Clothilda.

Clothilda did not play a role in any of the tragedies, but merely commented and interrupted with her songs in the interludes, and with her macabre laughter, transmitted by an amplifier, for instance after the death of Don Carlos or the Baron. She was the embodiment of death. Furthermore, the central chair at the table was empty. It was the chair in which characters died; they fell into the hands of death – Clothilda if they occupied it.

A cross was frequently projected either on the back wall or to one side, either when a character died (Don Carlos, Baron, Mozart), or when death was mentioned (the carriage with the victims of the plague passing, Leporello's mention of the statue's opinion of Don Juan's love for Dona Anna, the movement of the statue and its appearance to make its protest, the Baron's mention of his grave when talking about his fear of death), or at the mention of God and his blessing (the priest, the plea to save Margareta), or to warn Don Juan, when he shows no remorse for the murder of the Commandant, and he looks at the fainted Dona Anna through the magnifying glass (Figure 65).

> More and more frequently heroes freeze in front of the cross, shining out of the darkness, like a sign of retribution, like a request to come to one's senses. The meaning of sin and redemption, the understanding of the biblical Ten Commandments are for Lyubimov, and even more so for Pushkin, neither empty sound nor simple Christian moral, but an entire philosophy, interpreted in a moral programme of art.[24]

The roles were distributed between six actors (the seventh is Clothilda), four men and two women. All acted both positive and negative characters, victims and murderers,[25] and they were continually present on stage; if they were not participating in the action, they withdrew with their chairs to the back and resumed some fixed positions. However, their omnipresence was in this case not reminiscent of a carnival structure: the action was static, and the atmosphere depressed. The people were dying in the streets, and the characters on stage represented only a small segment of the crowd.

Music and sound were drawn from a wide range of sources: the amplified laughter of death by Clothilda, songs sung by Shatskaya and Saiko, Jewish melodies for the scene with the Jew, religious motifs, classical themes by Bach and Mozart in *Mozart and Salieri*, the film score of Mikhail Shveitser's *Little Tragedies* (1980; Vysotsky played the part of Don Juan), and Okudzhava's song "You cannot turn time back"[26] sung at Laura's party, as well as the music composed by Alfred Schnittke especially for the production. This music carried themes, accompanied, set counterpoints, underlined the rhythm and content of Pushkin's verse, spoken with regard to the caesura and according to sense and punctuation, rather than in a declamatory manner. The music did not, however, obtrude in the production, nor did it play an independent role. Text and music were inseparable, as in an opera, and indeed, as in opera, music accompanied almost the entire text. This intrinsic link between melody and word, the nearly operatic treatment of a text such as Pushkin's, which has a musical intonation itself, was most certainly not only a result of Lyubimov's theatre work, but also of his wide experience with opera productions in the West. It was therefore no coincidence that the name of the composer stood next to that of the director on the programme.

In the individual tragedies, certain aspects of the stage interpretation deserve special attention. *The Covetous Knight* was dominated by the metaphor of money: the Baron counted it on a tray; Albert plunged his hand into the pile of coins when considering that, if the Baron lives a long life, he might not receive his inheritance until he is himself an old man: the sound of the coins was rendered over an amplifier. Albert was noticeably eager to put money in his own pockets after managing to acquire some from the Jew: the father's obsession continues in the son, even if less strongly. The Baron even wept into his handkerchief at the thought that other people, including his son, might squander what he had saved, cherished and treasured: he sat on the table (representing a trunk), spitting in disgust at the audience as a potential owner. His obsession was emphasised as he looked at a doubloon through a magnifying glass in order to appreciate fully the beauty of the coin. When he died, coins were placed on his eyes.

Often characters said something contrary to what they were thinking; Lyubimov used here the device of the "Freudian slip". The Baron made up the story about his son as he spoke, thus filling with meaning the suspension points in Pushkin's text; he then shook his head in negation to the Duke's question as to whether he had any children, before answering "One son".[27]

His merits as a knight were subjected to strong doubt by the director: whereas the Baron sported a helmet to demonstrate his origin and rank, the Duke wore a simple hat; when mentioning his readiness to fight with his sword, he showed a fork to the Duke; hence also the omission from his speech of the lines expressing his concern about Honour, a moral value for knights, but not applicable to the Baron as portrayed on stage.

In *The Stone Guest*, Lyubimov sharpened the point about Don Juan's passion for women: his treatment of Laura as his property was made abundantly clear in the way he carried her around on his shoulders, and the finale of the second scene was sexually explicit with Laura lying over the table-bed, while Don Juan stretched and bent her legs. Leporello carried a list of his master's mistresses, arranged in alphabetical order. Property played an important role in the scene between Dona Anna and Don Juan: when Don Juan declared his readiness to sacrifice all his possessions for her, he removed his rings and dropped them upon a tray, a gesture which Dona Anna repeated, symbolically consenting to be purchased at that price. Later Don Juan held a magnifying glass above Dona Anna, who had fainted, as if to inspect his newly acquired property. The duel between Don Carlos and Don Juan over Laura had a similar effect; it took the form of a fist fight, which Don Carlos lost. He was then covered with the black cloth and his hat to mark his death, leaving Don Juan as the "owner" of Laura. When Dona Anna and Don Juan remarked that Don Juan had risked his life by coming, a piece of paper was burnt and the ashes were blown away by Don Juan, as if this symbolised the value of his life when confronted by a woman such as Dona Anna.

In *Mozart and Salieri*, candles played a significant role: they were lit and extinguished by Salieri when he decided to poison Mozart. Mozart later lit the candles again, but extinguished them when he left, poisoned, into the auditorium. The essence of this tragedy lay in the mutual incompatibility of murder and genius for Mozart, which made it impossible for the murderer Salieri ever to become a genius, which had been a prime motive for his killing of Mozart. Doubt was cast upon Salieri's "ear for music": when this was mentioned, the scraping sound of a tape could be heard, discordantly on fast forward.

An overall theme of the four tragedies was that they all highlighted a lack of character in the protagonists: the Baron's miserliness and his obsession with property, that deprives him of conscience and renders him the victim of his own passion; Don Juan's lack of respect for Laura,

Dona Anna, and the Commandant by treating them as objects, his passion for women which makes even murder unproblematic for him; Salieri's jealousy of Mozart's talent, which drives him to murder. Faust fits into this gallery of ruthless figures: he concluded a pact with the devil, and was infected by a psychological or mental form of plague.

The Feast looks also at human disregard for the effects of plague on the outside world, which leaves the guests untouched even by the appeal of the priest. These are all "little" tragedies, formally united as a whole by all the characters of the little tragedies becoming participants of the feast: it is the "little tragedies, which lead to the great tragedy – that of the plague".[28] Thus the motif of the plague, of impending death, is the core of the tragedy. The whole world seems to be infected. This image, both literally and symbolically, dominates the production: "The time, space and condition of existence of the guests at the feast is defined by one theme – plague or death".[29]

At the very beginning, the audience was reminded of the circumstances of plague, of the danger of infection, when a disinfector, wearing a gas mask, came to spray the stage, the table and the guests. All the characters covered their faces with white handkerchiefs, and the side wall of the auditorium was opened to let in some fresh air.[30] The guests at the table indicated with their heads the open wall when the Master of Revels (Antipov) spoke the lines "The plague clasps us, around us is quarantine, nowhere we can go... Our town is doomed to blazes and winds".[31] The wall opened up again in the second act, when the priest mentioned the "common grave",[32] into which the plague drives its victims, indicating at the same time that the plague was outside, in the city of Moscow, thus highlighting the contemporary relevance of these lines and of the entire theme of the play.

The priest, Mozart and the Commandant were the only figures who ever stepped into the auditorium; they are, notably, all essentially good and honest characters.

At the end of the epilogue of *Faust*, at Faust's words "Everything is sinking", interpreted by Mephistopheles as a direct command, a white curtain to the right side stage was inflated like a balloon, extending over the right half of the auditorium. The audience was thus drowned, threatened by the plague, infection and death. The cause was clear: the death of morality. Unfortunately, contemporary spectators had lost the habit of looking for the meaning behind allegories, symbols and metaphors, at a time of a more open journalistic style, with the overt exposure and discussion of problems. Aesopian language was no longer deemed a necessity. The short applause was rather for the actors than the production; the latter was largely disregarded by the critics. The only comprehensive review was published by Natalya Kazmina in *Teatr* in May 1990, an entire year after the première. She looked at the form of address to the audience and in her analysis provided clues for the lack of interest aroused by the production. When Faust says "I am bored, devil",[33] the lights went up in the auditorium:

> But there is no challenge, as there was before in *Godunov*... We are all "bored" (serious, wretched, terrible, fatal), we who have lost orientation and direction not only outside, but inside ourselves. Like the boat that Faust proposed to sink.[34]

Kazmina outlined Lyubimov's position in the changed situation of 1989. As in earlier years when he had directed the Taganka, he was again an outsider, standing outside the mainstream: "When all around raise the alarm and proclaim an anathema over the declining world, Yu. Lyubimov teaches us to live with the impossibility of real life".[35]

Without doubt, the combination of musical, visual and verbal elements in *The Feast during the Plague* reflects Lyubimov's experience as an opera director. The theme and form are general rather than specifically Russian, corresponding to the apocalyptic vision conveyed by the production, which also has a universal significance and is not restricted to a particular place or country. The production speaks about a widespread loss of moral values: in the ensemble, the theatre, the country and the world; it is a loss that threatens a theatre such as Lyubimov's which is based on moral values.

This production notably inverts all the creative devices formerly so relevant to Lyubimov's theatre. He always dwelt in his productions on the carnival atmosphere as a source for action; the movement on stage was so extensive that often choreography was needed to articulate it. He thereby introduced an optimistic – because active – element. Here, however, the carnival atmosphere was deliberately suppressed, the action was forcefully made static, and hence the dominant mood became pessimistic. The audience was threatened with drowning and disinfection, deprived of any space for action to bring about change. In that respect, the production of *The Feast during the Plague* is an extreme point of negativity, in the aesthetic sense, in Lyubimov's work. Yet while he perceives the collapse of personal and political principles, the cataclysm threatening the world, Lyubimov never loses the creative energy which responds to the life-force. His is the eternal struggle of man against his absurd existence; human existence may be limited by death, but man strives for eternal life. "Life resists death, as the soul resists the plague."[36]

Simultaneously, another aspect emerges in a rudimentary way in this production: the beauty of form, the aesthetics of art. As emotional and rational argument have failed to equip man with the moral values and the dignity to survive as a human being in our time, the beauty of form replaces the appeal, aesthetics replace ethics.

> Human dignity in an era of apocalypse – this is, in general terms, the main theme of contemporary high art. But to find and to understand the theme of the time is, although very important, still not enough. Form is needed ... the very special, imperative reliability of form.[37]

> [*The Feast during the Plague*] is about the conscience of art. About death, which awaits us all. About age, which we must not fear. About beauty, which, perhaps, saves the world. Or perhaps – it does not.[38]

Both *Boris Godunov* and *Feast* are tragedies of the nineteenth century. Both were written by Pushkin. The theatre's preoccupation with Pushkin echoes its previous predilection for Brecht. If Brecht was the founder of the epic theatre, then Pushkin may be considered as the founder of the *narodnyi teatr*, a popular theatre. Lyubimov is thus making a statement about taking a new direction. However, the *narod* in *Boris Godunov* is different from that in *Feast*: in the first instance it is active, in the second static. Yet both plays show their protagonists in extreme situations: how people live with murder – be it that of Dmitry, Don Carlos or Mozart, and with the responsibility for the death of the Baron or the people perishing in the plague.

Elektra and forgiveness

Lyubimov's turn to Sophocles's *Elektra* and thus to Greek tragedy came somewhat as a surprise in his repertoire, yet it logically reflects his persistent interest in characters in extreme situations: here, one murder has been committed, and it is revenge which is the central theme.

Agamemnon, King of Mycenae, sacrificed his daughter Iphigenia after upsetting the Gods by shooting their deer. Upon his return, he is killed by his wife Clytaemnestra and her lover Aegisthus. Elektra, his daughter, having sent her brother Orestes away lest he be murdered too, now awaits his return, so that he may take revenge. Her sister Chrysothemis refuses to take part in this vengeance. Orestes's death is reported, plunging Elektra into deep despair; yet this turns out to be a plot to ascertain Aegisthus's absence. Driven by his Elektra's need for revenge, Orestes kills Clytaemnestra, and later Aegisthus. For Elektra, revenge is her predicament, her destiny and her doom.

Elektra was premièred in Athens in May 1992, before opening in Moscow that September. Lyubimov brought this tragedy of ancient Greece to the present day by means of décor and costume (David Borovsky): the set consisted of corrugated metal panels with slits in them, which encircled the stage on three sides; in the central panel, a revolving glass door allowed access to and from the back stage. Above the door, neon letters indicated the name of a hotel, the title of the play: Elektra (Figure 66). The tragedy was thus transposed onto the streets of any city: the doors represented the entrance to a hotel as much as any palace doors.

> *Elektra* is consciously set in the bloodstained revolving door. In Athens, there is a hotel called *Elektra* which has just such a revolving door. Hence the name *Elektra* on top of the door. It is as though the action were happening outside the hotel, as really happens sometimes. There is a hint that such an action can occur in the present, too: the actors emerge and play outside the hotel *Elektra*.[39]

The palace doors were closed for Elektra, who, banned from the place where her father's assassins lived, crouched against the wall at the beginning of the production. The doors also fulfilled a more symbolic function: immersed in red light, they represented the turning of the wheels of fate. At the same time, they were reminiscent of a mincing-machine, into which Clytaemnestra and Aegisthus were thrown at the end of the play, when they were murdered by Orestes. The slits in the panels allowed onlookers to observe the scene: they could be spectators in the street, or observers in Mycenae, where constant caution was needed in order not to be overheard.

The costumes were equally contemporary and symbolic. They were dominated by the colour of blood. Elektra wore a red dress, Clytaemnestra a red raincoat, and Aegisthus a dressing gown. Props were scarce: an urn, a bowl of water, a picture of an ancient Greek head to underline Elektra's noble origin. Some scenes were rendered in a visually simplistic way: Orestes poured gravel onto a table, which he wiped away when he claimed that he would "purify and cleanse" the house of his fathers.

The music composed by Sofiya Gubaidulina accompanied most of the dialogue. Occasionally the sound of distorted voices from behind the metal wall produced an echo effect. There was one moment when the musical pattern underlying the production and serving to reinforce the heroine's emotional dilemma was disrupted: rock music was inserted in the scene between Elektra and Clytaemnestra. On the one hand, this demonstrated that Lyubimov was not concerned with who was right and who was wrong at this particular moment: Clytaemnestra claiming to have killed Agamemnon because he sacrificed her daughter, or Elektra arguing that her mother was guilty of committing the murder. Secondly, as the rock music was amplified, a young boy came on the stage: an observer, a casual passer-by who is sent away by the priest.

> An accidental tourist runs onto the scene. He sees a feast, a carnival, and timidly tries to join in, then realises that they are playing after all, apologises and leaves. This dislodges the action. The tourist enters centre stage at the point of culmination, when Elektra says: "If I could, I would commit the crime myself" when she is at the height of her revenge.[40]

The main parts in this production were played by Alla Demidova (Elektra), the Moscow Arts Theatre actress Ekaterina Vasilieva (Clytaemnestra). Both acted without pathos. Yet whereas Elektra was calm, determined in her fanaticism, Vasilieva was "vulgar, like market women and ladies of the demi-monde, like the criminal or bohemian and dissident audience".[41] Both actresses largely relied on gesture: they raised their arms in shock or horror, and this gesture was repeated by the chorus. Elektra's hand was often placed in a spotlight or onto a lightpath, indicating the symbolism of the hand as murder weapon; in a lightpath the hand became the emblem of fate: Elektra is following her destiny. She believes that her fate is to avenge her father's murder. She is doomed by this idea, and fails to realise that "vengeance, once started, cannot come to an end".[42]

A significant change in the interpretation of a Greek tragedy lies in the use of the chorus. In the play, the chorus of the women of Mycenae serves to comment, and to warn Elektra against pursuing her design. In the production, the chorus of women was dumb: they only expressed their attitude to a given situation by means of movement and gesture. The lines intended to be spoken by the chorus were given instead to an orthodox priest. While the chorus of women in Sophocles is supportive of the right moral choice and remains loyal to Elektra, in Lyubimov's production the chorus (the people) remain dumb: the people cannot give Elektra any support, they merely stand in silence, expressing shock or amazement, or repeating Elektra's gestures. Moral values in ancient Greece were clearly defined, they could easily be grasped by the people; moral choices in the twentieth century are much more complicated than mere adherence to a fixed moral code. Verbal support comes from the priest: in faith, not in the people, a human being finds support and moral guidance.

Elektra is obsessed by revenge and fails to listen to the priest's advice not to turn the wheel of vengeance further. Blood will have blood. There is the need to introduce an element of forgiveness and compassion, which is underlined in the production by the strength with which Chrysothemis refuses to participate in Elektra's vengeful plans. "The concept is simple: revenge brings no good, only blood. Revenge engenders revenge, nothing else. I rejected the heroic concept, the myth".[43] Both forgiveness and compassion are, however, concepts absent from Greek mythology, which is preoccupied with notions of honour and duty; these qualities belong to Christianity. Again, Lyubimov seems to warn of the danger of a loss of moral values, as he had done in *Feast*.

> The founder of the theatre has long seen the precipice that threatens to engulf his fellow citizens, and not for the first time he has sent them an alarm signal.[44]

Many reviewers grossly misinterpreted Lyubimov's conception of *Elektra*: they merely sought a political allegory in the production and thus overestimated the parallel to bloodshed in Russia. One critic even drew attention to the production's lack of eroticism, which was indeed an oddity in the Russian season of 1991/92, but hardly strange for a Greek tragedy. Lyubimov's *Elektra* was a "challenge to contemporary kitsch, ... to contemporary character fragmentation, ... to the stupiditys that governs the contemporary theatre"[45] and as such stood out from the Moscow theatre of that time.

Zhivago and doom

The same is true for Lyubimov's last production in the thirty years of the Taganka theatre discussed in this book, Pasternak's *Doctor Zhivago*. Upon his return to Moscow in January 1989 to rehearse *The Tough*, Lyubimov already spoke of his repertoire plans in terms of a production based on the poetry of Pasternak and Akhmatova. Indeed, Lyubimov's version of *Doctor Zhivago* concentrates more on the poems than the prose. Yet since the production was commissioned by a Western producer for the Vienna Festival, its commercial success very much depended on the title of the novel. Since any performance of the novel is bound by the copyright, which is held by the Italian publisher Feltrinelli, the production was entitled *Homage to Zhivago* (Vienna) or *Zhivago* (*Doctor*) (Moscow). The première took place in Vienna on 18 May 1993.

Inevitably, the novel had to be condensed to remove ephemeral characters and events. Yet, in any case, Lyubimov concentrated on the metaphorical rather than the descriptive aspect of the prose. His adaptation divided the work into two parts at the point where the novel breaks for the beginning of the second book with the arrival of the Zhivagos at Varykino. Whilst following the chronology of events in the novel, Lyubimov omitted only the last chapter and thereby the character of Tatyana, the daughter of Yury and Lara. Moreover, Lyubimov inserted Aleksandr Blok's poem *The Twelve* to complement Pasternak's description of the revolution and civil war and to create an analogy with the present.[46]

> I inserted Blok, because I did not want to depict realistic scenes of cruelty, despair, and bloodshed... I was annoyed with the interpretation of Blok's *Twelve* as a poem symbolic of the revolution, when it was the other way round: Blok showed his disgust for the revolution. There is only death, robbery, hooliganism, anarchy and sheer destruction. As Pasternak says: "the roof has flown away from the whole of Russia and we find ourselves under the open sky", with the subtext that we do not know what to do with this unexpected freedom. That is exactly what is happening in our country at the moment. The people are tormented, plunged into this nonsense by communism, idealism, nihilism, which destroyed everything: the personality, the family, the basis for life; everything is turned upside down.[47]

The set designed by Andrey von Schlippe was in many ways reminiscent of the décor for *Jenufa*: the bare stage was limited at the back by a backdrop behind which shadows appeared occasionally to illustrate the stage events with dance-like movements. Originally Lyubimov had intended to begin the production with the shooting of the Romanov family behind this backdrop, and for the Tsarevich's drawing of a sick bird to be projected; then, a red Soviet and a tricolour Russian flag were to be lowered. Indeed, "The Shades of the Past" and the scene with the banner dropping down in *Ten Days* seem to have served as models for Lyubimov. However, this prologue was omitted for technical reasons, although it seems likely that Lyubimov also realised the political emphasis he would thus be establishing from the very beginning of the production, visually reinforcing the one he set acoustically with the telephone conversation between Pasternak and Stalin on the theme of Mandelshtam's fate. At the end of this call, Pasternak had wanted to discuss with Stalin the topic of life and death, at which point Stalin terminated the conversation. It is this theme which preoccupied Pasternak in his entire work, and which made him so "dangerous" for the regime. During this scene, the visual side of the performance echoed the atmosphere of Stalinist terror by having all the characters covered by sacks, as though they were in prisoners' uniforms, and then led off stage.

The sides of the stage were limited by panels, which left gaps for the emergence and exit of characters, and which could turn round like revolving doors. The panels on the right side could close up to make a wall. The entire stage was raised towards the back and sloped down to the front (Figure 67).

Again, as in *Jenufa*, segments of the floorboards could be raised to form props. Some boards in the centre took the shape of a fence when

Yury mentions that the roof has flown away from Russia at the end of the war; or for the scene between Strelnikov and Zhivago at the station; or to represent how Yury is torn between Tonya and Lara when he returns to Varykino after meeting Lara again; or for his journey back from the partisans; and finally for his return to Moscow after Lara's departure. A book on a stand could also be lifted from the floorboards to underline references to Zhivago's diary. To the right, some boards could be sloped to form a bed for Zhivago when he is ill after his return from the partisans, or to create the space of Markel's flat after Zhivago's return to Moscow. Some props could be lowered into the scenic space: a white screen for projections of a window descended between two panels for the scenes in Yuryatin between Lara and Zhivago, when they are observed, literally, by Komarovsky, and symbolically by Strelnikov who keeps a protecting hand over Lara. A painting with a nude served as a screen for the seduction of Lara by Komarovsky. A frame with loops for people to hold on to was lowered for the scene when Zhivago suffers a heart attack in the trolleybus. Furthermore, a glass table could be lowered and inserted between panels on the left. This served as the sewing table for Madame Guichard's workshop; as her bed when she is ill with typhoid (in this scene, a white screen formed the wall to limit the stage-space to that of a room); it was Lara and Pavel Antipovs' home, and from here they watched Tonya giving birth to Zhivago's son; it served as a carriage for the journey to Varykino and immediately afterwards as a table (covered with a cloth) for the tea which is drunk after their arrival; it was the place where Strelnikov shoots himself, and finally Zhivago's coffin, upon which Lara placed her flowers at the end of the production.

The costumes matched the colour scheme of the set: they were black and blue-grey, like the glass or the backdrop. White banners were used, remaining within the non-colour scheme; yet for the scenes from *The Twelve*, red kerchiefs were held by the protagonists. A minor, yet important differentiation between Tonya and Lara was made through the length of their dress: Tonya's was short and practical, Lara's long, as dresses were in the past, underlining the archaic elements which dominate Lara's behaviour as well as her language.[48]

The production was subtitled "a musical parable", with music composed by Alfred Schnittke. Schnittke did not provide any solo musical scores, but offered choral music to accompany some of Pasternak's poems ("The Garden of Gethsemane", "Magdalene", "Holy Week", "Marriage", "Indian Summer", "August", "Christmas Star", "Meeting", "Winter Night") and *The Twelve*. This left Lyubimov with the problem of having only choral music, with no musical leitmotifs for the characters, who would have to speak their lines. Yet the commissioned performance was supposed to have an entirely musical form. This problem was overcome by using music which Schnittke had written for *Inspectorate Fairy Tales*. This music fulfilled two essential functions in the production: the Gogolian tunes equipped the main characters with rhythms and leit-motifs; whereas the choral music provided a unifying fabric for the people, who were almost omnipresent on stage, as in *Boris Godunov*. Indeed, as in *Boris Godunov*, all the characters emerged from the choir and returned to it. Only Yury Zhivago was occasionally alone on stage, for example when he recited "Hamlet", or after Lara had left him. However, in contrast to the linear function of the choir in *Boris Godunov*, in *Zhivago* the choir had a variety of functions and assumed a number of forms: it could consist either of women only, or men only, or be mixed. Although the choir was mainly dressed in black cloaks, some parts were sung by men or women in their ordinary costumes. This happened when the choir was composed of identifiable groups of the population, such as strikers or students, who were not clad in cloaks. At the beginning and end of each act, the choir wore black cloaks and was united with the main characters while singing stanzas of "The Garden of Gethsemane". During the funerals of Zhivago and Anna Gromeko, the choir consisted of women only, dressed in black cloaks, singing the orthodox chant "Eternal Memory"; they represented the mourning women, the *plakalshchitsy* of funeral rites. Most frequently, the choir's function was to comment on the events on stage, as in Greek or Epic theatre.

Pasternak had, both in his prose and his poetry, shown a preoc-cupation with sound. While in Dostoevsky characters had their individ-ual voices in terms of their understanding of the world, in Pasternak the individual is characterised by sound patterns and intonation. The voice creates the individuality of the human being. Lara is characterised by the vowel "a", Zhivago by the vowel "o". In the production, Lara echoed a melody based only on the sound "a": this was her theme. Strelnikov's speech and intonation are founded on consonant clusters; both Yury and Lara repeat these when they talk about him. The female voice Yury hears in his dream is Lara's; her voice replaces words and identifies her character. Zhivago is afraid of surrendering his entire soul merely by pronouncing her name. Lara, in turn, blushes at the sound of the name "Komarovsky". Similarly, Strelnikov repeats Lara's favourite phrase "*ne pravda li*" when he remembers her shortly before he commits suicide.

Some characters were identified by instrumental tunes. Tonya was often accompanied by the violin; Vakh was identified by a fast, but regular rhythm when mentioned by Anna Gromeko and taking the Zhivagos to Varykino. Both Komarovsky and Strelnikov had two leitmotifs, each of which represented two themes. Pavel is Antipov, Lara's husband, as well as Strelnikov, the revolutionary leader, the embodiment of an idea. Komarovsky is Lara's seducer and also her puppeteer who has some eternal control over Lara's life. The drum, often together with the Internationale, sounded for the revolutionary themes in scenes from *The Twelve* and in the partisan camp, as well as for Strelnikov. A waltz was played for the scene of the school memory and "Gaudeamus Igitur" reflected the climate of the student years of Tonya and Yury. Accentuated tunes with bells and a strict metronome accompanied the dream sequences.

Apart from providing leitmotifs for individual characters, music also served to underline the closeness of certain characters to one another. Both Zhivago and Lara speak of their desire to return to their families in Moscow when he, injured, is in the hospital where she works as a nurse: they were accompanied by the same tune and sang almost as a duet; they shared the same concern, the same fate. Both Zhivago and Lara sang several stanzas from "Magdalene": Lara before Pasha leaves her and her daughter, Zhivago when he speaks about people acting as if they were alive. Again, their fates are similar: both suffer from isolation, Lara within her family, Yury within society at large. The affinity between Yury and Lara at Varykino found expression in their duet of "Meeting". There is also a similarity between Tonya and Lara: Tonya's farewell letter and Lara's farewell to Yury by his coffin were accompanied by a tragic tune on the violin.

Yet music could also underline the contrast, the difference in attitudes between various characters. The violin and the cello acted as opposing voices when the Zhivagos arrive at Varykino where they are only gradually welcomed by the Mikulitsyns: only in the end did the instruments blend together. The dispute between orthodoxy and Judaism was also sustained on a strictly musical level: a Jewish chant competed with a Russian orthodox melody.

Finally, music was used as counterpoint. "Christmas Star" sounded parallel to Yury's and Lara's conversation about Tonya and Strelnikov. Then followed "Holy Week", which forced Lara to speak more and more loudly against the music. Since this is the only incident in the production where a voice fights against the music, the words deserve attention: Lara discusses Strelnikov, and as she speaks, she becomes increasingly convinced that he has fallen victim to the idea of revolution. For the sake of an idea, he has sacrificed his personality, abandoned the possibility of his – and her – potential happiness. This she cannot understand.

We, too, live in a period of collapse, the collapse of the most frightening of all utopias: the construction of heaven on earth, which has led us to the second collapse of an empire, this time the Soviet Empire. Only debunking, the death of utopia can give life to the living.[49]

The most poignant musical counterpoint in the whole production was, as in *Elektra*, a sudden loud burst of pop-music, composed by Andrey Schnittke. It was used when Zhivago tried to speak to Anna Gromeko about resurrection: he regurgitates something he has heard or read, but does not speak with his own voice and from his own experience. He speaks without conviction, and concludes "I have become a charlatan".

Acoustic elements were often juxtaposed to visual ones: a saw replaced a musical instrument. While the saw produced the sound, Marina and Zhivago cut firewood – without employing a real saw; but the wood still rolled down a slope on the other side of the stage. The melody played by Komarovsky on the saw/cello parodied Lara's theme from the film.

Movements were carefully choreographed. The plot of the novel in terms of the relationship between Lara, Pasha, Tonya and Yury was summed up in mime at the beginning; the "Dance of Death" was set against the background of upheaval and war: the men on the right killed the women who were running across the stage towards them, with spades which represented rifles.

Mime sequences accompanied Zhivago's dreams: while he suffered from typhoid fever, women performed grotesque doll-like movements; the same dolls appeared for the fever Zhivago endured upon his return from the partisans: the dolls placed shoes onto the stage and sat down, while Lara talked about her past: "and two shoes fell down" ("Winter Night"). The dance around the Christmas Tree for the party at the Zvenetskys' was characterised by a carnival atmosphere: the figures wore paper masks and danced to a fast mazurka.

Often, shadows behind the backdrop illustrated events on the stage, such as the seduction of Lara by Komarovsky. Movements or gestures also conveyed people's attitudes: Komarovsky held two sticks when described as a puppeteer who moves both Lara and Madame Guichard. A bottle rolled onto the frontstage both for Zhivago senior's addiction to alcohol, as well as Yury's when he loses Lara: Komarovsky left him the bottle before taking Lara away with him. The women in the workshop crossed their arms to signal that they were joining the workmen on strike.

Some metaphors from the novel were translated into theatrical images for the production: a candle was lit in Pavel's room at Lara's request: this was carried in on a spade. It was this candle which Zhivago saw as he went past the house to the Christmas party where Lara fired at Komarovsky; it was the same candle that inspired in him the line from "Winter Night" ("A candle is burning on the table ...".) Candles occurred again, as in the novel, when Pavel found Yury in Varykino: he identified the candles as those he had hidden there – war property. Strelnikov rolled them to Zhivago across the table. Zhivago lit one each for Tonya and Lara, which he placed on the edge of the table (Figure 68). When Strelnikov learned that Lara really loved him, he extinguished his candle in recognition that he has erred somewhere in life, and has irrevocably lost Lara. His next action is to shoot himself.

The rowanberry is another symbol of the novel. The bush leads Zhivago back from the partisans, and after Strelnikov has shot himself, his blood crystallises in the snow like rowanberries. In the production, the song of Kubarikha (who draws Zhivago's attention to the rowanberry bush), accompanied the rowanberry-theme. Rowanberries signify death: Pasha's death was reported to Lara in the hospital, and the tune sounded, unorchestrated. It also accompanied Pavel's suicide, when Zhivago threw red berries across the stage. Yet rowanberries also stand for life: they show Zhivago the way back, and here again, as he moved along the fence, Zhivago scattered rowanberries onto the stageboards.

Ambivalence (i.e. one object has different meanings) could also be inverted: a single meaning (movement or feeling) was rendered by different objects, signs or symbols: umbrellas were carried by the women's choir for both funerals; on each occasion, the rain represented the cleansing and also the sweeping force of water. During the first funeral, the choir knelt down, and while Yury remembered his father and reported how he died, the umbrellas turned ever faster, suggesting the movement of the wheels of a train, until the body of Zhivago senior rolled to the front. Here, the women in the choir folded up their umbrellas and, having become observers, pointed at the dead body. Yet the train's movement was also rendered differently: white banners were pulled diagonally across the stage, spotlights represented the wheels of a carriage and spades behind the banners moved to imitate the turning of the train's wheels as it takes the Zhivagos to Varykino. White banners were stretched horizontally across the stage to evoke the hospital, with the injured hanging their arms over the sheets in imitation of people lying in a hospital bed. A stretcher was used for Tonya to give birth and for Livery to sit on; yet both times the stretcher was positioned vertically, in the same way that the injured stood rather than lay.

Spades were another significant prop. They served as rifles in the prologue "Dance of Death", which summarises the background against which the novel is set. The grave for Zhivago's mother was dug with spades, which were then held to create a platform for Yury to step up on and speak about his childhood, before they formed a frame for Yury's face as he related the Zhivago family history. In the first of the scenes from Blok, spades were used to knock on the floor as Zhivago says "we are doomed". The extraordinary food supply Tonya and Zhivago receive was carried on spades from the back of the stage to front right, where a space between panels marks the Zhivagos' home. The spades were assembled to represent a Christmas tree (Figure 69), around which figures danced at the Zvenetskys'. Buckets were important for Lara and Marina, associated both with the carrying of water from a well or to Zhivago's flat respectively.

Zhivago was played by Valery Zolotukhin, who commented in alienation from his part on the background and the events; he assumed the narrator's stance, which enabled him to play at the same time the part of the poet, Pasternak, in the opening conversation with Stalin. Strelnikov, Lara and Tonya were played by Aleksandr Trofimov, Anna Agapova and Lyubov Selyutina respectively. All the other actors played several parts each, as in *Boris Godunov*.

Aesthetically, the visual and musical elements form a synthesis in *Zhivago*. Although not an opera, it is impossible to imagine *Zhivago* without its music, just as it was impossible to picture, for example, *The House on the Embankment* without its set. Music gives meaning to the words, and underlines the sound patterns of Pasternak's poetry. The music rather than the words identifies crossings of fate or the polarity between characters. Music was important in previous productions, but it had served mainly to accentuate and pace the rhythm. With *Boris Godunov*, unorchestrated music for the first time provided a unifying fabric for a production. In *The Feast* and *Elektra*, music was used consistently throughout, but the word was still spoken in *Elektra*; only in *The Feast* were some passages sung so that there was a unity between word and sound. This concept was perfected in *Zhivago*.

The images of the production served to emphasise a subjective perception of the phenomenal world; they allowed animation, as for example in the dream sequence, underlining the creative force of the imagination. The ambivalence of signifier and signified did not limit any image to one meaning, or any meaning to one image. This broadened Lyubimov's use of images, formerly restricted to a unilateral correspond-ence between signifier and signified. In these latest productions Lyubimov had ceased to use a set which contained, in the form of a meta-phor, the idea he would impose upon the text, and worked with a bare stage. Colours have disappeared almost entirely, making room for a black and white scheme. Lyubimov had always used genuine stage properties, such as the real skull in *Hamlet*. The properties in these most recent productions were almost all artificial: the fruit in *The Feast*, flowers in *Zhivago* and *The Feast*, and drinks in *Boris Godunov*. This is a clear indication that Lyubimov's theatre is no longer embedded in literal realities, but has moved onto a different, more abstract plane.

The production of *Zhivago* does not aim at a rendering of the events of the novel, but strives to represent in images and sound what preoccupied Pasternak and what preoccupied Zhivago: *"No kto my i otkuda ... a nas na svete net"* (But who are we, and where do we come from ...) is the key phrase echoed throughout the production and pronounced at its conclusion. The parallel between Christ, Hamlet and Zhivago, all accepting their fate and their suffering, is the main theme of the production. In that sense, *Zhivago* is "a liturgy about human life, about the human spirit, about the yearning of the human soul for immortality".[50]

Lyubimov's concern is no longer with human conscience, and the justifiability of an action, but with fate and the predicament of man, which receive full expression in this production. He speaks about the need to accept life whatever it may bring, and about the inability of any human being, be it the citizen of the 1960s or the revolutionary, society as a whole or the people in all their diversity, to effect any change. The wheels of fate have replaced the need for any appeal to act or take responsibility. Ethical issues have disappeared entirely in *Zhivago*, which is therefore highly unsymptomatic of its time. In an age of social upheaval and transformation Lyubimov contemplates fate, and the doomed individual.

For Lyubimov, beauty and perfection in art predominate over the necessity for art to equip man with moral guidelines and support him as a citizen. Therefore, images have receded to make room for sound, which strikes a different chord in the spectator.

> Music is high art. If it is genuine, music has a lofty pitch and raises the human soul. Feelings are fixed in the music, in the score. If played well, it is very precise. The word is dull and has no effect on anyone. Our century is so talkative, and all intelligent artists have moved against this verbosity.[51]

CONCLUSION

Lyubimov's theatre has usually been classified as political theatre. Yet, although most of his productions were deeply rooted in the political reality of their time, this alone does not create political theatre. Lyubimov has spent almost thirty years at the Taganka fighting for each production against either officials or press campaigns. Although this steeps some of his productions in a cloud of scandal, making him the "enfant terrible" of Soviet theatre, it does not mean that his opposition was essentially political.

> I think that the attitude to the Taganka theatre was wrong from the beginning. It did not become famous primarily because it resisted the régime. It did something completely different.[1]

Lyubimov embarked on his career as a director by rejecting the aesthetics imposed upon the Soviet theatre of the 1950s: the make-believe approach legitimised by Stanislavsky's "method" or rather the distortion of such ideas, the emotional lulling of the spectator rather than inviting him to think, and the illusion of political stability by means of Socialist Realist plays. The ideas of Brecht's epic theatre opposed all these fundamental elements of Soviet theatre: in Brechtian aesthetics, the naturalistic, emotional and illusionistic approach to theatre was rejected in favour of a demonstrative, rational, blatantly theatrical approach.

> The Taganka's success has to be analyzed clearly against its background. Other theatres were aesthetically quite different. Our theatre began with Brechtian aesthetics, which were new and had not yet been widely applied.[2]

For Lyubimov, there was never any barrier between the auditorium and the stage. His aesthetic principles are democratic: all art forms participate equally in a production, from circus to ballet, from sound to music, from set to property and costume design, from spotlight to innovative lighting techniques ("light curtain" and "light path"), and all this makes for a synthetic theatre. Elements of Bakhtin's carnivalesque, Brecht's street theatre and Pushkin's popular theatre (*narodnyi teatr*) underline these democratic structures.

The Taganka theatre was, however, the only theatre of its time to tread this path. Other directors contributed to the development of other strands of Russian theatre. Thus, Anatoly Efros continued the techniques of Mikhail Chekhov, Oleg Efremov and Oleg Tabakov followed those of Stanislavsky, Valentin Pluchek and Yury Zavadsky emulated Meyerhold, and Ruben Simonov – Vakhtangov.

Lyubimov's concern has always been with the individual and the people, with man's predicament under particular historical, social or personal conditions. If theatre is political simply because it directs an appeal to the audience, whether it be to ameliorate society, or to act in a way that does not demean the human conscience, or to accept fate, then Lyubimov may be called political.

Yet in all this he remained a convinced socialist, except that his view of socialism and equality comprised principles of democratic participation which clashed with the Soviet distortion of the socialist ideal. Lyubimov always recognised the danger of any idea, political or otherwise: if such an idea dominated human behaviour, it could wreak destruction.

For Lyubimov, aesthetics rather than ideas gradually assumed prime importance. Visual aspects remained still in the foreground, but the musical element became stronger as the Taganka moved into the post-Soviet era. In a synthetic theatre the emphasis on the visual proved too intellectual an approach to generate a spiritual rebirth. The focus therefore was shifted to music, which might reach the audience on a different and higher plane than images or words.

> The audience is raised to a higher pitch, which I wanted in view of the degrading and collapsing empire, its debris. Only a lofty pitch can attract people. Only from an exalted position can art prove influential and helpful, if indeed it is ever able to offer help. It may help through beauty, through many things, and I hope *Zhivago* will achieve this.[3]

The Taganka theatre had occupied a special place in society: its audience was composed of dissidents and members of the liberal intelligentsia, former prisoners and workers, teenagers and pensioners, Party and state officials, and foreign visitors. Encouraged by the Artistic Council and the intelligentsia, under constant pressure from the authorities, struggling to exist in a totalitarian state, the Taganka theatre played a powerful role in social and cultural life.

> The Taganka ... became an island of freedom ... in a chained and ice-bound country with an almost alcoholic indifference to human values, to freedom of speech. ... The border between the Taganka and the Moscow Party Organs was transparent, but the war was real, total and destructive. ... The Taganka led Russia out of the prison cell of socialist realism, into the fresh wind of the

twentieth century... Lyubimov returned. And they took the theatre away from the Master. .... And, believe it or not, the mayor and the ministry of fine arts, and the presidential circles simply let this happen, and the public didn't give a damn. For me, there is now a gaping hole in Moscow. As in the 1930s, when people failed to recognize Moscow without the Church of Christ the Saviour.[4]

After the collapse of the Soviet Union and the split in his theatre Lyubimov tried to restore the Taganka to its function as a place where people could find moral and spiritual support. Yet it seems that all the audience ever wanted to hear from the Taganka stage was criticism of politics. And they could now see political views expressed in another arena: the political. For spiritual support they could turn to the Church. And so Lyubimov sought to appeal to the people's sense of aesthetics in order to enrich their lives with at least one higher dimension. However, "theatres are like people; they pass through different phases: they are born and they die. A theatre does not have a second life".[5]

NOTES

Introduction

1. The People's Committee (later Ministry) for Internal Affairs (NKVD) was the Security Section of the State.
2. For a list of his roles, see Appendix 2, i.
3. Lyudmila V. Tselikovskaya (b. 8 September 1919): People's Artist of the RSFSR (1963); films and Vakhtangov theatre; daughter of the conductor V. V. Tselikovsky (Music and Drama Theatre, Kirghizia).
4. Yury Lyubimov, "Algebra garmonii", *Avrora* 10 (1974): 60.
5. Yury Lyubimov, Interview, Berlin: 8 August 1988.
6. Lyubimov, Interview, Berlin: 8 August 1988. Although there are no debts properly speaking in a planned economy, there can be an accumulative deficit (expenditure higher than planned and income lower than planned), which is what is referred to here by "debts".
7. *Feu* 63–65. Applications for a change of name were made in 1965, 1971 and 1974 (TsGALI 2485/2/9, 38 and 55). The Kirov District Committee had approved of the change in 1966, but the Main Administration refused to alter the name (TsGALI 2485/2/38).
8. TsGALI 2329/25/300 (Statutes of the Theatre Administration of the USSR Ministry of Culture, 1969).
9. The *Glavnoe Upravlenie Kul'tury ispolkoma Mossoveta* (Main Administration) controlled all the theatres except for the Bolshoi Theatre, Maly Theatre and MKhAT, which were subordinated to the USSR Ministry of Culture, and the Kirov (Mariinsky) Theatre, Leningrad and Vakhtangov Theatre, Moscow, which were subordinated to the RSFSR Ministry of Culture.
10. See Appendix 2, iii.
11. Main Administration of Matters of Literature and Publishing (*Glavnoe upravlenie po delam literatury i izdatel'stv*), later Main Administration for the Protection of Military and State Secrets in Print (*Glavnoe upravlenie po okhrane voennykh i gosudarstvennykh tain v pechati*), commonly referred to as *Glavlit*, both under the USSR Council of Ministers.
12. The Taganka theatre was subordinated to the Kirov District Committee of the Party; after the reorganisation of districts in 1968 the Zhdanov District Committee.

13. Yury Lyubimov, "V zashchitu professii i professionalov", *Teatr* 11 (1973): 32–35; "Algebra garmonii", *Avrora* 10 (1974): 60–64; "Ya – za antidekoratsiyu", *Khudozhnik. Stsena. Ekran.* (Moskva: n.p., 1975) 20–21. The first and second article are translated by A. Werth in *Culture* 5.2 (1978): 64–81.
14. Lyubimov, "Algebra garmonii", 60.
15. Lyubimov, "Ya – za antidekoratsiyu", 20.
16. Rimma Krechetova, "Lyubimov", *Portrety rezhisserov* (Moskva: Iskusstvo, 1977) 138, 140.
17. Berezkin, "David Borovsky", *Sovetskie khudozhniki teatra i kino '75* (Moskva: Sovetskii khudozhnik, 1977) 51.
18. Berezkin, "Stsenograf i veshch' ", *Dekorativnoe iskusstvo* 11 (1972): 31.
19. Lyubimov, "Algebra garmonii", 60. My italics.
20. *Feu* 78.
21. Lyubimov, "Algebra garmonii", 62.
22. *Feu* 78.
23. Lyubimov, "Algebra garmonii", 64.
24. Lyubimov, "The duty of art is to talk simply, candidly and straight-forwardly", Interview with Z. Zinik, *The Listener* 22 September 1983: 3.
25. Lyubimov, "V zashchitu professii i professionalov", *Teatr* 11 (1973): 33.
26. David Samoilov, "Chto takoe poeticheskii teatr", *Literaturnaya gazeta* 10 January 1968.

1. The Development of a Poetic Theatre

1. Anna Alekseevna Orochko: actress (People's Artist of the RSFSR) and pupil of Vakhtangov.
2. Konstantin Simonov, "Vdokhnovenie yunosti", *Pravda* 8 December 1963.
3. Order No. 10 (24 Jan. 1964) by B. Rodionov, Head of the Main Administration of Culture of the Moscow City Council Executive Committee; confirmed by the City Council's Decision No. 7/6 (18 Feb. 1964) by V. Promyslov, chairman of the Executive Committee, and A. Pegov, secretary of the Executive Committee (TsGALI 2485/2/2).
4. A. Demidova, B. Goldaev, A. Kolokol'nikov, L. Komarovskaya, V. Kliment'ev, I. Kuznetsova, I. Petrov, M. Politseimako, Z. Slavina and L. Voziyan all transferred to the Taganka theatre with Lyubimov.
5. A large number of Brecht's plays and theoretical writings were published in Russian translation in 1956/57. Productions of Brecht's plays in the Soviet Union are listed in Hecht and Hahn, eds., *Brecht 81* (Berlin: Henschel, 1981), and discussed in Konstantin Rudnitsky, *Spektakli raznykh let* (Moskva: Iskusstvo, 1974) 286–342.

6. *Feu* 216.

7. V. Sakhnovsky-Pankeev, "Molodo, smelo, talantlivo!" *Yunost'* 2 (1964): 101–102.

8. Bertolt Brecht, *Schriften zum Theater* (Frankfurt: Suhrkamp, 1983) 94.

9. Lyubimov, Interview, Berlin: 8 August 1988.

10. *Feu* 63.

11. By 1966, no production by Plotnikov remained in the repertoire. *The Good Person* ran up to 70 times annually at the Taganka theatre; see Appendix 1, iii.

12. Yury Lyubimov and Nikolay Erdman, *Mikhail Yu. Lermontov: Geroi nashego vremeni* (Moskva: VUOAP, 1965).

13. October 1964–April 1966; see Appendix 1, iii.

14. Lyubimov and Erdman, *Lermontov: Geroi*, 49–50.

15. "Na stsene – geroi Lermontova", *Teatral'naya Moskva* 34a (1964): 4.

16. Inna Vishnevskaya, "Geroi nashego vremeni", *Vechernyaya Moskva* 10 November 1964.

17. Lyubimov had a so-called "light curtain" installed in the theatre. It consisted of a line of footlights in a trough at the front stage (which can be lowered into the floor) which are directed at the balcony, where special black "traps" literally "caught" the beams and made them visible. The effect was that the light formed a curtain between the stage and the auditorium.

18. Cf. A. Mar'yamov, "Natka, Pechorin i vremya", *Teatr* 3 (1965) 23. *Zanni* is a male servant mask of the Commedia dell'Arte.

19. K. Zamoshkin, "Poisk i mysl'", *Smena* 7 (1965): 16.

20. Mar'yamov, "Natka, Pechorin i vremya", 23.

21. Vishnevskaya, "Geroi nashego vremeni".

22. G. Petrova, "Nakanune dnya tret'ego...", *Sovetskaya Rossiya* 28 November 1964.

23. Lyubimov, Interview, Berlin: 8 August 1988.

24. Yury Aikhenval'd, "'Geroi nashego vremeni' v teatre na Taganke", *Moskovskii komsomolets* 30 December 1964.

25. Mar'yamov, "Natka, Pechorin i vremya".

26. Lyubimov, Interview, Berlin: 8 August 1988; Stanislav Lesnevsky, "Poet i teatr", *Moskovskii komsomolets* 28 January 1965.

27. Lyubimov, Interview, Berlin: 8 August 1988; examples of this practice are: Viktor Rozov and Mikhail Roshchin for the Sovremennik, Aleksandr Vampilov for the Ermolova Theatre.

28. Yury Geriya, "Dykhanie vremeni", *Sovetskaya Abkhaziya* 13 July 1966; (my italics).

29. Lesnevsky, "Poet i teatr".

30. Geriya, "Dykhanie vremeni".

31. Yury Golubensky, "Vozderzhavshikhsya net", *Smena* 20 April 1965.

32. Lesnevsky, "Poet i teatr".

33. Vernita Mallard Batchelder, *The Theatre Theory and Theatre Practice of Jurij Lyubimov: 1964–1971* (Ann Arbor: UMI, 1978) 240; cf. N. Gorenkova, "Teatr na Taganke", *Teatral'naya zhizn'* 14 (1966): 17.

34. Andrey Voznesensky, *Antimiry* (Moskva: VUOAP, 1966) 2.

35. Yu. Lyubimov, S. Kashtelyan, I. Dobrovol'sky, Yu. Dobronravov, *Desyat' dnei, kotorye potryasli mir* (Moskva: VAAP, 1977).

36. John Reed, *Ten Days that Shook the World* (Harmondsworth: Penguin, 1986) 175; 194–196.

37. Len Karpinsky, "V tvorcheskom poiske", *Pravda* 16 May 1965.

38. Boris Galanov, "Eto vremya gudit telegrafnoi strunoi... ", *Literaturnaya gazeta* 22 April 1965.

39. Part I: 1. Interludes in the Foyer; 2. Prologue; 3. Change of the Red Guard; 4. Song of Truth; 5. Pantomime "Eternal Flame"; 6. Transition to Senate-scene; 7. Meeting of the U.S. Senate Commission; 8. W. Wilson's song; 9. Music-hall singers; 10. Pantomime "Bitter Fate"; 11. Invalids' song; 12. Transition to the scene "Noble Meeting"; 13. Buffet at Noble Meeting; 14. Song about Russia; 15. Prisons; 16. Allegory: "Bureaucrat and Dignitary"; 17. Fall of the 300-year-old House of the Romanovs; 18. Pantomime: "The Tearing of the Banner"; 19. Speech of Premier Kerensky; 20. Women's Battalion; 21. Song of Power; 22. Queue for bread; 23. White Guard; 24. Pierrot; 25. Chaos; 26. Shades of the Past. Part II: 1. Hands of the Fathers of the City: Debates in the City Duma; 2. Song "When Nectar..."; 3. Diplomats; 4. Den of the Counter-Revolution; 5. Soldiers' Trenches; 6. Street Meetings; 7. Last Meeting of the Provisional Government; 8. Kerensky's Flight; 9. Those who are Provisional, step down!; 10. Song: "Those who are Provisional,... "; 11. Decrees; 12. Song: Blok's "Twelve"; 13. In the Capital for Truth; 14. Smolny; 15. Pantomime: "Hive of the Revolution"; 16. Finale.

40. This was sharply criticised as "simplification of historic truth" by Len Karpinsky, "V tvorcheskom poiske".

41. V. Frolov, "Spektakl' o plamennykh dnyakh", *Izvestiya* 29 May 1965.

42. For further details of the use of light, see Béatrice Picon-Vallin, " 'Les dix jours qui ébranlèrent le monde' au Théâtre Taganka de Moscou", *Les Voies de la Création Théâtrale* 3 (1972): 344–377.

43. Cf. Robert Russell, *Russian Drama of the Revolutionary Period*, (London: Macmillan, 1989) 24.

44. *Desyat' dnei* 10.

45. *Desyat' dnei* 10, 14.

46. *Desyat' dnei* 12.
47. Personal notes, 4 January 1987.
48. *Desyat' dnei* 69.
49. *Desyat' dnei* 71, 73.
50. Ya. Varshavsky, "V poiske", *Vechernyaya Moskva* 18 June 1965.
51. M. Savel'ev, "Revolyutsiyu slavya", *Vodnyi transport* 3 July 1965.
52. Aleksandr Anikst, "Zrelishche neobychaineishee", *Teatr* 7 (1965): 30.
53. *Desyat' dnei* 31.
54. *Desyat' dnei* 70.
55. T. Sharoeva, "Chtoby shelest stranits, kak shelest znamen", *Molodezh' Gruzii* 30 June 1966.
56. Anikst, "Zrelishche neobychaineishee", 36.
57. A. Mar'yamov, "S Arbata na Taganku", *Yunost'* 7 (1965): 93.
58. Picon-Vallin, "Les dix jours...", 365; 363.
59. Galanov, "Eto vremya gudit..."
60. *Zheltyi tsyplenok* ("Yellow Chicken"), *Zemlyanka* ("The Dug-out"), *Vstavai, strana...* ("Country, rise..."), *Dal'nevostochnaya* ("Far-Eastern"), *Chizhika pyzhika*.
61. Gerhard Schaumann, "Der lyrische Held auf der Bühne", *Theater der Zeit* 11 (1967): 29.
62. Ruf' Tamarina, "Zhivye – pavshim", *Leninskaya smena* 5 October 1973.
63. Natal'ya Krymova, "Pavshikh pamyati svyashchennoi", *Teatr* 4 (1966): 50.
64. Rimma Krechetova, "Lyubimov", *Portrety rezhisserov* (Moskva: Iskusstvo, 1977) 134.
65. Krymova, "Pavshikh pamyati svyashchennoi"; Evgeny Evtushenko, "Ne do ordena – byla by rodina...", *Sovetskaya kul'tura* 30 November 1965.
66. TsKhSD, 5/36/151 (1965).
67. Aksenova, *Teatr na Taganke...* , 5; Yury Lyubimov, "Kto – korol'? Kto – prem'er? Kto – tot? Kto – etot?... ", Interview with A. Glezer, *Strelets* 10 (1986): 36–37.
68. "*Net, ne iz knizhek nashikh skudnykh...*", published as part of the cycle "Vozvrashchenie", never appeared in any edition under the title it is here referred to. I am obliged to Dr. Katherine Hodgson for the information about the 1965 edition.
69. TsKhSD, 5/36/151.
70. TsGALI 2485/2/310.
71. Anastas Mikoyan (1895–1978), member of the Politburo and President of the Supreme Sovet (1964–1965). His son was present at the last viewing. Aksenova's argument that Burlatsky and Andropov

intervened in favour of the production (as remembered by Delyusin)
refers to an earlier stage in the discussions (September 1965). Cf.
Aksenova, *Teatr na Taganke...*, 8.

72. Aksenova, *Teatr na Taganke...*, 11: B. Pokarzhevsky, "Kommunist v
tvorcheskoi organizatsii", *Sovetskaya Rossiya* 6 June 1968; "Teatr bez
aktera", *Komsomolskaya pravda* 18 September 1968; N. Tolchenova,
"Na ezopovom yazyke", *Ogonek* 33 (1968): 27–29; Yu. Zubkov,
"Kogda zabyvaetsya glavnoe", *Krasnaya zvezda* 5 October 1968.

73. Fedor Burlatsky and Len Karpinsky, "Na puti k prem'ere", *Komsomolskaya pravda* 30 June 1967.

74. Brecht, *Stücke* 8 (Berlin: Suhrkamp, 1957) 205.

75. D. Zolotnitsky, "Mudraya molodost' teatra", *Smena* 8 May 1967.

76. Nately Lordkipanidze, "Ispytanie razumom", *Nedelya* (suppl.) 28 May
1966.

77. I. Vishnevskaya, "Zhizn' Galileya", *Vechernyaya Moskva* 13 June 1966.

78. Brecht, *Stücke* 8, 201.

79. Cf. M. Stroeva, "Zhizn' ili smert' Galileya", *Teatr* 9 (1966): 13–14 and
Rudnitsky, *Spektakli raznykh let* 323.

80. Konstantin Rudnitsky, "Iskusstvo zhit' na zemle", *Radio. Televidenie*
29 (1966): 11.

81. Vishnevskaya, "Zhizn' Galileya".

82. Lordkipanidze, "Ispytanie razumom".

83. Stroeva, "Zhizn' ili smert' Galileya", 14.

84. T. Lanina, "Zhizn' Galileya", *Vechernii Leningrad* 10 May 1967.

85. Brecht, *Stücke* 8, 205.

86. Cf. TsGALI 2485/2/331.

87. T. Shakh-Azizova, "Mayakovskomu", *Teatr* 12 (1967): 16.

88. For a full list of works quoted in the production, see Ol'ga
Sharyaeva's version of Yury Lyubimov and Veniamin Smekhov, *V.
Mayakovsky: Poslushaite!*, Stsenicheskii variant 1967 goda. ([Moskva]:
ts., n.d.).

89. V. Frolov, "Poslushaite. Mayakovsky", *Sovetskaya kul'tura* 30 May 1967.

90. Frolov, "Poslushaite... ".

91. Shakh-Azizova, "Mayakovskomu", 18.

92. Batchelder, 259.

93. Only Sharyaeva's version makes the distinction between the five
different characters/actors. [1], [5–6].

94. Cf. Shakh-Azizova, "Mayakovskomu", 19; Sharyaeva, [86–88]; Yu.
Lyubimov, and V. Smekhov, *Vl. Mayakovsky: Poslushaite!* ([Moskva]:
ts., n.d.) 92–94.

95. Shakh-Azizova, "Mayakovskomu", 20.

96. Sharyaeva, [63].

97. Sharyaeva, [69–70]; this was not the case for the initial production as it passed the authorities.

98. TsGALI 2485/2/328: 53; Lyubimov.

99. Sharyaeva, [62].

100. In the lines "Below, we spread a carpet of compliments; if you have it in for someone, we will do him in. We put Lunacharsky's laurel wreaths into the common comradely soup..." the reference to "someone" is replaced by a reference to Zubkov, and the reference to Lunacharsky by one to the Main Administration (Sharyaeva, [57]). Yury Zubkov was at the time the editor of *Teatral'naya zhizn'*, and author of the defamatory article "Poiski na Taganke", *Sovetskaya kul'tura* 10 December 1966.

101. Nina Velekhova, "Tam zhili poety... ", *Literaturnaya gazeta* 7 February 1968.

102. Shakh-Azizova, "Mayakovskomu", 19.

103. B. Galanov, "Mayakovsky no Taganke", *Literaturnaya gazeta* 14 June 1967.

104. G. Yurasova, "Mayakovsky na Taganke", *Teatral'naya zhizn'* 19 (1967): 10–13.

105. Cf. TsGALI 2485/2/331 and 328.

106. TsGALI 2485/4/550 (review by the Main Administration).

107. Batchelder, 261.

108. TsGALI 2485/2/328: 42; Lyubimov.

109. Yury Lyubimov, "The crosses Yuri Lyubimov bears", Interview with Bryan Appleyard, *The Times* 5 September 1983.

110. Publication by Svetlana Sidorina "Dve intermedii k 'Pugachevu'", *Teatr* 5 (1989): 121–125.

111. David Samoilov, "Chto takoe poeticheskii teatr", *Literaturnaya gazeta* 10 January 1968.

112. TsGALI 2485/2/368. Order No. 226 of Mossovet.

113. Yury Lyubimov during a rehearsal in February 1982; quoted in "Posleslovie" to "Dve intermedii k 'Pugachevu'", ed. S. Sidorina, *Teatr* 5 (1989): 125.

115. Later, the text of the interludes was added, at least partly.

116. M. Sabinina, "Novye puti sinteza", *Sovetskaya muzyka* 5 (1983): 62–72.

117. Vysotsky remembering at a concert between 1976 and 1978; quoted in Sidorina "Dve intermedii... ", 125.

118. Natal'ya Krymova,"...s raskosymi i zhadnymi ochami", *Teatr* 4 (1968): 19.

119. Alla Demidova, *Vladimir Vysotsky* (Moskva: STD, 1989) 67.

120. Samoilov, "Chto takoe poeticheskii teatr".

121. Stanislav Lesnevsky, "Ya khochu videt' etogo cheloveka!" *Moskovskii komsomolets* 21 December 1967.
122. Krechetova, "Lyubimov", 128.

2. 1968 and After: The Crushing of a Repertoire

1. Len Karpinsky and Fedor Burlatsky, "Na puti k prem'ere", *Komsomol'skaya pravda* 30 June 1967.
2. The kolkhoz (collective farm) was headed by a chairman, but all decisions about farming were taken at the District (*raion*) or the hierarchically superior Province (*oblast'*) in the Executive Committees of the Party. The kolkhoz workers had no income other than the share of grain left once the amount required by the economic plan had been sold to the state (often this amount exceeded the actual harvest) and the share of the net earnings from the sale of the harvest (sold at very low prices set by the state) – both distributed once a year and depending on the number of workdays. The kolkhoz workers were entitled to the *ogorod* (garden or farmstead), where they would grow extra grain which they could use for themselves or sell on the market at free prices. Although passports had been introduced in 1932, the kolkhoz workers were not entitled to possess them until 1974 and therefore could neither move nor seek work outside the kolkhoz.
3. V. Kondratovich, "Po stranitsam 'Novomirskogo dnevnika'", *Teatral'naya zhizn'* 1 (1989): 23. Mozhaev was called in to Polyansky (USSR Council of Ministers) on 21 March 1968.
4. Valery Zolotukhin, Interview, Vienna: 22 May 1993.
5. The documents which give evidence for the procedures described in the following are located in the Central State Archive for Literature and Art (fond 2485); partly published by Aksenova in "Teatr na Taganke: 68-i i drugie gody", *Gorizont* 4 (1989): 46–64, revised and reprinted in *Teatr na Taganke: 68-i i drugie gody* (Biblioteka Ogon'ka 5: 1991): 28–47, and by Kondratovich in *Teatral'naya zhizn'* 1 (1989): 22–24.
6. Veniamin Smekhov, "Skripka Mastera", *Teatr* 2 (1988): 105.
7. Boris Mozhaev in an interview with Olga Martynenko, " 'Zhivoi' ostaetsya zhivym", *Moskovskie novosti* 5 March 1989.
8. Lyubimov, Conversation, Berlin: 22 September 1990; Smekhov, "Skripka Mastera", 105.
9. Valery Zolotukhin, "Den' shestogo nikogda", *Teatr* 7 (1989): 23–28.
10. TsKhSD 5/81/85 (Grishin in a letter to the Central Committee, 14 March 1969). My italics.
11. Galina Aksenova, "Teatr na Taganke: 68-i i drugie gody", *Gorizont* 4 (1989): 56.

12. Kalinin (Deputy Minister of Agriculture), Kukhar (Vladimir Ilich kolkhoz), Isaev (Gorky kolkhoz) and Tsarev (editor of *Sel'skaya zhizn'*) respectively. Cf. Hermann Pörzgen, "Die Literatur mit der Egge gemessen", *Frankfurter Allgemeine Zeitung* 25 November 1975; Nicole Zand, "Pourquoi 'la vie de Fedor Kouzkine' n'a pas franchi le barrage de la censure", *Le Monde* 13 November 1975; Liubimov, "I will not work under such conditions any more... ", Interview with M. Fillimore, *Index on Censorship* 1 (1985): 58; Galina Aksenova, "Teatr na Taganke: 68-i i drugie gody", *Gorizont* 4 (1989): 46–64; TsGALI 2485/2/493.

13. TsKhSD, 5/68/619 (2 July 1975).

14. TsKhSD, 5/68/619 (Mozhaev in a letter to Brezhnev, 30 June 1975).

15. Final dress rehearsal, 21 February 1989; Mozhaev, [*Zhivoi*], ([Moskva]: ts., [1990]). The words quoted are recorded by Valery Zolotukhin, "Den' shestogo nikogda", *Teatr* 7 (1989): 27 and attributed to Furtseva.

16. *teper' zhit' mozhno/vezde zhit' mozhno*. Boris Mozhaev, *Starye istorii* (Moskva: Sovremennik, 1978) 130.

17. The main versions are: (a) [Mozhaev], [*Zhivoi*], Moskva: ts., 1968 (theatre archive); (b) TsSGALI 2485/4/687 (1968); (c) TsGALI 2485/4/686 (1974); (d) Boris Mozhaev, *Zhivoi* (*po stranitsam "Iz zhizni Fedora Kuz'kina"*). *Dramaticheskoe predstavlenie v 2-kh deistviyakh*, Moskva: ts., 1988; and (e) the final version: [Boris Mozhaev], [*Zhivoi*], [Moskva]: ts., [1990].

18. Boris Mozhaev on 26 September 1967. In: Galina Aksenova, "Teatr na Taganke: 68-i i drugie gody", *Gorizont* 4 (1989): 46.

19. Final dress rehearsal, 21 February 1989; Mozhaev, [*Zhivoi*], [1990], 4–5, 63, 76–77.

20. Mozhaev, [*Zhivoi*], [1990], 30.

21. Aksenova, "Teatr na Taganke: 68-i i drugie gody", 47; Boris Mozhaev and Yu. Lyubimov: February–March 1968.

22. Aleksandr Minkin, "Zhivoi. O spektakle, arestovannom na 21 god", *Teatral'naya zhizn'* 17 (1989): 5.

23. Viktor Gul'chenko, "Znaki prepinaniya", *Teatr* 7 (1989): 30, 34.

24. Gul'chenko, "Znaki... ", 32.

25. L. Petrov, "Akkurat ochko!", *Vechernyaya Moskva* 2 March 1989.

26. Tat'yana Bachelis, "Skaz o pravdolyubtse Kuz'kine", *Izvestiya* 27 February 1989.

27. Minkin, "Zhivoi... ", 4.

28. Minkin, "Zhivoi... ", 5.

29. Boris Mozhaev, "Chem shchi khlebat'?" *Teatr* 7 (1989): 19.

30. Minkin, "Zhivoi... ", 5.

31. Minkin, "Zhivoi... ", 4.

32. Minkin, "Zhivoi... ", 4.

33. *Glavrepertkom* controlled the theatre repertoires between 1923 and 1953, when the Ministry of Culture was established and took over this function.

34. Letter from Stalin to Stanislavsky, 9 November 1931. Nikolay Erdman, *P'esy, intermedii, pis'ma, dokumenty, vospominaniya sovremennikov* (Moskva: Iskusstvo, 1990) 283–284.

35. Yury Lyubimov, Mikhail Vol'pin, Ruben Simonov, Nikolay Okhlopkov, Sergey Yutkevich, Boris Messerer and Dmitry Shostakovich served in the same unit.

36. These attempts were in 1965, 1971 (TsGALI) and 1981/88 (Freedman, SEEDTF 8 (2 and 3), December 1988), when the Satire Theatre was granted permission to stage the play.

37. I, 15 (Kalabushkin's repetition of how wonderful life is); IV, 9 and 15 are slightly shortened; IV, 17 and 18 are translated into mime; V, 1 and 3 are omitted and IV, 19 follows V, 2.

38. This is done in the manner of Pustoslavets of the *Scenes to the vaudeville by D. Lensky "Lev Gurych Sinichkin"* Erdman, *P'esy...*, 173–185.

39. *Intermedii k spektaklyu po tragedii U. Shekspira "Gamlet"*, Erdman, *P'esy...*, 186–191.

40. Mikhail Bulgakov to Stalin, 4 February 1938. Erdman, *P'esy...*, 293–294.

41. Meyerhold wrote to Molotov on 2 and 13 January 1940. Cf. Edward Braun, "Meyerhold: The Final Act", *New Theatre Quarterly* 33 (1993): 8, 10 and *Teatral'naya zhizn'* 5 (1989).

42. The set design by I. Leistikov for Meyerhold's production also envisaged lines of washing for Act IV.

43. J. B. Molière, *Tartuffe* (Paris: Larousse, 1971).

44. For a detailed analysis of the production, see Jacqueline Jomaron, " 'Le Tartuffe' mis en scène par lioubimov", *travail* théâtral 4 (1971): 158–162.

45. S. Velikovsky, "O derzosti i robosti ozorstva", *Teatr* 4 (1969): 27.

46. Aleksandr Ninov, "Dva Mol'era", *Neva* 3 (1974): 208.

47. Jomaron, "Le Tartuffe...", 159–160; S. Povartsev, " 'Tartyuf' poprezhnemu molod", *Omskaya pravda* 15 September 1983; L. Rondeli, "Bednyi Mol'er", *Teatral'naya zhizn'* 12 (1974): 25; performance of 18 January 1987.

48. Jomaron, "Le Tartuffe...", 161–162.

49. Velikovsky, "O derzosti i robosti ozorstva", 28.

50. Ninov, "Dva Mol'era", 208.

51. Yury Zubkov, "Grani poiska", *Teatral'naya zhizn'* 5 (1969): 6.

52. N. Efremova, "Mol'er v teatre na Taganke i u nas v gostyakh", *Vpered* 20 November 1969.

53. O. Ul'yanova, "Tartyuf na Taganke", *Nauka i religiya* 6 (1969): 83.

54. Molière, *Tartuffe* 147.

55. Lyubimov, Interview, Berlin: 8 August 1988.

56. Evgeny Surkov, "A Tartyuf?...", *Ogonek* 13 (1969): 26–27.

57. S. Velikovsky, "O derzosti i robosti ozorstva", *Teatr* 4 (1969): 24–29.

58. N. Lavrenyuk, "Ne tol'ko o 'Tartyufe'", *Sovetskaya kul'tura* 3 April 1969.

59. Galina Kuz'ko, "Eshche raz o 'Tartyufe'", *Ogonek* 17 (1969): 19. My italics. The same word (harmful) had been used by Stalin to condemn Erdman's *The Suicide* in a letter to Stanislavsky (1931).

60. N. Tolchenova, "Na ezopovom yazyke", *Ogonek* 33 (1968): 27–29.

61. E. Surkov, "Shivorot- navyvorot", *Ogonek* 35 (1969): 26.

62. A. Ninov, "Dva Mol'era", *Neva* 3 (1974): 206–212.

63. Nina Velekhova, "Uslovnost'? Net, uproshchenie", *Literaturnaya gazeta* 6 August 1969.

64. Lyubimov, Interview, Berlin: 8 August 1988.

65. TsGALI 2485/2/281 (Rodionov compiled a list with remarks on 27 November 1968).

66. Yury Lyubimov and Boris Glagolin, *M. Gor'ky: Mat'* (Moskva: VAAP, 1977).

67. Lyubimov and Glagolin, *Gor'ky: Mat'* 55 (I, 5 and II, 3).

68. Lyubimov and Glagolin, *Gor'ky: Mat'* 3, 54.

69. B. Byalik, "Obrashchayas' k Gor'komu", *Literaturnaya gazeta* 25 June 1969; Byalik lists the following sources: *The Complaint, My Universities, The Life of Klim Samgin, Childhood*.

70. David Borovsky, "Ot Gor'kogo k Gor'komu", *Tvorchestvo* 7 (1970): 12–13. Also in "Podpisi k kartinkam", *Teatral'naya zhizn'* 5 (1994): 13.

71. A. Anastas'ev, "V soglasii s Gor'kim", *Teatr* 9 (1969): 15.

72. TsGALI 2485/2/420 (Miringof, 2 July 1970).

73. TsGALI 2485/2/419 and 420 (Miringof).

74. TsGALI 2485/2/422, document 39.

75. Yury Lyubimov, *N.G. Chernyshevsky: Chto delat'?* (Moskva: VAAP, 1977). The "prologue" of the script is for practical purposes called here the "introduction".

76. Lyubimov, *Chernyshevsky: Chto delat'?* 6–7.

77. V. Abramova, "Chto delat'?" *Teatr* 4 (1971): 9.

78. Abramova, "Chto delat'?" 11.

79. O. Radishcheva, "Povtorenie proidennogo", *Teatr* 9 (1971): 60.

80. N. Kidina, "Gde zhe vy, 'novye lyudi'?" *Teatral'naya zhizn'* 2 (1971): 25.

81. It was originally planned in 1966/67 under the title *Man* (TsGALI 2485/2/434-a and 1501). The first reading took place on 18 April 1968 with the title *Protect your [own] Face* (TsGALI 2485/2/1501-a). The play

was rehearsed with the title *Antiface* and announced with the final title *Protect Your Faces!*. Voznesensky had submitted the text to the theatre in April 1967, and the project was agreed with the Administration in February 1969; the text received authorisation from *Glavlit* in June 1969 (TsGALI 2485/4/473).

82. The archival version (TsGALI 2485/2/440) is incomplete. The versions which were put at my disposal are: the author's version *Protect your Faces!* (*Beregite vashi litsa!*), [Moskva]: ts., n.d., which was made available by Svetlana Sidorina; and the theatre's versions of *Antiface* (*Antilitso* [Moskva]: ts., n.d., [20 and 18 pages] and *Antilitso*, [Moskva]: ts., n.d., [25 and 22 pages]), which were made available by Boris Glagolin. The versions differ notably in the sequence and the choice of poems.

83. The play is subtitled *litsezrelishche* in two *litsedeistvo*. This is a play on words. *litsedei* = hypocrite, *litso* = face; in obsolete use: *litsedei* = actor, *litsedeistvo* = act, *litsezret'* = to behold with one's own eyes.

84. *Feu* 120.

85. Andrey Voznesensky, *Antilitso* ([Moskva]: ts.[38 pages], n.d.), II: 4; *Antilitso* ([Moskva]: ts.[47 pages], n.d.), II: 5.

86. *Feu* 156. TsKhSD 5/62/87 (letter from the Moscow City Committee to the Central Committee, 25 February 1970).

87. TsGALI 2485/4/473 (Panfilov and Barulina, 9 February 1970).

88. TsGALI 2485/2/438.

89. TsGALI 2485/2/437 and 1503 (3 February 1970) and 2485/2/1503 (6 February 1970).

90. David Borovsky, Conversation, Paris: 6 February 1994.

91. TsKhSD 5/62/87 (Viktor Grishin in a letter to the Central Committee, 25 February 1970).

92. TsGALI 2485/2/33 (Main Administration of Culture, Order No. 16).

93. Evgeny Evtushenko, *Oruzh'e bezoruzhnykh* ([Moskva]: ts., n.d.). The text was made available by Boris Glagolin.

94. Rima Shore, "Under the Skin of the Statue of Liberty", *Drama Review* 17 (1973): 139.

95. TsGALI 2485/2/457–461.

96. Evtushenko, *Oruzh'e bezoruzhnykh*, [Moscow]: ts., n.d.

97. TsGALI 2485/2/460 (Puchkova, Party Committee).

98. Evtushenko, Letter to the Editor of *The New York Times*, 15 January 1973, as quoted by P. R. Ryder, "Liubimov/Yevtushenko: Under the Skin of the Statue of Liberty", *Drama Review* 17 (1973): 136.

99. Evtushenko, Letter to the Editor, 136.

3. The Individual in the Present and in the Past

1. Boris Vasil'ev, Interview, London: 30 October 1987.
2. Yury Lyubimov and Boris Glagolin, *Boris Vasil'ev: A zori zdes' tikhie* . . . (Moskva: VUOAP, 1971).
3. Boris Vasil'ev, "A zori zdes' tikhie . . .", *Izbrannye proizvedeniya* 1 (Moskva: Khudozhestvennaya literatura, 1988): Chapters 7, 8, 10 and Chapters 1, 2 respectively.
4. Lyubimov and Glagolin, *Vasil'ev: A zori zdes' tikhie* . . . Scenes 1, 2 and 3, 4 respectively.
5. Lyubimov and Glagolin, *Vasil'ev: A zori zdes' tikhie* . . . Scenes 31, 33, 36, 39, 41 respectively.
6. Vasil'ev, Interview, London: 30 October 1987.
7. Cf. E. Stishova, "Status professii", *Teatr* 4 (1977): 53–57.
8. Lyubimov and Glagolin, *Vasil'ev: A zori zdes' tikhie* . . . 3.
9. Vydmantas Silyunas, "A zori zdes' tikhie . . .", *Teatr* 6 (1971): 8.
10. Silyunas, "A zori zdes' tikhie . . .", 13.
11. Aleksandr Shtein, "Rampa – liniya ognya . . .", *Komsomol'skaya pravda* 5 March 1971.
12. Cf. V. Berezkin, "Itogi sezona", *Teatr* 3 (1972): 61–67.
13. Liza's death is followed by "*Ya rastsvel kak makov tsvet* . . .", Sonya's by "*Kogda budesh' bol'shaya* . . .", Galya's by "*Matushka, matushka, chto vo pole pyl'no* . . .", Zhenya's by "*Ne kukui, gor'ka kukushka* . . ." and Rita's by "*Oi, ne rastet trava zimoyu, polivai, ne polivai* . . .".
14. Silyunas, "A zori zdes' tikhie . . .", 8–10.
15. "*S berez ne slyshen, nevesom sletaet zheltyi list* . . .".
16. Lyubimov, "Praviteli i teatr", Interview with John Glade, *Vremya i my* 98 (1989): 170–171.
17. Cf. Maya Turovskaya, " 'Zori' na Taganke", *Yunost'* 4 (1971): 92.
18. Nina Velekhova, "Vospitanie chuvstv", *Literaturnaya gazeta* 16 February 1972.
19. Rimma Krechetova, "Zhivym o pavshikh", *Trud* 22 January 1971.
20. TsGALI 2485/4/464. Blok's line is from the poem "Rozhdennye v goda glukhie" (1914) contained in the cycle *Rodina*.
21. Anatoly Golubev, "Tikhie zori Rossii", *Smena* 12 (1971): 20–22.
22. TsGALI 2485/2/184.
23. The cubes for *Listen!*; the executioner's block for *Pugachev*; the eternal flame for *The Fallen and the Living*.
24. Vasil' Bykov, *Perekrestok* (Moskva: VAAP, 1977).
25. Elizaveta Pul'khritudova, "Etot strannyi 'kozel otpushcheniya'", *Literaturnoe obozrenie* 7 (1980): 85–86.

26. Lyubimov, Interview, Berlin: 8 August 1988; TsGALI 2485/2/27; Appendix 1, ii; *Feu* 141–142.
27. [Yury Lyubimov and Aleksandr Anikst], *Khroniki* (Moskva: ts., 1968). The text was made accessible by the Taganka archive, and contains 151 pages with 53 scenes.
28. TsGALI 2485/4/14 (Samarin).
29. Lyubimov, Seminar in Berlin (1988).
30. Insertions between prologue and I, 1; I, 2 and I, 3; III, 3 and III, 4.
31. David Borovsky, Conversation, Moscow: 25 January 1987.
32. Cf. Tat'yana Bachelis, "Gamlet – Vysotsky", *Voprosy teatra* 11 (Moskva: STD, 1987): 128.
33. Aleksandr Anikst, "Tragediya: garmoniya, kontrasty", *Literaturnaya gazeta* 12 January 1972 and Tat'yana Bachelis, "Gamlet – Vysotsky", 128.
34. Béatrice Picon-Vallin, " 'Hamlet' à moscou", *travail théâtral* 8 (1972): 154.
35. "Hamlet" formed part of *Doctor Zhivago*, which was still prohibited at this time in the Soviet Union.
36. Mikhail Miringof, "Gamlet na Taganke", *Teatral'naya zhizn'* 6 (1972): 20.
37. Yu. Khanyutin, "Gamlet epokhi kinematografa", *Nedelya* 6–12 December 1971.
38. Vydmantas Silyunas, "Muzhestvo sovesti", *Trud* 19 December 1971.
39. Picon-Vallin, " 'Hamlet' à moscou", 156.
40. Miringof, "Gamlet na Taganke".
41. Anikst, "Tragediya: garmoniya, kontrasty".
42. Miringof, "Gamlet na Taganke", 20.
43. Bachelis, "Gamlet – Vysotsky", 132.
44. Anikst, "Tragediya: garmoniya, kontrasty".
45. Bachelis, "Gamlet – Vysotsky", 141.
46. TsGALI 2485/2/224, 76 (Lyubimov).
47. TsGALI 2485/4/883.
48. Documents and statements made accessible by the Lyric show that this change was initiated by the theatre, who thought Dostoevsky staged by a Russian director would be more attractive for a British audience.
49. Shakespeare, *Hamlet* (I, 2): 1.131–2.
50. Shakespeare, *Hamlet* (III, 1): 1.78–82.
51. Jerzy Stefan Stawinski, (b. 1921): writer, film director and scenarist. The adaptation was by Veniamin Smekhov, *Stavinsky, Ezhi Stefan: Chas Pik* ([Moskva]: ts., n.d.).
52. TsGALI 2485/2/410.
53. M. Krupina, "Moskva. Chas Pik", *Teatr* 5 (1970): 172.
54. Cf. Gershkovich, *Teatr na Taganke* 111; Krupina, "Moskva. Chas Pik", 172.

55. Krupina, "Moskva. Chas Pik", 172.

56. O. Kuchkina, "Chelovek v 'Chas Pik'", *Komsomol'skaya pravda* 6 February 1970.

57. Krupina, "Moskva. Chas Pik", 172.

58. Cf. Krupina, "Moskva. Chas Pik", 172.

59. V. Karnaukhov, "Neveselyi itog priyatnoi vo vsekh otnosheniyakh zhizni", *Vechernii Omsk* 15 September 1983.

60. Karnaukhov, "Neveselyi itog... "

61. Fedor Abramov, *Sobranie sochinenii* 3 (Leningrad: Khudozhestvennaya literatura, 1980–1982).

62. Fedor Abramov, *Derevyannye koni: P'esa v 2 deistviyakh* (Moskva: VAAP, 1974) 7–9, 17.

63. Abramov, *Derevyannye koni* 16–18; 20–23.

64. Abramov, *Derevyannye koni* 9.

65. Abramov, *Derevyannye koni* 17.

66. Abramov, *Derevyannye koni* 20–23.

67. David Borovsky, "Podpisi k kartinkam", *Teatral'naya zhizn'* 5 (1994): 26–27.

68. This applies to performances on the old stage only; after the transfer to the new stage, where the production ran during the 1980s, this entrance was impossible for technical reasons.

69. Cf. M. Sabinina, "Novye puti sinteza", *Sovetskaya muzyka* 5 (1983): 65–66.

70. TsGALI 2485/2/237, 38: Abramov.

71. Yu. Chernichenko, "Zhivaya voda", *Teatr* 11 (1974): 27.

72. Natal'ya Krymova, "Chto perezhito...", *Komsomol'skaya pravda* 19 June 1974.

73. Chernichenko, "Zhivaya voda", 23.

74. S. Nagnibeda, "V poiskakh 'zhivoi vody'", *Vechernii Omsk* 10 September 1083.

75. TsGALI 2485/2/237.

76. TsGALI 2485/2/241 (Rozov, 15 March 1974).

77. Cf. Fedor Abramov, "Samyi nadezhnyi sud'ya – sovest'", *Neva* 5 (1984): 146.

78. TsGALI 2485/2/298.

79. A. Demidov wrote in his article "...Pokuda serdtse b'etsya" that the parts of Lena and Dmitriev were played both by Alla Demidova/ Leonid Filatov and Inna Ulyanova/Aleksandr Vil'kin. According to Vil'kin, Filatov/Demidova rehearsed only once, but never played in the production.

80. Yury Trifonov and Yury Lyubimov, "Obmen", *Teatr pisatelya* (Moskva: Sovetskaya Rossiya, 1982) 54, 55 and 61.

81. Michael McLain, "Trifonov's Exchange at Lioubimov's Taganka", *SEEA* 3.1 (1985): 163.
82. Demidov, "...Pokuda serdtse b'etsya", 41–42.
83. Trifonov and Lyubimov, "Obmen", 74, 81.
84. Trifonov/Lyubimov, "Obmen", 55, 56, 65, 84.
85. Trifonov/Lyubimov, "Obmen", I: 50–55; II: 55–71; III: 71–89; IV: 89–95. My divisions.
86. Trifonov/Lyubimov, "Obmen", 69–70.
87. Trifonov/Lyubimov, "Obmen", 69. The father then continues to narrate the episode with Mar'ya Petrovna and the red ball.
88. McLain, "Trifonov's Exchange...", 165.
89. Demidov, "...Pokuda serdtse b'etsya", 44.
90. Ol'ga Trifonova, Conversation, Moscow: 15 January 1987.
91. Cf. Konstantin Rudnitsky, "Kentavry", *Teatr* 6 (1979): 48.
92. Yu. Skvortsov, "Semeinaya drama inzhenera Dmitrieva", *Trud* 25 July 1976.
93. Evgeny Evtushenko, "Besposhchadnost' k 'besposhchadnosti'", *Sovetskaya kul'tura* 6 July 1976.
94. Demidov, "...Pokuda serdtse b'etsya", 39.
95. Yury Karyakin, *Prestuplenie i nakazanie* ([Moskva]: ts., n.d.).
96. Yury Lyubimov and Yury Karyakin, *Fedor Dostoevsky. Crime and Punishment*, English version by Nicholas Rzhevsky, (London/Lyric Theatre: ts., n.d.) 70. Subsequently referred to as "Rzhevsky".
97. Konstantin Rudnitsky, "Priklyucheniya idei", *Dostoevsky i teatr* (Leningrad: Iskusstvo, 1983): 443.
98. Anatoly Smelyansky, "Ispytanie Dostoevskim", *Teatr* 8 (1981): 95.
99. A light path was created by means of a spot placed on one side of the stage at a slight angle to the floor, directed diagonally across the stage, so that a path would be lit.
100. Rzhevsky, 10.
101. Richard Allen Cave, "Doorways and thresholds", *Times Higher Education Supplement* 2 September 1983.
102. Smelyansky, "Ispytanie Dostoevskim", 97–99.
103. Smelyansky, "Ispytanie Dostoevskim", 98.
104. Martin Esslin, "Crime and Punishment", *Plays and Players* 11 (1983).
105. Smelyansky, "Ispytanie Dostoevskim", 96. The distinction in Russian is made by the use of verbal aspect to refer to either repetitive or unique actions.
106. Galina Aksenova, "Prestuplenie i nakazanie", *Ekran i stsena* 23 August 1990.
107. Robert Brustein, "Hallucination and Moral Dissent", *New Republic* 16 February 1987.

108. Yury Trifonov and Yury Lyubimov, "Dom na naberezhnoi", *Teatr pisatelya* (Moskva: Sovetskaya Rossiya, 1982) 108–109, 114, 115, 122, 126, 129, 136, 138.

109. Trifonov/Lyubimov, "Dom na naberezhnoi", 104, 104–105, 107, 122.

110. Trifonov/Lyubimov, "Dom na naberezhnoi", 102; 97–98; 110.

111. Trifonov/Lyubimov, "Dom na naberezhnoi", 97; 102; 108–109.

112. Cf. Susanne Gelhard, *Die Dramatisierung von Jurij Valentinovič Trifonovs Roman "Das Haus an der Moskva" am Moskauer Taganka-Theater*, (Diss), (Mainz: Liber, 1984) 89.

113. Trifonov/Lyubimov, "Dom na naberezhnoi", 109.

114. Trifonov/Lyubimov, "Dom na naberezhnoi", 99.

115. Trifonov/Lyubimov, "Dom na naberezhnoi", 101–102.

116. Trifonov/Lyubimov, "Dom na naberezhnoi", 102.

117. Trifonov/Lyubimov, "Dom na naberezhnoi", 118: Sonya.

118. Gelhard, *Dramatisierung*, 95–99. TsGALI 2485/4/488 (licence of 23 April 1980).

119. Trifonov/Lyubimov, "Dom na naberezhnoi", 108.

120. Trifonov/Lyubimov, "Dom na naberezhnoi", 103–104.

121. Film by Vladimir Sukhobokov (1948) based on a screenplay by Sergey Mikhalkov.

122. A term introduced in 1947 to denounce someone expressing positive views of the non-communist West, as opposed to patriotism for the Soviet Union; mainly, though, a euphemism for "Jew".

123. David Borovsky, Conversations, Moscow: 25 January 1987 and 20 April 1990.

124. The House used to accommodate members of the *nomenklatura*, and is located on the embankment of the Moscow river, opposite the Kremlin, by the Kamenny Bridge. Anikst pointed out in one of the discussions with Marianna Druzhinina of the Main Administration of Culture that, if for each person who lived in the House and who was killed during the Stalinist years, a memorial plate were installed outside, the House would be covered entirely in marble: Borovsky, Conversation, Moscow: 20 April 1990 and Smekhov, "V epokhu 'dvukh Yur'", *Ekran i stsena* 24 May 1990.

125. This function was introduced by Borovsky; when he tried to enter the House before completing the set design, he was thrown out several times by the lift operators. Borovsky, Conversation, Moscow: 20 April 1990.

126. Gelhard, *Dramatisierung* 120 (interview with Lyubimov).

127. A. Demidov, "Minuvshee", *Teatr* 7 (1981): 107.

128. For a detailed account, see Gelhard, who devoted a section of her dissertation to the use of music and provided the song texts in an appendix.

129. Gelhard, *Dramatisierung* 129. She also notes a sharp change in the musical tunes for Shulepa and Glebov at their encounter when they recall their wartime experience: 127.
130. Gelhard, *Dramatisierung* 123.
131. Daniel Vernet, "Les ombres du passé", *Le Monde* 9 July 1980.
132. Cf. Demidov, "Minuvshee", 102.
133. Demidov, "Minuvshee", 102.
134. Demidov, "Minuvshee", 98–99.
135. According to Gelhard, they are actually kept in the theatre, a legacy of Trifonov.
136. Demidov, "Minuvshee", 101.
137. Demidov, "Minuvshee", 104.
138. Gelhard, *Dramatisierung* 172, 174 (interview with Lyubimov).
139. Cf. Natan Eidel'man, "Svidanie s Pushkinym", *Trud* 20 May 1973.
140. Lyudmila Tselikovskaya and Yury Lyubimov, *Tovarishch, ver'*... (Moskva: VAAP, 1974); see also Figure 31.
141. Pushkin in fact met only the two Tsars Aleksandr I and Nikolay I; the meeting with Pavel (1796–1801) is fictitious.
142. "Liberty" (1817), "The Rose" (pre-1817), "Farewell" (1817), "Epistle to the Censor" (1822), "Travel Complaints" (1830), "Winter Evening" (1825), "The Prophet" (1826), "The Upas-Tree" (1828), "The Demons" (1830), "To the Poet" (1830), "Remembrance" (1828), "The Pilgrim" (1835), "19 October" (1825).
143. From both scenes entitled "Palace of the Tsar", from "Night. The Garden. The Fountain", "Square in front of the Cathedral in Moscow", "Place of Execution" and "The Kremlin. House of Boris. A Guard on the Steps".
144. Eidel'man, "Svidanie s Pushkinym".
145. Stanzas XX–XXV and XXIX–XXX from Chapter I; cf. V. Kuleshov, "Ot tlen'ya ubezhav", *Literaturnaya gazeta* 30 May 1973.
146. Eidel'man, "Svidanie s Pushkinym".
147. Tselikovskaya and Lyubimov, *Tovarishch, ver'*...4.
148. Yury Zubkov, "Sluzhen'e muz ne terpit suety", *Moskva* 2 (1974): 195.
149. Kuleshov, "Ot tlen'ya ubezhav".
150. Vl. Voronov, "Vremya vybora", *Yunost'* 7 (1973): 80.
151. Tselikovskaya and Lyubimov, *Tovarishch, ver'*... 5–6.
152. Cf. Eidel'man, "Svidanie s Pushkinym".
153. Voronov, "Vremya vybora", 81.
154. Viktor Komissarzhevsky, "Chitaya svitok vernyi...", *Komsomol'skaya pravda* 20 April 1973.
155. Kuleshov, "Ot tlen'ya ubezhav".
156. TsGALI 2485/2/386.
157. TsGALI 2485/2/396 (Rozov and Pokarzhevsky).

158. TsGALI 2485/2/396 (Svetlakova).
159. TsGALI 2485/4/618 (licence).
160. The parts are distributed to actors as "for Pushkin", or "instead of Pushkin" [za Pushkina].
161. Yury Lyubimov, Boris Glagolin, Aleksandr Vil'kin, Veniamin Smekhov, *Benefis* ([Moskva]: ts., [1973]); TsGALI 2485/2/216. The plays were structured in the following manner: Part I – *The Storm* (I–III) with fragments from *A Festive Dream* and *The Diary of a Scoundrel* as well as the characters Schatslivtsev and Neschastlivtsev from *The Forest* (1871); *A Festive Dream* (I, II) followed by fragments of *The Storm* (IV) and *A Festive Dream* (III); and finally *The Diary of a Scoundrel* (I) followed by *The Storm*. Part II – *The Diary of a Scoundrel* (II–V) with the endings of *The Storm* and *A Festive Dream* inserted between acts, in such a manner that *The Storm* finished the production. The version was preceded by a prologue about the unsuccessful 25th anniversary of Ostrovsky the playwright.
162. Inna Vishnevskaya, "Benefis", *Komsomol'skaya pravda* 11 January 1974.
163. Yury Zubkov, "I vse okazalis' v ovrage...", *Ogonek* 9 (1974): 22.
164. Zubkov, "I vse okazalis' v ovrage...", 23.
165. Vishnevskaya, "Benefis".
166. Yury Lyubimov, [*Vecher Gogolya (Revizskaya Skazka)*] ([Moskva]: ts., n.d.). The text was made available by Svetlana Sidorina. It contains excerpts from: *Arabesques* (*Diary of a Madman, Nevsky Prospect, The Portrait*), *The Nose, The Overcoat, Dead Souls; The Government Inspector, The Gamblers, After the Play; Author's Confession and Selected Passages from Correspondence with Friends*.
167. In 1985/86 Lyubimov staged the production in Vienna. This version [Nikolai Gogol and Yuri Lyubimov, *Tote Seelen*, transl. Peter Urban (Wien: Burgtheater, 1985/86)] differs slightly from the Russian text. The play does not start with the completion of a theatrical performance of *The Government Inspector*, but with comments by the two Gogols. The sequence of short stories is the same, except that the scene of the decision to order a new overcoat is expanded. The choice of themes taken from *Dead Souls* differs slightly: Gogol introduces the characters, the childhood of Chichikov is related and the order of the landowners from whom Chichikov buys dead souls differs, with the addition of Koshkarev and Kostanzhoglo. The theme of *The Gamblers* is entirely omitted: the second act forms merely an epilogue rather than a second act properly speaking, which shows Poprishchin and Gogol going mad and being committed to a psychiatric clinic. These changes may have been made in

view of an audience less familiar with Gogol's work than the Moscow audience.

168. Konstantin Rudnitsky, *Russian and Soviet Theatre* (London: Thames and Hudson, 1988) 192.

169. M. Lyubomudrov, "Problemy klassiki", *Ogonek* 31 (1982): 21.

170. Oksana Korneva, "Fantazii ne na temu", *Teatral'naya zhizn'* 15 (1979): 29–30; and Galina Kozhukhova, "A Gogol' molchit ...", *Pravda* 29 January 1979.

171. Kozhukhova, "A Gogol' molchit..."

172. Anatoly Smelyansky, "Chelovecheskoe slyshitsya vezde", *Literaturnoe obozrenie* 2 (1979): 90. My italics.

173. Korneva, 28.

174. Korneva, 30.

175. M. Lyubomudrov, "Problemy klassiki", 21.

176. G. Makogonenko, quoted in Lyubomudrov, "Problemy klassiki", 22.

177. Lubimov, *A Stage Adaptation of M. A. Bulgakov's "The Master and Margarita"* (London: Overseas Publications, 1985) 10.

178. These attempts were in 1971, 1972 and 1975; see Appendix 1, ii.

179. David Borovsky, Conversation, Moscow: 20 April 1990.

180. Interestingly enough, the production was not only delayed until the *thirteenth* anniversary of the theatre, but, as a compilation of the dates of performances shows, the production was played in almost every month on the 13th, although also often on the 3rd or the 26th.

181. Borovsky, Conversation, Moscow: 20 April 1990.

182. Nikolay Potapov, " 'Seans chernoi magii' na Taganke", *Pravda* 29 May 1977.

183. Borovsky, Conversation, Moscow: 20 April 1990.

184. Borovsky, Conversation, Moscow: 20 April 1990; Lyubimov describes the phenomenon of theatre tickets, especially for *The Master and Margarita*, having more value than banknotes in *Feu* 105–106.

185. In 1973 V. A. Dyachin submitted a play called *Assembly, or Under the Clear Skies*; the play was not accepted, but Lyubimov then invited him to adapt *The Master and Margarita*.

186. The events at flat No. 50, the adventures of Behemoth and Koroviev and the long description of the flight have been omitted as well as the epilogue. Many occurrences have either been shortened (such as Bezdomny's persecution of Woland, the first meeting of the Master and Margarita, the breakfast after the rout, and Arthanius's murder of Judas) or totally omitted (such as Sokov's visit to the doctor, Margarita's meeting with Woland before the ball or her adventures on the flight).

189. Anna Tamarchenko, "Roman na stsene: 'Master i Margarita' v teatre na Taganke", *Canadian-American Slavic Studies* 15.2–3 (1981): 369, 371.
190. Nicholas Rzhevsky, "Magical Subversions: 'The Master and Margarita' in Performance", *Modern Drama* 30.3 (1987): 329.
191. Tamarchenko, "Roman na stsene", 361.
192. T. Zlotnikova, "Chtoby mayatnik ne ostanovilsya", *Komsomolets Uzbekistana* 6 October 1982.
193. Rzhevsky, "Magical Subversions", 337.
194. Lubimov, *Master* 90.
195. Lyubimov changed the production for the 1989/90 season and shortened it by merging the second and third acts, thereby losing the emphasis on the "manuscripts" by the break of action. This shortening was necessitated by the actors' loss of the initial energy with which they had played, and because the production, lasting four hours, became too long for the audience: many spectators left after the second act.
196. Lubimov, *Master* 99.
197. Lubimov, *Master* 48.
198. Rzhevsky, "Magical Subversions", 338.

4. Individual and Artist in Crisis

1. B. Poyurovsky, "Rabota est' rabota", *Sovetskaya estrada i tsirk* 7 (1977): 19.
2. Yury Medvedev, Conversation, Munich: 30 September 1990.
3. Marina Yur'eva, "Sud'ba, sud'by, sud'be … ", *Sovetskaya kul'tura* 26 December 1989.
4. Grigory Baklanov and Yury Lyubimov, *Pristegnite remni. (Chetyre minuty v efir)* ([Moskva]: ts., 1975); TsGALI 2485/2/357.
5. Cf. M. Sabinina, "Novye puti sinteza", *Sovetskaya muzyka* 5 (1983): 69–70; Alla Demidova, "Roli i gody", *Literaturnoe obozrenie* 1 (1983): 91.
6. G. Danilova, "Spros osobyi", *Teatral'naya zhizn'* 20 (1975): 11.
7. "Razgovor posle spektaklya", *Teatral'naya zhizn'* 17 (1975): 24–26.
8. "Razgovor posle spektaklya", Suvorova.
9. "Razgovor posle spektaklya", Fedonyuk.
10. Baklanov and Lyubimov, *Pristegnite remni* 58, 70.
11. Baklanov and Lyubimov, *Pristegnite remni* 65: Director.
12. Bert Brecht, *Stücke* 14 (Frankfurt: Suhrkamp, 1967) 134.
13. The only written record of the production is Galina Aksenova's *Printsessa Turandot* (Leningrad State Institute of Theatre, Music and Film: Course Work, 1979). The quotation is from p. 6.
14. Aksenova, *Printsessa Turandot* 5.

15. Aksenova, *Printsessa Turandot* 7–8.

16. TsGALI 2485/4/90 (a letter by Anurov, head of the Main Administration, reproaches the theatre for diverging from the agreed text. If such a distortion occurred again, Anurov threatened to stop further performances. Probable date: June 1981).

17. TsGALI 2485/2/513.

18. TsGALI 2485/4/90 and 639.

19. Yury Lyubimov and Grigory Faiman, *Teatral'nyi Roman* (Moskva: ts., 1983). The text was made available by Svetlana Sidorina. The dress rehearsal took place on 9 June 1983.

20. Lyubimov and Faiman, *Teatral'nyi Roman:* annotated supplement with distribution of roles, dated 7 February 1983.

21. These are: Chichikov (*Dead Souls, Diaboliad*) and Don Quixote (*Don Quixote*); Bunsha (*Ivan Vasilievich*) and Louis (*Molière*); Benckendorf and Nicholas I (*The Last Days*). An episode of *Egyptian Mummy* is rehearsed by Ivan Vasilievich.

22. Lyubimov, Artistic Council, 1 August 1980: 2.

23. Gerald S. Smith, *Songs to Seven Strings* (Bloomington: Indiana UP, 1984) 158.

24. Lyubimov, Artistic Council, 1 August 1980: 2.

25. *Poeticheskoe predstavlenie "V. Vysotsky" v teatre na Taganke* (Moskva: ts., [1981]) 6. Subsequently referred to as "Vysotsky".

26. The theatre version had four sections (Sections II–V below). The critic Aleksandr Gershkovich noted five: I–V below (Aleksandr Gershkovich, *Teatr na Taganke* 155–162). The final version falls into seven sections: *Vysotsky* 1–14 (I), 14–23 (II), 23–32 (III), 32–41 (IV), 41–51 (V), 51–57 (VI) and 57–66 (VII).

27. Songs: "Someone Wanted the Fruit", "Song about the Earth", "On Bolshoi Karetnyi Ryad". Poems: "I Stay Awake", "The Strained Rope", "I Love you Now".

28. "Sad Romance", "The Masked Ball", "Ninka", "The Fellow-Traveller", "That Evening, I neither Drank nor Sang", "From Childhood" and "When I Read the Burial Service and Go Out".

29. The songs comprise: "In No Man's Land", "From the Diary of a Journey", "Half a Year, Half the World...", "March about the End of the War", "Song about the New Age", "We Turn the Earth", "If Somewhere, in the Silent Night...", "White Waltz", "Half an Hour before Attack". The questionnaire was compiled by A. Men'shikov: see Alla Demidova, "Roli i gody", 90.

30. An enactment of "The Sea-Cove's Gone for Good", "Tale about the Unhappy Inhabitants of the Woods", "The Wild Boar"; recordings of "The House" and "Give Meat to the Dogs".

31. "I Retired", "Stupid Dream", "Apples from Paradise", "Again, I am Shivering", "I Live in the Best of Worlds", "My Fate...".

32. *Vysotsky* 20: stage directions.

33. *Vysotsky* 15.

34. The harshest public criticism of Vysotsky was published in *Sovetskaya Rossiya* in 1968.

35. *Vysotsky* 32–35.

36. Lyubimov, Conversation, Berlin: 27 July 1988.

37. "Kak eto delalos'", *Yunost'* 11 (1988): 79–82; Svetlana Sidorina, "Ozhidanie dlilos', a provody byli nedolgi...", *Sovremennaya dramaturgiya* 3 (1991): 155–174 and 4 (1991): 179–201; T. Domrachova, "Soobshchaetsya v poryadke informatsii", *Literaturnaya gazeta* 15 April 1992.

38. "Kak eto delalos'", 79 (Samoilenko, 27 July 1981).

39. Domrachova, "Soobshchaetsya v poryadke informatsii".

40. Yury Zubkov, "Grani poiska", *Teatral'naya zhizn'* 5 (1969): 6.

41. Domrachova, "Soobshchaetsya..."; TsKhSD, 5/84/1014.

42. "Kak eto delalos'", 81 (Schnittke, 13 October 1981).

43. "Kak eto delalos'", 82 (Lyubimov, 31 October 1981).

44. On 2 November 1981 a reprimand was issued by Anurov. Later, special permission was granted by the chief of the KGB, Andropov, that a memorial evening could take place for the anniversary of Vysotsky's birth and death (under severe militia control): Gershkovich, *Teatr na Taganke* 151; Lyubimov, "Kabala svyatosh", interview with A. Minkin, *Ogonek* 27 (1990): 8, 26–29; Smekhov, "Skripka Mastera", *Teatr* 2 (1988): 106–107.

45. Yury Lyubimov, "The crosses Yury Lyubimov bears", Interview with Bryan Appleyard, *The Times* 5 September 1983.

46. A. Anisimov, "Teatr na Taganke: Sud'ba starogo moskovskogo kvartala", *Arkhitektura SSSR* 2 (1984): 52–55.

47. A. Shaikhet, "Teatr na Taganke", *Stroitel'stvo i arkhitektury Moskvy* 10 (1979): 12–14; Yury Gnedovsky, "Teatr v krupnom gorode", *Stsenicheskaya tekhnologiya i tekhnika* 5 (1975): 18–20.

48. Gnedovsky, "Teatr v krupnom gorode", and "Teatr i gorod", *Arkhitektura SSSR* 10 (1979): 10–11; "Teatr novogo tipa", *Arkhitektura SSSR* 6 (1973): 9–14.

49. Mikhail Shcherbachenko, "Dialogi o teatral'noi arkhitekture", *Teatr* 6 (1982): 81–88; *Feu* 109.

50. Yury Pogrebnichko had joined the Taganka as an actor for the 1967/68 season; he was invited to work there as a director by Lyubimov around 1977 (Vampilov's *The Elder Son* on the Small Stage). He works with the set designer Yury Kononenko and recently took over the

artistic direction of the theatre studio "Na Krasnoi Presne", where he staged successful "versions" of Gogol and Chekhov.

51. Lyubimov, Seminar, Berlin: 4 August 1988. Pogrebnichko, Conversation, Moscow: 10 April 1990. According to Pogrebnichko, Lyubimov introduced Denisov's background music, and the opening of the side wall, and also worked on the role of Masha. Whereas Pogrebnichko had rehearsed the play for about a year, Lyubimov completed the production within twelve days.

52. In the initial version, a bed stood there and it was the residence of Anfisa; it was thereby a place visible, yet supposedly invisible, to the audience. Yury Kononenko, Conversation, Moscow: 25 November 1986.

53. Andrey Karaulov, "Rekviem", *Teatr* 10 (1982): 115.

54. Karaulov, "Rekviem", 115.

55. Marianna Stroeva, "Voennaya muzyka", *Teatr* 10 (1982): 121.

56. Lyubimov, Seminar, Berlin: 4 August 1988.

57. *van'ka vstan'ka*: cork-tumbler; a doll with weight attached to its base which causes it always to recover its standing position.

58. Anton Chekhov, *Tri sestry* (Moskva: ts., n.d.) 25, 26.

59. Cf. G. Zamkovets, "Variatsii pod orkestr", *Teatral'naya zhizn'* 23 (1981): 28–29.

60. Karaulov, "Rekviem", 115.

61. Stroeva, "Voennaya muzyka", 125.

62. Vadim Zitser, "Esli by znat'", *Smena* 16 January 1983.

63. Karaulov, "Rekviem", 115; and Zitser, "Esli by znat'". Vasily Kachalov (1875–1948) played Tuzenbakh in the 1901 production at the Moscow Art Theatre; Sergey Yursky (b. 1935) and Emma Popova played Tuzenbakh and Irina in Tovstonogov's 1965 production at the Leningrad Bolshoi Dramatic Theatre.

64. Three real-life drunkards were drinking vodka outside as the side panels opened on one occasion (Lyubimov: Berlin, 4 August 1988; *Feu* 110).

65. Stroeva, "Voennaya muzyka", 122.

66. Stroeva, "Voennaya muzyka", 125.

67. Chekhov, *Three Sisters* (II): Masha; (transl. E. Fen).

68. Alla Demidova, *Vtoraya real'nost'* (Moskva: Iskusstvo, 1980) 102–106.

69. Anatoly Gorelov, "Novy srok –'s pravom perepiski'", *Novoe vremya* 8 (1990): 46.

5. In Exile

1. When Evseev died during a debate before he could speak in support of Lyubimov, the discussion was not even interrupted: another official began to chair the meeting; *Feu* 150–151.

2. TsGALI 2485/4/184 (Lyubimov in a discussion of *Inspectorate Fairy Tales*, 1 June 1978).

3. *Feu* 137.

4. I am indebted to John Roberts, then director of the GB-USSR Association, for this information.

5. Galina Aksenova, "Kak eto bylo", *Russkaya mysl'* 13 October 1991.

6. Lyubimov quoting Mr. Filatov's words after the publication of the interview in *The Times* in "I will not work in such conditions any more ..." *Index on Censorship* 1 (1985): 55.

7. *Feu* 168.

8. Vladimir Maksimov, "Besy", *Sobranie sochinenii* 5 (Frankfurt: Possev, 1979) 233–331.

9. Yury Karyakin, *Iz provintsial'noi khroniki XIX veka* (Moskva: ts., 1979).

10. Yury Lyubimov, *The Possessed*, translated by Richard Crane (London: ts., 1984). References in the text are to acts and scenes of this version; in subsequent footnotes referred to as "Crane".

11. Crane, I, 1: 29 and 16.

12. Crane, II, 17: 190.

13. Programme *The Possessed*, Almeida Theatre.

14. Edward Braun, *The Director and the Stage* (London: Methuen, 1982) 119.

15. Paola Dionisotti, "Lyubimov's *Crime and Punishment*", *drama* 151.1 (1984): 22.

16. Crane, 73.

17. Brecht, *Schriften* 252.

18. Crane, I, 2: 46.

19. Crane, I, 1: 6.

20. Crane, 174.

21. Crane, 11.

22. Crane, 108, 51 and 16.

23. Crane, 3, 23 and 24.

24. *Feu* 169–170.

25. *Feu* 169.

26. Crane, 254 (stage directions).

27. Martin Cropper, "Comic and grotesque", *The Times* 23 March 1985.

28. Eric Shorter, "Russian mannerisms", *The Daily Telegraph* 22 March 1985.

29. Cropper, "Comic and grotesque".

30. Shorter, "Russian mannerisms".

6. Lyubimov at the Opera

1. Jürg Stenzl, "Azione Scenica und Literaturoper", *Musikkonzepte* 20: *Luigi Nono* (München: text + kritik, 1981) 45–57.

2. "Tochki nad 'i' ", *Literaturnaya gazeta* 8 March 1978.

3. Published in the form of an interview between the correspondent Maksimov and Yury Lyubimov under the title "Ya vozmushchen makhinatsiyami organizatorov 'Biennale' ", *Literaturnaya gazeta* 2 November 1977.

4. Algis Juraitis [Zhuraitis], "V zashchitu 'Pikovoi damy' ", *Pravda* 11 March 1978.

5. "La 'Pravda' refuse de publier la réponse de M. Lioubimov aux attaques dont il a été l'objet", *Le Monde* 16–17 April 1978; Aleksandr Minkin, "Pikovaya Dama", *Ogonek* 9 (1989): 20–23.

6. Minkin, "Pikovaya dama", 23.

7. Hans-Klaus Jungheinrich, "Einer wird gerettet, die andern bleiben gefangen", *Frankfurter Rundschau* 30 November 1985.

8. A. Frenkin, " 'Tat'yana za reshetkoi'...", *Literaturnaya gazeta* 20 May 1987.

9. Reinhard Beuth, "Schattenspiele aus russischer Seelenlandschaft", *Süddeutsche Zeitung* 17 March 1987.

10. Ulrich Schreiber, "Laterna Magica als Bewußtseinstheater", *Frankfurter Rundschau* 18 March 1987.

11. H. D. Terschueren, "Tatjana hinter Gittern", *Bonner Rundschau* 17 March 1987.

12. Edward Greenfield, "Ring in the new", *The Guardian* 1 October 1988.

13. Bayan Northcott, "Going for gold", *The Independent* 1 October 1988.

14. "A Russian Ring", *The Independent* 28 September 1988: Lyubimov.

7. The Return of the Master

1. Anatoly Efros (1925–1987) was a pupil of Mariya Knebel. When she took over the artistic direction of the Central Children's Theatre in Moscow in 1956, he was invited to direct there. His productions were so successful that, in 1963, Efros was appointed Chief Artistic Director of the Lenin Komsomol Theatre, where he continued to direct the works of the new generation of dramatists. After a "scandalous", because absurdist, production of Chekhov's *Seagull* in 1967 he was dismissed and given the inferior post of director at the Theatre on Malaya Bronnaya. In 1984 he succeeded Lyubimov as Chief Artistic Director of the Taganka theatre. Efros was never a Party member.

2. Demidova, "Teatr na Taganke: Utraty i nadezhdy", *Izvestiya* 14 April 1987; Smekhov, "Skripka Mastera", *Teatr* 2 (1988); Smelyansky, "Master bez skripki", *Moskovskie novosti* 6 March 1988; Gershkovich "Lyubimov i Efros", *Teatral'naya zhizn'* 10 (1991).

3. Gershkovich mentions this in "Lyubimov i Efros".

4. The following productions were dropped from the repertoire in 1984: *Fallen, Listen, Mother, Comrade, House, Master, Crime; Work* was removed because Mezhevich left the theatre when Efros took over; *Rush Hour* was dropped when Smekhov left the theatre. Oddly, *Ten Days* and *Dawns* remained in the repertoire, probably because of their widespread popularity. A strange occurrence is the disappearance of *House*, while *Exchange* remained in the repertoire, yet the themes of *House* are much more controversial; it was, however, the first production to be revived in 1986 at Gorbachev's request. For the 1984/85 season, the following productions by Lyubimov remained in the repertoire: *Good Person, Ten Days, Tartuffe, Dawns, Horses, Exchange* and *Three Sisters*. See also Appendix 1.

5. See Efros's Letter to the Editors of *Kontinent* 46 (1985).

6. The letter "Let Gorbachev give us proof" was subsequently published in *Moskovskie novosti* 13 (1987), 29 March 1987.

7. D. Pevtsov, "Na volne prezhnei slavy?", *Moskovskaya pravda* 25 October 1988; K. Shcherbakov, "Dolg chesti", *Moskovskie novosti* 6 November 1988; N. Velekhova, "Troyanskii kon' u vorot Taganki", *Moskovskaya pravda* 27 November 1988; Yu. Smelkov, "A tak li vse prosto?", *Moskovskaya pravda* 1 December 1988; B. Shestakov, "Eshche raz o Taganke", – "G. Borovikova, "Postupok", – I Taranenko, "Fakty ne bessporny", – L. Dmitrieva, "Svet umershei zvezdy", *Moskovskaya pravda* 1 December 1988.

8. See Appendix 2.

9. The experiment was launched on 1 January 1987 following the USSR Ministry of Culture's Order No. 330 (6 August 1986). The new law on theatre management was introduced by Directive No. 297 of the Council of Ministers of the RSFSR (31 May 1991).

10. There were, at that time, approximately 250 people on the Taganka payroll. One-third were actors, and two-thirds production personnel and administration. Many of the actors had not been in any production for several years; such was the system of Soviet theatre management.

11. With a few exceptions all those who joined the Fellowship were not leading actors; many of them had never played a substantial part and, indeed, would probably not have been kept in the troupe if a contract system had been introduced.

8. Musical Harmony and the Doomed Individual

1. Andropov had been in the Navy, and the pretender Dmitry wore a sailor's shirt; *Feu* 148.

2. Fried Neumann, "Zaren sterben, aber das Volk bleibt", *Die Welt* 29 January 1983.

3. Elena Levikova (ed.), "Deistvuyushchie litsa i ispolniteli...", *Sovremennaya dramaturgiya* 4 (1988): 208–223.

4. TsGALI 2485/4/210.

5. Several attempts had been made to obtain permission for staging Erdman's *The Suicide* (not then published); in 1983, after the Satire Theatre had been granted permission to rehearse the play, Lyubimov was still refused permission. *The Possessed* had been rehearsed for six weeks in 1982 before rehearsals were stopped by the Main Administration (Cf. *Feu* 168).

6. Incomplete versions were staged in 1870 at the Aleksandrinsky Theatre, in 1880 at the Maly Theatre in Moscow and in 1907 at the Moscow Art Theatre by Nemirovich-Danchenko. In 1934, B. Sushkevich produced the complete play for the first time at the Pushkin Academic Theatre in Leningrad. In 1937, to mark the centenary of Pushkin's death, several theatres planned a production. In Moscow, Meyerhold worked on the play at his own theatre and Radlov rehearsed it at MKhAT, but both abandoned their projects before the première; only Kokhlov premièred *Boris Godunov* in the same year at the Maly Theatre. Anatoly Efros unsuccessfully staged the play in 1957 at the Central Children's Theatre, but made a more successful film version of it in 1970. For a full account of the stage history, see *Sovremennaya dramaturgiya* 4 (1988): 205–206.

7. Konstantin Rudnitsky, "Shest' let spustya", *Izvestiya* 23 June 1988.

8. Nicholas Rzhevsky, "Adapting Drama to the Stage", *SEEA* 3.1 (1985): 173.

9. Rzhevsky, "Adapting Drama to the Stage", 174.

10. Rimma Krechetova, "Lyubimov", 137. Leonid Velekhov gave an account of the ten days' rehearsal of *Boris Godunov* in May 1988 in "Desyat' dnei", *Teatr* 2 (1989): 52–62. An example of how contemporary certain phrases can sound is a performance I saw in Moscow in April 1990, shortly after the economic blockade against Lithuania: the passages on the relations between Russia and Lithuania sounded as if they had been written especially for the current situation, which was not, of course, the case.

11. Rzhevsky, "Adapting Drama to the Stage", 173.

12. Rzhevsky, "Adapting Drama to the Stage", 175.

13. "Deistvuyushchie litsa i ispolniteli... ", *Sovremennaya dramaturgiya* 4 (1988): 213; Mozhaev.

14. Leonid Velekhov, "Prostranstvo tragedii", *Moskovskaya pravda* 24 June 1988.

15. Velekhov, "Desyat' dnei", 59.

16. Rudnitsky, "Shest' let spustya".

17. Mikhail Shvydkoy, "Prostranstvo tragedii", *Sovetskaya kul'tura* 16 July 1988.

18. Lyubimov, Interview, Berlin: 8 August 1988.

19. Velekhov, "Desyat' dnei", 62.

20. The Stockholm production used white dresses for Clothilda and Laura/Mary, a white tablecloth and black panels for the wall. A skull was lit under the table, and a skeleton was hanging on the side of the stage.

21. In the first scene of *The Covetous Knight*, Albert's fighting in tournaments, his doubts about taking money from the Jew and his accusing the Jew of being a thief have been omitted. In *The Stone Guest*, the lengthy debate between Don Juan and Leporello about the success of the disguise for the return to Madrid (Scene I) has been deleted.

    A few songs from *The Feast* have been replaced by others. Some lines spoken in the original by one character are shared with some of the characters of *The Feast*: Albert's speech at the beginning of scene II is split up between him and Clothilda; Mephistopheles's part has been distributed among all the actors.

22. Ol'ga Korshunova, "Podglyad", *Teatral'naya zhizn'* 17 (1989): 3; Lyubimov.

23. Aleksandr Pushkin, *Pir vo vremya chumy* ([Moskva]: ts., [1988]) 2. Subsequently: *Pir*.

24. Natal'ya Kaz'mina, "Dar", *Teatr* 5 (1990): 75.

25. Cf. Yury Apter, "Pir vo vremya chumy", *Komsomol'skaya pravda* 24 September 1989.

26. "Byloe nel'zya vorotit' ": the lines "A vse taki zhal', chto nel'zya s Aleksandrom Sergeichem...".

27. *Pir* 13.

28. Apter, "Pir vo vremya chumy".

29. Apter, "Pir vo vremya chumy".

30. The Swedish production emphasised this atmosphere with grave-diggers and Samaritans who crossed the auditorium, and the theatre staff wearing protective masks. Most Swedish critics were strongly reminded of the impending threat of new diseases like AIDS and nuclear contamination.

31. *Pir* 1.

32. *Pir* 39.

33. *Pir* 49; "Mne skuchno, bes".

34. Kaz'mina, "Dar", 76.

35. Kaz'mina, "Dar", 70.

36. Kaz'mina, "Dar", 73.
37. Tat'yana Bachelis, "Zametki o teatral'noi forme", *Teatral'naya zhizn'* 22 (1989): 7.
38. Bachelis, "Zametki o teatral'noi forme", 9.
39. Lyubimov, Interview, Vienna: 23 May 1993.
40. Lyubimov, Interview, Vienna: 23 May 1993.
41. Boris Zingerman, "Molenie o mire", *Teatr* 2 (1993): 43.
42. Zingerman, "Molenie o mire", 43.
43. Lyubimov, Interview, Vienna: 23 May 1993.
44. Zingerman, "Molenie o mire", 42.
45. Lev Anninsky, "Elektra: shok", *Argumanty i fakty* 40 (1992): 5.
46. The first of these insert occurs when Yury returns to Moscow at the end of the war, the second during Yury's time with the partisans.
47. Lyubimov, Interview, Vienna: 21 May 1993.
48. Her use of the phrase *ne pravda li* (is it not true) is an example of such archaic language.
49. Yury Lyubimov, *Doktor Zhivago* (ts., Jerusalem, 1991).
50. Valery Zolotukhin, (interview with Yuliya Marinova), "Ot 'Zhivogo' k 'Zhivago'", *Teatral'naya zhizn'* 6 (1994): 3.
51. Lyubimov, Interview, Vienna: 21 May 1993.

Conclusion

1. Lyubimov, Interview, Vienna: 21 May 1993.
2. Lyubimov, Interview, Vienna: 21 May 1993.
3. Lyubimov, Interview, Vienna: 21 May 1993.
4. Yury Chernichenko, "Pravilo dlya kontsa sveta", *Kuranty* 27 October 1993.
5. Yury Lyubimov, Interview, Berlin: 8 August 1988.

APPENDIX 1
THE REPERTOIRE

(i) *List of Productions by Yury Lyubimov* **(in alphabetical order)**

Productions at the Taganka Theatre

Antiworlds (*Antimiry*). By Andrey Voznesensky. Adapt. by Andrey Voznesensky. Assistant Director: Petr Fomenko. Set design by Enar Stenberg. Music by B. Khmelnitsky, A. Vasil'ev, V. Vysotsky. Première on 2 February 1965; in repertoire until January 1979.

Boris Godunov. By Aleksandr Pushkin. Set design by Yury Lyubimov. Music by Dmitry Pokrovsky. Première in December 1982 to 19 May 1988. (Censored in 1982; official première in May 1988).

Comrade, Believe ... (*Tovarishch, ver'* ...). Based on works by Aleksandr Pushkin. Adapt. by Lyudmila Tselikovskaya and Yury Lyubimov. Assistant Director: Efim Kucher. Set design by David Borovsky. Music by Grigory Pyatigorsky, Yury Butsko, Ivan Dykhovichny. Première on 11 April 1973; in repertoire until May 1984.

Crime and Punishment (*Prestuplenie i nakazanie*). By Fedor Dostoevsky. Adapt. by Yury Lyubimov and Yury Karyakin. Assistant Director: Yury Pogrebnichko. Set design by David Borovsky. Music by Edison Denisov. Première on 12 February 1979; in repertoire until May 1984; revived in December 1989. (First directed by Lyubimov at Vigszinhaz, Budapest in 1978).

Crossroads (*Perekrestok*). By Vasil' Bykov. Adapt. by Vasil' Bykov. Assistant Director: Boris Glagolin. Set design by David Borovsky. Première on 6 October 1977; in repertoire until March 1979.

But the Dawns here are so Calm ... (*A zori zdes' tikhie* ...). By Boris Vasil'ev. Adapt. by Yury Lyubimov and Boris Glagolin. Assistant Director: Boris Glagolin. Set design by David Borovsky. Music by Yury Butsko. Première on 6 January 1971; in repertoire until May 1990.

Elektra. By Sophocles. Set design by David Borovsky. Music by Sof'ya Gubaidulina. Première on 13 September 1992. (First performed in Athens in May 1992).

The Exchange (*Obmen*). By Yury Trifonov. Adapt. by Yury Lyubimov and Yury Trifonov. Assistant Director: Efim Kucher. Set design by David

Borovsky. Music by Edison Denisov. Première on 20 April 1976. (Directed by Lyubimov in Solnek/Hungary in 1979).

The Fallen and the Living (*Pavshie i zhivye*). Adapt. by Yury Lyubimov, David Samoilov, Boris Gribanov. Assistant Director: Petr Fomenko. Set design by Yury Vasil'ev. Music by Shostakovich, Okudzhava, Vysotsky, Levitansky. Première on 4 November 1965; in repertoire until June 1984.

Fasten Your Seat Belts (*Pristegnite remni!*). By Grigory Baklanov and Yury Lyubimov. Assistant Director: Efim Kucher. Set design by David Borovsky. Music by Grigory Pyatigorsky and Luigi Nono. Première on 2 January 1975; in repertoire until May 1977.

The Feast during the Plague (*Pir vo vremya chumy*) (Little Tragedies). By Aleksandr Pushkin. Set design by David Borovsky. Music by Alfred Schnittke. Première on 30 May 1989.

The Gala (*Benefis*). Based on Aleksandr Ostrovsky. Adapt. by Yury Lyubimov, Boris Glagolin, Aleksandr Vil'kin and Veniamin Smekhov. Assistant Directors: Boris Glagolin, Aleksandr Vil'kin, Veniamin Smekhov. Set design by Enar Stenberg. Music by N. Sidel'nikov. Première on 7 July 1973; in repertoire until June 1975.

The Good Person of Szechwan (*Dobryi chelovek iz Sezuana*). By Bertolt Brecht. Trans. I. Yuzovsky and E. Ionova. Set design by Boris Blank. Music by B. Khmelnitsky and A. Vasil'ev. Première on 23 April 1964.

Hamlet (*Gamlet*). By William Shakespeare. Trans. by Boris Pasternak. Set design by David Borovsky. Music by Yury Butsko. Première on 29 November 1971; in repertoire until Vysotsky died in July 1980.

A Hero of Our Time (*Geroi nashego vremeni*). By Mikhail Lermontov. Adapt. by Nikolay Erdman and Yury Lyubimov. Set design by V. Dorrer. Music by M. Tariverdiev. Première on 14 October 1964; in repertoire until April 1966.

The House on the Embankment (*Dom na naberezhnoi*). By Yury Trifonov. Adapt. by Yury Lyubimov and Yury Trifonov. Assistant Director: Boris Glagolin. Set design by David Borovsky. Music by Edison Denisov. Première on 12 June 1980; in repertoire until April 1984; revived in December 1986.

Inspectorate Fairy Tales (*Revizskaya Skazka*). By Nikolay Gogol'. Adapt. by Yury Lyubimov. Assistant Director: Boris Glagolin. Set design by Eduard Kochergin. Music by Alfred Schnittke. Première on 9 June 1978; in repertoire until March 1983.

From the Life of Fedor Kuz'kin (*Zhivoi: Iz zhizni Fedora Kuz'kina*). By Boris Mozhaev. Adapt. by Boris Mozhaev. Assistant Director: Boris Glagolin. Set design by David Borovsky. Première on 23 February 1989. (Banned in 1968).

The Life of Galileo (*Zhizn' Galileya*). By Bertolt Brecht. Trans. by Lev Kopelev. Set design by Enar Stenberg. Music by D. Shostakovich, B. Khmelnitsky, A. Vasil'ev. Première on 17 May 1966; in repertoire until October 1977.

Listen! (*Poslushaite!*). By Vladimir Mayakovsky. Adapt. by Yury Lyubimov and Veniamin Smekhov. Set design by Enar Stenberg. Music by Edison Denisov. Première on 16 May 1967; in repertoire until April 1984; revived in May 1987 and in repertoire until June 1989.

The Master and Margarita (*Master i Margarita*). By Mikhail Bulgakov. Adapt. by Yury Lyubimov and V. Dyachin. Assistant Director: A. Vil'kin. Set design by M. Anikst, S. Barkhin, D. Borovsky, E. Stenberg. Music by Edison Denisov. Première on 6 April 1977; in repertoire until May 1984; revived in October 1987.

The Mother (*Mat'*). By Maksim Gor'ky. Adapt. by Yury Lyubimov and Boris Glagolin. Assistant Director: Boris Glagolin. Set design by David Borovsky. Music by Yury Butsko. Première on 23 May 1969; in repertoire until May 1984; revived in October 1987 and in repertoire until May 1990.

Protect Your Faces! (*Beregite vashi litsa!*). By Andrey Voznesensky. Songs by V. Vysotsky. Première on 10 February 1970. (Closed by Mossovet after the première).

Pugachev. By Sergey Esenin. Adapt. by Nikolay Erdman. Assistant Director: V. Raevsky. Set design by Yury Vasiliev. Music by Yury Butsko. Première on 17 November 1967; in repertoire until February 1984.

The Rush Hour (*Chas Pik*). By Jerzy Stawinski. Trans. by Zinaida Shatalova. Adapt. by Veniamin Smekhov. Assistant Director: A. Burov. Set design by David Borovsky. Costumes by I. Malygina. Choreography by V. Bokkadoro. Première on 4 December 1969; in repertoire until September 1985.

In Search of a Genre (*V poiskakh zhanra*). *Tvorcheskii vecher* by Vladimir Vysotsky, Valery Zolotukhin, Leonid Filatov, Dmitry Mezhevich, Alla Demidova. Set design by David Borovsky. Première on 8 March 1978.

Tartuffe (*Tartyuf*). By Jean-Baptiste Molière. Trans. by Mikhail Donskoy. Set design by Mikhail Anikst and Sergey Barkhin. Music by A. Volkonsky. Première on 14 November 1968.

Ten Days that Shook the World (*Desyat' dnei, kotorye potryasli mir*). By John Reed. Adapt. by Yury Lyubimov, Yu. Dobronravov, I. Dobrovolsky, S. Kashtelyan. Set design by I. Tarasov. Music by N. Karetnikov. Première on 2 April 1965; in repertoire until May 1990. (Directed by Lyubimov in Havana in 1977).

Three Sisters (*Tri sestry*). By Anton Chekhov. Assistant Director: Yury Pogrebnichko. Set design by Yury Kononenko. Music by Edison Denisov. Première on 16 May 1981.

Turandot, or the Congress of Whitewashers (*Turandot ili kongress obelitelei*). By Bertolt Brecht. Trans. by L. Fradkin. Assistant Director: Efim Kucher. Set design by David Borovsky. Music by Alfred Schnittke. Première on 20 December 1979; in repertoire until April 1981.

Under the Skin of the Statue of Liberty (*Pod kozhei statui svobody*). By Evgeny Evtushenko. Adapt. by Evgeny Evtushenko. Assistant Directors: B. Glagolin, A. Vasil'ev, V. Smekhov, L. Filatov. Set design by David Borovsky. Music by V. Arusmanov, G. Pyatigorsky, A. Vasil'ev, D. Mezhevich. Première on 18 October 1972; in repertoire until April 1974.

The Suicide (*Samoubiitsa*). By Nikolay Erdman. Set design by David Borovsky. Music by Edison Denisov. Première on 24 July 1990.

Vladimir Vysotsky. By Yury Lyubimov. Set design by David Borovsky. Music by Vladimir Vysotsky. Première on [27 July] 1981. (Performed in private four times on the anniversary of Vysotsky's birth and death; first official performance in May 1988).

What is to be Done? (*Chto delat'?*). By Nikolay Chernyshevsky. Adapt. by Yury Lyubimov. Assistant Directors: B. Glagolin, G. Primak. Set design by David Borovsky. Music by Yury Butsko. Première on 18 September 1970; in repertoire until May 1982.

The Wooden Horses (*Derevyannye koni*). By Fedor Abramov. Adapt. by Fedor Abramov. Assistant Directors: Boris Glagolin, Aleksandr Vil'kin. Set design by David Borovsky. Music by N. Sidel'nikov. Première on 16 April 1974; in repertoire until June 1992.

Work is Work (*Rabota est' rabota*). Choreography by I. Burova. Music by Dmitry Mezhevich (songs by Bulat Okudzhava). Première on 21 April 1976; in repertoire until March 1984; revived for the 1989/90 season under the title "Daughter, Father and Guitarist".

Zhivago. By Boris Pasternak. Adapt. by Yury Lyubimov. Set design by Andrey von Schlippe. Music by Alfred Schnittke. Première in June 1993. (First performed in Vienna on 18 May 1993).

Productions at other theatres

Al gran sole carico d'amore. By Luigi Nono. La Scala, Milan: 4 April 1975. Conducted by Claudio Abbado. Set design by David Borovsky. Choreography by L. Yakobson.

Boris Godunov. By Modest Mussorgsky. [Version by Paul Lamm]. La Scala, Milan: December 1979. Conducted by Claudio Abbado. Set design by David Borovsky.

The Comedians. Based on Aleksandr Ostrovsky. Adapt. by Yury Lyubimov. Set design by Andrey von Schlippe. Music by Edison Denisov. Finnish National Theatre, Helsinki: November 1992.

Crime and Punishment. By Fedor Dostoevsky. Lyric Theatre, Hammersmith, London: 5 September 1983. Adapt. by Yury Karyakin and Yury Lyubimov. Trans. by Nicholas Rzhevsky. Set design by David Borovsky. Music by Edison Denisov.

Crime and Punishment. By Fedor Dostoevsky. Akademietheater, Vienna: 12 October 1984. Adapt. by Yury Karyakin and Yury Lyubimov. Trans. by Peter Urban. Set design by David Borovsky. Music by Edison Denisov.

Crime and Punishment. By Fedor Dostoevsky. Arena del Sol, Bologna: December 1984. Adapt. by Yury Lyubimov and Yury Karyakin. Trans. by S. Vitale. Set design by David Borovsky. Music by Edison Denisov.

Crime and Punishment. By Fedor Dostoevsky. Arena Stage, Washington: January 1987. Adapt. by Yury Karyakin and Yury Lyubimov. Trans. by Michael H. Heim. Set design by David Borovsky. Music by Edison Denisov.

Dead Souls. By Nikolay Gogol'. Burgtheater, Vienna: 30 January 1986. Adapt. by Yury Lyubimov. Trans. by Peter Urban. Set design by Yury Lyubimov and David Cunningham. Music by Alfred Schnittke.

Don Giovanni. By Wolfgang Amadeus Mozart. Opera House, Budapest: 25 May 1982. Conducted by I. Fischer. Set design by David Borovsky.

Eugene Onegin. By Petr Tchaikovsky. Opernhaus, Bonn: 15 March 1987. Conducted by Maximiano Valdes. Set design by Paul Hernon. Costumes by Alexandre Vasiliev. Choreography by Cristina Hamel.

The Feast during the Plague. (Little Tragedies). By Aleksandr Pushkin. Kungliga Dramatiska Teatern, Stockholm: 28 September 1986. Trans. by Lars Erik Blomqvist. Music by Daniel Bell. Set and costumes designed by Bo Ruben Hedwall.

Fidelio. By Ludwig van Beethoven. Staatstheater, Stuttgart: 28 November 1985. Conducted by Janos Kulka/Dennis Russell Davies. Set and costumes designed by Stefanos Lazaridis. Lighting designed by Hanns-Joachim Haas.

The Good Person of Szechwan. By Bertolt Brecht. Habima Theatre: 24 July 1988. Trans. by Shimon Sandbank. Set design by Yoseph Yekerson. Costumes by Anat Mesner. Lighting design by Natan Panturin. Music by A. Vasil'ev and B. Khmelnitsky.

Hamlet. By William Shakespeare. Haymarket Theatre, Leicester: 14 September 1989. Set design by David Borovsky. Lighting designed by Krystof Kozlowski. Choreography by Chang Ching.

Jenufa. By Leos Janaček. Opernhaus, Zurich: 4 May 1986. Conducted by
    Christian Thielemann. Set design by Paul Hernon. Costumes by
    Clare Mitchell. Choreography by Eleanor Fazan.

Jenufa. By Leos Janaček. Royal Opera House, Covent Garden, London: 17
    November 1986, 10 February 1988, 20 April 1993. Conducted by
    Christian Thielemann. Set design by Paul Hernon. Costumes by
    Clare Mitchell. Lighting design by Paul Hernon and Robert Bryan.
    Choreography by Romayne Grigorova.

Khovanshchina. By Modest Mussorgsky [Version by Dmitry
    Shostakovich]. La Scala, Milan: 24 February 1981. Conducted by
    Raitchev. Set design by David Borovsky.

Lady Macbeth of Mtsensk. By Sergey Prokof'ev. Staatsoper, Hamburg: 18
    February 1990. Set design by David Borovsky.

Lulu. By Alban Berg. Teatro Regio, Turin: 27 May 1983. Conducted by Zoltan
    Pesko. Set design by David Borovsky. Choreography by Susanna Egri.

Lulu. By Alban Berg. Lyric Opera, Chicago: November 1987.

The Master and Margarita. By Rainer Kunad, based on Mikhail Bulgakov.
    Badisches Staatstheater, Karlsruhe: 9 March 1986. Conducted by
    Peter Sommer. Set design by Heinz Balthes. Costumes by Renate
    Schmitzer. Choreography by Yolande Straudo.

The Master and Margarita. By Mikhail Bulgakov. Kungliga Dramatiska
    Teatern, Stockholm: 18 December 1988. Adapt. by Yury Lyubimov.
    Trans. by Lars Erik Blomqvist. Set design by Jan Lundberg, after the
    idea of Yury Lyubimov. Music by Edison Denisov. Lighting design
    by Krzystof Kozlowski.

St Matthew Passion. By Johann Sebastian Bach. La Scala/San Marco,
    Milan: 6 June 1985.

The Possessed. By Fedor Dostoevsky. Almeida Theatre London/Theatre
    d'Europe, Paris: 16 February 1985. Adapt. by Yury Lyubimov. Trans.
    by Richard Crane. Set design by Stefanos Lazaridis. Costumes by
    Clare Mitchell. Music by Alfred Schnittke. Lighting designed by
    David Cunningham. Choreography by Jacky Lansley.

I Quattro Rusteghi. By Ermanno Wolf-Ferrari. Bayerische Staatsoper
    Munich: 18 April 1982. Conducted by Alberto Zedda. Set design by
    David Borovsky. Choreography by Peter Marcus.

The Queen of Spades. By Petr Tchaikovsky. [New version by Alfred
    Schnittke and Yury Lyubimov]. Badisches Staatstheater, Karlsruhe:
    10 November 1990. Conducted by V. Sinaisky. Set Design and
    Costumes by David Borovsky.

A Raw Youth. By Fedor Dostoevsky. Adapt. by Yury Lyubimov. Set
    design by Andrey von Schlippe. Music by Edison Denisov. Finnish
    National Theatre, Helsinki: October 1991.

Rheingold. By Richard Wagner. Royal Opera House, Covent Garden, London: 28 September 1988. Conducted by Bernard Haitink. Set design by Paul Hernon. Lighting design by Robert Bryan.

Rigoletto. By Guiseppe Verdi. Maggio Musicale, Florence: May 1983. Conducted by Hans Graf. Set design by Stefanos Lazaridis.

Salammbô. By Modest Mussorgsky. [Version by Zoltan Pesko]. Teatro San Carlo, Naples: April 1983. Conducted by Zoltan Pesko. Set design by David Borovsky.

Salammbô. By Modest Mussorgsky. [Version by Zoltan Pesko]. Grand Opéra at Palais Garnier, Paris: 16 June 1986. Conducted by Zoltan Pesko. Set and costumes designed by David Borovsky. Choreography by Pierre Darde. Lighting designed by David Cunningham.

The Sunset. By Isaak Babel'. Habima Theatre: 2 August 1986. Trans. by Nilli Mirsky. Set design by Yoseph Yekerson. Costumes by Anat Mesner. Music by Poldi Schätzman. Lighting design by Natan Panturin.

Tannhäuser. By Richard Wagner. [Parisian version]. Staatstheater Stuttgart: 7 May 1988. Conducted by Garcia Navarro. Set and costumes designed by Paul Hernon. Choreography by Valery Panow. Lighting design by Hanns-Joachim Haas.

The Threepenny Opera. By Bertolt Brecht and Kurt Weill. Vigszinhaz, Budapest: 1981. Set design by David Borovsky.

Tristan and Isolde. By Richard Wagner. Teatro Communale, Bologna: 1 December 1983. Conducted by Zoltan Pesko. Set design by Stefanos Lazaridis.

Yaroslavna. By Boris Tishchenko. Little Opera and Ballet Theatre, Leningrad: 1974. Conducted by P. Bubel'nikov. Choreography by O. Vinogradov.

(ii) Production Histories[1]

PRODUCTION	REF	READING	ART COUNCIL	PROD CONF	MOSSOVET	MINISTRY	PREMIÈRE
Hero	1964	15 June 64			17 Nov. 64		14 Oct. 64
Antiworlds	1965						2 Feb. 65
10 Days	1964	11 June 64	20 Mar. 65	20 Mar. 65 / 8 Apr. 65 / 29 Sept.65 / 2 Nov. 67	13 June 64	17 June 64	2 Apr. 65
Fallen & Living			July/Aug. 65 / 22 Nov. 69		24 Mar. 65 / 30 June 65 / 9 Sept.65	Oct. 65	4 Nov. 65
Galileo			Feb. 66	20 May 66	16 May 66		17 May 66
Listen!		16 Feb. 66 / 29 Mar. 68 / May 68	Apr. 66 / Mar./Apr. 67 / 22 Nov. 69	Mar. 67 / 3 Nov. 67	Apr.-May 67 / 17 May 67	17 May 67	16 May 67
Pugachev	1966		10 Jan. 67 / 17 Oct. 67 / 13 Nov. 67	Sept.-Oct. 67	16 Nov. 67 / 17 Nov. 67		17 Nov. 67
Tartuffe	1968		May-Oct. 68	June-Nov. 68	Oct.-Nov. 68		14 Nov. 68
Mother		18 Nov. 68	25 Feb. 69 / 15 May 69	12 May 69	27 Nov. 68 / 16 May 69 / 22 May 69	16 May 69 / 22 May 69	23 May 69
Rush Hour	1968,69		June-Nov. 69	Oct.-Nov. 69	28 Nov. 69 / 3 Dec. 69	28 Nov. 69	4 Dec. 69
Protect Faces	1966,69, 70,71	18 Apr. 68	25 Dec. 69 / 27/8 Jan. 70	2 Feb. 67	3 Feb. 70		10 Feb. 70
What...?	1970		29 Dec. 69 / Feb.-June 70	6 June 70	11/12 June 70 / 2 July 70 / 14 Sept. 70	11/12 June 70	18 Sept.70
Dawns			22 Dec. 70		26 Dec. 70		6 Jan. 71
Hamlet/Chronicles	1968		27 Nov. 70 / 25 June 71 / 10 Nov. 71	25 June 71	22 Nov. 71		29 Nov. 71
Statue of Liberty	1969,71, 72	13 Mar. 71	1972		6 June 72 / 9 July 72 / 15 Sept.72 / 10 Oct. 72	6 June 72 / 9 July 72	18 Oct. 72
Comrade	1971,72, 73	9 Mar. 71	18 May 72 / 21/3 Dec. 72 / 3 Mar. 73 / 27 Mar. 73	June-Oct. 72	28 Mar. 73 / 2 Apr. 73		11 Apr. 73
Gala	1973		27 Oct. 72 / 5 June 73	29 Oct 72			7 July 73
Wooden Horses	1973,74		23 Mar. 74		8 Apr. 74 / 12 Apr. 74	1974	16 Apr. 74
Seat Belts	1975	6 Dec. 74	24 Dec. 74	6 Dec. 72	30 Dec. 74		2 Jan. 75
Exchange	1975,76	28 Nov 75	1 Dec. 75 / 10 Apr. 76		13 Apr. 76	13 Apr. 76	20 Apr. 76
Master	1971,72, 75	1975					6 Apr. 77
Crossroads		29 June 76					6 Oct. 77
Fairy Tales	1973	2 Dec. 73		2 Dec. 73			9 June 78
Crime	1972	Sept./Oct.76					12 Feb. 79
Turandot	1973,74, 76	29 Oct. 73		22 Nov. 73			20 Dec. 79
House							12 June 80
Vysotsky		.	13 Oct. 81 / 31 Oct. 81		21 July 81		12 May 88
Godunov			7 Dec. 82		10 Dec. 82		19 May 88
Tough	1968,71, 74,75	30 Jan. 67	19 Dec. 67		Feb. 68	6 Mar. 69 / 24 June 75	23 Feb. 89
Suicide	1965,71						24 July 90

[1] "reference": mention of the production in official letters and applications for rehearsal permission; "reading": reading by Lyubimov or the author, usually at the beginning of the rehearsal process; "Art. Council": discussions with the (enlarged) artistic council (often classified as meetings with the 'intelligentsia'); "prod. conf.": production conference, an administrative and internal meeting; "Mossovet": discussions with the representatives of Mossovet's Central Directorate of Culture; "Ministry": discussions with representatives of the USSR or/and RSFSR Ministry of culture.

Compiled on the basis of fond 2485 of the Central State Archive of Literature and Arts, Moscow.

(iii) Repertoire Statistics 1964–1994[1]

Title	1964	1965	1966	1967	1968	1969	1970	1971	1972	1973	Total
4 under Roof	25 (11*)										25 (11)
Housing Estate	39 (5*)	21 (2*)									60 (7)
Ghosts	39 (3*)	29 (2*)	4								72 (7)
Jean	22 (22*)	29 (29*)									51 (51)
Kettle/Moon	51 (1*)	42	30 (5*)	1							124 (6)
Good Person	61	70	46	38	25	28 (1*)	21 (1*)	19 (2*)	21 (2*)	14 (2*)	343 (8)
Hero	22 (4*)	41 (18*)	10 (10*)								73 (32)
Antiworlds		37 (25*)	66 (40*,16#)	55 (28*,22#)	49 (34*,12#)	43 (12*,29#)	48 (11*,36#)	36 (8*,26#)	38 (6*,32#)	31 (5*,25#)	403 (367)
Ten Days		62	62	55 (2*)	50 (2*)	39 (3*)	42 (6*)	37 (4*)	33 (10*)	27 (5*)	407 (32)
Fallen/Living		12	43 (8*)	44 (14*)	37 (17*,1#)	25 (12*)	27 (14*)	21 (6*)	17 (5*)	14 (3*)	240 (80)
Telegrams			36 (9*)	33 (14*)	36 (14*)	6 (4*)					111 (41)
Galileo			30	38 (1*)	34 (1*)	29 (3*)	23	17 (1*)	16 (1*)	8 (1*)	195 (8)
Investigation			1	13 (1*)							14 (1)
Listen!				33 (2*)	35	21 (1*)	13 (2*)	12 (4*)	10 (2*)	14 (5*)	138 (16)
Pugachev				7	42 (11*)	31 (8*)	38 (14*)	20 (9*)	16 (6*)	13 (3*)	167 (51)
Taruffe					4 (2*)	40 (19*)	21 (8*)	30 (17*)	20 (9*)	20 (11*)	135 (66)
Mockinpott						17 (4*,2#)	7 (5*)				24 (11)
Mother						14	37 (3*)	17 (2*)	14 (3*)	13	95 (8)
Rush Hour							42 (5*)	24 (2*)	22 (3*)	27 (8*)	115 (18)
What ?							11 (1*)	23 (4*)	11 (3*)	1 (1*)	46 (9)
Dawns								39 (4*)	47 (5*)	34 (6*)	120 (15)
Hamlet								1	43	29	73 (-)
Statue									9	24 (4*,1#)	33 (5)
Comrade										25 (3*)	25 (3)
Gala										11	11 (-)
Annual Perf	259	343	328	317	312	293	330	296	317	305	

[1]Repertoire statistics 1964–1989: number of total annual performaces (matinée performances marked with asterisks, late night performances at 10 pm with apostrophe; both are included in the preceding figure).
Compiled on the basis of announcements published in *Vechernjaya Moskva*, *Teatral'naya Moskva* and *Teatral'no-Kontsertnaya Moskva*; the internal Taganka repertoires (in TsGALI) were not accessible at the time of research. The number of annual performances for 1988 and 1989 have been compared with internal Taganka statistics. The so-called "tselevye" and "shefskie" performances are not included.

Title	1974	1975	1976	1977	1978	1979	1980	1981	1982	1983	Total
Good Person	12 (2*)	15	9	10 (2*)	11 (2*)	6 (1*)	14 (2*)	17 (1*)	15 (1*)	13	122 (11)
Antiworlds	25 (2*,23#)	24 (5*,19#)	12 (4*,8#)	12 (5*,7#)	10 (3*,7#)	1 (1*)					84 (84)
Ten Days	21 (3*)	24 (4*)	18 (3*)	16 (3*)	15 (2*)	13 (6*)	17 (5*)	15 (2*)	11 (2*)	19 (1*)	169 (31)
Fallen/Living	13 (5*)	14 (5*)	13 (5*)	11 (8*)	15 (9*)	10 (5*)	16 (6*)	18 (6*)	15 (9*)	26 (20*)	151 (78)
Galileo	6	4	7	1							18 (-)
Listen!	7 (3*)	6 (3*)	10 (2*)	13 (6*)	12 (2*)	13 (7*)	12 (5*)	13 (8*)	12 (4*)	13 (3*)	111 (43)
Pugachev	7 (1*)	10 (1*)	3 (2*)	9 (5*)	9 (4*)	4 (1*)	2 (1*)	15 (2*)	10 (4*)	5 (2*)	74 (23)
Tartuffe	12 (5*)	15 (8*)	12 (7*)	18 (12*)	15 (9*)	14 (6*)	6 (2*)	11 (4*)	7 (5*)	8 (4*)	118 (62)
Mother	7 (1*)	8	9 (3*)	10 (1*)	13 (1*)	9 (2*)	12 (1*)	10 (1*)	4	13 (1*)	95 (11)
Rush Hour	15 (4*)	12 (3*)	14 (3*)	17 (1*)	14 (5*)	17 (6*)	9 (4*)	11 (5*)	10 (3*)	15 (4*)	134 (38)
What?		3 (2*)	12 (2*)	9 (2*)	7 (2*)	10 (3*)	6 (5*)	6 (2*)	6 (2*)		59 (20)
Dawns	23 (6*)	22 (3*)	23 (6*)	18 (4*)	19 (6*)	16 (4*)	19 (2*)	12 (2*)	16 (4*)	18 (4*)	186 (41)
Hamlet	15	12	18	17	19	17	8				106 (-)
Statue	7 (4*)										7 (4)
Comrade	23	18 (1*)	14 (2*)	12 (1*)	13 (2*)	10 (2*)	11 (2*)	11	8	8 (1*)	128 (11)
Gala	25	11 (2*)									36 (2)
Horses	11 (1*)	22 (1*)	16	19 (1*)	17 (1*)	16 (3*)	14 (3*)	18 (2*)	11 (1*)	14 (2*)	158 (15)
Seat Belts		29 (4*)	17	9							55 (4)
Orchard		8 (1*)	14 (5*)	9 (3*)	11 (2*)	8 (3*)	6 (1*)				56 (15)
Exchange			17	33	21 (1*)	15 (4*)	11 (4*)	13 (5*)	10 (4*)	17 (10*)	137 (28)
Work			2 (1#)	31 (31#)	27 (1*,25#)	22 (1*,21#)	21 (1*,20#)	8 (1*,7#)	6 (6#)	14 (7*,7#)	131 (129)
Master				23	35	31	24	29	13	34	189 (-)
Crossroads				9 (2*)	20 (10*)	4 (3*)					33 (15)
Fairy Tales					11 (1*)	14 (2*)	12 (6*)	7 (2*)	4	6 (2*)	54 (13)
Crime						20	20	11 (1*)	9	15	75 (1)
Turandot						1	22 (4*)	6 (5*)			29 (9)
House							14	20 (2*)	14 (1*)	26 (2*)	74 (5)
Orchestra								18 (6*,10#)	12 (9*,2#)	35 (26*,5#)	65 (58)
Babel								2 (2#)	8 (5*,3#)	24 (23*)	34 (33)
3 Sisters									24	26	70 (-)
Annual Perf.	229	257	240	306	314	271	276	291	225	349	

Repertoire Statistics 1964–1994 (continued)[7]

Title	1984	1985	1986	1987	1988	1989	1990	1991	1992	1993	Total
Good/Person	24 (2*)	18 (1*)	14 (2*)	21 (5*)	18 (7*)	14 (4*)	12 (4*)	10 (3*)	15	6	152 (28)
Ten Days	27 (4*)	26 (5*)	21 (4*)	25 (10*)	19 (10*)	16 (9*)	7 (7*)				141 (49)
Fallen/Living	21 (9*)										21 (9)
Listen!	23 (6*)	7 (4*)		15 (3*)	16 (4*)	10 (5*)					71 (22)
Pugachev	14 (2*)	5 (2*)									19 (4)
Tartuffe	21 (6*)	31 (14*)	29 (17*)	41 (23*)	35 (14*)	26 (14*)	27 (15*)	17 (14*)	31 (5*)	7	265 (122)
Mother	8 (1*)			5 (1*)	12 (2*)	8 (1*)	6				39 (5)
Rush Hour	36 (5*)	19 (2*)									55 (7)
Dawns	23 (8*)	23 (8*)	19 (9*)	23 (2*)	15 (4*)	8 (1*)	5				116 (32)
Comrade	10 (3*)										10 (3)
Horses	23 (4*)	24 (1*)	19 (4*)	23 (8*)	13 (2*)	13 (1*)	18 (3*)	9	8 (1*)		150 (24)
Orchard		13	30	16	10 (1*)	7	3	2			81 (1)
Exchange	32 (15*)	29 (16*)	22 (13*)	20 (14*)	16 (5*)	23 (15*)	22 (9*)	19 (9*)	18 (6*)	4	205 (102)
Work	11 (6*,1#)					18 (3*)	15 (4*)	19 (1*)			63 (15)
Master	15 (1*)			15	24	31	32	25	31	13	186 (1)
Search					18 (1*, 17#)	26 (5#)	6 (1*)	9 (2*)	2		61 (26)
Crime	9					1	26 (1*)	16	13	8	73 (1)
House	9			29 (2*)	25 (4*)	30 (4*)	24 (2*)	17 (2*)	21	5	160 (14)
Orchestra	41 (16*,5#)	35 (25*,2#)	35 (21*)	47 (15*)	42 (14*)	32 (7*)		8 (3*)	5 (1*)		245 (109)
Babel	40 (24*,2#)	37 (17*,18#)	42 (13*,8#)	41 (16*)	32 (8*)	23 (6*)	25 (10*)	32 (24*)	24 (5*)	8	304 (151)
3 Sisters	33	24 (1*)	20	21 (1*)	14 (3*)	9	6	8	6	1	142 (5)
Lower Depths		38	32	21	13 (3*)	8	6				118 (3)
War		28 (2*)	37 (14*)	34 (14*)	26 (15*)	18 (10*)	1				144 (55)
Picnic		12	19								31 (-)
15 sq.m.			18 (2*)	31 (18*)	13 (9*)						62 (29)
Dreamer			12 (2*)	13 (4*)							25 (6)
Misanthrope			13	29 (1*)	27 (1*)	26 (6*)	16 (4*)	16 (11*)	8 (3*)	1	136 (26)
Blond Girl			9 (2*)	10 (1*)							19 (3)
Vysotsky					13	15	4	10	16	8	66 (-)
Godunov					10	23	19	12	23	8	95 (-)
Phaedra					8	18 (4#)	17	9	4	2	58 (4)
Kuzkin						21	18	23	21	8	91 (-)
Feast						12	25	15	15	5	72 (-)
Suicide							9	20	20	8	57 (-)
Elektra									11	9	20 (-)
Zhivago										2	2 (-)
Annual Perf.	420	369	391	480	419	436	349	296	292	103	

Repertoire Statistics 1964–1994 (continued)[7]

(iv) Evaluation of Repertoire Statistics [1]

PRODUCTION	PREMIERE	LAST PERFORMANCE	TOTAL PERF	MATINEES IN %	YEARS IN REPERTOIRE	AVERAGE PERF. P.A
Good Person	23 Apr 1964		617	8	30	21
Hero	14 Oct 1964	IV/66	73	44	2	36
Antiworlds	2 Feb. 1965	I/79	487	93	14	35
Ten Days	2 Apr 1965	V/90	717	16	25	29
Fallen/Living	4 Nov 1965	VI/84	412	40	19	22
Galileo	17 May 1966	X/77 (X 74/5,76/7)	213	4	9	24
Listen[1]	16 May 1967	IV/84 R: V/87-VI/89	320	25	19	17
Pugachev	17 Nov. 1967	II/84 (X 79/80)	260	30	16	16
Tartuffe	14 Nov. 1968		518	48	25	21
Mother	23 May 1969	V/84 R. X/87-V/90	229	10	18	13
Rush Hour	4 Dec. 1969	IX/85	304	21	16	19
What ?	18 Sept 1970	V/82 (X 73-75)	105	28	9	12
Dawns	6 Jan. 1971	V/90	422	21	19	22
Hamlet	29 Nov. 1971	VII/80	179	0	9	20
Statue	18 Oct. 1972	IV/74	40	22	2	20
Comrade	11 Apr. 1973	V/84	163	10	11	15
Gala	7 July 1973	VI/75	47	4	2	23
Horses	16 Apr 1974	VI/92	308	13	18	17
Seat Belts	2 Jan. 1975	V/77	55	7	2	27
Orchard	30 June 1975	V/80 R X/85-II/91	137	12	11	12
Exchange	20 Apr 1976		342	38	18	19
Work	21 Apr 1976	III/84 R: IX/89-VII/91	194	74	10	19
Master	6 Apr. 1977	V/84 R. X/87	375	0	14	27
Crossroads	6 Oct 1977	III/79	33	45	2	16
Search	8 Mar. 1978	II/92 (not announced till 1988)	61	43	4 (14)	15
Fairy Tales	9 June 1978	III/83	54	24	5	11
Crime	12 Feb. 1979	V/84 R XII/89	148	1	10	15
Turandot	20 Dec. 1979	IV/81	29	31	2	14
House	12 June 1980	IV/84 R: XII/86	234	8	12	19
Orchestra	24 Dec. 1980		310	54	14	22
Babel	18 Jan. 1981		338	54	13	26
3 Sisters	16 May 1981		212	2	13	16
Vysotsky	12 May 1988		66	0	6	11
Godunov	19 May 1988		95	0	6	16
Phaedra	9 June 1988		58	7	6	10
Kuzkin	23 Feb. 1989		91	0	5	18
Feast	30 May 1989		72	0	5	14
Suicide	24 July 1990		57	0	4	14
Elektra	13 Sept 1992		20	0	2	10
Zhivago	16 June 1993		2	0	1	-
Lower Depths	24 Jan. 1985		118	2	9	13
War	2 May 1985		144	38	9	16
Picnic	18 Oct. 1985	X/86	31	0	1	-
1.5 sq. m.	28 Apr 1986	VI/88	62	47	2	31
Dreamer	13 Sept 1986	I/88	25	24	2	12
Misanthrope	27 Sept 1986		136	19	8	17
Blond Girl	5 Oct. 1986	V/87	19	16	1	-

[1] List of productions, premières, last performances; total number of performances, percentage of matinée performances, years in repertoire and average number of annual performances. R stands for Revival; X for except.

APPENDIX 2
LYUBIMOV, THE TAGANKA AND THE SYSTEM

(i) *Chronology of events*

30 IX 1917	Yury Petrovich Lyubimov born in Yaroslavl
1922	Lyubimov moves to Moscow
1931–1933	Technical school (electrician)
1934–1936	School of MKhT II (closed in 1936)
1936–1940	Shchukin School (Vakhtangov Theatre): actor
1941–1947	Song and Dance Ensemble of the NKVD
1947–1964	Actor at the Vakhtangov Theatre[1]

Roles in the Theatre

1937	*The Man with the Gun* (N. Pogodin): Signaller
1939	*A Straw Hat* (E. Labiche): Felix
1939	*The Road to Victory* (A. Tolstoy): Officer
1940	*Much Ado About Nothing* (W. Shakespeare): Claudio
1947	*The Young Guard* (A. Fadeev) [B. Zakhava][2]: Oleg Koshevoy
1947	*Deep Roots* (J. Gow, A. D'Usseau) [A. Gabovich]: Negro
1948	*On the Eve* (I. Turgenev) [R. Simonov][3]: Shubin
1948	*All My Sons* (A. Miller) [A. Remizov]: Chris
1949	*The Doomed Conspiracy* (N. Virta): Mark Pino
1950	*Early Joys* (K. Fedin) [B. Zakhava]: Kirill Izvekov
1950	*The Missouri Waltz* (N. Pogodin): Robin
1950	*Les Misérables* (V. Hugo) [A. Remizov]: Enjolras
1951	*No Ordinary Summer* (K. Fedin) [B. Zakhava]: Kirill Izvekov
1951	*Cyrano de Bergerac* (E. Rostand): Cyrano
1951	*Egor Bulichev and Others* (M. Gorky) [B. Zakhava]: Tyatin (Stalin State Prize of the USSR)

---

[1]The list of roles is based on information provided by Svetlana Sidorina and published details in *Le Feu Sacré*. Authors are given in brackets, directors in square brackets, Lyubimov's parts after the colon.

[2]Boris Zakhava (1896–1976), director and actor of the Vakhtangov theatre.

[3]Ruben Simonov (1899–1968), actor and director; chief artistic director of the Vakhtangov theatre from 1939–1968; from 1968, his son Evgeny Simonov headed the theatre.

1952   *Much Ado About Nothing* (W. Shakespeare): Benedict
1952   *The Two Gentlemen of Verona* (W. Shakespeare): Valentin
1954   *The Seagull* (A. Chekhov) [B. Zakhava]: Treplev
1954   *The Man with the Gun* (N. Pogodin) [R. Simonov]: Dymov
1954   *Before Sunrise* (G. Hauptmann) [A. Remizov]: son
1956   *Foma Gordeev* (M. Gorky) [R. Simonov]: Young man
1956   *Romeo and Juliet* (W. Shakespeare) [I. Rapoport]: Romeo
1956   *Filomena Marturano* (Eduardo de Filippo) [E. Simonov]: son
1957   *After separation* (Tur Brothers): Raymond
1957   *Two Sisters* (F. Knorre): Anatoly
1958   *Eternal Fame* (B. Rymar): Gritsenko
1958   *The Idiot* (F. Dostoevsky) [A. Remizov]: Ivolgin
1959   *Little Tragedies* (A. Pushkin) [E. Simonov]: Mozart
1959   *The Irkutsk Story* (A. Arbuzov) [E. Simonov]: Viktor
1950   *The Twelfth Hour* (A. Arbuzov) [R. Simonov]: Ulybshev
1962   *Aleksey Berezhnoy* (K. Simonov): Aleshka
1962   *The History of One Family* (L. Kruczkovsky): Willy

Roles in Films:

1941   *Coloured stories*: Prince – swineherd
1941   *Snow Princess*: Narrator. (N. Erdman, based on Andersen)
1945   *Days and Nights*: Myslennikov. [A. Stolper] (based on
           K. Simonov)
1946   *An Agitated Household*: La Rochelle. [M. Zharov]
1946   *Our Heart*: Yakov. [A. Stolper]
1947   *Robinson Crusoe*: Friday. [A. Andrievsky]
1948   *Blue Ways*: Vetkin. [V. Braun]
1948   *The Boy from the Border*: Pilot. [V. Zhuravlev]
1949   *Michurin*: Translator. [A. Dovzhenko]
1950   *Kuban Cossacks*: Plyasoz. [I. Pyriev]
1956   *On the Stage Boards*: Zefimov. [K. Yudin] (based on
           vaudeville by D. Lensky, scenario by N. Erdman)
1959   *Man from the Planet Earth*: Pharmacist. [B. Buneev] (based
           on the life of Tsiolkovsky)
1960   *Three Encounters*: Young scientist. [V. Pudovkin]
1963   *Kain XVIII*: Prime Minister. [N. Kosheverova] (N. Erdman,
           based on E. Shvarts)
1970   *A Farm in the Steppe*: Bachey. [B. Buneev] (based on Kataev)
1975   *Some Words in Defence of Monsieur de Molière*: Molière
           [A. Efros] (for television)
1952   State Prize of the USSR

1953	Member of the Communist Party[4]
1954	''Merited Artist of the RSFSR''
1958–1964	Teacher at the Shchukin School and presents in 1963 *The Good Person of Szechwan*
1959	Director of Aleksandr Galich's *How much Does Man Need?* at the Vakhtangov Theatre

The Taganka Theatre[5]

1964

23 April	*The Good Person of Szechwan* (Bertolt Brecht)
May	*Fearless Jean* (T. Gabbe) [B. Breev]
August	Taganka to Ryazan
14 Oct.	*A Hero of Our Time* (Mikhail Lermontov)
Dec.	*Mr Kettle and Mrs Moon* (J. B. Priestley) [S. Birman, revival]

1965

2 Feb.	*Antiworlds* (Andrey Voznesensky)
2 April	*Ten Days That Shook the World* (John Reed)
April	Taganka to Leningrad
4 Nov.	*The Fallen and the Living*
	The Suicide (Nikolay Erdman): censored

1966

31 Jan.	*Telegrams Only* (V. Osipov) [T. Vulfovich]
April	Taganka to Tula
17 May	*The Life of Galileo* (Bertolt Brecht)
June/July	Taganka to Georgia (Tbilisi and Sukhumi)
26 Dec.	*The Investigation* (Peter Weiss) [P. Fomenko, L. Eidlin]

1967

April	Taganka to Leningrad
16 May	*Listen!* (Vladimir Mayakovsky)
17 Nov.	*Pugachev* (Sergey Esenin)
	Marat/Sade (Peter Weiss): banned

---

[4]The date is dubious: the Soviet Encyclopaedia gives 1952; the Theatre Encyclopaedia 1947, and memoirs 1953 [Gershkovich in *Teatr na Taganke* (Benson, Vermont: Chalidze, 1986) and Lioubimov, *Le Feu Sacré* (Paris: Fayard, 1985)].

[5]Authors are given in brackets, director(s) in square brackets; for productions directed by Lyubimov, no indication is made.

1968

February	Lyubimov in East Berlin: 70th anniversary of Bertolt Brecht
30 April	*From the Life of Fedor Kuzkin* (Boris Mozhaev): censored
14 Nov.	*Tartuffe* (J. B. Molière)
	The Chronicle Plays (W. Shakespeare): banned

1969

15 Feb.	*How Mr. Mockinpott was Relieved of his Sufferings* (Peter Weiss) [M. Levitin]
23 May	*The Mother* (Maksim Gorky)
4 Dec.	*The Rush Hour* (Jerzy Stawinski)
	Lyubimov in Havana as member of festival jury

1970

10 Feb.	*Protect Your Faces!* (Andrey Voznesensky): censored
18 Sept.	*What is To Be Done?* (Nikolay Chernyshevsky)
	Lyubimov as advisor on *Ten Days* in Brno (CSSR)

1971

6 Jan.	*But the Dawns Here are so Calm* (Boris Vasiliev)
summer	Taganka to German Democratic Republic
Sept.	Taganka to Kiev
29 Nov.	*Hamlet* (William Shakespeare)

1972

June/July	Taganka to Leningrad
18 Oct.	*Under the Skin of the Statue of Liberty* (Evgeny Evtushenko)

1973

11 April	*Comrade, believe!* (Aleksandr Pushkin)
7 July	*The Gala* (Aleksandr Ostrovsky)
June/July	Taganka to Georgia (Tbilisi, Sukhumi)
Sept./Oct.	Taganka to Alma Ata and Tashkent

1974

16 April	*The Wooden Horses* (Fedor Abramov)
June/July	Taganka to KAMAZ, Naberezhnye Chelny
Sept.	Taganka to Vilnius and Riga
Oct.	Taganka to Leningrad
	Yaroslavna (Boris Tishchenko), Leningrad: Little Theatre of Opera and Ballet

1975

2 Jan.	*Fasten Your Seat Belts* (Grigory Baklanov)
March	Taganka to Tallinn

4 April	*Al gran sole carico d'amore* (Luigi Nono), Milan: La Scala
June	*The Tough: From the Life of Fedor Kuzkin*: censored
30 June	*The Cherry Orchard* (Anton Chekhov) [A. Efros]
Sept./Oct.	Taganka to Vladimir, Pskov, Rostov
Sept.	Taganka to Bulgaria

1976

20 April	*The Exchange* (Yury Trifonov)
21 April	*Work is Work*
spring	Taganka to Klin, Siberia, Kamchatka
July	*Yaroslavna* shown at Festival d'Avignon
Sept.	BITEF [Belgrad International Theatre Festival] (*But the Dawns ...*, *Hamlet*, *Ten Days*): First Prize for *Hamlet*
Oct./Nov.	Taganka to Hungary
	Lyubimov participates in UNESCO conference on "Artists in Totalitarian Countries"

1977

6 April	*The Master and Margarita* (Mikhail Bulgakov)
6 Oct.	*Crossroads* (Vasil Bykov)
Nov.	Taganka to France (Paris, Lyons, Marseilles)
	Ten Days that Shook the World, Havana

1978

8 March	*In Search of a Genre*
9 June	*Inspectorate Fairy Tales* (Nikolay Gogol)
June	*Book of Complaints* (Anton Chekhov) [E. Kucher]
	Crime and Punishment (Dostoevsky), Budapest: Vigszinhaz
July	Taganka and Lyubimov in East Berlin
Mar./Apr.	*The Queen of Spades* cancelled at the Grand Opéra, Paris

1979

12 Feb.	*Crime and Punishment* (Fedor Dostoevsky)
June	Taganka to Minsk
Sept./Oct.	Taganka to Georgia (Tbilisi)
20 Dec.	*Turandot* (Bertolt Brecht)
Dec.	*Boris Godunov* (Modest Mussorgsky), Milan: La Scala
	The Exchange in Hungary, Solnek

1980

May	Taganka to Poland
12 June	*The House on the Embankment* (Yury Trifonov)
25 July	Death of Vladimir Vysotsky
summer	Taganka to Chelyabinsk, Ufa

24 Dec.   *The Little Orchestra of Hope* (Petrushevskaya, Volodin, Zlotnikov) [S. Artsybashev]

1981

18 Jan.   *Five Tales by Babel* (Isaak Babel) [E. Kucher]
24 Feb.   *Khovanshchina* (Modest Mussorgsky), Milan: Scala
16 May   *Three Sisters* (Anton Chekhov) [co-dir. Yury Pogrebnichko]
27 July   *Vladimir Vysotsky*: censored
summer   Taganka to Tyumen
6 Dec.   *Vassa Zheleznova* (Maksim Gorky) [A. Vasiliev]
                The Threepenny Opera (Brecht/Weill), Budapest: Vigszinhaz

1982

Feb.   Taganka to Bryansk
18 April   *I Quattro Rusteghi* (Wolf-Ferrari), Munich
May/June   Taganka to Finland
25 May   *Don Giovanni* (Mozart), Budapest Opera House
Sept.   Taganka to Tashkent
Dec.   *Boris Godunov* (Aleksandr Pushkin): censored
                The Possessed (Fedor Dostoevsky): censored
                The Suicide (Nikolay Erdman): censored
                The Elder Son (A. Vampilov) [Yu. Pogrebnichko]

1983

23 April   Official Inauguration of the New Building for the Taganka
                Theatre
April   *Salammbô* (Modest Mussorgsky), Naples: Teatro San Carlo
27 May   *Lulu* (Alban Berg), Turin: Teatro Regio
9 June   *Theatrical Novel* (Mikhail Bulgakov): dress rehearsal
August   Taganka to Omsk
Sept.   Old Stage reopens after restoration
5 Sept.   *Crime and Punishment*, London: Lyric Theatre
1 Dec.   *Tristan und Isolde* (Richard Wagner), Bologna: Teatro
                Comunale

1984

24 Jan   *London Evening Standard* Award for best production
6 March   Lyubimov dismissed as Chief Artistic Director
7 March   Efros becomes Chief Artistic Director of the Taganka
                Theatre
9 May   Old Stage closed for restoration
May   *Rigoletto* (Verdi), Florence: Maggio Musicale
26 July   Lyubimov deprived of Soviet citizenship

| 12 Oct. | *Crime and Punishment*, Vienna: Burgtheater |
| Dec. | *Crime and Punishment*, Bologna: Arena del Sole |

1985

24 Jan.	*The Lower Depths* (Maksim Gorky) [A. Efros]
16 Feb.	*The Possessed* (Fedor Dostoevsky), London: Almeida Theatre
2 May	*War has no Female Face* (S. Aleksievich) [A. Efros]
6 June	*Matthäuspassion* (Bach), Milan
summer	Lyubimov meets the Habima Theatre, Israel
October	Taganka to BITEF
18 Oct.	*Beautiful Sunday for a Picnic* (T. Williams) [V. Sarkisov]
28 Nov.	*Fidelio* (Beethoven), Stuttgart
	Cerceau (V. Slavkin) [A. Vasiliev]

1986

30 Jan.	*Dead Souls* (Nikolay Gogol), Vienna: Burgtheater
9 March	*The Master and Margarita* (Kunad), Karlsruhe: Badisches Staatstheater
28 April	*One and a Half Square Meters* (B. Mozhaev) [S. Artsybashev, A. Efros]
4 May	*Jenufa* (Janaček), Zurich
16 June	*Salammbô*, Paris: Palais Garnier
2 Aug.	*The Sunset* (Isaak Babel), Israel: Habima Theatre
Sept.	Taganka to Kuibyshev
13 Sept.	*Notes of a Dreamer* (Fedor Dostoevsky) [V. Sarkisov]
27 Sept.	*Misanthrope* (J. B. Molière) [A. Efros]
5 Oct.	*Blond Girl round the Corner* (A. Chervinsky) [T. Kazakova]
Oct.	*Jenufa*, London: Covent Garden
Nov.	Taganka to Poland
Dec.	*Little Tragedies* (Aleksandr Pushkin), Stockholm: Royal Dramatic Theatre

1987

Jan.	*Crime and Punishment*, Washington: Arena Stage
13 Jan.	death of Anatoly Efros
Feb.	Taganka to Paris
15 March	*Eugene Onegin* (Petr Tchaikovsky), Bonn
May	Taganka to Milan
24 Nov.	*Lulu*, Chicago

1988

| Feb. | *Jenufa* revived at London Covent Garden |
| March | Taganka to Madrid (*The Mother*); meeting with Lyubimov |

May	*Tannhäuser* (Wagner), Stuttgart
May	*Boris Godunov* (Pushkin). Revival of the production closed in 1982
June	*Phaedra* (Marina Tsvetaeva) [R. Viktyuk]
24 July	*The Good Person of Szechwan* (Bertolt Brecht), Israel: Habima Theatre
July/Aug.	seminar on *Hamlet* in West Berlin
28 Sept.	*Rheingold* (Wagner), London: Covent Garden
Sept.	Taganka to Novosibirsk
Oct.	Taganka to Greece
Dec.	*The Master and Margarita* (Bulgakov), Stockholm: Royal Dramatic Theatre
Dec.	Taganka to Stockholm and Helsinki (*Boris Godunov*)

1989

24 Jan.	Lyubimov arrives in Moscow
23 Feb.	*The Tough* (B. Mozhaev)
30 May	*The Feast During the Plague* [*Little Tragedies*] (A. Pushkin)
May	Taganka to Greece
June	Taganka to Zurich (*Boris Godunov*)
14 Oct.	*Hamlet*, Leicester: Haymarket Theatre
23 Dec.	*Crime and Punishment*: revival

1990

18 Feb.	*Lady Macbeth of Mtsensk*, Hamburg: Staatsoper
March	Taganka to Helsinki
June	Taganka to Israel
24 July	*The Suicide* (Nikolay Erdman)
Sept./Oct.	Taganka to Germany (Berlin, Munich)
10 Nov.	*The Queen of Spades* (Tchaikovsky/Schnittke), Karlsruhe: Badisches Staatstheater

1991

March	Taganka to Stuttgart (*Boris Godunov*)
	Taganka to Spain (Pamplona, Madrid)
April	Taganka to Portugal
September	New Season: Performances on the Old Stage only.
December	Taganka to Prague
October	*A Raw Youth* (Dostoevsky), Helsinki: Finnish National Theatre
8 Dec.	Lyubimov signs contract with G. Popov as Artistic Director until December 1993

1992

12 Jan.	General Meeting and split between Lyubimov and Gubenko
April	Restricted access to theatre for Gubenko
6 April	Letter to Luzhkov asking for division
April/May	Rehearsals for *Elektra* in Greece
13 Sept.	*Elektra* (Sophocles) opens in Moscow
23 Sept.	Eltsin's resolution to hold secret ballot and act accordingly
27–30 Oct.	Secret ballot (146 for, 27 against division out of total 267)
19 Nov.	Mossovet confirms division
Nov.	*The Comedians* (based on Ostrovsky), Helsinki: Finnish National Theatre

1993

March	Taganka to Japan
April/May	Rehearsals for *Doctor Zhivago* in Vienna
28 April	Mossovet allocates part of the building to Gubenko and the Fellowship
16 June	*Doctor Zhivago* opens in Moscow
29 June	Moscow Arbitration Court confirms division and allocation of premises to Gubenko and the Fellowship
17 July	Gubenko occupies the New Stage and shuts off all connecting doors on the basis of the above decision
August	Taganka in Bonn
30/31 Aug.	Lyubimov cannot open the season in these circumstances
27 Sept.	Appeals Court decides in favour of Lyubimov
Oct./Nov.	Taganka in Hamburg and Munich
Nov./Dec.	Taganka in Spain
15 Dec.	Higher Arbitration decides in favour of Gubenko

1994

Jan./Feb.	Taganka in Paris
15 March	Old stage closed (fire doors are blocked)
28 April	Luzhkov (Moscow Government) returns the entire premises to Lyubimov
26 May	Moscow Arbitration Court decides in favour of Gubenko
21 July	Appeals Court decides in favour of Lyubimov
12 Sept.	Higher Arbitration Court decides the two sides should try to reach a settlement
14 Oct.	Taganka vacates the new building by 24 October

(ii) *The Taganka: Actors and Artistic Council*[6]

THE ACTORS

Name	DoB	School	Taganka
Andreev, I. A.	1953	Shchukin	1976
Antipov, Feliks N.	1942	Shchukin	1968
Balushkova, N. Yu.	1949	Yaroslavl	1978
Belyaev, Yury V.	1947	Shchukin	1975
Bogina, Alla M.	1945	Shchepkin	1974
Boiko, L. G.	1946	Kiev	1976
Bokhon, V. F.	1957	Shchepkin	1981
Bortnik, Ivan S.	1939	Shchukin	1966
Chernyaev, V. N.	1949	Sverdlovsk	1975
Chernova, Alla A.	1937	MGU	1964
Chub, Nina E.	1949	Shchukin	1972
Davydov, Aleksandr V.	1951	Shchukin	1973
Davydova, L. A.	1947	Shchukin	1973
Demidova, Alla S.	1936	Shchukin	1964
Dodina, Taisiya V.	1939	MKhAT Studio	1962
Doktorova, M. N.	1921	Shchukin	1945
Durova, E. L.	1959	GITIS	1980
Dykhovichny, Ivan V.	1947	Shchukin	1970
Dzhabrailov, Rasmi Kh.	1932	GITIS	1965
Farada, Semen L.	1933	MVTU im. Baumana	1972
Filatov, Leonid A.	1946	Shchukin	1969
Frolova, I. Ya.	1940	Saratov	1972
Gabets, Elena N.	1955	Shchukin	1976

---

[6]This list is based on information contained in TsGALI file 2485/4/880 (1983).
Shchukin School: affiliated to the Vakhtangov Theatre [Boris Shchukin, 1894–1939, actor of Vakhtangov Studio theatre].
Shchepkin School: affiliated to the Maly Theatre [Mikhail Shchepkin, 1788–1863, actor of Maly Theatre].
VGIK (im. Gerasimova): All-Union State Institute of Cinematography [Vsesoyuznyi Gosudarstvennyi Institut Kinematografii].
GITIS (im. Lunacharskogo): State Institute of Theatre Arts (Moscow) [Gosudarstvennyi Institut Teatral'nogo Iskusstva].
GABT: State Academic Bolshoi Theatre [Gosudarstvennyi Akademicheskii Bol'shoi Teatr].
MVTU: Moscow Technical High School [Moskovskoe Vysshee Tekhnicheskoe uchilishche].
LGITMiK: Leningrad State Institute of Cinematography, Music and Theatre [Leningradskii Gosudartsvennyi Institut Teatra Muzyki i Kinematografii].
MKhAT: Academic Moscow Art Theatre [Moskovskii Khudozhestvennyi Akademicheskii Teatr].

Grabbe, Aleksey N.	1947	Shchukin	1971
Grabbe, Ekaterina N.	1954	Shchukin	1975
Gulynskaya, O. P.	1948	Shchukin	1972
Gubenko, Nikolay N.	1941	VGIK	1964, 1980
Grudneva, G. B.	1950	MKhAT	1976
Ivanenko, Tat'yana V.	1941	VGIK	1966
Kazancheev, Oleg A.	1956	Shchukin	1978
Khmel'nitsky, Boris A.	1940	Shchukin	1964
Kholmogorov, Stanislav I.	1946	Shchukin	1970
Kornilova, E. K.	1938	VGIK	1964
Kovaleva, N. P.	1954	GITIS	1979
Komarovskaya, Lyudmila G.	1937	Shchukin	1964
Krasil'nikova, N. B.	1956	GITIS	1980
Kuznetsova, Irina S.	1940	Shchukin	1964
Lebedev, Mikhail S.	1945	LGITMiK	1976
Leont'ev, Avangard S.	1957	GITIS	1980
Lukyanova, Tat'yana S.	1939	Shchukin	1966
Makhova, T. M.	1923	MGU	1959
Manysheva, Elena Yu.	1956	Shchepkin	1981
Matyukhin, Vladimir V.	1946	Shchukin	1972
Medvedev, Yury D.	1941	Circus	1964
Mezhevich, Dmitry E.	1040	Shchukin	1968
Mulina, O. I.	1948	GITIS	1973
Osipov, Yu. N.	1957	Shchukin	1980
Petrov, Igor' A.	1941	Shchukin	1964
Politseimako, Maria V.	1938	Shchukin	1965
Pogorel'tsev, V. A.	1940	Shchepkin	1964
Podkolzin, S. M.	1940	Shchukin	1969
Pyl'nova, Z. V.	1947	Odessa	1968
Radunskaya, Viktoriya A.	1937	GABT/Choreography	1966
Roninson, Gotlib M. (d. 1992)	1916	Shchukin	1945
Sabinin, Aleksandr I.	1932	Shchukin	1967
Saiko, Natalya P.	1948	Shchukin	1970
Savchenko, S. A.	1946	Shchukin	1970
Savchenko, Lidiya K.	1941	GITIS	1967
Selyutina, Lyubov' S.	1952	Shchepkin	1976
Semenov, V. S.	1943	VGIK	1966
Semin, A. B.	1957	Shchukin	1978
Serenko, A. M.	1939		1976
Sidorenko, Tat'yana I.	1949	Shchukin	1971
Shapovalov, Vitaly V.	1939	Shchukin	1968
Shatskaya, Nina S.	1940	GITIS	1964

Shcheblykin, V. I.	1948	Kazan'	1975
Shcherbakov, Dal'vin A.	1938	VGIK	1965
Shkol'nikov, O. Ya.	1947	Circis	1968
Shteinraikh, Lev A.	1923	GITIS	1945
Shternberg, Viktor V.	1936	Shchukin	1972
Shulyakovsky, V. L.	1945	Shchukin	1974
Slavina, Zinaida A.	1940	Shchukin	1964
Smekhov, Veniamin B.	1940	Shchukin	1962
Smirnov, Yury N.	1938	Shchukin	1963
Sobolev, Vsevolod N.	1939	Shchepkin	1963
Trofimov, Aleksandr A.	1952	Shchukin	1974
Ul'yanova, Inna I.	1934	Shchukin	1964
Vlasov, Leonid M.	1954	GITIS	1980
Vlasova, Galina N. (d.1993)	1916	Len. Art Studio	1955
Vlasova, S. Yu.	1952	Circus	1972
Vil'kin, Aleksandr M.	1953		
Vysotsky, Vladimir S. (d.1980)	1938	MKhAT Studio	1964
Yarmol'nik, L. I.	1954	Shchukin	1976
Zaitsev, A. A.	1939	Shchukin	1978
Zheldin, Konstantin B.	1933	Shchukin	1966
Zhukova, Tat'yana I.	1939	GITIS (1962)	1966
Zolotareva, G. V.	1956	GITIS	1979
Zolotukhin, Valery S.	1941	GITIS/Operetta	1965

THE ARTISTIC COUNCIL

a. Members of the Artistic Council of the Taganka Theatre (1964–1990)

Artistic Council in 1964

THEATRE: *ex officio*: Nikolai Dupak (adm. dir.), Yury Lyubimov (art. dir.), Ella Levina (lit. adviser). *Actors*: Alla Demidova, Petr Fomenko, Nikolai Gubenko, A. Kolokolnikov, Inna Ulyanova, Leonid Veitsler, Galina Vlasova.

INTELLIGENTSIA: N. Fedosova, Nikolai Karetnikov (composer), A. Maryamov (critic), Enar Stenberg (designer), Valentin Tolstykh (philologist), Georgy Vladimov (writer), Andrey Voznesensky (poet).

Artistic Council in 1977

THEATRE: Yury Belyaev, Nina Chub, Alla Demidova, Ivan Dykhovichny, Leonid Filatov, Boris Khmelnitsky, Efim Kucher, A. Kolokolnikov, Mariya Politseimako, Zinaida Slavina, Venyamin

Smekhov, Vsevolod Sobolev, Vitaly Shapovalov, Galina Vlasova, Aleksandr Vilkin, Vladimir Vysotsky, Tatyana Zhukova, Valery Zolotukhin.
INTELLIGENTSIA: Sergey Averintsev (philosopher), Aleksandr Anikst (critic), Aleksandr Bovin (correspondent), Edison Denisov (composer), Evgeny Evtushenko (poet), S. P. Kapitsa (mathematician), Yury Karyakin (critic), Feliks Kuznetsov (critic), Boris Mozhaev (writer), David Samoilov (poet), Boris Slutsky (poet), Yury Trifonov (writer), V. Shubkin (philologist), Andrey Voznesensky, Boris Zingerman (critic).

Artistic Council in 1981
THEATRE: *Actors*: Yury Belyaev, Nina Chub, Alla Demidova, Leonid Filatov, Boris Khmelnitsky, Mariya Politseimako, Zinaida Slavina, Veniamin Smekhov, Vsevolod Sobolev, Vitaly Shapovalov, Galina Vlasova, Tatyana Zhukova–Kirtbaya, Valery Zolotukhin. *Directors*: Sergey Artsybashev, Efim Kucher, Yury Pogrebnichko.
INTELLIGENTSIA: Fedor Abramov (writer), Bella Akhmadulina (poet), Aleksandr Anikst, Aleksandr Bovin, Edison Denisov, Evgeny Evtushenko, Yury Karyakin, S. P. Kapitsa, Boris Mozhaev, Alfred Schnittke (composer), Andrey Voznesensky.

Artistic Council in 1983
THEATRE: *Actors*: Yury Belyaev, Viktor Bokhon, Nina Chub, Aleksey Grabbe, Mikhail Lebedev, Tatyana Lukyanova, Mariya Politseimako, Aleksandr Sabinin, Vsevolod Sobolev, Veniamin Smekhov, Aleksandr Trofimov, Galina Vlasova, Konstantin Zheldin, Tatyana Zhukova. *Directors*: Sergey Artsybashev, Efim Kucher, Yury Pogrebnichko, Anatoly Vasiliev.
INTELLIGENTSIA: Aleksandr Anikst, Bella Akhmadulina, Aleksandr Bovin, Lev Delyusin (historian), Edison Denisov, Evgeny Evtushenko, Mikhail Eremin (lit. critic), Grigory Faiman (lit. critic), S. P. Kapitsa, Yury Karyakin, Viktor Loginov (historian), Boris Mozhaev, Bulat Okudzhava (poet), V. Shubkin, Alfred Schnittke, Andrey Voznesensky, Boris Zingerman.

Artistic Council in 1989/90
THEATRE: Yury Belyaev, Aleksandr Davydov, Alla Demidova, Semen Farada, Leonid Filatov, Boris Glagolin, I. Kulevskaya, Mariya Politseimako, Aleksandr Sabinin, Dmitry Shcherbakov, Zinaida Slavina, Veniamin Smekhov, Yury Smirnov, Vsevolod Sobolev, Aleksandr Trofimov, Aleksandr Vilkin, Galina Vlasova, Tatyana Zhukova, Valery Zolotukhin.

*b. Members of the Enlarged Artistic Council of the Taganka
Theatre* (1964–1990)

Abramov, Fedor A.	writer, critic (1920–1983)
Akhmatova, Anna A.	poet (1889–1966)
Akhmadulina, Bella A.	poet (b. 1937)
Aliger, Margarita I.	poet (1915–1992)
Anastav'ev, Arkady N.	theatre critic [*Teatr*] (b. 1914)
Ancharov, Mikhail L.	writer (b. 1923)
Andronikov, Irakly L.	[Andronikashvili] writer and lit. critic, master of oral recital (b. 1908)
Anikst, Aleksandr A.	lit. critic (1910–1989)
Arbuzov, Aleksey N.	playwright (1908–1986)
Bachelis, Tat'yana I.	theatre and film critic
Baklanov, Grigory Ya.	writer; editor of *Znamya* (b. 1923)
Barkan, Semen A.	director of theatre "Romen"
Bartoshevich, Aleksandr	lit. critic, Shakespeare expert
Borovsky, David L.	set designer (b. 1934)
Borshchagovsky, Aleksandr M.	writer, critic (b. 1913)
Bovin, Aleksandr E.	correspondent [Izvestiya] (b. 1930)
Boyadzhiev, Grigory N.	theatre critic (1909–1974)
Burlatsky, Fedor M.	journalist, writer; formerly correspondent [*Pravda*]; chief editor of *Literaturnaya gazeta* since 1990 (b. 1927)
Butsko, Yury M.	composer
Byalik, B. A.	Gor'ky Institute of Literature
Chernichenko, Yury D.	writer and journalist, ed. board of *Znamya* and *Ogonek* (b. 1929)
Chukhray, Grigory N.	film director (b. 1921)
Dashkevich, Vladimir S.	composer (b. 1934)
Delyusin, Lev P.	historian, expert on China
Denisov, Edison V.	composer (b. 1929)
Donskoy, Mikhail A.	translator
Efremov, Oleg N.	actor and artistic director of MKhAT im. Chekhova; founder of "Sovremennik" theatre (b. 1927)
Eidel'man, Natan Ya.	writer, historian (1930–1989)
Erdman, Nikolay R.	playwright (1902–1970)
Eremin, Mikhail P.	literary critic
Evtushenko, Evgeny A.	poet (b. 1933)
Fedorov, Vasily D.	poet (1918–1984)

Flerov, Georgy N.	physicist, Academy member (b. 1913)
Frolov, Vladimir V.	theatre critic (b. 1917)
Gerasimov, Sergey A.	director, playwright, critic (1906–1985)
Ginzburg, Lev V.	writer and translator (1921–1980)
Gribanov, Boris M.	editor *Khudozhestvennaya literatura*
Ikramov, Kamil' A.	writer (b. 1927)
Iskander, Fazil' A.	writer (b. 1929)
Kapitsa, Andrey P.	geographer, Academy member (b. 1931)
Kapitsa, Petr L.	physicist, Academy member (1894–1984)
Kapitsa, S. P.	physicist and mathematician, Academy member
Karetnikov, Nikolay N.	composer (b. 1930)
Karpinsky, Len V.	correspondent [*Pravda*], secretary to Central Committee under Khrushchev; after 1969: dissident; now political observer for *Moscow news* (b. 1929)
Karyakin, Yury F.	lit. critic, journalist, historian, Institute of International Workers' Movement (b. 1930)
Kassil', Lev A.	writer (1905–1970)
Kataev, Valentin P.	writer (1897–1986)
Katanyan, Vasily A.	literary critic, Mayakovsky expert (b. 1902)
Kirsanov, Semen I.	poet (1906–1972)
Khutsiev, Marlen M.	film director (b. 1925)
Klimov, Elem	film director (b. 1933)
Komissarzhevsky, V. G.	theatre critic
Kopelev, Lev Z.	writer (b. 1912); exiled to Germany in 1980
Korzhavin, N. M.	poet (b. 1925); exile 1973
Krechetova, Rima P.	theatre critic
Krymova, Natal'ya A.	theatre critic; wife of A. Efros
Kucher, Efim M.	director
Kuleshov, Vasily I.	lit. critic (b. 1919)
Kuznetsov, Feliks F.	lit. critic (b. 1931)
Lakshin, Vladimir Ya.	lit. critic, editor of *Znamya* (1933–1993)
Levina, Ella P.	head of lit. dept. of Taganka theatre from 1964–1980
Levitansky, Yury D.	poet and translator (b. 1922)
Levitin, Mikhail Z.	chief director of "Ermitazh" theatre
Loginov, Viktor T.	writer, journalist, historian (b. 1925)
L'vov, Mikhail D.	poet (b. 1916/17)
L'vov-Anokhin, Boris A.	director and theatre critic; since 1963 chief director of Stanislavsky Theatre (b. 1926)

Lyubimov, Boris N.	theatre critic, teacher at GITIS
Mal'tsev, Elizar Yu.	writer (b. 1916/17)
Mar'yamov, Aleksandr M.	writer and theatre critic (b. 1909)
Mikhailov, Aleksandr A.	critic of cont. poetry (b. 1922)
Mozhaev, Boris A.	writer (b. 1923)
Narovchatov, Sergey S.	poet and lit. critic (1919–1981)
Nechkina, Militsa V.	historian, Academy member (1901–1985)
Neizvestny, Ernst I.	sculptor (b. 1926)
Nekrasov, Viktor P.	writer (b. 1911); exile in 1974
Nilin, Pavel F.	writer, screenplays (1908–1981)
Okudzhava, Bulat Sh.	writer and singer (b. 1924)
Paperny, Zinovy S.	lit. critic and parodist, Mayakovsky expert (b. 1919)
Pluchek, Valery N.	director of the Satire Theatre since 1957 (b. 1909)
Pospelov, Gennady N.	lit. critic (b. 1899)
Rozhdestvensky, Robert I.	poet (b. 1932)
Rozov, Viktor S.	writer, dramatist (b. 1913)
Rozovsky, Mark G.	director and writer
Rudnitsky, Konstantin L.	theatre critic (1920–1988)
Samoilov, David S.	poet (1920–1990)
Shatrov, Mikhail F.	playwright (b. 1932)
Shchedrin, Rodion K.	composer (b. 1932)
Shcherbakov, K. A.	critic, chief editor *Iskusstvo kino*
Shklovsky, Viktor B.	writer and lit. critic (1893–1984)
Shostakovich, Dmitry D.	composer (1906–1975)
Schnittke, Alfred G.	composer (b. 1934)
Simonov, Konstantin M.	writer and social (1915–1979)
Silyunas, Vidmantas Yu.	theatre critic
Shubkin, V. N.	philologist
Slutsky, Boris A.	poet (1919–1986)
Smoktunovsky, Innokenty M.	actor of MKhAT (b. 1925)
Solopov, M. V.	stage-manager of Taganka theatre
Soloukhin, Vladimir A.	writer (b. 1924)
Spetsivtsev, Vyacheslav S.	director, actor at Taganka theatre in 1965/66
Stantso, V. V.	editor of *Zhizn i khimiya*
Stenberg, Enar G.	set designer
Stroeva, Marina N.	theatre critic
Tendryakov, Vladimir F.	writer (1923–1984)
Tol'stykh, Valentin I.	cinema critic (b. 1929)
Trifonov, Yury V.	writer (1925–1981)

Trubin, Vladimir N.	lit. critic
Turovskaya, Maya I.	film critic (b. 1924)
Vasil'ev, Boris L.	writer (b. 1924)
Vasil'ev, Sergey A.	poet (1911–1975)
Vol'pin, Mikhail D.	poet, writer, scenarist (b. 1902)
Voronov, Nikolay P.	writer (b. 1926)
Voroshilov, V. Ya.	
Voznesensky, Andrey A.	poet (b. 1933)
Vul'fovich, Teodor Yu.	film director (Mosfilm); (b. 1923)
Yashin, Aleksandr Ya.	writer (1913–1968)
Yutkevich, Sergey I.	director and film critic (1904–1985)
Zalygin, Sergey P.	writer, chief editor of *Novy mir* since 1986 (b. 1913)
Zingerman, Boris I.	theatre critic (b. 1928)
Zlobin, S. P.	writer (1903–1965)

(iii) *The State and Party Apparatus*[7]

THE SYSTEM OF CONTROL OVER THE THEATRES

A. The Party
Central Committee, Secretariat for Ideology

Furtseva, Ekaterina	1956–60
Il'ichev, Leonid	1961–65
Demichev, Petr	1965–74
Zimyanin, Mikhail	1976–87
Ligachev, Egor	1987–90

Central Committee, Department of Culture

Polikarpov, Dmitry	1956–65
Shauro, Vasily	1965–86
Voronov, Yury	1986–90

Central Committee, Department of Agitprop

Il'ichev, Leonid	1958–61
Tyazhelnikov, Evgeny	1977–86
Yakovlev, Aleksandr	1986–90

---

[7]The information compiled here is based on the TsGALI fond 2485. The dates are approximate; the status of the listed people is attributed on the basis of references in the minutes of the discussions, but they may well contain inaccuracies; however, it has proved impossible to find more precise informations on this issue.

Moscow Party Committee

Grishin, Viktor	1967–86
El'tsin, Boris	1986–87
Chausov, M. L.	Inspector (c. 1964–72)
Puchkova, M. I.	Head of Dept. of Agitprop, (c. 1969–72)

B. The State

USSR Ministry of Culture

Furtseva, Ekaterina	Minister of Culture (1960–74)
Voronkov, K. V.	Deputy Minister of Culture (c. 1967–75)
Demichev, Petr	Minister of Culture (1974–86)
Zakharov, Vasily	Minister of Culture (1986–89)
Gubenko, Nikolay	Minister of Culture (1989–91)
Afanas'ev, R. M.	Chief Editor of Repertoire Dept (c. 1964–70)
Goldobin, V. Ya.	Chief Editor of Repertoire Dept (c. 1964–75)
Seleznev, V. P.	Senior Inspector of Theatre Dept (c. 1974)

RSFSR Ministry of Culture

Melent'ev	Minister of Culture (c. 1970–77)
Evseev, F.	Head of Theatre Dept
Kropotova, N. I.	Senior Inspector of Theatre Dept (c. 1966–76)
Panfilov, A. P.	Inspector (c. 1969–72)
Shkodin, M. S.	Deputy Head of Theatre Dept (c. 1964–75)
Svetlakova, M. A.	Deputy Head of Theatre Dept (c. 1964–75)
Sychev, A. S.	Chief Editor of Repertoire Dept (c. 1982)

Main Administration of Culture (*Executive Committee of Mossovet*)

Rodionov, Boris E.	Head (c. 1964–70)
Pokarzhevsky, Boris V.	Head (c. 1971–75)
Anurov, V.	Head (c. 1976–81)
Shchadrin, Valery I.	Head (c. 1982–84)
Sapetov, N. K.	Deputy Head (c. 1967–71)
Seleznev, V. P.	Deputy Head (c. 1982)
Dikikh, A.	Head of Theatre Dept (c. 1972–74)
Druzhinina, Marina G.	Head of Theatre Dept (c. 1981–82)
Kuleshov, A. A.	Deputy Head of Theatre Dept (c. 1969–73)
Miringof, M. M.	Senior Inspector (c. 1968–71)
Rozov, V. I.	Head of Theatre, Music and Concert Board (c. 1973–4)
Sadkovoy, N. P.	Deputy Head of Theatre, Music and Concert Board (c. 1974–76)

Samoilenko, V. M.	Deputy Head of Theatre and Concert Board (c. 1981)
Smirnova, A. A.	Inspector (c. 1964–76)
Viren, V. N.	Head of Repertoire Dept (c. 1969–76)
Zakshiver, I. B.	Deputy Head of Theatre Dept (c. 1968–72)

PARTY

Politburo	
General Secretary	
Central Committee Secretariats	• Dept of Culture
	• Dept of Agitprop
• Secretariat for Ideology	
Central Committee	
Moscow Party Committee	

STATE

Supreme Soviet	
Council of Ministers	*Glavlit*
USSR Ministry of Culture	
• Theatre Dept	
• Repertoire Dept	
Committee for State Security (KGB)	
RSFSR Ministry of Culture	
Main Administration of Culture	
Moscow City Council Executive Committee	
Moscow City Council	

State and Party control over theatres

SELECT BIBLIOGRAPHY

I have had access to the Taganka theatre's own versions of all the productions. These are not listed in the bibliography: some versions have been published by VAAP [Vsesoyuznoe agenstvo po avtorskim pravam], or its predecessor VUOAP [Vsesoyuznoe upravlenie po okhrane avtorskikh prav] and can be found in the Library of the Theatre Workers' Union, Moscow and/or the Lenin State Library; others are unpublished and have been made accessible to me by the staff of the Taganka theatre (Boris Glagolin, Tat'yana Vashkina, Petr Leonov, Nina Shatskaya), by Svetlana Sidorina, Yury Apter, Veniamin Smekhov, and Yury Karyakin. The Central State Archive of Literature and Art of the USSR (TsGALI, since 1992 *Russian* State Archive) holds most of the production scripts.

For a detailed bibliography of the productions and history of the Taganka theatre, see Ol'ga Lysyak's *Bibliograficheskii ukazatel'*. Listed below are the major publications. After bibliographical information follows the production(s) referred to; it is placed behind suspension points if the publication is not entirely concerned with the production(s) listed; specific aspects dealt with are also given in brackets; no comment is given if the publication is of a general nature.

Abramova, V. "Chto delat'?" *Teatr* 4 (1971): 8–11. (What).

Aikhenval'd, Yury. " 'Geroi nashego vremeni' v teatre na Taganke". *Moskovskii komsomolets* 30 December 1964. (Hero).

Aksenova, Galina. "Teatr na Taganke: 68-i i drugie gody". *Gorizont* 4 (1989): 46–64. (Kuzkin).

—— "Prestuplenie i nakazanie". *Ekran i stsena* 23 August 1990. (Crime).

—— *Printsipy instsenizatsii sovremennoi sovetskoi prozy v teatre dramy i komedii na Taganke.* Diplomnaya rabota; VI kurs. ts. Leningrad: Leningrad State Institute of Theatre, Music and Film, 1981.

—— 'Printsessa Turandot, ili kongress obelitelei'. B. Brecht. *Teatr dramy i komedii na Taganke. Rezh. Yu. P. Lyubimov.* Kursovaya rabota; III kurs. ts. Leningrad: Leningrad State Institute of Theatre, Music and Film, 1979. (Turandot).

—— "Tak bylo... A zori zdes' tikhie". *Teatral'naya zhizn'* 5 (1994): 20–23. (Dawns).

—— "Tak bylo... Tartyuf". *Teatral'naya zhizn'* 5 (1994): 8–12. (Tartuffe).

—— Teatr na Taganke: 68-i i drugie gody. *Biblioteka Ogon'ka* 5 (1991).

Anastas'ev, A. "V soglasii s Gor'kim". *Teatr* 9 (1969): 12–15. (Mother).

Anikst, Aleksandr. "Zrelishche neobychaineishee". *Teatr* 7 (1965): 24–37. (10 Days).

—— "Tragediya geniya". *Moskovskii komsomolets* 17 September 1966. (Galileo).

—— "Tragediya: garmoniya, kontrasty". *Literaturnaya gazeta* 12 January 1972. (... Hamlet).

Anisimov, A. "Kakim budet Teatr na Taganke". *Teatr* 2 (1973): 139–141. (Building).

—— "Teatr na Taganke. Sud'ba starogo moskovskogo kvartala". *Arkhitektura SSSR* 2 (1984): 52–55. (Building).

Anninsky, Lev. "Elektra: shok". *Argumenty i fakty* 40 (1992): 5. (Elektra).

Apter, Yury. "Pir vo vremya chumy". *Komsomol'skaya pravda* 24 September 1989. (Feast).

Bachelis, Tat'yana. "Skaz o pravdolyubtse Kuz'kine". *Izvestiya* 27 February 1989. (Kuzkin).

—— "Uroki Taganki". *Teatral'naya zhizn'* 5 (1994): 25, 28, 29.

—— "Gamlet – Vysotsky". *Voprosy teatra* 11. Moskva: STD, 1987. 123–142. (Hamlet).

—— "Umom i talantom". *Izvestiya* 6 June 1989. (Feast).

—— "Zametki o teatral'noi forme". *Teatral'naya zhizn'* 22 (1989): 6–9.

Baklanov, Grigory. "Prichashchayas' pamyati". *Nedelya* 5–11 July 1971. (Dawns).

Bartoshevich, A. "Zhivaya plot' tragedii". *Sovetskaya kul'tura* 14 December 1971. (Hamlet).

Batchelder, Vernita Mallard. *The Theatre Theory and Theatre Practice of Jurij Ljubimov: 1964–1971*. Diss. University of Georgia, 1978. Ann Arbor: UMI, 1978. 7901657.

Bazhenova, Lyudmila. " 'Dobryi chelovek iz Sezuana', 'Zhizn' Galileya' ". *Teatr* 4 (1976): 17–21. (Good Person, Galileo).

Benyash, Raisa. "Yury Lyubimov". *Zvezda* 3 (1973): 181–191.

Berezkin, V. "Stsenograf i veshch' ". *Dekorativnoe iskusstvo* 11 (1972): 28–31. (Design).

—— "David Borovsky". *Sovetskie khudozhniki teatra i kino* 1975. Moskva: Sovetskii khudozhnik, 1977. 48–57.

—— "Ststenografiya Davida Borovskogo". *Voprosy teatra* 11. Moskva: STD, 1987. 97–122.

—— "Stsenografiya vtoroi poloviny 70-kh godov". *Voprosy teatra '81*. Moskva: VTO, 1981. 153–180. (Design).

—— "Itogi sezona". *Teatr* 3 (1972): 61–67. (... set of Dawns).

Billington, Michael. "The crime to fit the punishment". *The Guardian* 13 May 1983. (Crime/London).

——"The devil in Dostoevsky". *The Guardian* 18 February 1985. (Possessed).

Borovsky, David. "Ot Gor'kogo – k Gor'komu". *Tvorchestvo* 7 (1970): 11–13. (... Mother).

——"Podpisi k kartinam". *Teatral'naya zhizn'* 5 (1994): 6–7; 13; 18–19; 24; 26–27; 30. (Design).

Borshchagovsky, Aleksandr. "Nepredvidennyi Pushkin". *Nedelya* 23–29 April 1973. (Comrade).

Bott, Marie-Luise. "Die 'Drei Schwestern' in Moskau – eine Groteske". *Theater Heute* 3 (1984): 18–20. (3 Sisters).

Boyadzhiev, Grigory. "Staya molodykh nabiraet vysotu... ". *Sovetskaya kul'tura* 3 April 1965. (10 Days). [Reprinted as "My nash, my novyi mir postroim" in Boyadzhiev's *Ot Sofokla do Brekhta za sorok teatral'nykh vecherov* (Moskva: Prosveshchenie, 1969): 278–283, and (Moskva: Prosveshchenie, 1988): 274–280.]

Budgen, David. "Farandole, farce and vortex". *Times Literary Supplement* 5 April 1985. (Possessed).

Burlatsky, Fedor, and Len Karpinsky. "Na puti k prem'ere". *Komsomol'skaya pravda* 30 June 1967.

Byalik, B. "Obrashchayas' k Gor'komu". *Literaturnaya gazeta* 25 June 1969. (Mother).

Cave, Richard Allen. "Doorways and thresholds". *Times Higher Education Supplement* 2 September 1983. (Crime/London).

Chernichenko, Yury. "Zhivaya voda". *Teatr* 11 (1974): 22–27. (Horses).

——"Pravilo dlya kontsa sveta". *Kuranty* 27 October 1993.

Cournot, Michel. "La magie russe et ses mystères". *Le Monde* 19 February 1985. (Possessed).

——"Lioubimov et sa lampe de poche". *Le Monde* 24 November 1977. (Hamlet).

Cropper, Martin. "Comic and grotesque". *The Times* 23 March 1985. (Possessed).

Danilova, G. "Myatezh vzdymaet parusa... ". *Teatral'naya zhizn'* 7 (1968): 22. (Pugachev).

——"Spros osobyi". *Teatral'naya zhizn'* 20 (1975): 8–11. (... Belts).

Degrada, Francesco, ed. *Al gran sole carico d'amore. Nono Ljubimov Borovskij Abbado Degrada Aulenti Pestalozza*. Milan: Ricordi, 1978.

Demidov, A. "Minuvshee". *Teatr* 7 (1981): 97–107. (House).

——"... Pokuda serdtse b'etsya". *Teatr* 9 (1976): 38–46. (Exchange).

Demidova, Alla. *Vtoraya real'nost'*. Moskva: Iskusstvo. 1980.

——"Roli i gody". *Literaturnoe obozrenie* 1 (1983): 89–93.

——Interview with Vladimir Simonov. "Ozhidanie v otele 'Elektra'". *Literaturnaya gazeta* 3 February 1993 (Elektra).

Demidova, Alla. *Vladimir Vysotsky, kakim znayu i lyublyu*. Moskva: Soyuz teatral'nykh deyatelei RSFSR, 1989.

—— *Teni zazerkal'ya*. Moskva: Prosveshchenie, 1993.

Denisov, Viktor. "Doiti do samoi suti". *Nezavisimaya gazeta* 22 June 1993. (Zhivago).

Dieckmann, Friedrich. "Stanzija Taganskaya". *Theaterbilder*. Berlin: Henschel, 1979. 145–169.

"Differend entre MM. Liebermann et Rostropovitch sur 'La Dame de Pique'". *Le Monde* 21 June 1977. (Queen, Paris).

Dionisotti, Paola. "Lyubimov's Crime and Punishment". *Drama* 151.1 (1984): 21–22. (Crime/London).

Dondey, Marc. "Dostoievski–Lioubimov: le metteur en scène et son double". *Théâtre en Europe* 4 (1984): 15–18.

Eidel'man, Natan. "Svidanie s Pushkinym". *Trud* 20 May 1973. (Comrade).

Erdman, Nikolay. *P'esy, intermedii, pis'ma, dokumenty, vospominaniya sovremennikov*. Moskva: Iskusstvo, 1990.

—— "Dve intermedii k 'Pugachevu'". Ed. S. Sidorina. *Teatr* 5 (1989): 121–125. (Pugachev: interludes).

"Eshche raz o poiskakh na Taganke". *Sovetskaya kul'tura* 21 February 1967.

Esslin, Martin. "Crime and Punishment". *Plays and Players* 11 (1983). (Crime/London).

Evtushenko, Evgeny. "Ne do ordena – byla by rodina…". *Sovetskaya kul'tura* 30 November 1965. (Fallen).

—— "Besposhchadnost' k 'besposhchadnosti'". *Sovetskaya kul'tura* 6 July 1976. (Exchange).

Freedman, John. "Three Soviet Suicides". *Soviet and East European Performance* 11 (2) Summer 1991: 37–45. (Suicide).

Frenkin, A. "'Tat'yana za reshetkoi', ili bonnskie skandaly Yu. Lyubimova". *Literaturnaya gazeta* 20 May 1987. (Onegin).

Frolov, V. "Spektakl' o plamennykh dnyakh". *Izvestiya* 29 May 1965. (10 Days).

—— "Poslushaite. Mayakovsky". *Sovetskaya kul'tura* 30 May 1967. (Listen).

Gaevsky, Vadim. "Poslednyaya rol'". *Sovetskii teatr* 1 (1989): 42–44. (Vysotsky).

—— "Lyudi i teni". *Pravda* 18 July 1988. [Reprinted in *Sovetskii teatr* 2 (1989): 33–35.] (Godunov).

—— "Plennoi mysli razdrazhen'e". *Moskovskii nablyudatel'* 1 (1992): 22–31.

—— *Fleita Gamleta*. Moskva: Soyuzteatr, 1990.

Galanov, B. "Eto vremya gudit telegrafnoi strunoi…". *Literaturnaya gazeta* 22 April 1965. (10 Days).

—— "Pobeda starshiny Vaskova". *Literaturnaya gazeta* 27 January 1971. (Dawns).

—— "Mayakovsky na Taganke". *Literaturnaya gazeta* 14 June 1967. (Listen).

Gelhard, Susanne. *Die Dramatisierung von Jurij Valentinovic Trifonovs Roman "Das Haus an der Moskva" am Moskauer Taganka-Theater*. Diss. University of Mainz, 1984. Mainzer Slavistische Veröffentlichungen Slavica Moguntiaca 5. Mainz: Liber, 1984.

Gershkovich, Aleksandr. *Teatr na Taganke* (1964–1984). Benson, Vermont: Chalidze, 1986. [Translation *The Theatre of Yuri Lyubimov* by Michael Yurieff, New York: Paragon House, 1989]; published in Russian by Solyaris in 1993.

—— "Sud'ba 'Borisa Godunova' ". *Russkaya mysl'* 8 April 1983. (Godunov).

—— "V teatre na Taganke, s utra do vechera". *Kontinent* 38 (1983): 285–317.

—— "The Taganka: Russian Political Theater, 1964–1984". Kennan Institute for Advanced Russian Studies. Occasional Papers. #225. 1988. [Reprinted in: *Aspects of Modern Russian and Czech Literature*. Ed. Arnold McMillin. Columbus: Slavica, 1989. 79–95.]

—— "Lyubimov i Efros" *Teatral'naya zhizn'* 10 (1991): 14–15, 26–27.

Gnedovsky, Yury. "Teatr v krupnom gorode". *Stsenicheskaya Tekhnologiya i Tekhnika* 5 (1975): 18–20. (... Building).

—— "Teatr i gorod". *Arkhitektura SSSR* 10 (1979): 10–11. (... Building).

—— "Novyi oblik teatra na Taganke". *Stroitel'stvo i Arkhitektura Moskvy* 7 (1972): 31–33. (Building).

—— "Teatr novogo tipa". *Arkhitektura SSSR* 6 (1973): 9–14. (Building).

Gorenkova, N. "Teatr na Taganke". *Teatral'naya zhizn'* 14 (1966): 15–18.

Golovashenko, Yury. "Poeticheskaya geroika". *Sovetskaya kul'tura* 14 December 1967. (Pugachev).

Grayson, Jane. "Transgressions". *Times Literary Supplement* 23 September 1983. (Crime/London).

Greenfield, Edward. "Ring in the new". *The Guardian* 1 October 1988. (Rheingold).

Griffiths, Paul. "Vivid staging is killed by excess". *The Times* 18 November 1986. (Jenufa, London).

—— "Dream ticket offers bumpy ride". *The Times* 30 September 1988. (Rheingold).

Grinevich, A. "Tochki s zapyatoi". *Sovetskaya kul'tura* 28 February 1989. (Kuzkin).

Gubenko, Nikolay "Taganka – eto vera". Interview with Mar'ya Dement'eva. *Ogonek* 30 (1988): 17–19. [Partly also in *Kul'tura i zhizn'* 12 (1988): 27–28.]

Gul'chenko, Viktor. "Znaki prepinaniya". *Teatr* 7 (1989): 28–34. (Kuzkin).

—— "Metamorfozy Smutnogo vremeni". *Teatr* 2 (1989): 37–39. (Godunov).

Jomaron, Jacqueline. " 'Le Tartuffe' mis en scène par Lioubimov". *Travail théâtral* 4 (1971): 158–162. (Tartuffe).

Jongh, Nicholas de. "The Possessed". *The Guardian* 26 March 1985. (Possessed).

"Kak eto delalos' ". *Yunost'* 11 (1988): 79–82. (Vysotsky).

Karaulov, Andrey. "Rekviem". *Teatr* 10 (1982): 113–117. (3 Sisters).

Karpinsky, Len. "V tvorcheskom poiske". *Pravda* 16 May 1965. (10 Days).

Kaz'mina, Natal'ya. "Dar". *Teatr* 5 (1990): 70–76. (Feast).

Kennedy, Michael. "Ring of promise". *The Daily Telegraph* 1 October 1988. (Rheingold).

Kenyon, Nicholas. "Ringing the changes". *The Observer* 2 October 1988. (Rheingold).

Khemlin, Margarita. "Vsego zhivitel' i vinovnik". *Segodnya* 18 June 1993. (Zhivago).

Khemlin, Margarita and Maksim Andreev. "Sbor truppa". *Nezavisimaya gazeta* 22 January 1992 (minutes of meeting).

Khmara, Irina. "Doktor Zhivago zapel". *Komsomol'skaya pravda* 19 June 1993. (Zhivago).

Kidina, N. "Gde zhe vy, 'novye lyudi'?" *Teatral'naya zhizn'* 2 (1971): 23–25. (What).

Komissarzhevsky, Viktor. "Obmenu ne podlezhit". *Literaturnaya gazeta* 23 June 1976. [Reprinted in *Teatr, kotoryi lyublyu*. (Moskva: VTO, 1981): 124–130]. (Exchange).

—— "Chitaya svitok vernyi...". *Komsomol'skaya pravda* 20 April 1973. (Comrade).

Kondratovich, V. "Po stranitsam 'Novomirskogo dnevnika' Alekseya Kondratovicha". *Teatral'naya zhizn'* 1 (1989): 22–24.

Kopelew, Lew. "Moskau: Ljubimov und die Tradition der Avantgarde". *Theater Heute Jahrbuch* 1971. 114–118.

Korneva, Oksana. "Fantazii ne na temu". *Teatral'naya zhizn'* 15 (1979): 28–30. (Tales).

Korshunova, Ol'ga. "Podglyad, ili na repetitsiyakh u Yuriya Lyubimova". *Teatral'naya zhizn'* 17 (1989): 2–3. (Feast).

—— "Tri sestry na Taganke". *Teatral'naya zhizn'* 9–10 (1992): 8–10 and 11 (1992): 9–11.

—— "Realii znakomykh vremen". *Sovetskaya kul'tura* 26 November 1988.

Kozhukhova, Galina. "A Gogol' molchit...". *Pravda* 29 January 1979. (...Tales).

Krechetova, Rimma. "Lyubimov". *Portrety rezhisserov*. Moskva: Iskusstvo, 1977. 123–159.

—— "Zhivym o pavshikh". *Trud* 22 January 1971. (Dawns).

—— "Poiski edinstva". *Teatr* 2 (1973): 58–67. (Hamlet, Statue).

—— "Prizvanie". *Sovetskaya kul'tura* 30 September 1977.

—— "Monolog v ozhidanii istorii". *Teatral'naya zhizn'* 5 (1994): 2ff.

—— "Paradoksy Lyubimova". *Ekran i stsena* 36–37 (1992): 8–9.

Krupina, M. "Moskva. Chas Pik". *Teatr* 5 (1970): 171–172. (Hour).

Krymova, Natal'ya. "O Vysotskom". *Avrora* 8 (1981): 98–115.

—— "Etot strannyi, strannyi mir teatra". *Novyi mir* 2 (1980): 245–265. (Prose).

—— "Tri spektaklya Yuriya Lyubimova". *Imena. Rasskazy o lyudyakh teatra*. Moskva: Iskusstvo, 1971. 144–173.

—— "Chto perezhito...". *Komsomol'skaya pravda* 19 June 1974. (Horses).

—— "Brekht na ulitse Vakhtangova". *Teatr* 3 (1964): 42–50. (Good Person).

—— "Pavshikh pamyati svyashchennoi". *Teatr* 4 (1966): 49–52. (Fallen).

—— "... s raskosymi i zhadnymi ochami". *Teatr* 4 (1968): 17–23. (Pugachev).

Kuleshov, V. "Ot tlen'ya ubezhav". *Literaturnaya gazeta* 30 May 1973. (Comrade).

Kustow, Michael. "Dostoevsky discovered". Letter to the Editor. *The Sunday Times* 31 March 1985. (Possessed).

Kuz'ko, Galina. "Eshche raz o 'Tartyufe'". Letter to the Editor. *Ogonek* 17 (1969): 19. (Tartuffe).

"La 'Pravda' refuse de publier la réponse de M. Lioubimov aux attaques dont il a été l'objet". *Le Monde* 16–17 April 1978. (Queen, Paris).

Lavrenyuk, N. "Ne tol'ko o 'Tartyufe'". *Sovetskaya kul'tura* 3 April 1969. (... Tartuffe).

Law, Alma. "The trouble with Lyubimov". *American Theatre* 4 (1985): 4–11.

—— "Yuri Lyubimov directs in Helsinki". *Slavic and East European Performance* 13/1 (1993): 13–27. (Comedians, Raw Youth).

Lehmann, Barbara. "Ljubimows 'Dämonen'". *Osteuropa* 10 (1985): 717–725. (Possessed).

Leonov, Petr. "Yury Lyubimov repetiruet 'Borisa Godunova'". *Teatr* 2 (1989): 40–51. (Godunov).

Lesnevsky, Stanislav. "Poet i teatr". *Moskovskii komsomolets* 28 January 1965. (Antiworlds).

—— "Ya khochu videt' etogo cheloveka!" *Moskovskii komsomolets* 21 December 1967. (Pugachev).

Levikova, Elena, ed. "Deistvuyushchie litsa i ispolniteli...". *Sovremennaya dramaturgiya* 4 (1988): 196–223. (Godunov).

Lioubimov, Youri. *Le Feu Sacré*. Paris: Fayard, 1985.

Litavrina, Marina. "Klyuch ot royalya". *Moskva* 7 (1983): 172–182. (3 Sisters).

Lordkipanidze, Nately. "Ispytanie razumom". *Nedelya* 22–28 May 1966. 22–23. (Galileo).

Lordkipanidze, Nately. "Igraite tak, chtoby spektakl' zakryli". *Ekran i stsena* 19 July 1990. 1, 8–9. (Suicide).

—— *Rezhisser stavit spektakl'*. Moskva: Iskusstvo, 1990.

Lubimov, Yuriy. *A Stage Adaptation of M. A. Bulgakov's "The Master and Margarita"*. London: Overseas Publications Interchange Ltd., 1985.

Lungina, Evgeniya. *Dostovernaya uslovnost' Yuriya Lyubimova*. Kursovaya Rabota, IV kurs. Moscow State Institute of Theatre Arts. ts. n.d.

Lysyak, Ol'ga, ed. *Moskovskii Teatr Dramy i Komedii na Taganke* 1964–1984. *Bibliograficheskii Ukazatel'*. Moskva: Ministerstvo kul'tury SSSR – Gosudarstvennaya tsentral'naya teatral'naya biblioteka, 1989.

Lyubimov, Yury. "V zashchitu professii i professionalov". *Teatr* 11 (1973): 32–35.

—— "Algebra garmonii". *Avrora* 10 (1974): 60–64.

—— "The Algebra of Harmony: A Meditation on Theatre Aesthetics followed by A Note on Actors and the Acting Profession". *Culture* 5.2 (1978): 64–81. [Translation of the above articles by A. Werth.]

—— "Pervyi shag sdelan". *Sovetskaya Rossiya* 16 January 1964.

—— "Ya – za antidekoratsiyu". *Khudozhnik, stsena, ekran*. Moskva: n.p., 1975. 20–21.

—— "Kazhdyi shag – kak poslednii". *Sovetskii ekran* 1 (1977): 8–9.

—— "Ya vozmushchen makhinatsiyami organizatorov 'Biennale'". *Literaturnaya gazeta* 2 November 1977.

—— "Popytaemsya posmotret' na veshchi real'no". *Teatral'naya zhizn'* 5 (1994): 14–15, 18.

Lyubimov, Yury. "The crosses Yuri Lyubimov bears". Interview with Bryan Appleyard. *The Times* 5 September 1983.

—— "Pora konchat' s sovetskim infantilizmom". Interview with M. Andreev. *Nezavisimaya gazeta* 14 December 1991.

—— "V takikh usloviyakh ya bol'she rabotat' ne budu...". Interview with M. Fillimor. *Strana i mir* 1–2 (1984): 127–138. [Translated by R. Porter in *Index on Censorship* 1 (1985): 55–60.]

—— "Home thoughts from exile". Interview with Mark Frankland. *The Observer* 9 November 1986.

—— "On Nikolai Erdman". Interview with John Freedman. *SEEDTF* 8 (2–3) December 1988: 9–16.

—— "Praviteli i teatr". Interview with John Glade. *Vremya i my* 98 (1989): 165–179.

—— "Kto – korol'? Kto – prem'er? Kto – tot? Kto – etot?..." Interview with A. Glezer. *Strelets* 10 (1986): 34–39.

—— "Interv'yu s Yuriem Petrovichem Lyubimovym". Interview with Natal'ya Gorbanevskaya. *Kontinent* 44 (1985): 411–443.

—— "Poeziyu truda vydumali bezdel'niki". Interview with Yury Kovalenko. *Izvestiya* 25 June 1994.

—— "Kabala svyatosh". Interview with Aleksandr Minkin. *Ogonek* 27 (1990): 8ff.

—— "They Treat Artists Like Waiters". Interview with N. Nagorski. *Newsweek* 23 April 1984: 56.

—— "Domoi, na Taganku...". Interview with A. Polyukhov. *Novoe vremya* 46 (1988): 42–43.

—— "Yury Lyubimov: prostye istiny iskusstva". Interview with A. Shcherbakov. *Teatr* 7 (1988): 143–148.

—— "Vstrecha". Interview with Egor Yakovlev. *Moskovskie novosti* 22 May 1988.

—— "The duty of art is to talk simply, candidly and straightforwardly". Interview with Zinovy Zinik. *The Listener* 22 September 1983: 2ff.

Lyubomudrov, M. "Uroki klassiki". *Zvezda* 1 (1978): 200–212. (... Comrade).

—— "Problemy klassiki". *Ogonek* 31 (1982): 19–22. (... Tales).

—— *Protivostoyanie. Teatr, vek XX: tragedii – avangard.* Moskva: Molodaya gvardiya, 1991.

Mal'tseva, O. "Boris Godunov Yuriya Lyubimova". *Rezhisser i vremya.* Leningrad: MK RSFSR and LGITMIK, 1990; 126–143. (Godunov).

Makarova, G. "Enar Stenberg". *Teatr* 8 (1969): 72–75.

—— "David Borovsky". *Teatr* 2 (1972): 118–120.

Marchenko, Tat'yana. "Teatr ulits i ploshchadei". *Iskusstvo byt' zritelem ili priglashenie k sporu.* Moskva, Leningrad: Iskusstvo, 1966. 110–142.

Marinova, Iyuliya. "Ot Zhivogo k Zhivago...". Interview with Valery Zolotukhin. *Teatral'naya zhizn'* 6 (1994): 2–5. (Zhivago) .

Markov, Pavel A. *O teatre.* 4 vols. Moskva: Iskusstvo, 1974–1977.

Mar'yamov, A. "S Arbata na Taganku". *Yunost'* 7 (1965): 91–93. (10 Days).

—— "Natka, Pechorin i vremya". *Teatr* 3 (1965): 20–26. (Hero).

McLain, Michael. "Trifonov's Exchange at Lioubimov's Taganka". *Slavic and East European Arts* 3.1 (1985): 159–169. (Exchange).

Metelkina, Adelaida. "Nemnogo o tebe, Elektra". *Nezavisimaya gazeta* 17 September 1992. (Elektra).

Minkin, Aleksandr. "Zhivoi. O spektakle, arestovannom na 21 god". *Teatral'naya zhizn'* 17 (1989): 4–5. (Kuzkin).

—— ed. "Pikovaya Dama". *Ogonek* 9 (1989): 20–23. (Queen, Paris).

Miringof, Mikhail. "Gamlet na Taganke". *Teatral'naya zhizn'* 6 (1972): 19–20. (Hamlet).

Mozhaev, Boris. "Chem shchi khlebat'?" *Teatr* 7 (1989): 19–23. (Kuzkin).

Nikolaevich, Sergey. "Teatr na Taganke: poslednyaya mizanstsena". *Ogonek* 38 (1993).

Northcott, Bayan. "Going for gold". *The Independent* 1 October 1988. (Rheingold).

"Obrashchenie akterov teatra na Taganke. Pis'mo Yuriya Lyubimova truppe teatra na Taganke". *Moskovskie novosti* 37 (1993).

Panfilova, N. and O. Fel'dman. "Boris Godunov na Taganke". *Voprosy teatra* (Ministerstvo kul'tury SSSR and VNII-STD RSFSR) 1990: 288–328. (Godunov) .

Patrikeeva, Irina. "Otryad starshiny Vaskova". *Teatral'naya zhizn'* 12 (1971): 6–8. (Dawns).

—— "Mayatnik i paradoks". *Teatral'naya zhizn'* 21 (1970): 23–25. (. . . Hour, Mother).

—— "Chto vo pole vidno? . . .". *Teatral'naya zhizn'* 20 (1973): 20–21. (Comrade, Statue).

Pavlova, Lyudmila. "Vladimir Vysotsky: My govorim Taganka – podrazumevaem Lyubimov". *Literaturnaya gazeta* 22 June 1993.

Peter, John. "Yuri Lyubimov's Hamlet, or What You Will". *The Sunday Times* 24 September 1989. (Hamlet/Leicester).

—— "Lyubimov's puppets". *The Sunday Times* 24 March 1985. (Possessed).

Picon-Vallin, Béatrice. " 'Les dix jours qui ébranlèrent le monde' au Théâtre Taganka de Moscou". *Les Voies de la Création Théâtrale* 3 (1972): 344–377. (10 Days, Good Person, Antiworlds, Fallen, Listen).

—— "'Hamlet' à Moscou". *Travail théâtral* 8 (1972): 153–156. (Hamlet).

—— "Lioubimov et le théâtre soviétique". *Théâtre en Europe* 4 (1984): 20–27.

Polonsky, Georgy. "Prizyv k muzhestvu". *Nedelya* 26 May–1 June 1963. (Good Person).

Polyakova, E. *et al.* "Vokrug Taganki". *Mir iskusstv*. Moskva: GITIS and VNII, 1991: 9–56.

Potapov, N. " 'Seans chernoi magii' na Taganke". *Pravda* 29 May 1977. (Master).

Potter, Lois. "And then, the curtain". *Times Literary Supplement* 29 September 1989: 1063. (Hamlet/Leicester).

Poyurovsky, B. "Po–vakhtangovski!" *Moskovskii komsomolets* 15 December 1963. (Good Person).

—— "Rabota est' rabota". *Sovetskaya estrada i tsirk* 7 (1977): 18–19. (Work).

Pul'khritudova, Elizaveta. "Pushkin – geroi dramy". *Teatr* 6 (1974): 65–74. (. . . Comrade).

—— "Etot strannyi 'kozel otpushcheniya' ". *Literaturnoe obozrenie* 7 (1980): 84–89. (Prose).

"Razgovor posle spektaklya". *Teatral'naya zhizn'* 17 (1975): 24–26. (Belts).

Rondeli, L. "Bednyi Mol'er". *Teatral'naya zhizn'* 12 (1974): 24–25. (. . . Tartuffe).

Rudnitsky, Konstantin. "Iskusstvo zhit' na zemle". *Radio. Televidenie* 29 (1966): 11. (Galileo).

—— "Priklyucheniya idei". *Dostoevsky i teatr*. Leningrad: Iskusstvo, 1983. 426–462. (. . . Crime).

—— "Shest' let spustya". *Izvestiya* 23 June 1988. [Reprinted in *Kul'tura i zhizn'* 12 (1988): 25–26.] (Godunov).

—— "Kentavry". *Teatr* 6 (1979): 46–52. (Prose).

—— *Spektakli raznykh let*. Moskva: Iskusstvo, 1974.

—— *Proza i stsena*. Moskva: Znanie, 1981.

—— *Teatral'nye syuzhety*. Moskva: Iskusstvo, 1990.

Ryder, Paul Ryan, ed. "Lyubimov/Yevtushenko: Under the Skin of the Statue of Liberty". *Drama Review* 17 (1973): 134–137. (Statue).

Rzhevsky, Nicholas. "Magical Subversions: 'The Master and Margarita' in Performance". *Modern Drama* 30.3 (1987): 327–339. (Master).

—— "The Program as Performance Text". *Slavic and East European Arts* 4.1 (1986): 97–101. (Design: Programme).

—— "Adapting Drama to the Stage: Liubimov's Boris Godunov". *Slavic and East European Arts* 3.1 (1985): 171–176. (Godunov).

Sabinina, M. "Novye puti sinteza". *Sovetskaya muzyka* 5 (1983): 62–72. (. . . Music).

Sakhnovsky–Pankeev, V. "Molodo, smelo, talantlivo!" *Yunost'* 2 (1964): 101–102. (Good Person).

Sands, Sarah. "Wayward Russian falls from the Ring". *London Evening Standard* 15 October 1988. (Ring).

Samoilov, David. "Chto takoe poeticheskii teatr". *Literaturnaya gazeta* 10 January 1968. (Pugachev).

Shakh–Azizova, T. "Mayakovskomu". *Teatr* 12 (1967): 16–21. (Listen).

Shatskov, V. "Nenavist' dobrogo cheloveka". *Komsomol'skaya pravda* 14 August 1963. (Good Person).

Shcherbakov, Konstantin. "Dolg chesti". *Moskovskie novosti* 6 November 1988.

—— "Chest' soldata". *Sovetskaya kul'tura* 23 January 1971. (Dawns).

—— "Gamlet". *Komsomol'skaya pravda* 26 December 1971. (Hamlet).

Shklovsky, Viktor. "Slova Lenina obnovlyayut teatr". *Nedelya* 11–17 April 1965. (10 Days).

—— "Pobeda poezii". *Izvestiya* 9 June 1967. (Listen).

Shore, Rima. "Under the Skin of the Statue of Liberty". *Drama Review* 17 (1973): 138–142. (Statue).

Shorter, Eric. "Russian mannerisms". *The Daily Telegraph* 22 March 1985. (Possessed).

Shvydkoy, Mikhail. "Prostranstvo tragedii". *Sovetskaya kul'tura* 16 July 1988. (Godunov).

Silina, I. "Iz pepla". *Teatr* 2 (1989): 63–67. (Godunov).

Silyunas, Vydmantas. "A zori zdes' tikhie . . . " *Teatr* 6 (1971): 7–14. (Dawns).

—— "Muzhestvo sovesti". *Trud* 19 December 1971 (Hamlet).

Simonov, Konstantin. "Vdokhnovenie yunosti". *Pravda* 8 December 1963. (Good Person).

Smekhov, Veniamin. "Nakanune". *Teatr* 9 (1982): 113–119.

—— "Oborachivat'sya pridetsya vpered". *Teatral'naya zhizn'* 14 (1983): 18–19 (. . . Listen).

—— "Skripka Mastera". *Teatr* 2 (1988): 97–124.

—— *Skripka Mastera*. Biblioteka Ogonek 37 (1988).

—— "Taganka: malen'kie i bol'shie tragedii". *Ogonek* 23 (1989): 17–19.

—— "V epokhu 'dvukh Yur' ". *Ekran i stsena* 24 May 1990. (House).

—— "Erdman na Taganke". *Ekran i ststena*. 1 March 1990, 12–13. (Suicide).

—— " . . . zhila-byla Taganka". *Vremya i my* 117 (1992): 250–270.

—— *Taganka. Zapiski zaklyuchennogo*. Moskva: Polikom, 1992.

Smelyansky, Anatoly. "Mozhet li proza stat' poeziei?" *Literaturnaya gazeta* 11 August 1976. (. . . Gala).

—— "Chelovecheskoe slyshitsya vezde". *Literaturnoe obozrenie* 2 (1979): 85–91. (. . . Tales).

—— *Nashi sobesedniki*. Moskva: Iskusstvo, 1981.

—— "Ispytanie Dostoevskim". *Teatr* 8 (1981): 89–101. (. . . Crime).

——"Master bez skripki". *Moskovskie novosti* 6 March 1988.

—— "Spektakl', kotoryi ne zakroyut". *Moskovskie novosti* 5 August 1990. (Suicide).

Smith, Gerald S. *Songs to Seven Strings*. Bloomington: Indiana University Press, 1984.

Sokolova, Natal'ya. "Mir – oblagodetel'stvovan ego izgnaniem . . ." *Teatral'naya zhizn'* 17 (1989): 5–7.

Solopov, M., V. Titov, and K. Pan'shin. "Svetovoi zanaves v moskovskom teatre dramy i komedii". *Stsenicheskaya tekhnika i tekhnologiya* [Referativnaya seriya.] 2nd ed. Moskva: Ministerstvo kul'tury SSSR – Gosudarstvennyiinstitutpoproektirovaniyuteatral'no-zrelishchnykh predpriyatii "giproteatr", 1966: 23–25. (Design: Light Curtain).

Stenzl, Jürg. " 'Azione scenica' und Literaturoper". *Musikkonzepte* 20: *Luigi Nono*. München: text+kritik, 1981. 45–57. (. . . Al gran sole).

Stishova, E. "Status professii". *Teatr* 4 (1977): 53–57.

Stroeva, Marianna. "Zhizn' ili smert' Galileya". *Teatr* 9 (1966): 11–16. (Galileo).

—— "Voennaya muzyka". *Teatr* 10 (1982): 118–125. (3 Sisters).

—— "Smena rezhisserskikh form". *Teatral'nye stranitsy*. Moskva: Iskusstvo, 1979. 83–125.

—— "Sofokl posle Chekhova". *Ekran i stsena* 38–39 (1992). (Elektra).

Surkov, E. "A Tartyuf?..." *Ogonek* 13 (1969): 26–27. (Tartuffe).

—— "Shivorot – navyvorot". *Ogonek* 35 (1969): 26–27. (... Tartuffe).

Sutcliffe, Tom. "Putting on the style". *The Guardian* 19 November 1986. (Jenufa, London).

Tamarchenko, Anna. "Roman na stsene: 'Master i Margarita' v Teatre na Taganke". *Canadian–American Slavic Studies* 15.2–3 (1981): 355–381. (Master).

Tarshis, Nadezhda. "Vernost' istorii". *Teatr* 5 (1980): 57–65. (... Dawns).

—— "Muzyka spektaklya". *Teatr* 1 (1974): 46–51. (... Music for Dawns).

Terschüren, H. D. "Tatjana hinter Gittern". *Bonner Rundschau* 17 March 1987. (Onegin).

"Tochki nad 'i' ". *Literaturnaya gazeta* 8 March 1978.

Tolchenova, N. "Prostota. Velichie. Chuvstvo". *Teatr* 6 (1973): 3–11.

—— "Na ezopovom yazyke" *Ogonek* 33 (1968): 27–29.

Tolstykh, V. "Kritika 'neobosnovannykh predpolozhenii' ". *Sovetskaya kul'tura* 16 February 1967. [Reply to Zubkov, "Poiski na Taganke".]

Trifonov, Yury. *Teatr pisatelei: Tri povesti dlya teatra.* Moskva: Sovetskaya Rossiya (Biblioteka "v pomoshch' khudozhestvennoi samodeyatel'nosti" No. 7), 1982. (Exchange, House).

Turovskaya, Maya. " 'Zori' na Taganke". *Yunost'* 4 (1971): 90–92. (Dawns).

Varshavsky, Ya. "V poiske". *Vechernyaya Moskva* 18 June 1965. (10 Days).

Vasil'ev, Boris. "V nachale byla voina". *Sovremennaya dramaturgiya* 1 (1985): 227–233. (... Dawns).

—— *A zori zdes' tikhie. Spektakl' Moskovskogo teatra dramy i komedii na Taganke.* Melodiya, M40 44043–46, 1982.

Velekhov, Leonid. "Prostranstvo tragedii". *Moskovskaya pravda* 24 June 1988. (Godunov).

—— "Desyat' dnei". *Teatr* 2 (1989): 52–62. (Godunov).

Velekhova, Nina. "Ischezayushchee prostranstvo". *Teatr* 5 (1973): 23–40. (Hamlet, Dawns).

—— "Vospitanie chuvstv". *Literaturnaya gazeta* 16 February 1972. (... Dawns).

—— "Uslovnost'? Net, uproshchenie". *Literaturnaya gazeta* 6 August 1969. (... Tartuffe).

—— "Tam zhili poety...". *Literaturnaya gazeta* 7 February 1968. (... Listen).

—— "Troyanskii kon' u vorot Taganki". *Moskovskaya pravda* 27 November 1988.

Velikovsky, S. "O derzosti i robosti ozorstva". *Teatr* 4 (1969): 24–29. (Tartuffe).

Vishnevskaya, I. "Zhizn' Galileya". *Vechernyaya Moskva* 13 June 1966. (Galileo).

—— "Geroi nashego vremeni". *Vechernyaya Moskva* 10 November 1964. (Hero).

—— "Benefis". *Komsomol'skaya pravda* 11 January 1974. (... Gala).

Vitez, Antoine. "Lioubimov ou l'audace". *Théâtre en Europe* 4 (October 1984): 18–20.

Volkov, Solomon. "At the scene of Lyubimov's 'crime'". *American Theatre* 4 (1987): 12–18. (Crime/Washington). [Shortened version of publication in *Kontinent* 52 (1987)].

—— "Yury Lyubimov v Vashingtone". *Kontinent* 52 (1987): 309–325. (Crime/Washington).

Vysotsky, Vladimir. *Pesni i stikhi.* 2 vols. Ed. Boris Berest. New York: Literaturnoe zarubezh'e, 1981–1983.

—— *Sobranie stikhov i pesen.* 3 vols. New York: Apollon Foundation & Russica Publications Inc., 1988.

—— "Gamlet. Spektakl' Moskovskogo teatra dramy i komedii na Taganke". Album 20 and 20 bis. *Svetloi pamyati Vladimira Vysotskogo.* London: Odeon, 1984.

—— "Vladimir Vysotsky. Spektakl' Moskovskogo teatra dramy i komedii". *Svetloi pamyati Vladimira Vysotskogo.* Album 21 and 21 bis. London: Odeon, 1984.

Wardle, Irving. "Alas, poor Will is lost". *The Times* 21 September 1989. (Hamlet/Leicester).

Yurasova, G. "Mayakovsky na Taganke". *Teatral'naya zhizn'* 19 (1967): 10–13. (Listen).

Yur'eva, Marina. "Sud'ba, sud'by, sud'be...". *Sovetskaya kul'tura* 26 December 1989. (Work).

"Youri Lioubimov ne montera pas 'la Dame de Pique' à Paris". *Le Monde* 1 April 1978. (Queen, Paris).

Yutkevich, S. "Gamlet s Taganskoi ploshchadi". *Shekspirovskie chteniya* 1978. Moskva: Nauka (AN SSSR), 1981. 82–89. (Hamlet).

Zaionts, Marina. "Dvoe v komnate – ya i Stalin". *Moskovskie novosti* 10 (1993): 11–12. (Zhivago).

Zaitsev, N. "Dni, kotorye potryasli mir". *Vechernii Leningrad* 21 April 1965. (10 Days).

—— "Dialog s potomkami". *Neva* 2 (1975): 196–206. (... Comrade).

Zalygin, Sergey. "Literatura i stsena: 'Derevyannye koni' v teatre na Taganke". *Literaturnaya gazeta* 15 May 1974. (Horses).

Zamkovets, G. "Variatsii pod orkestr". *Teatral'naya zhizn'* 23 (1981): 28–29. (3 Sisters).

Zand, Nicole. "Pourquoi 'la vie de Fedor Kouzkine' n'a pas franchi le barrage de la censure". *Le Monde* 13 November 1975. (Kuzkin).

—— "A Moscou, Lioubimov monte 'le maître et Marguerite', de Boulgakov". *Le Monde* 5 April 1977. (Master).

—— "Vivre à Moscou aujourd'hui". *Le Monde* 3 July 1976. (Exchange).

—— "Attachez vos ceintures. Une satire à Moscou". *Le Monde* 9–10 March 1975. (Belts).

Zhuraitis [Juraitis], Al'gis. "V zashchitu 'Pikovoi damy' ". *Pravda* 11 March 1978. (Queen, Paris).

Zingerman, Boris. "Zametki o Lyubimove". *Teatr* 1 (1991): 37–61.

—— "Molenie o mire" *Teatr* 2 (1993): 42–44. (Elektra).

Zingerman, Boris and Vladimir Kolyazin. "Yury Lyubimov: Russkii klyuch k Brekhtu". *Teatral'naya zhizn'* 4 (1991): 10–11.

Zolotukhin, Valery. "Den' shestogo nikogda". *Teatr* 7 (1989): 23–28. (Kuzkin).

—— "Vinovatogo nuzhno iskat' v sebe". Interview with I. Kozhokhina. *Teatral'naya zhizn'* 17 (1991): 18–19.

—— *Vse v zhertvu pamyati tvoei*... Moskva: Soyuzteatr 1992.

—— *Drebezgi*. Moskva: Soyuzteatr, 1991.

Zubkov, Yury. "Poeticheskaya letopis' epokhi". *Moskva* 9 (1971): 190–194. (... Dawns).

—— "Grani poiska". *Teatral'naya zhizn'* 5 (1969): 3–7. (... Tartuffe).

—— "Sluzhen'e muz ne terpit suety". *Moskva* 2 (1974): 192–196. (... Comrade).

—— "I vse okazalis' v ovrage... ". *Ogonek* 9 (1974): 22–23. (... Gala).

—— "Poiski na Taganke". *Sovetskaya kul'tura* 10 December 1966.

—— "Obrashchenie k proze". *Moskva* 8 (1970): 181–186. (... Mother).

—— "Kogda zabyvaetsya glavnoe...". *Krasnaya zvezda* 5 October 1968.

INDEX

Other titles in the Contemporary Theatre Studies series:

This book is part of a series. The publisher will accept continuation orders which may be cancelled at any time and which provide for automatic billing and shipping of each title in the series upon publication. Please write for details.